WITHDRAWN

MUSIC AND THE
CULTURES OF PRINT

CRITICAL AND CULTURAL MUSICOLOGY
VOLUME I
GARLAND REFERENCE LIBRARY OF THE HUMANITIES
VOLUME 2027

CRITICAL AND CULTURAL MUSICOLOGY
MARTHA FELDMAN, *Series Editor*
University of Chicago

MUSIC AND THE CULTURES OF PRINT
edited by Kate van Orden

MUSIC AND THE CULTURES OF PRINT

EDITED BY
KATE VAN ORDEN

AFTERWORD BY
ROGER CHARTIER

GARLAND PUBLISHING, INC.
A MEMBER OF THE TAYLOR & FRANCIS GROUP
NEW YORK & LONDON
2000

Published in 2000 by
Garland Publishing, Inc.
A Member of the Taylor & Francis Group
19 Union Square West
New York, NY 10003

10   9   8   7   6   5   4   3   2   1

Library of Congress Cataloging-in-Publication Data is available
from the Library of Congress.

van Orden, Kate.
        Music and the cultures of print / edited by Kate van Orden.

        Includes index.
        ISBN 0–8153–2574–6 (alk. paper)

Cover: Nineteenth-century opera arrangement.
Photo courtesy of Thomas Christensen

Printed on acid-free, 250-year-life paper.
Manufactured in the United States of America

Contents

Critical and Cultural Musicology
MARTHA FELDMAN

Musicology has undergone a sea change in recent years. Where once the discipline knew its limits, today its boundaries seem all but limitless. Its subjects have expanded from the great composers, patronage, manuscripts, and genre formations to include race, sexuality, jazz, and rock; its methods from textual criticism, formal analysis, paleography, narrative history, and archival studies to deconstruction, narrativity, postcolonial analysis, phenomenology, and performance studies. These categories point to deeper shifts in the discipline that have led musicologists to explore phenomena that previously had little or no place in musicology. Such shifts have changed our principles of evidence while urging new understandings of existing ones. They have transformed prevailing notions of musical texts, created new analytic strategies, recast our sense of subjectivity, and produced new archives of data. In the process, they have also destabilized canons of scholarly value.

The implications of these changes remain challenging in a field whose intellectual ground has shifted so quickly. In response to them, this series offers essay collections that give thematic focus to new critical and cultural perspectives in musicology. Most of the essays contained herein pursue their projects through sustained research on specific musical practices and contexts. They aim to put strategies of scholarship that have developed recently in the discipline into meaningful exchanges with one another while also helping to construct fresh approaches. At the same time they try to reconcile these new approaches with older methods, building on the traditional achievements of musicology in helping to forge new disciplinary idioms. In both ventures, volumes in this series also attempt to press new associations among fields outside of musicology, making aspects of what has often seemed an inaccessible field intelligible to scholars in other disciplines.

In keeping with this agenda, topics treated in the series include music and the cultures of print; music, art, and synesthesia in nineteenth-century Europe; music in the African diaspora; relations between opera and cinema; Marxism and music; and music in the cultural sensorium. Through enterprises like these, the series hopes to facilitate new disciplinary directions and dialogues, challenging the boundaries of musicology and helping to refine its critical and cultural methods.

Introduction

KATE VAN ORDEN

THE CULTURES OF PRINT

This is a book about the cultures that coalesced around printed music in previous centuries. Its chronological boundaries have been determined by two technological revolutions: the advent of music printing in 1501 and the rise in the early twentieth century of phonographic recordings, which, like prints of music, profoundly altered the transmission of musical texts.

One goal of this collection has been to sketch a history of printed music that takes account of the theoretical framework established by contemporary historians of the book. Until recent decades, historians favored paleographic work on manuscripts and less often pursued bibliographic work on printed books. For at a time when most literary critics attempted to edit texts in such a way as to represent the final intentions of the author, printed texts seemed to obstruct this end. The variants introduced by earlier editors, the errors of compilers and typesetters, and the abbreviations used in early printed books all stood in the way of recovering the author's authentic text. Printed books contained errors that needed to be identified and erased. Manuscript sources, on the other hand, promised a version of the text that seemed closer to the author's original or final intentions (a version commonly referred to by musicians as an *Urtext* after the series launched by G. Henle Verlage in the 1940s that produced "clean" editions of Bach, Haydn, Mozart, Beethoven, and others). Textual criticism, then, revolved around content and tended to focus on an ideal redaction of the text—the text itself—while excluding criticism of the forms in which the text was contained. Only rarely did these modern editors consider how the formal characteristics of a book—its page layout, foliation, size, format, and the technology used to produce it—shaped its content, to say nothing of its readership or circulation.

When historians and literary scholars did turn their attention to printed books, their work was oriented toward descriptive bibliographies designed to serve textual critics and editors. Study of editions, dates, and the authorship of books produced bibliographies describing the extant sources of an author's oeuvre, and, alongside bibliographies, catalogues of printed books accounted for the output of individual presses or the presses of an entire city, further refining the scholar's control of source material. Far from clarifying the history of authorship, however, such bibliographies and catalogues brought to light a wealth of material evidence that ultimately called for new histories and historical methods, evidence that complicated the literary critic's notion of authorship, the "work," and audience even as it attracted the eye of a new breed of historian interested in the history of mentalities, feelings, and everyday life. The Annales school was one locus of a new historiography that transformed the study of print in the years following World War II. With the publication of *L'apparition du livre* in 1958, Lucien Febvre and his student Henri-Jean Martin challenged historians to open the history of print and printing to the social sciences.[1] Just as Annales moved history away from narratives of power and toward social history (the full title of the journal that gave the school its name is *Annales: Economies, Sociétés, Civilisations*), so too the authors of *L'apparition du livre* saw printed books as part of social systems, launching the study of what we have now come to think of as the many "cultures of print."

Since the publication of *L'apparition du livre*, historians of the book such as Martin, Roger Chartier, and Robert Darnton have been exploring the unique modes by which print organized the presentation of texts, the conception of written works, and the ways in which texts were read and disseminated.[2] Some of the most fruitful inquiries have examined the audiences for print, for, as we are beginning to understand, the ways in which printed matter targets its readers, anticipating and trying to shape their tastes and reading habits, can largely be discerned from prints themselves. To cite one example, Renaissance dedications to princes reveal how printing added a tacit third party to the exchange between prince and subject, namely the buyer. Publishers recognized that any purchaser of a printed book could become in effect a spectator to the act of dedication and, by buying the book, could also in essence rededicate it to him- or herself. Princely dedications thus flattered an aspiring nobility that made up one potential public for printed books.[3] At the same time, prefaces directly addressing anonymous readers slowly but surely supplanted dedications in printed books, revealing the broad public on which printing relied for economic support. Another example of what bibliographic work can reveal about the audiences for print is offered by cheap compendia of works by well-known authors issued alone or in inexpensive collections. Publishers shaped such compilations in order to respond directly to consumers, circumventing authors and putting together financially advantageous books on their own. By studying forms of print such as these we come closer to understanding their writers, printers, compilers, backers, readers, dedicatees, and sellers, and, moreover, the practices that interconnect them in social complexes shaped by new ideologies, new forms of exchange and circulation, and new technologies.

TEXT AND PERFORMANCE

What sets music apart from literature and, indeed, what suggests the need for a book specifically devoted to music and the cultures of print, is the fact that musical texts are performative texts. Musical texts presume a musical performance, with the result that music as manifest in print leads a dual life as text and performance. The meanings of musical texts unfold twice as they are "read" both by musicians and then by audiences. In the first instance, the black signs cast across the pages of musical scores give musicians instructions for how to perform a given piece; the notes help musicians to produce a reading of a piece, public or private, whether with instruments, voice, or both. As we well know, this kind of reading is not a transparent rendition of a musical text. Musicians interpret scores when they read, making the piece their own, creating "variant readings" with each performance, impressing their individual marks upon the works they play. We speak of Leonard Bernstein's "Beethoven Five" and Glenn Gould's *Goldberg Variations*, linking the names of composers and works with those of the artists who perform them. In this sense, the notion that readers appropriate texts—an idea of current interest among historians of print—is a given when it comes to music. Performers embody the music they read, acting out musical texts like the scripts for a play. Yet unlike stage actors, musicians also mediate what for many listeners is an illegible text, pages of hieroglyphs that require special literacy: the score. Notation alone sets music apart from literature.

With performance, the musical text becomes available to an audience of listeners who in turn "read" the music they hear, responding to it, making sense of it, multiplying its meanings. A night at the symphony, ballet, or opera produces hundreds of simultaneous readings of a given work by those present. In this sense, then, musical works come to light through an aural act of "publication." Long before print transformed the literary culture of early modern Europe by mobilizing and multiplying texts and their readers, musical performances "published" musical texts as a matter of course. This is not to deny that literary texts were also read aloud like music, for certainly in the period before Gutenburg and thereafter, composers, minstrels, poets, and playwrights served their patrons in day-to-day performances that were not recorded in print. Occasional verse, songs, and motets celebrated events in the lives of city notables and turned the wheels of sociability at European courts, also without going to press. Even as printing professionalized writing in such a way that composers and poets could extend the lines of patronage through print and thus loosen the ties that bound them to courts and noble households, in-person performance was not immediately superceded. Eventually, however, literature became virtually synonymous with its texts—with written literature, that is—whereas music did not, at least not before the advent of sound recordings; and it is this insistence of musical texts upon being performed that so richly complicates the cultures surrounding printed music. During the seventeenth and eighteenth centuries, when print drew solitary individuals together into a Republic of Letters and changed the nature of reading and authorship, composers continued to work for their living within the institutions of court, church, salon, and theater, as well as in the street, tavern, and square, never establishing a musical institution that relied upon print in the manner of the Republic of European intellectuals that formed and functioned across great distances through newspapers, pamphlets, and books.

From the very outset, printed texts have been remaking social life. The Reformation, humanism, the Renaissance—scholars regularly interrogate the connections between these vast cultural transformations and the sixteenth-century printed books that disseminated the new ideologies. Did printed music intersect and shape culture in similar ways? In 1457, two years after the publication of the Bible, Gutenberg's associates Johann Fust and Peter Schöffer printed a *Psalterium* with musical staves on which notes were added by hand. Soon afterwards, other printers began to use a double impression method for music, first printing the staves and then overlaying the notes. In 1501, Ottaviano de' Petrucci produced the first print of polyphonic music in this way, the *Harmonice musices Odhecaton A*, a collection of nearly 100 secular songs, and in 1529 Pierre Attaingnant published the first musical prints employing moveable type that joined notes to their staff lines and thus enabled a single impression method for the printing of music. This technological advance greatly improved the legibility of printed music at the same time as it made music publishing more cost effective, so that after 1529, music began to fly from European presses by the ream. In this way the printing of music kept pace with the printing of other texts. But did the invention of music printing change the actual music and the process of music-making? The multiplication of musical texts in print surely initiated a rise in musical literacy, but it never produced significant cultural institutions independent of public performance. Of course private music-making continued and expanded: nobles supplemented lessons on the lute or viola da gamba with printed tutors in the sixteenth century, just as simple piano sonatas and Lieder supported the *Hausmusik* culture of the nineteenth. Yet even in these cases, printed music perpetuated traditions of performance in such a way that print stood alongside performance in the triangle it formed with composers and audiences. Before recording technology made it possible to transport, store, and access musical performances at will, there was no real musical analogue to reading a literary text in silence.

Given that in earlier times music reached its broadest public through performance, any history of the musical cultures of print must engage performative issues. While performance per se is not the focus of these essays, its modes inform the methods of the present collection, in which we highlight the performative nature of printed music. Here our book extends ongoing studies of print culture in their current performative direction. Performance points up the mobility of musical texts and their dynamic transmission of information, offering a conceptual ground upon which to examine the inventiveness of interpretation and the way in which certain kinds of interpretation triangulate the paths between author and reader traversed by nonmusical texts. This is not to say, of course, that literary texts are any less subject to the creative appropriation associated with performance than are musical ones. It is instead to observe that the appearance of music in print disrupts the linear continuum between composer and audience in the same way that musical performances do. Print complicates and expands this middle ground by multiplying the material forms of texts and thereby multiplying their meanings. As Roger Chartier says in *Forms and Meanings: Texts, Performances, and Audiences from Codex to Computer,* "When the 'same' text is apprehended through different mechanisms of representation, it is no longer the same. Each of its forms obeys specific conventions that mold and shape the work according to the laws of that form and connect it, in differing ways, with other arts, other genres, and other texts. If we want to understand the appropriations and interpretations of a text in their full historicity we need to identify the effect, in terms of meaning, that its material forms produced."[4] Performance and print both shape the way music conveys its meaning; yet while historians of music have long been cognizant of the former—that performers interpret and mold the meaning of the texts they realize—they have rarely theorized the implications of print in similar terms. By conceiving of print as performative, we hope to use the written text to reflect back upon the past performances it shaped in new social histories that include not just authors, publishers, and readers, but composers, performers, and listeners as well.

This collection of essays is organized according to three broad rubrics that roughly correspond to the subjects "printing," "authorship," and "reception." The essays themselves tend to resist these groupings by keeping all three subjects in play; in the introductions that follow I try to suggest the ways they exemplify and move among the categories containing them. The first four essays, on "Printing the New Music," show how new musical genres stressed the resources of contemporary music publishers in ways both technological and economic. These difficulties illuminate the clefts between what publishers were ready or able to send to press at any given time and what composers and editors wished to print. The efforts exerted to print new kinds of music thus cast into relief not only the difficulties involved in printing music, but, most importantly, the aspirations of those engaged in bringing music to press. The second section of the book, "Authors and Entrepreneurs," presents three essays that explore how musical authorship changed in the face of the new social and material economies produced by print. Finally, "Music in the Public Sphere" pairs two essays on the reception and performance of musical prints in two very different public contexts: the salon and the street. These essays acknowledge the argument made by Jürgen Habermas that print extended the social systems of local gathering places into a public sphere constructed through print rather than speech, yet they also suggest that that musical performances continued to shape the forms and uses of print circulating in and beyond European salons and squares.[5]

PRINTING THE NEW MUSIC

One of the first stumbling blocks for music printing came right around 1600 when virtuoso solo song first issued in print. Up until that time, the only genres of vocal music commonly available in print were polyphonic Masses and motets, and vernacular songs for two or more voices. In short, vocal music meant vocal polyphony, which was issued first in choirbook format and later, beginning in the 1520s, in partbooks, but never in scores. The "new music," as Italian solo song or monody has come to be called, required new technology to produce vocal/instrumental scores and, even more troublesome, a new range of note values to capture the rapid flourishes and coloratura of the new style. Without written-out embellishments, the essence of the new music would have been lost. Yet, in "Printing the 'New Music,'" Tim Carter concludes that the typographical innovations inspired by monody sometimes serve to widen rather than close the gap between text and realization. Their graphic beauty promoted monody with books designed to please the connoisseur's eye more than his or her ear, withholding in the process the professional trade secrets that singers revealed only in performance. Carter's essay shows how uncertain the benefits of print appeared to the professional singer-composers who developed the new style and how their anxieties over print produced scores that hide as much as they reveal of the singer's art.

The story of how monody first came to print actually conflates two innovations: new ways of writing down the improvisations of singers, and new ways of printing these transcriptions. It reminds us that musical notation itself was, alongside print, a rapidly developing technology in the centuries covered by this study. One impetus for writing down music was to stabilize musical repertories; one result of writing was that musical texts often became objects laden with special authority. Probably the most famous story about the writing down of a musical repertory is the legend of Pope Gregory (reigned 590–604), which tells the story of a holy dove that sang chants into the mouth of St. Gregory, who sang them out again for a scribe to write them down. This tale explains the origin of the corpus of Gregorian plainchant, but it also does much more, for the story itself came into being during the ninth century when Charlemagne was busy attempting to standardize the liturgy of his vast empire. The implementation of Roman chant aimed to erase other chant dialects in the realm, and the legend of St. Gregory validated Roman chant as the most holy and "authentic" rite in use. In fact, the written versions of Gregorian chant were new, not from Gregory's time, and musical notation was itself an invention inspired by Charlemagne's desire to regularize sacred rituals north and south of the Alps. Thus, our first written examples of music—the corpus of Gregorian chant—resulted from a political reform championing the Roman rite throughout Christendom.[6] In her essay, "Elite Books, Popular Readers, and the Curious Hundred-Year History of the *Liber Usualis,*" Katherine Bergeron looks at the mid-nineteenth century to study another moment at which the promulgation of the Roman rite became a *cause célèbre.* A group of Benedictine monks at the Monastery of Solesmes devoted their lives to resuscitating the lost traditions of the Roman liturgy. Their research into the tradition of chanting led them to revise their collections of plainchant, first in manuscript, and finally in print. The printing of the *Liber Gradualis* (1883) produced the first authoritative edition of the Roman gradual, complete with neumes specially crafted to achieve an antique scriptlike appearance and the image of a singing St. Gregory on the title page (see Fig. 2.4, p. 49). Once again, St. Gregory presided over a technological innovation born in the service of liturgical reform.

Our third essay on printing "new music" examines a case in which public demand motivated a new form of print. Thomas Christensen's essay, "Public Music in Private Spaces: Piano-Vocal Scores and the Domestication of Opera," traces how the pan-European craze for opera eventually led publishers to press the music of entire operas into a friendly format for home use: the piano-vocal score. With these scores, operas and opera excerpts could be played and replayed for private delectation, and a large repertory quickly became available for home study and entertainment. The piano-vocal score, Christensen suggests, perfectly fit the new attention to the parlor as a principal site of sociability in the late eighteenth and early nineteenth centuries. But one outcome of the explosion of opera arrangements and transcriptions was a radical transformation of theatrical music as it was relocated to the home. Transcription turned arias into songs and overtures into sonatas, changing the way audiences heard opera in the theater after it had become commonplace at home. It is this destabilization of operatic reception that print enabled, and Christensen's concern is to explore how the domestic context shaped the form of piano-vocal scores and reshaped the meanings of the works they conveyed.

Robert Holzer's essay, "Alban Berg Remembers Emil Hertzka: Composer and Publisher between Real and Ideal," reveals the ambivalent kinds of relationships that composers often developed with their publishers. As managing director of Universal Editions in Vienna during a tumultuous period of musical change, Hertzka had gambled and won on the music of the Second Viennese School of composers, shepherding so many works of Arnold Schoenberg, Anton Webern, and others into print. The problems involved in printing this new music were more economic than typographical, for as Berg himself admitted, "it is a tall order for a businessman—and a publisher has to be that—to dispose of a product that the consumer has rejected as unpalatable." Certainly the success of Universal in the face of public opposition to the works they published is a testimony to Hertzka's business acumen, but even given the surprising skill with which Universal managed to market the new music, Berg's relationship with his publisher was not always a friendly one. One of Holzer's most intriguing conclusions is that Hertzka gave a face to Berg's difficult relationship with print. Even while Universal's cunning admixture of art and business kept alive the "ideal of the new music," the philistinism of musical commerce darkened Berg's spirit.

AUTHORS AND ENTREPRENEURS

Composers had long worried about how circulating a work in print might devalue it. Print represented a loss of control, and in many dedications Renaissance composers refer to their printed works as children sent out alone into the world. Dedications might implore a noble patron to protect the work, but nobles, too, often had a vexed relationship with print owing to its lack of exclusivity.

In this light, the ambition and ability of Orlando di Lasso to navigate the burgeoning sixteenth-century systems of print is all the more remarkable. Lasso was the first composer to combine a court appointment with an active international publishing career that spanned the continent from Antwerp to Rome and from Munich to Nuremberg, Paris, and Venice. In "Orlando di Lasso, Composer and Print Entrepreneur," James Haar reconstructs the composer's publishing ventures beginning with his "Opus 1" of 1555, a portfolio advertising the young composer's versatility with a wealth of musical styles and genres. Haar goes on to show how, after landing a comfortable position with the imperial court, Lasso expanded his publishing career with two extraordinary personal privileges: the first was granted by Charles IX of France in 1571 and permitted the composer to oversee the printing of his music in French territories, and the second was granted by Emperor Rudolf II in 1580–1581 for publications in imperial territories. Lasso asked for these personal privileges in order to choose his publishers himself and thus control the printing and reprinting of his works. Haar's study demonstrates that long before the demise of court society forced composers to earn their livings by publishing (at least in part), some exceptional composers such as Lasso reaped financial gain from the new trade in music.

"Lasso" had become something of a brand name early on in the composer's career as printers began to cash in on its good value by using it to sell anthologies "by Orlando di Lasso and others." Certainly the privileges the composer secured attempted to regain control of this "trademark"; they also introduce the fraught issues of authorship, authority, and naming in the age before copyright. Publication not only tore the musical work from its original context, it often severed the authorial ties binding the composer's name to it. In her "Authors and Anonyms: Recovering the Anonymous Subject in *Cinquecento* Vernacular Objects," Martha Feldman calls our attention to the nameless in an affirmative light, observing that anonymity was a marked and sometimes positive category for certain kinds of pieces and prints in the sixteenth century, especially collections of vernacular song. The subject under investigation in her study is not the author per se, then, but the author as what she calls "a typological subject, reducible enough to be packaged up, represented, and—at least within the present analytic—typified within print media" in ways that are still discernible today. Her essay suggests reasons for publishing works without attributions that reveal the logic, character, and conditions by which anonymous works entered mass circulation through print.

There is no question that the mass production of print created new figures of the author, yet even as print seemed, perhaps, to offer unlimited opportunities for self-creation and promotion, the industry quickly rigidified along an almost monolithic set of codes that structured the forms of print and publication. Those new to publishing found it a challenge to craft a wholly unique identity in print. Nonetheless, those willing to work within its constraints found in print a medium that was still available to minorities, whether social, political, or racial. In early twentieth-century America, black composers found social and professional advancement in the printing industry, discovering in it not only a tool to further their careers, but one for racial uplift more broadly. Thomas Bauman begins his essay, "Enterprise and Identity: Black Music, Theater, and Print Culture in Turn-of-the-Century Chicago," with the story of black vaudevillians on the South Side of Chicago who created the first entirely black-run and black-owned musical theater in the country. The print images employed by Robert T. Motts, owner of the Pekin Temple of Music, promoted his establishment as a locus of black enterprise and identity. Bauman's study of the program books, newspaper criticism, and sheet music that came out of the Pekin illustrates how the adoption of (largely white) mechanisms of print by black entrepreneurs initiated a deeply ambivalent discourse about community and identity among blacks in the urban North during the Progressive Era.

MUSIC IN THE PUBLIC SPHERE

In *The Structural Transformation of the Public Sphere: An Inquiry into a Category of Bourgeois Society*, Jürgen Habermas argues that during the seventeenth and eighteenth centuries, new forms of sociability arose in cities, engaging bourgeois citizens in intellectual debates in salons, coffeehouses, and academies. Print contributed greatly to the rise of a bourgeois public sphere, particularly in the form of periodicals and newspapers in which ideas about current affairs could be expressed. Eventually, this reading public turned its attention to matters that formerly had not been up for discussion, such as issues of government and religious questions. A literary public thus became politicized and took over the public sphere that—according to Habermas—had previously been the sole domain of the monarch.

The last two essays in our collection study music in a bourgeois public sphere still in the process of formation, but one already relying on print to amplify its systems of sociability and social critique. So doing, they expand upon Christensen's essay, which posits a musical component to the debates of European bourgeois. In her essay entitled "Bénigne de Bacilly and the *Recueil des plus beaux vers, qui ont esté mis en chant* of 1661," Lisa Perella situates this renowned collection of song texts in the culture of Parisian salons that produced and consumed it. On any given night during the mid-seventeenth century, participants gathered at the twilight hour in the salons of the greatest Parisian mansions for poetry readings, poetry contests, song, cards, and conversation. As part of a widespread campaign to civilize society, the women who invited guests into their salons for such entertainment stressed the sorts of refined etiquette and politeness for which the court of Louis XIV subsequently became so famed. Salons were the center of literary criticism in seventeenth-century France and, for smaller genres such as the *air*, the center of musical criticism as well. Music and poetry here intersected with social aims, and print with the representation of what went on behind closed doors. Bacilly's book of song texts made public what previously had been private and published the music of the salons—at that time a manuscript repertory—before a curious public. At the same time, it linked the participants of the salons together through print. Bacilly's *Recueil* thus served a literary culture that avidly consumed poetry and music, even as it sold salon songs publicly and divulged the identities of their upper-class authors, who usually remained masked behind the thin veil of initials.

Habermas offers a rich explanation of the connections between Enlightenment thought, its dissemination in print, and the French Revolution, showing how the intellectual sociability engendered through print fostered political discourse. Habermas situated this politicization of the bourgeois public sphere in the eighteenth century, seeing its origins in the interactions that took place in cafes and academies where newspapers and periodicals were read. In my own essay, "Cheap Print and Street Song following the Saint Bartholomew's Massacres of 1572," I reconsider Habermas's model of politicization in order to suggest that the sovereign public which opposed absolutism at the end of the eighteenth century may have emerged fleetingly two centuries before to voice its political opinions during the peasant revolts of the French Wars of Religion. Mine is not a corrective to Habermas, but an attempt to recover the strains of sixteenth-century political thought that were sung in the streets of Lyon in the form of political songs. The texts of these songs were printed in cheap pamphlets and on posters, from which they were sung in city streets and squares. Unlike the eighteenth-century Republic of silent readers, however, the participants in the sixteenth-century bourgeois public sphere that I delineate listened and perhaps even sang together. My paper concludes that singing galvanized the citizens of Lyon and surrounding villages in ways that silent reading never could. The prints upon which I base my study, then, resemble political literature, but are in fact musical "scores," reminding us of the great divide between music and its texts.

NOTES

[1]*L'apparition du livre* (Paris: Éditions Albin Michel, 1958, 1971), available in English as *The Coming of the Book: The Impact of Printing 1450–1800*, trans. David Gerard (London: Verso, 1984).

[2]A few of the many notable studies include Henri-Jean Martin and Roger Chartier, *Histoire de l'édition française*, 4 vols. (Paris: Promodis, 1982–1986); Roger Chartier, *The Cultural Uses of Print in Early Modern France*, trans. Lydia G. Cochrane (Princeton: Princeton University Press, 1987); idem, *L'ordre des livres* (Paris: Editions Alinea, 1992), in English as *The Order of Books: Readers,*

Authors, and Libraries in Europe between the Fourteenth and Eighteenth
Centuries, trans. Lydia G. Cochrane (Stanford: Stanford University Press, 1994);
idem, *Forms and Meanings: Texts, Performances, and Audiences from Codex to
Computer* (Philadelphia: University of Pennsylvania Press, 1995); Natalie
Zemon Davis, *Society and Culture in Early Modern France* (Stanford: Stanford
University Press, 1975); Robert Darnton, *The Kiss of Lamourette: Reflections in
Cultural History* (New York: Norton, 1990); and *Printing the Written Word: The
Social History of Books, circa 1450–1520*, ed. Sandra L. Hindman (Ithaca and
London: Cornell University Press, 1991). A select bibliography of relevant publi-
cations can be found in Chartier, *Forms and Meanings*, 115–121.

[3]See Chartier, "Princely Patronage and the Economy of Dedication" in
Forms and Meanings, 25–42.

[4]Ibid., 2.

[5]Jürgen Habermas, *The Structural Transformation of the Public Sphere: An
Inquiry into a Category of Bourgeois Society,* trans. Thomas Burger with Frederick Lawrence (Cambridge, Mass.: MIT Press, 1989).

[6]This argument is advanced by Richard Taruskin in his *Music in the Western
World* (Oxford and New York: Oxford University Press, forthcoming).

PART I

Printing the New Music

reissued by the music presses of Italy since the advent of single-impression letterpress music printing in the second quarter of the sixteenth century. The great Venetian printing houses of Antonio Gardane and Girolamo Scotto and their successors, emulated by a number of smaller presses in other Italian cities, nurtured a market for their products by the cunning commercial strategies of an emerging music "industry."[3] They understood and exploited concepts of advertising, niche marketing, and brand loyalty, controlling supply and manipulating demand while distributing their products across the length and breadth of Italy and beyond. Most bookshops had music on the shelves; most music-lovers bought this music for their libraries or music rooms. And although the tradition of manuscript copying and dissemination by no means died (indeed, it may have been healthier than many have assumed), music became conditioned and controlled by what might conveniently be called a "print culture."

    The advertising ploy explicit in Caccini's title is obvious enough. It also reflects a standard deception on the composer's and/or printer's part: as with earlier "new" musics (Adrian Willaert's *Musica nova* of 1559 is only the most obvious example), these songs were by no means new when they appeared from the press:[4] indeed, there is a clear sense that such music was printed only as it ceased to have currency in more immediate performance contexts. Presumably Caccini turned to print specifically in 1601–1602 chiefly because of the claims and counterclaims of precedence in inventing the "new" styles (solo song and recitative) that were then a matter of hot debate in Florence. But whatever his motives, he was one of the first of many monodists to exploit the power of print in order to establish his wares in the musical market-place. Three new publications containing solo songs were issued in 1602 (two were by Domenico Maria Melli), two more in 1606 (by Bartolomeo Barbarino—a reprint of a now lost first edition—and Domenico Brunetti), four in 1607 (Barbarino, Lodovico Bellanda, Severo Bonini, Francesco Lambardi), one in 1608 (Francesco Rasi), five in 1609 (Bonini, Giovanni Ghizzolo, Sigismondo d'India, Melli, Jacopo Peri), and six in 1610 (Barbarino, Bellanda, Ghizzolo, Johann Hieronymus Kapsberger, Enrico Radesca da Foggia, Rasi).[5] By the mid-1610s, most composers had jumped on the bandwagon, publishing secular (and, we should not forget, sacred) music in the new styles for voice(s) and instruments:[6] some 200 editions of solo songs by over 100 composers appeared in the first third of the seventeenth century.[7] Those whom the trend left behind could only mutter darkly about the perils of fashion, the decline of taste, and the loss of respect in the art and craft of musical composition.[8]

Many editions of solo songs bear all the hallmarks of luxury consumption, being as carefully and elegantly presented as contemporary printing technology would allow. The significant use of upright folio formats may have been dictated by performance needs—with singer and accompanist sharing the score (if indeed they were not one and the same person)—but it also makes these volumes stand apart from the cheaper, more functional quarto or octavo partbooks conventionally adopted for multi-voice (and later, some solo-voice) secular and sacred music in the sixteenth and seventeenth centuries. In terms of paper alone—the major cost of printing in this period—such editions were expensive to produce; they also seem to have sold (in Florence, at least) for two to three times the price of a set of partbooks.[9] And consumers got for their money more than just the musical notes. The grand title pages, dedications, prefaces, postfaces, tables of contents, and other paratextual matter found in these editions clearly drew on conventions established in earlier music prints. But they increasingly sought to confer distinction and to offer explanation to "readers" (for the moment, I use the term loosely) needing introduction to new aesthetic and performing worlds.

A great deal more archival work needs to be done before we can answer fundamental questions concerning the production and consumption of these (and for that matter, earlier) music prints. We know too little about the financial arrangements and trading practices that brought these works from the composer's pen to the consumer's bookshelf. At one extreme is the notion of a "vanity press," with composers and/or their patrons (or some other third party) paying the total costs of a small-scale print run produced at no financial risk to the printer and/or publisher. At the other, some printers, in particular Giacomo Vincenti of Venice, appear to have issued solo songs and related repertories on their own initiative, whether as prestigious loss-leaders or for commercial gain. The middle ground was probably occupied by a complex range of temporary or semi-permanent relationships between patrons, composers (and their associates), publishers, and printers, all hoping to attract an audience so as to recoup in whatever way their investment of time, effort, and money.

Certainly there appears to have been a market for this music: Melli's first book of *Musiche* (Venice: Giacomo Vincenti, 1602) was reissued by Vincenti in 1603 and 1609, and Caccini's *Le nuove musiche* appeared in Venice in 1607 (printed by Alessandro Raverii), 1608 (the arias only; printed by Giacomo Vincenti) and 1615 (by Vincenti). Even operas such as Jacopo Peri's *Euridice* (Florence: Giorgio Marescotti, 1600; Venice: Alessandro Raverii, 1607) and Claudio Monteverdi's *Orfeo* (Venice: Ricciardo Amadino, 1609, 1615)—which would seem to be "vanity"

items *par excellence*—went to a second edition. One is struck by the
commerce in music that would seem on the face of it to have little selling
power. The striking persistence of the "new music" in print cannot be explained simply by those collections (numerous at least from the 1610s)
clearly catering to singers of modest achievement, with simple tunes and
pleasant ditties sung to the strummed chords of the Spanish guitar.
Rather, much of this repertory made demands that would have taxed se-
verely even the professional virtuosos now entertaining Giustiniani's
Roman gentlemen. Yet those concerned with these editions clearly hoped
that someone somewhere would procure and somehow use them, for all
the difficulties they presented.[10] So the question remains, what real benefits were to be gained from printing and publishing this music?

PUBLISH OR PERISH?

A portion of the monody repertory—in particular music directly associated with specific singers or their patrons—remained in manuscript.[11]
But the sheer number of monodists turning to print suggests significant
pressure to publish their music from patrons, peers, and even the marketplace. The fixity of print, its ability to standardize a musical text in multiple copies, and the prestige associated with it were alluring indeed. But
monodists were typically performer-composers and often approached
print with a sense of anxiety that seems more than just conventional,
however much false modesty might play a part: witness the care lavished
on the design of their collections, on the choice of favorite poetry to set
to music, and on the dedications and prefaces expressing concern for the
fruits of their labors and giving useful information on how to realize
them in performance. In particular, this prefatory material—whether by
composers themselves or by friends, associates, or even professional
writers and secretaries—offers significant insights into the pleasures and
the perils of publishing.[12]
    To take one example from many, in 1626 the Tuscan composer An-
tonio Brunelli had the Venetian printer Bartolomeo Magni issue his
*Prima parte delli fioretti spirituali a 1.2.3. quatro & cinque voci per con-
certare nell' Organo,* a set of partbooks of pieces in mixed scorings (1–5
voices and continuo) setting spiritual and devotional texts in Latin.
Brunelli had studied in Rome with Giovanni Maria Nanino and then in
Florence with Giulio Caccini;[13] he pursued a career of moderate distinction in Pisa and Prato, ending up back in Pisa as *maestro di cappella* of
the Knights of St. Stephen. His fifteen opus numbers (six or seven are

lost) include sacred music in the concertato style and three books of *Arie, scherzi,* [or *Scherzi, arie,*] *canzonette e madrigali* published in Venice by Giacomo Vincenti (1613, 1614[14], 1616[12]), containing solo songs, duets, and trios plus instrumental music; he also wrote three student manuals.[14] The *Prima parte delli fioretti spirituali* is dedicated to Maria Magdalena, Archduchess of Florence and one of the three regents ruling Tuscany in the 1620s on behalf of the young Grand Duke Ferdinando II: her fierce religiosity was doubtless enough to persuade Brunelli to produce a volume of this kind in her honor. He also provided it with a revealing preface:

The Author to the courteous Readers[15]

Publishing new compositions [lit. "Bringing new compositions to light"] is nothing other than opening eyes and minds to search in them with all subtlety every tiniest imperfection. The intelligent and those of goodwill cannot, and know not how to, blame praiseworthy works, but the enthusiasts, and those who presume greatly of themselves, accommodate themselves to them with difficulty; and when they find nothing striking, or to show that they have superiority of intellect, they pronounce this decision:

There are no miracles here: one could do better.

And so, if they take a general view, some of these fine intellects might at first assume that these concertos of mine, because of the quantity and quality of the *passaggi,* would turn out [to be] difficult to sing; but if they apply their minds well, they will find them to be very manageable for those, however, who have the rule and manner of singing, given that such compositions [are] like those put into practice by all my pupils, in regard of whom I composed the greater part of them, just as the same will also succeed in singing clearly with [but] a simple glance the good compositions of others even if they have *passaggi* and are difficult. And just as I pride myself on those lively intellects who have learnt such a faculty from me, so I feel myself obliged to commend the admirable virtuous skill, well-placed in honor of God, of the two most noble and sacred virgins of the Monastery of S. Matteo (or of Pisa) for the excellent disposition and sweetness of voice that one hears in them, since one—the Very Reverend Donna Maddalena Cini, pupil of a worthy teacher and taken further by me—and the other—the Very Reverend Donna Canente Agostini, my pupil since her beginnings—concertizing together with soprano and alto voices, have enlivened the divine offices and have honored these labors of mind, which the Most Serene Highnesses of Tuscany have on many occasions enjoyed during their time staying in Pisa. Let the testimony of Signora Francesca [Caccini], daughter of the famous Signor Giulio Romano, suffice as confirmation of this truth, who—as a *maestra* of good and graceful singing, and as such, as for other most noble qualities and virtuous skills, recognized and admired by the world—having many times enjoyed their concerto can bear of what I have recounted to you, kind Readers, full and undoubtable witness. I have wished for many reasons to advise you of everything so that you can defend him who merits [it] and give praise to those who, daily advancing themselves in the path of virtuous skills, do honor to themselves and bring glory to him who teaches them, and may you live happily.

Brunelli's rhetorical strategies merit close analysis. He appears anxious to defend himself both from personal attack and from the prejudice of those who do not believe that mere singing teachers can produce significant musical works. The mention of his two pupils, both nuns, provides a context for this music and also assures the reader that although it might appear difficult on the page, it can indeed be performed by relative beginners given proper training in the art of singing. This, in turn, offers some manner of advertisement for Brunelli's teaching skills. The mention of Maddalena Cini and Canente Agostini also initiates a standard rhetorical trope of invoking patronal protection for works now travelling abroad in the world: the sequence continues through an indirect reference to the dedicatee, Archduchess Maria Magdalena (one of "the Most Serene Highnesses of Tuscany"), and thence to Francesca Caccini—the famous virtuoso soprano and daughter of the ostensible founder of the "new music"—of whom Brunelli writes in glowing terms.[16] It may be significant that Brunelli appeals so extensively to specific women: his music thereby colonizes a feminized space and also curries critical favor because it would not be gallant to treat it disparagingly. That, in turn, seems clearly designed to win the reader over to Brunelli's side and to counterbalance the evident, if slightly mannered, nervousness with which he approaches the act of publication.

The *Prima parte delli fioretti spirituali* also contains (in the organ partbook) a set of "Avvertimenti per concertare la detta opera." These "instructions" contain advice on how to perform these songs for different voice combinations by octave displacement (the soprano to tenor, and alto to bass), and with or without the organ (which may or may not transpose). Such recommendations on flexible performance practices are not uncommon in this period and were presumably intended to increase sales. For example, in Enrico Radesca da Foggia's *Canzonette, madrigali et arie a 3, 2, et 1* (Venice: Giacomo Vincenti, 1618), the signatory of the preface, Lodovico Caligaris, says that he has asked three things of the composer: first, to avoid difficult *passaggi* so as to make this music widely performable (Caligaris notes that the best *passaggi* are always improvised anyway); second, to ensure that the pieces for three voices can be sung by one (soprano or tenor) or two (soprano or tenor and bass); and third, to allow the bass part to be sung an octave higher (presumably so as to permit performance by just women or boys). Similar issues are raised by those prints that present music in dual formats, such as Paolo Quagliati's madrigals for solo voice or four-voice ensemble in his *Il primo libro de' madrigali a quattro voci* (Venice: Giacomo Vincenti, 1608), and Pietro Maria Marsolo's four-voice arrangements of well-known solo songs, including works by Giulio Caccini, in his *Secondo libro de' madrigali a quattro voci* (Venice: Giacomo Vincenti, 1614).[17]

But although Brunelli is anxious to facilitate the performance of his music, his "Avvertimenti" reveal that something more is required. His repeated emphasis here on the need for a "buona maniera di cantare" (and for a good teacher) returns to the point made in his preface, where he notes "the rule and manner of singing," the "admirable virtuous skill," and the "excellent disposition and sweetness of voice" cultivated in and by his two pupils. He does not define or explain further these various terms: indeed, he suggests that only a good teacher can make them clear in practice.[18] Thus there is an additional, and not uncommon, rhetorical strategy in play: although Brunelli needs to counter the impression that his music might be difficult to perform, the account of Maddalena Cini's and Canente Agostini's vocal virtuosity cuts both ways, simultaneously closing and widening the distance between musical text and musical rendition. The composer cannot lose: those who succeed in performing this music do so because of its quality; those who do not, fail because they, not the music, are lacking.

EXPLAINING THE "NEW MUSIC"

Contemporary readers (and modern scholars) seeking enlightenment on "the rule and manner of singing," "admirable virtuous skill," and "excellent disposition and sweetness of voice" would presumably turn to the treatises that proliferate in this period. In the late sixteenth century, the number of primers appearing from the music presses increased sharply in response to the broadening market for music prints and to the shift of music theory from the science of number to the practice of art. In a similar vein, the long preface to Caccini's *Le nuove musiche* presents an account of the rise of monody and the reception of his songs, and then gives detailed instructions on performance covering vocal embellishment—including devices unamenable to musical notation (for example, the *esclamazione* and the *crescere e scemare della voce*)—and realization of the continuo. Other prefaces to monody books tread similar ground, if on a more compressed scale, again in an apparent attempt to make the new and the strange seem both feasible for and approachable by the consumers at which these prints were aimed.

For example, in 1618, the Roman singer-composer Giovanni Domenico Puliaschi had his associate, the composer Giovanni Francesco Anerio, publish a collection of his songs, *Gemma musicale dove si contengono madrigali, arie[,] canzoni, et sonetti, a una voce*, at the press of Giovanni Battista Robletti (= 1618[13]; the dedication from Anerio to Puliaschi is dated 1 May). Puliaschi, a member of the papal chapel and a touring virtuoso, had by all accounts a remarkable voice of a kind singled out for special praise by Vincenzo Giustiniani as capable of singing in both tenor and bass registers.[19] But the printer did the composer no service: Puliaschi claimed that he was so horrified by the misprints in the volume that he immediately commissioned a second edition, *Musiche varie a una voce sola*, from the press of Bartolomeo Zannetti (1618[14]). The dedication of the *Musiche varie* to Cardinal Borghese (signed by Puliaschi and dated 1 June 1618) contains the conventional defensive tropes by the composer concerning songs done as "recreation" which he is greatly reluctant to expose in the theater of the world, and Puliaschi claims he would not have done so without the support of Anerio (some of whose motets are also included). However, Puliaschi is less shy of coming forward in his postface. The following translation is fairly literal: its tortuous convolutions are the composer's own.

The Author to the Readers[20]

> Kind Readers, I know that it will not surprise those who have heard me sing one of these songs of mine to see that they touch on so many notes in the bass and tenor [registers], the voice now moving quickly on and now stopping in all these passages [*passi*] which are found in the work, given that the Lord God has graced me with such a voice and disposition. However, if some virtuoso who has not heard me should desire to know the manner in which I sing them, even though it is difficult to

represent it in words for the reason that many aspects of the voice are better understood in hearing them done rather than described, nevertheless so as to satisfy whomever has such a desire, I will not refrain from offering some particular instructions with which everyone can, the voice being apt, with practice reach such perfection that these same works can be performed not only in the way in which I myself sing them but even better, since it is easy to add to things already invented.[21] Now to begin, I will say that in addition to using a different tempo in grave and joyful arias, as well as speeding it up in some passages and slowing it down [in others], and placing and controlling the voice and reciting in song to express the word and the sense and the affect according to the subject, and at its [proper] time the passion and joyfulness of the singing, and [using] soft and loud in such a way that the voice does not lose its sweetness, and doing *passaggi* now with their flowing movement and with trills, which should stand out in a lively way, and adding a dot now to the first note, now to the second as the passage requires, and also other effects which graceful singers are wont to do, I am wont to accompany my voice with different types of consonances, sometimes fuller and sometimes thinner according to the passage; in particular when the part I sing descends under the instrumental bass I avail myself of few consonances, those being the ones that better accompany that passage. Nor do I always avail myself of consonances, since as everyone can see for himself in the work, in some passages I very much like causing the listener to delight in the dissonances done with the voice such that they not offend the ear harshly, adopting a similarity to syncopation, which gives them grace so that they make an effect which everyone who has heard me on many occasions knows very well; and how true this is I will leave to be said by whomever is a friend of the truth. Whence having seen from experience what great delight is given to the listener by some passages done against the rules of counterpoint, for this [reason] I have not tied myself to such rules in this work of mine but only observed graceful singing and the ending of a passage with grace, even if one might move from B *molle* to B *quadro* [i.e., directly from the soft to the hard hexachord] or the opposite; nor have I considered spoiling a passage because of two fifths or two octaves, since it is not necessary here, given that I avail myself of the instrumental bass only to accompany the voice, which when one sings the simple bass makes everything emerge as unisons, and for such a reason on those few occasions I have not been concerned, nor even about two fifths in such composition. And although I could adduce examples from composers who have published works for several voices to sing with the organ where one sees that it seems that they wish to bring into use two fifths and two octaves and two unisons, having used them on many occasions, and likewise having the bass and the contralto sound together in a seventh, nevertheless I have not wished to avail myself of such an example, because I do not judge it well done. The reason I have been moved thus to publish this work has already been spoken of enough in the dedication. These few instructions that I have offered, I felt it appropriate to give only for those who wish to know them, just as on other occasions they have been requested of me; however, I do not intend to lay down the law to so many valiant men learned in this noble profession, to whom I profess myself to be a true friend and servant. May you live happily.

Puliaschi was well aware of the rhetoric of prefaces to publications of the "new music": there are clear echoes of Caccini in the references to "recitar cantando" and to the fact that the rules of counterpoint (e.g., prohibiting consecutive fifths and octaves) might justifiably be relaxed in solo song.[22] The latter is also a convenient excuse for the unschooled composer, anticipating any criticism of lack of technique. The notion that Puliaschi's style will already be familiar to those who have heard him sing is typical self-advertisement, as is the claim that good singing is much better heard than described. But although Puliaschi makes an apparent effort to explain his art, he does so in a dense, obscure way that seems to reflect more than just the inadequacy of words to describe performance, or his discomfort with writing prose. For example, one may or may not expect him to define the problematic term "disposizione," which was in common currency (compare Brunelli, above), but he deliberately leaves hanging at the end of his discussion of the voice the "other effects which graceful singers are wont to do." And in general the "kind reader" is left impressed by the details of the art of performance but bewildered as to how to put them fully into practice: the notion that anyone who heeds his advice might sing these songs as well as if not better than Puliaschi himself is clearly specious. The *Musiche varie* may be designed as a written record of a great virtuoso's performance, to be studied and admired accordingly, but its status as a blueprint for future performances is more open to question. Did, indeed could, just anyone really sing this music?

NOTATING THE "NEW MUSIC"

Specific virtuoso singers are often associated with prints of the "new music": we have already seen Antonio Brunelli referring to Francesca Caccini, and earlier, the Roman soprano Vittoria Archilei is regularly cited endorsing the work of Peri, Caccini, Marco da Gagliano, Sigismondo d'India and others.[23] The importance to the "new music" of the performance act is also emphasized by the repeated claims in dedications and prefaces that the score is a poor substitute for live rendition: thus Cristofano Marescotti, the Florentine printer and editor of Jacopo Peri's *Le varie musiche* of 1609, says that despite all his efforts in accurately printing Peri's songs, "it would be necessary to hear the composer play and sing them himself to fully appreciate their perfection."[24] There are also numerous examples of composers, editors, or printers seeking to notate specific performances (or at least, specific performance styles) by particular singers. Luzzasco Luzzaschi's *Madrigali . . . per cantare, et sonare a uno, e doi, e tre soprani* (1601) made public for the first time, and more than a decade after the event, the secrets of Duke Alfonso II d'Este's famous *concerto di donne* of Ferrara.[25] Similarly, at the center of Caccini's *Le nuove musiche* (between the madrigals and arias) lies music for the final chorus of *Il rapimento di Cefalo,* an opera staged for the wedding of Maria de' Medici and Henri IV of France in Florence in October 1600. Two related five-voice sections frame three central stanzas for solo voice and continuo (the first two followed by a repeat of the opening chorus as a refrain) which were sung, respectively, by the bass Melchior Palantrotti and the two tenors Jacopo Peri and Francesco Rasi (Peri's and Rasi's stanzas are strophic variations). Caccini claims in a prefatory note that in all three cases he wrote the *passaggi* notated in his print. The rubrics to each stanza then explain that Palantrotti sang "with the *passaggi* as given," Peri "with different *passaggi,* according to his own style," and Rasi "with some of the *passaggi* as given and some according to his own taste."[26] Another example of a song purportedly notated as performed is Giovanni Ghizzolo's setting of Giambattista Guarini's "O Mirtillo, Mirtillo anima mia" (*Il pastor fido,* I.4) included in his *Il terzo libro delli madrigali, scherzi et arie. A una, et due voci* (Milan: Filippo Lomazzo, 1613):[27] this florid setting (ranging from *B'* to *e'*) is printed as "sung . . . with the same *passaggi*" by the Milanese virtuoso bass Ottavio Valera.[28] All these examples, and there are many others, combine homage, reportage, and instruction to varying degrees. However, performing these songs as written is another matter: in the case of the Ghizzolo, the notion of a virtuoso bass enunciating the delicate sentiments of Guarini's lovesick nymph, Amarilli, is at best faintly ridiculous. One wonders why this song was written for Valera in the first place.

In such cases it is musical notation, rather than prose, that seeks to articulate and explain the subtleties of the "new music": the resulting changes in notational systems and practices merit an essay in themselves. It is clear that prints of solo songs and related repertories stretched printing houses to the limit, requiring greater resources (an expanded font with a wider range of note values, ties, and slurs) and typesetting skills (aligning the vocal part, text, and basso continuo) than the conventional partbook. Puliaschi's account of the fiasco over the printing of his *Gemma musicale/Musiche varie* suggests—unless it was just a ploy to get two books for the price of one—that some music printers were ill-equipped to meet these technical demands. Again, contemporary prefaces reveal the pressures. Don Bassano Casola, "close friend" of Francesco Rasi and editor of his *Vaghezze di musica per una voce sola* printed by the Gardano press in Venice in 1608,[29] distances the composer from this edition of his music—Rasi is "intent on other studies" and holds these madrigals in "slight regard"[30]—and begs pardon for the errors in those songs: "It remains for me to find excuse, if they are not sufficiently correct, in the fact that the keen desire of others and urgency have transported me."[31]

Francesco Rasi, whom we have already seen mentioned in *Le nuove musiche,* was a virtuoso tenor trained in Florence and Rome and working at the Gonzaga court in Mantua:[32] he took the title role in Monteverdi's *Orfeo* in February 1607, and according to Casola his "excellence in solo singing is known to the world." Clearly the 1608 collection (Rasi's first) was designed to demonstrate his skills as a composer, performer, and poet (he also wrote a good number of the texts set here). It is worth looking at one of its songs closely, "Indarno Febo il suo bell'oro eterno" (see Figure 1.1). The conventional pastoral poem by Gabriello Chiabrera contrasts the lover's unhappy state with the delights of nature, and where the text speaks of the "sound" ("suono") of a bubbling stream, Rasi initiates a long roulade for obvious word painting. The roulade continues in straightforward *semicrome* (16th notes) until measure 29 (counting whole notes)—running over the fourth and the last system of the first page—which contains two curious note formations in close succession: a stem flagged with what looks like a figure 3, and a stem with a reverse flag bending back on itself (producing in conjunction with the stem the figure 4). Notes bearing the 3-shape flag also appear in measure 30. Neither flag is commonly found in the fonts of earlier (or many contemporary) music printers. But the newly emerging problem of notating values smaller than the *semicroma* was clearly an issue, given composers' attempts to notate diminution and ornamentation practices that lay at the performing heart of the "new music."

The 3- and 4-shape flags are in fact mentioned and used in the chief diminution treatise of this period, Girolamo dalla Casa's *Il vero modo di diminuir, con tutte le sorti di stromenti,* printed in Venice by Angelo Gardano in 1584:[33] Dalla Casa calls them respectively "treplicate" (with 24 to the whole note, i.e., triplet 16th notes) and "quadruplicate" (32 to the whole note, i.e., 32nd notes). Rasi's *Vaghezze di musica* was also printed at the Gardano press: hence the appearance of characters (sorts) which Angelo Gardano must have designed and cast for Dalla Casa's treatise and then kept in stock for himself and his heirs. In Rasi's songbook, however, *treplicate* usually represent 32nd notes, not Dalla Casa's triplet 16th notes. And neither note value for the 3-shape flag actually fits the apparent duration of the conclusion of the "suono" roulade in "Indarno Febo" (two whole notes): the twelve *treplicate* in measure 30 last either a half note (twelve triplet 16th notes following Dalla Casa) or a dotted quarter note (twelve 32nd notes) rather than the whole note in the bass. The preceding measure 29 is still more problematic: four *semicrome,* four *treplicate,* four *semicrome,* and eight *quadruplicate* (here meaning 64th notes?) do not add up to one whole note by any reckoning.

Certainly this poses a problem for any modern editor of Rasi's songs, who will need somehow to "correct" the aberrant notation (presumably relying on the all-too-comfortable assumption of one or more printing errors). But the virtuoso performer would doubtless have been less constrained by the arithmetic. Indeed, the notation may be precise in its lack of precision. All Rasi wants, it seems, and all his editor and printer notate, is a fast *passaggio* to the cadence: the various flags have no rhythmic (still less, metrical) significance other than to indicate that "something fast happens with these pitches," with only the requirement that the singer should synchronize with the accompaniment for the final D whole note (measure 31). The problematic gap here between notation and performance is precisely what Caccini would have located in the realms of "sprezzatura," that effortless grace and willingness to "bend" the rhythm which he claims is crucial to any stylish performance of his songs.[34] However, it takes some skill to realize the point: the dense notation, like Puliaschi's dense prose, creates a resistance to performance, losing the literal-minded in a welter of ungrammatical *semicrome, treplicate,* and *quadruplicate.*

Figure 1.1 Francesco Rasi, "Indarno Febo il suo bell'oro eterno," in *Vaghezze di musica per una voce sola* (1608), fols. 2r-2v. Reproduced by kind permission of Garland Publishing.

Figure 1.1 (*continued*)

READING THE "NEW MUSIC"

Casola printed Rasi's songs "both to delight those who understand this art, and to be of use to those who study it." His reference to "intendenti" and "studiosi" reveals something of the desired readership of these prints: they were not always used by professional singers, some of whom may have been uncomfortable with musical notation and who anyway would doubtless have preferred music less obviously in the public domain and more exclusive to their individual use.[35] The score format of most monody prints did indeed permit the leisurely contemplation or study of a composer's works in ways not possible with partbooks—these songs need not be realized in or through performance, or scored up or intabulated, to get the measure of their achievement—and it also allowed the user to follow a specific performance to gauge the artistry of the musician(s) involved. But the single-impression letterpress printing adopted for Rasi's *Vaghezze di musica* (and indeed for most music prints of this period) does not make for easy reading: it was designed for different styles and repertories. Copper-plate or wood-cut engraving was more effective, permitting more precise note groupings (e.g., by beaming), alignment, and text underlay, although it was expensive and technically demanding.[36] Composers publishing in Rome, in particular, had this option given the presence there of skilled engravers catering most frequently to the highly developed art market: Simone Verovio, Martin van Buyten, Christoforo Ab Andlaw, Nicolò Borboni, Christopherus Blancus and others produced superb examples of engraved musical calligraphy. Their editions of songs and of keyboard music (a genre still less amenable to letterpress) by Luzzaschi, Ottavio Durante, Girolamo Frescobaldi, and others offer visual delight in ways that surely made them collectors' items.

Christoforo Ab Andlaw engraved Johann Hieronymus Kapsberger's *Libro primo di arie passaggiate* in 1612. Kapsberger was a virtuoso lutenist and chitarrone player in Rome, and his book of songs for voice and continuo (the latter also in tablature) revels in the possibilities of displaying all the traits of the new music through the art and craft of the engraver: the notated diminutions and ornamentation, plus the carefully intabulated accompaniments, of these "arie passaggiate" offer a remarkable illustration (in both senses) of contemporary performance practices. Not for nothing does Kapsberger set poetic texts focusing on vocal virtuosity, including the example *sans pareil,* Guarini's "Mentre vaga angioletta" (see Figure 1.2).

Figure 1.2 Johann Hieronymus Kapsberger, "Mentre vaga angioletta," in *Libro primo di arie passaggiate* (1612), 19. Reproduced by kind permission of the British Library, London.

Guarini's poem, headed "Gorga di cantatrice" ("The Singer's Throat") in his 1598 *Rime,* was written, it seems, in Ferrara in 1581 and specifically as an evocation of the ravishing sopranos of Duke Alfonso II d'Este's *concerto di donne.*

> *Mentre vaga angioletta*
> *ogni anima gentil cantando alletta,*
> *corre il mio core e pende*
> *tutto dal suon di quel soave canto;*
> *e non so come intanto*
> *musico spirto prende*
> *fauci canore e seco forma e finge,*
> *per non usata via,*
> *garrula, e maestrevol armonia.*
> *Tempra d'arguto suon pieghevol voce,*
> *e la volve e la spinge,*
> *con rotti accenti e con ritorti giri,*
> *qui tarda e là veloce;*
> *e talor mormorando*
> *in basso e mobil suono e alternando*
> *fughe e riposi e placidi respiri,*
> *or la sospende e libra,*
> *or la preme, or la frange, or la raffrena;*
> *or la saetta e vibra,*
> *or in giro la mena,*
> *quando con modi tremuli e vaganti,*
> *quando fermi e sonanti.*
> *Così cantando e ricantando il core,*
> *o miracol d'amore,*
> *è fatto un usignolo,*
> *e spiega già per non star meco il volo.*[37]

[While the lovely little angel / delights every soul with her singing, / my heart runs and hangs / wholly on the sound of that sweet song; / and I know not how, at the same time, / the spirit of music takes on / a singer's throat, and forms within itself and feigns, / in an unaccustomed manner, / a loquacious and masterful harmony. / It tempers with clever sound its pliable voice, / and turns it and pushes it, / with broken accents and with contorted turns, / here slowly, there quickly; / at times murmuring / in low and pliable sounds, and alternating / imitations and

rests and calm breaths, / it now suspends and frees it, / now pushes it,
now breaks it, now slows it down; / now it shoots it and makes it shake,
/ now leads it in turns, / at times in a tremulous and wandering manner,
/ at times firmly and resonantly. / Thus singing and singing again the
heart, / oh miracle of love, / becomes a nightingale / and already, in
order to leave me, takes flight.]

This is one of a large number of poems from this period that seeks to capture the essence and describe the pleasure of virtuoso singing, documenting in verse what Vincenzo Giustiniani noted in prose.[38] Its convolutions
not only reflect the difficulties of describing musical performance in
words (compare Puliaschi's prose efforts discussed above); they also enhance the mystique by focusing the attention on a fragmented succession
of key words that either draw upon the technical vocabulary used in
singing treatises to describe the virtuoso "pieghevol voce" (*accenti, giri,
fughe, riposi, respiri*) or exploit more metaphorical language to invoke
the seductive warbling of the singer's throat.

Guarini intended his "canzonetta" for music—he claimed that Duke
Alfonso's "Musico" (Luzzaschi?) would find much in it to do himself
honor[39]—and six settings do indeed survive in print: aside from Kapsberger's, there are those for six voices by Giorgio Florio (1589) and
Tiburtio Massaino (1604), for five by Giovanni Battista Caletti (1604),
for three voices, two violins, and continuo by Francesco Turini (1629),
and for two tenors and continuo by Monteverdi in his eighth book of
madrigals, the *Madrigali guerrieri, et amorosi* (Venice: Alessandro Vincenti, 1638). Curiously, only Kapsberger's version for solo voice (soprano clef) and continuo invokes the ensemble seemingly described by
Guarini. But his heavily ornamented monody certainly reveals some of
the tricks of the singer's trade, if not always in expected ways. The opening (seen in Figure 1.2) is reasonably effective, and there is a predictable
flourish on "cantando," using ornamentation to invoke the power of song.
Kapsberger also responds obviously enough to the opportunities for
word painting: an abrupt shift down an eleventh for "per non usata via,"
whole notes for "qui tarda" shifting abruptly to 16th and 32nd notes for
"veloce," a low register for the "basso e mobil suono," brief imitation between voice and bass for "fughe," roulades for "hor in giro la mena" and
so on, leading to a shift to triple time at "o miracol d'amore" for rhetorical emphasis, and concluding *passaggi* (in duple time) to represent the
heart flying from the breast. However, Kapsberger's setting of "Tempra
l'arguto [*sic*] suon pieghevol voce, / e la volve e la spinge, / con rotti

accenti e con ritorti giri" (see Example 1.1(a)) raises more interesting
questions. Conventionally enough, 16th notes paint "pieghevol," a turn
"volve," an upward scale "spinge," a leap "rotti," and roulades "ritorti."
But Kapsberger leaves two key words relatively uninflected, "accenti"
and "giri," even though these are technical terms borrowed from singing
treatises. True, when "hor in giro . . ." occurs later in the text, Kapsberger
notates what Caccini would have called a *giro di voce,* but at this point in
the poem the word is used more in its metaphorical sense than in its technical one. And in the following ". . . la mena, / quando con modi
tremol'e vaganti, / e [*sic*] quando fermi e sonanti," Kapsberger places the
written-out *trillo* on "mena" rather than "tremol[i]" (see Example
1.1(b)). Thus he seems happy to write out ornamentation when it serves
to reflect Guarini's metaphorical invocations of vocal virtuosity, but he
resists presenting too exact a response to Guarini's technical terms. Any
intendente or *studioso* admiring this song would not be able to identify
precisely an *accento, giro,* and *tremolo* as cued in the poem, even though
all three are present elsewhere in Kapsberger's setting. Similarly, any
singer performing it—and despite the notated embellishments—would
still have ornaments to add (precisely, one or more *accenti, giri,* and
tremoli as noted in the text).

Perhaps Kapsberger's imprecision—and for that matter the rather
stereotypical nature of his notated ornamentation—is due to incompetence or lack of musical commitment. Matters seem less equivocal in
Monteverdi's well-known setting of Guarini's poem.[40] This has a striking
opening for unaccompanied solo voice: the continuo then makes a dramatic entrance at "musico spirto prende"; and at "garrula" we hear for
the first time the second voice (off-stage, as it were, and in echo?). This
virtuosic (in both senses) setting also appears more open in its representation of vocal techniques covering, it seems, the full range of contemporary embellishment practices. Moreover, *accenti, giri,* and *tremoli* are
approximately notated at the appropriate words (see Example 1.2(a) and
(b)), although, and rightly, there is no ornamental *giro* at "hor in giro la
mena." As a result, Monteverdi gets much closer to Guarini's meaning,
but even he does not score consistent high marks for verisimilitude: after
all, the virtuoso female singing so splendidly evoked by Guarini's narrator (admittedly, a man) is realized here by two tenors.

A paradox begins to emerge. The vocal partbooks that make up the bulk
of the printed repertory in the sixteenth century were, for obvious commercial reasons, somewhat neutral in their performance specifications or

requirements: for example, embellishment and the use of instruments to double or replace the voices tend to pass unrecorded, and accordingly the music presents an image of uniformity that does scant justice to the rich variety of contemporary performance practices known from other documentary evidence of the time. This was doubtless a deliberate ploy to enhance the marketability of these prints, presenting the music in as transparent, and therefore as adaptable, a format as possible. However, towards the end of the sixteenth century and into the seventeenth, music prints became more precise in terms of describing and notating such matters as ornamentation, instrumentation, tempo and dynamic markings, articulation, and so forth. There is a clear sense of composers wishing to exert greater control over the realization of their music, incorporating within its fabric, and therefore specifying, performance details previously considered matters of convention or choice. This may have been partly due to stylistic changes, and also to developing concepts of the "work." But it also appears to be in response to the demands, and anxieties, of print. As increasingly complex music became more widely disseminated in fragmented worlds beyond the narrow circles of a composer and his immediate performing environment, it required more accurate transmission by way of more efficient and informative notation, and more careful explanation by way of prose. Yet for all the explication and clarification, this music becomes in many senses harder, not easier, to perform. And one might go further still. In all the above examples by Brunelli, Puliaschi, Rasi, Kapsberger, and others—examples which, I now freely admit, have been chosen to suit my case—we have found singers, instrumentalists, and composers variously being obscure where they might have been clear, almost willfully refusing to reveal the secrets of their art and distracting our attention elsewhere.[41] Whether the medium is verbal prose or musical notation, each of my case studies gives with one hand and takes away with the other: *intendenti* and *studiosi*—nay, even performers—are told something, but never enough. Not for nothing did music printing decline in the second quarter of the seventeenth century as secular repertories reverted to manuscript transmission.

We all know that there is always a significant gap between a musical text and its realization in performance, and that the gap widens still further the more one seeks to fix an essentially improvisatory art on the printed page. Perhaps the performer-composers associated with the "new music" were obscure simply because of the limitations of their chosen medium, be it prose or notation, to convey the subtleties of their art. But there may be more at stake here, with the anxieties of print focusing their

Example 1.1 Johann Hieronymus Kapsberger, "Mentre vaga angioletta," in
Libro primo di arie passeggiate (1612), 19-21 (tablature omitted).

Example 1.1 (*continued*)

(b)

hor   in   gi -   -   -   -   ro   la

me - - - - - - -

-   -   -   -   -   -   -

na, Quan-do con mo - di tre -   mo-l'e_____ va - gan -

ti,   E quan -   do fer - mi_e_____ so - nan - ti.

Example 1.2 Claudio Monteverdi, "Mentre vaga angioletta," in *Madrigali guerrieri, et amorosi . . . libro ottavo* (1638).

Example 1.2 (*continued*)

minds in specific ways. Many musicians involved in the "new music" appear defensive, hiding behind colleagues or friends as editors, or behind fellow performers and patrons as witnesses to their art. However, the retreat into (deliberate, I now submit) obscurity may in fact be more aggressive. The reputation of a Caccini, Rasi, Puliaschi, or Kapsberger was largely based on their performing abilities, which had to be, and had to be seen to be, better than any rival's. Certainly they sought kudos in having their music published—impressing patrons and the wider world—and it helped them set several records straight over the authorship, content, and performance of their songs.[42] But if the virtuoso art of the "new music" could be captured fully on the printed page, it would be a feeble art indeed. Moreover, for these performer-composers to reveal all would be to expose themselves to unwelcome scrutiny ("There are no miracles here: one could do better"!), and indeed could threaten their very livelihood. Why pay them to sing and play these songs if others could do so to perfection?

All scores resist their realization in sound, inhabiting a nebulous musical present between a performed past and an about-to-be-performed future. However, disadvantage could be turned to advantage as early seventeenth-century performer-composers established their reputation yet sought to shield what gave rise to it, willingly imprisoning themselves precisely in that nebulous present by way of systemic notational and verbal ambiguity to protect their art from the past and for the future. The more one works with these songbooks the more one realizes that they are not so much neutral transmitters of information from composer to performer as iconic representations of specific or generalized performance acts that need to be handled as carefully as any other iconographical evidence from this period. One also starts to realize that for better or for worse they serve as much to distance us from the sound of this music as to bring it closer to our ears.

NOTES

[1]Vincenzo Giustiniani, *Discorso sopra la musica,* in Angelo Solerti, *Le origini del melodramma* (Turin: Fratelli Bocca, 1903; reprint, Bologna: Forni, 1969), 98–128, at p. 121; my translation differs slightly from *Hercole Bottrigari, "Il Desiderio . . .";* Vincenzo Giustiniani, *"Discorso sopra la musica,"* trans. Carol MacClintock, Musicological Studies and Documents no. 9 (n.p.: American Institute of Musicology, 1962), 76.

[2]Giulio Caccini, *Le nuove musiche* (Florence: I Marescotti, 1601 [= 1602]). Caccini's dedication is dated 1 February 1601 (*stile fiorentino*, i.e., 1602) but a note by the printer explains that publication was delayed by the death of Giorgio Marescotti. Thus it is more by accident than design that the first printed book of solo songs was in fact Domenico Maria Melli's *Musiche . . . per cantare nel chittarone, clavicembalo, & altri instromenti* (Venice: Giacomo Vincenti, 1602), the dedication of which is dated 26 March.

[3]There are an increasing number of bibliographical and typographical studies of individual music printers in sixteenth- and early seventeenth-century Italy, most notably on Antonio Gardane (see Mary S. Lewis, *Antonio Gardano, Venetian Music Printer 1538–1569: A Descriptive Bibliography and Historical Study*, 2 vols. to date [New York and London: Garland Publishing, 1988, 1997] 1: 1538–1549, 2: 1550–1559) and Girolamo Scotto (see Jane A. Bernstein, *Music Printing in Renaissance Venice: The Scotto Press (1539–1572)* [New York and Oxford: Oxford University Press, 1998]). But the broader issues are only gradually emerging. I made some preliminary remarks in my *Music in Late Renaissance and Early Baroque Italy* (London: Batsford [Portland, Oregon: Amadeus Press], 1992), 40–44; and see also my "The Music Trade in Late Sixteenth-Century Florence," in *Atti del XIV congresso* [*Bologna, 1987*] *della Società Internazionale di Musicologia: trasmissione e recezione delle forme di cultura musicale,* ed. Angelo Pompilio et al., vol. 1, *Round Tables* (Turin: EDT, 1991), 288–294.

[4]Caccini made clear in his preface that at least some of the songs in *Le nuove musiche* had been composed in the mid 1580s. For *Musica nova,* see most recently Richard Agee and Jessie Ann Owens, "La stampa della *Musica nova* di Willaert," *Rivista italiana di musicologia* 24 (1989): 219–305; Martha Feldman, *City Culture and the Madrigal at Venice* (Berkeley and Los Angeles: University of California Press, 1995), *passim.* Much of Willaert's music here seems to have been composed in the 1540s. It is also significant, in the context of the argument developed below, that although *Musica nova* was printed in conventional partbooks, the repertory appears to have been designed for performance by solo voice (the virtuoso soprano Polissena Pecorina) and instrumental accompaniment. Similarly, Luzzasco Luzzaschi's *Madrigali . . . per cantare, et sonare a uno, e doi, e tre soprani* (Rome: Simone Verovio, 1601; facsimile edition, Florence: S.P.E.S., 1979) contains music dating back a decade or more.

[5]For the repertory, the best studies remain Nigel Fortune, "Italian Secular Monody from 1600 to 1635: An Introductory Survey," *The Musical Quarterly* 39 (1953): 171–195; idem, "Italian Secular Song from 1600 to 1635: The Origins and Development of Accompanied Monody" (Ph.D. diss., University of Cambridge, 1954). The relevant prints are listed in idem, "A Handlist of Printed Ital-

ian Secular Monody Books, 1602–1635," *Royal Musical Association Research Chronicle* 3 (1963): 19–37; 4 (1964): 98.

    [6]See the statistics in Tim Carter, "Music Publishing in Italy, c.1580–c.1625: Some Preliminary Observations," *Royal Musical Association Research Chronicle* 20 (1986–1987): 19–37.

    [7]Of course, we do not know the average print runs of these editions, which is a thorny issue in general for the period. But instinct suggests that they were rarely as high as the 1,023 copies of John Dowland's *Second Booke of Songs or Ayres, of 2. 4. and 5. Parts* (1600) which the London printer Thomas East was contracted to produce; see Margaret Dowling, "The Printing of John Dowland's *Seconde Booke of Songs or Ayres*," *The Library* ser. 4, 12 (1932): 365–382.

    [8]Compare the comments discussed in Robert R. Holzer, "'Sono d'altro garbo . . . le canzonette che si cantano oggi': Pietro della Valle on Music and Modernity in the Seventeenth Century," *Studi musicali* 22 (1992): 253–306. See also Severo Bonini in his *Discorsi e regole sovra la musica* (c.1650, Florence, Biblioteca Riccardiana, MS 2218; given in Carter, *Music in Late Renaissance and Early Baroque Italy,* 242): "Do you not see that today one is only concerned with composing little arias for one and two voices concerted with harpsichords or similar instruments? Madrigals to be sung at the table without instruments have been sent to oblivion, as is church music, all of which are too composed, and so little by little one will carry on losing this art, because today hard work seems somewhat unhealthy, having given the boot to the rules of Zarlino and to however many books one finds by rule-givers, with [musicians] acting according to their whim, believing in this idiotic maxim, that he who composed the rules is a man like any other."

    [9]For Florence, see Tim Carter, "Music-Printing in Late Sixteenth- and Early Seventeenth-Century Florence: Giorgio Marescotti, Cristofano Marescotti and Zanobi Pignoni," *Early Music History* 9 (1989): 27–72, at pp. 63–64. However, prices appear to have come down through the century: in the catalogue issued by Alessandro Vincenti in 1649 (see Oscar Mischiati, *Indici, cataloghi e avvisi degli editori e librai musicali italiani dal 1591 al 1798,* Studi e testi per la storia della musica no. 2 [Florence: Leo S. Olschki, 1984], 163–186), monody books appear to be priced on a par with madrigal books, although prices in this catalogue vary to the extent that paper no longer seems the main consideration (which in turn perhaps reflects the fact that much of the music in this catalogue is old).

    [10]Perhaps significantly in the context of my developing argument, surprisingly few surviving copies of early seventeenth-century songbooks show signs of significant use. One exception may prove the rule. The copy of Vincenzo Calestani's *Madrigali et arie . . . a una, e due voci* (Venice: Giacomo Vincenti, 1617) that survives in the Biblioteca Nazionale Centrale, Florence, has a signifi-

cant number of manuscript annotations reflecting corrections to and amplifications of the notation: clearly its owner had some difficulty understanding various conventions. I intend to make this the focus of a future study. Another example is also revealing. On 11 June 1616, Domenico Belli sent to Duke Ferdinando Gonzaga of Mantua copies of his *Il primo libro dell'arie a una, e a due voci* and his *Orfeo dolente,* both published in Venice in that year by Ricciardo Amadino; he hopes that Ferdinando will have these works sung by his musicians, thereby countering those critics who had recently judged them unperformable on account of the excessive number of *crome* in the bass lines, "se bene del continuo mi affatico di disgannare con farle sentire da chi l'ho dedicate, et insegnarli il modo, e la vera maniera che vanno cantate" ("even though I repeatedly strive to disabuse [them] by having them [the songs] heard by those to whom I have dedicated them, and by teaching them the way and true manner in which they are to be sung"); given in Alessandro Ademollo, *La bell'Adriana, ed altre virtuose del suo tempo alla corte di Mantova* (Città di Castello: S. Lapi, 1888), 216.

[11]See, for example, the sources discussed in John Walter Hill, *Roman Monody, Cantata, and Opera from the Circles around Cardinal Montalto,* 2 vols. (Oxford: Clarendon Press, 1997).

[12]For example, the dedication of Caccini's *Le nuove musiche* to Lorenzo Salviati (we do not know about its famous preface) was ghost-written by the poet Michelangelo Buonarotti "il giovane"; see Warren Kirkendale, *The Court Musicians in Florence during the Principate of the Medici, with a Reconstruction of the Artistic Establishment,* "Historiae Musicae Cultores" Biblioteca no. 61 (Florence: Leo S. Olschki, 1993), 144.

[13]See H. Wiley Hitchcock, "A New Biographical Source for Caccini," *Journal of the American Musicological Society* 26 (1973): 145–147.

[14]*Regole utilissime . . . sopra la pratica della musica* (Florence: Volcmar Timan, 1606); *Regole et dichiarationi di alcuni contrappunti doppii* (Florence: Cristofano Marescotti, 1610); *Varii esercitii . . . per una, e due voci* (Florence: Zanobi Pignoni, 1614).

[15]"L'Autore à cortesi Lettori // Il mandar nuove compositioni alla luce altro non è, che aprir gl'occhi e le menti per ricercare in esse con ogni sottigliezza ogni minima imperfetione. Gl'intelligenti, e ben affetti non possono ne sanno biasimare l'opera lodevole, ma gl'appasionati, e che molto presumono di loro stessi, difficilmente, vi si accomodono, e quando non trovano nissuno appice o per mostrare d'haver superiorità d'ingegno pronuntiano questa decisione. / Non ci sono Miracoli, si poteva far meglio. / E cosi se la passano per la generale, alcuni di questi belli ingegni haverebbe potuto à prima vista supporre, che questi miei concerti per la quantità, e qualità de passaggi tornassero difficili a cantarsi, ma se v'applicheranno ben l'animo troveranno essere molto agevoli a quelli però, che

hanno regola, e maniera di cantare, essendo così fatti componimenti già come tali
messi in pratica da tutti li miei scolari, a contemplazione de' quali composi la
maggior parte di essi, oltre ch'alli medesimi riuscirà il cantare franchissima-
mente con una semplice veduta anco l'altrui buone compositioni ben che passaggiate, e difficili. E si come mi pregio di quei vivaci ingegni, che da ma hanno
appreso tal facoltà, cosi mi sento obligato a commendare l'ammirabil Virtù ben
collocata in honor di Dio nelle due Nobilissime e Sacre Vergini del Monast[e]rio
di San Matteo o di Pisa per l'ottima dispositione, e soavità di voce, che in loro si
sente, poi che l'una, ch'è la Molto Reverenda Donna Maddalena Cini allieva di
valoroso Maestrò, è da me più oltre incamminata, e l'altra la Molto Reverenda
Donna Canente Agostini mia scolare sino da primi principij concertate insieme
con voce di Soprano, e di Contralto hanno ne i divini offizzi avvivate, & honorate
queste mie fatiche, si come più volte ancora hanno gustato l'Altezze Serenissime
di Toscana nel tempo, che hanno dimorato in Pisa. Vagliami per confermatione di
questa verità il testimonio della Signora Francesca figliola del famoso Signor
Giulio Romano, la quale come Maestra di bene, e gratiosamente cantare, e come
tale, e per altre nobilissime qualità, è Virtù conosciuta, & ammirata dal Mondo,
havendo più volte gustato del concerto loro, può fare di quanto ho raccontato à
voi benigni Lettori piena, & indubitata fede, Ho voluto per molti rispetti farvi del
tutto avvisati, acciò possiate difendere chi merita, e donar lode à coloro, che gior-
nalmente avanzandosi nel sentiero delle Virtù fanno honore à se stessi, & appor-
tano gloria à chi gl'insegna e vivete felice."

[16]There may be an additional subtext here, given that Francesca Caccini was
falling out of favor in Florence; see Tim Carter, *Jacopo Peri (1561–1633): His
Life and Works* (Ph.D. diss., University of Birmingham, 1980; reprint, New York
and London: Garland Publishing, 1989), 97–99. Brunelli seems to be bolstering
her support.

[17]Paolo Quagliati, *Il primo libro de' madrigali a quattro voci,* ed. Judith
Cohen, Recent Researches in the Music of the Baroque Era no. 79 (Madison:
A-R Editions, 1996); Pietro Maria Marsolo, *Secondo libro de' madrigali a quattro voci,* ed. Lorenzo Bianconi, Musiche Rinascimentali Siciliane no. 4 (Rome:
Edizioni De Santis, 1973). A similar impetus is apparent in those scores that present simple and embellished versions of the same piece: "Possente spirto e formi-
dabil nume" from Act III of Monteverdi's *Orfeo* is the classic example, but there
are a number of others, including motets by Bartolomeo Barbarino in his *Il secondo libro delle motetti . . . da cantarsi à una voce sola* (Venice: Bartolomeo
Magni, 1614), although here the simple versions are for those who can add *passaggi,* and the passaged ones for those who cannot.

[18]Compare Cesare Marotta to Enzo Bentivoglio, Rome, 3 March 1614, referring to a newly composed "Romanesca bastarda," so called because "in many

places it must be sung with passion [*cantato con affetto*] and in others with sustained notes, short embellishments, and other niceties [*con tenute di voci, accenti, et altre diligenze*] that cannot be written but require the spoken word" (given in Hill, *Roman Monody, Cantata, and Opera*, 1: 128).

[19]*Hercole Bottrigari, "Il Desiderio . . ."; Vincenzo Giustiniani, "Discorso sopra la musica,"* trans. MacClintock, 71. For the repertory, including songs by Caccini, see H. Wiley Hitchcock, "Caccini's 'Other' *Nuove musiche," Journal of the American Musicological Society* 27 (1974): 438–460, at pp. 447–453. A diarist reporting on a performance by Puliaschi in Florence in 1620 noted that he sang "with three voices, namely contralto, tenor and bass" (loc. cit., 447).

[20]"L'Autore a i lettori // Benigni Lettori io sò che non apportarà maraviglia à chi hà sentito cantar da me alcuna di queste mie opere il veder, che tocchino tante corde di Basso, e di Tenore hora sfuggendo, hora fermando la voce in tutti quelli passi, che nell'opera si trovano, havendomi il Signore Iddio aggratiato di tal voce, e dispositione: però se alcun virtuoso non mi havendo sentito desiderasse saper il modo con che le canto ancor che sia difficile rappresentarlo in parole per cagione, che molti motivi di voce meglio si comprendono in sentirli portare, che in raccontarli; con tutto ciò, per sodisfare à chi havesse simil desiderio, non restarò di dire alcuni avvertimenti particolari con i quali ciascuno potrà trovandosi la voce atta, con l'essercitio venir in tal perfettione, che queste istesse opere le potrà far sentire, non solo nel modo ch'io stesso le canto, mà anco meglio, essendo facile nelle cose già inventate l'accrescere. Hora per dar principio dirò; che oltre l'usar diverso tempo di battuta tra l'arie gravi, & allegre, come anco in alcuni passi stringerla & allentarla; & metter, e regger la voce, e recitar cantando, che esprima la parola, & il senso: e l'affetto secondo il proposito, & al suo tempo l'ardire, & allegrezza del cantare: & il piano, e forte in modo, che la voce non perda la dolcezza: & il portar de passaggi hora col suo andar corrente, & con li trilli, che spicchino vivaci; & hora col punteggiare la prima nota, hor la seconda si come richiede il passo; & oltre l'altri effetti, che sogliono fare li legiadri cantanti; soglio accompagnar la mia voce con diversa maniera di consonanze quando più piene, e quando più vote secondo il passo; & in particolare, quando la parte ch'io canto discende sotto il Basso da sonare mi servo di poche consonanze, e quelle, che più accompagnano quel passo: ne sempre mi servo delle consonanze; poiche come ogn'uno potrà da se stesso vedere nell'opera, in alcuni passi stimo assai il far gustar à chi sente le disonanze portate con la voce in modo, che non offendino aspramente l'orecchio, adoprando una somiglianza d'andar sincopato, che le da gratia, che faccino effetto, come ogn'uno che m'hà più volte udito, sà benissimo; il che quanto sia vero lo lascierò dire à chi è amico della verità: onde havendo visto per esperienza, quanto diletto habbino dato à chi sente alcuni passi fatti contra le regole del contrapunto, per questo non mi son

legato in queste mie opere à tali regole; mà solo hò osservato il leggiadro cantare, & il far concludere un passo con gratia, ancorche camini di b, molle in b, quadro, ò per il contrario; nè hò stimato il guastar un passo per causa di due quinte, ò due ottave, non essendo necessario in questo; servendomi del Basso da sonare solo per accompagnamento della voce, il che quando si canta il semplice Basso tanto vengono ad'esser tutti unisoni, e per tal ragione alcune poche volte non mi son curato, ne anco delle doi quinte in questa simil compositione: & se bene potrei addurre essempio di autore, che hà dato in luce opere à più voci da cantar con organo, dove si vede, che due quinte, e due ottave, e due unisoni par che li voglia porre in uso havendoli usati più volte, come anco nell'andar in sù il Basso, & Contr'Alto battere insieme in settima, con tutto ciò non voglio servirme di tal'essempio, perche non lo giudico ben fatto: la causa che mi hà mosso à dar in luce così quest'opera; già nella dedicatoria si è detto à bastanza: questi pochi avvertimenti, che hò detti mi è parso di dirli solo per quelli, che desiderano saperli, come altre volte me ne è stato fatto istanza; non intendendo però di voler dar legge à tanti valent'huomini dotti di questa nobil professione, à i quali professo esser vero amico, e servitore. Vivete felici."

[21]That is, *facilis inventis addere,* a stock Latin proverb.

[22]Compare Caccini's preface to *L'Euridice composta in musica* (Florence: Giorgio Marescotti, 1600): "Nor, too, have I avoided the juxtaposition of two octaves and two fifths when two sopranos singing with other inner parts produce *passaggi,* thinking that thus, with their charm and novelty, they will delight more greatly, and especially since without these *passaggi* all the parts are without such errors"; given in *Composing Opera: From "Dafne" to "Ulisse errante,"* trans. Tim Carter, Practica Musica no. 2 (Kraków: Musica Iagellonica, 1994), 39.

[23]Kirkendale, *The Court Musicians in Florence,* 272–275.

[24]Translated in Jacopo Peri, *"Le varie musiche" and Other Songs,* ed. Tim Carter, Recent Researches in the Music of the Baroque Era no. 50 (Madison: A-R Editions, 1985), xxxviii. Marco da Gagliano said the same of Peri in the preface to his *La Dafne* (Florence: Cristofano Marescotti, 1608): "Then Signor Iacopo Peri discovered that artful manner of sung speech which all Italy admires. I will not toil at praising it, given that there is no one who does not give it infinite praise and no lover of music who does not have always before him the songs of Orpheus. [But] I will indeed say that he who has not heard them sung by him himself cannot entirely comprehend the gentility and force of his arias, since he gives them such a grace, and in a way impresses upon others the emotion of those words, that one is forced to weep and to grow happy according to his wishes" (*Composing Opera,* trans. Carter, 53). Similarly, Bernardo Bizzoni notes in a letter to Enzo Bentivoglio (Rome, 28 August 1607; given in Hill, *Roman Monody, Cantata, and Opera,* 1: 308) that "l'Arie qui di Roma riescono più a sentirle

cantare, che à scriverle" ("the arias here of Rome succeed more in hearing them sung than in writing them down"). And the printer of Sigismondo d'India's third book of *Musiche* (Milan, 1618), Filippo Lomazzo, says that he has gone to some lengths to procure the volume and print it well so that those who practice this noble art and who unfortunately are unable to hear d'India sing them himself can at least see his music in print.

[25]The repertory is discussed in Anthony Newcomb, *The Madrigal at Ferrara, 1579–1597,* 2 vols. (Princeton: Princeton University Press, 1980).

[26]The music is edited in Giulio Caccini, *Le nuove musiche (1602),* ed. H. Wiley Hitchcock, Recent Researches in the Music of the Baroque Era no. 9 (Madison: A-R Editions, 1970), 101–113.

[27]Reprinted in vol. 4 of *Italian Secular Song 1606–1636,* ed. Gary Tomlinson, 7 vols. (New York and London: Garland Publishing, 1986).

[28]Other pieces sung by Valera "con gli istessi Passaggi" are included in the second part of Francesco Rognoni Taeggio's *Selva de varii passaggi . . . divisa in due parti* (Milan: Filippo Lomazzo, 1620; facsimile edition, Bologna: Forni, 1983), 2: 72–75.

[29]Rasi's songbook is reprinted in vol. 5 of *Italian Secular Song 1606–1636,* ed. Tomlinson. Casola was Duke Vincenzo Gonzaga of Mantua's vice-*maestro di cappella;* he is now known primarily for the letter in which he describes the "great studiousness and difficulty" of Monteverdi's *Missa "In illo tempore"* that the composer published with his *Vespers* in 1610.

[30]Again, this is a conventional trope, particularly from composers who claimed noble status for whom publication would appear a vulgar act.

[31]"A i lettori. // Questi Madrigali del Signor Francesco Rasi L'eccellenza di cui nel cantare solo è nota al mondo sono stati raccolti da me mentre egli intento ad altri suoi dilettosi studij ne teneva poco conto; Io che mi ritrovo seco congionto (oltre al desiderio di servirlo) con stretta amicitia ho preso ardire di porre in luce le presente sue compositioni si per dilettare gl'intendenti di questa arte, come per giovare a gli studiosi, sicuro che non meno stimeranno la vaghezza delle parole che la leggiadria della Musica fra le cui poesie alcune ve ne ha delle sue; Resta ch'io trovi scusa se non fossero à pieno corette perche il soverchio desiderio d' l'altri e la prestezza m'hano trasportato; cui bacio la mano."

[32]See the biography in Kirkendale, *The Court Musicians in Florence,* 556–603.

[33]There is a facsimile edition (Bologna: Forni, 1980).

[34]In the preface to *Le nuove musiche,* Caccini speaks of "that noble manner (as I call it) which, not submitting to strict time but often halving the value of the notes according to the ideas of the text, gives rise to that kind of singing with

so-called 'negligence' [*sprezzatura*]"; given in Caccini, *Le nuove musiche (1602)*, ed. Hitchcock, 55.

[35]For singers learning repertory by rote, see Hill, *Roman Monody, Cantata, and Opera,* 1: 128–129; the context here is that of training beginners, although it is clear that in general singers were expected to perform without scores which, when available, were only intended as an *aide-mémoire.* Curiously, just as I was writing this essay English newspapers were enjoying the scoop that the great operatic tenor Luciano Pavarotti has been claimed not to be able to read music (see *The Guardian,* Friday 25 July 1997, 2: 16–17). The notion of professionals and their patrons keeping such music secret is well documented as regards the *concerto di donne* of Ferrara; see also Cesare Marotta's comments on Cardinal Montalto's attempts to restrict access to Marotta's "libro delle musiche" so as to avoid others stealing his songs, made in a letter from Marotta to Enzo Bentivoglio, Rome, 3 March 1614, given in Hill, *Roman Monody, Cantata, and Opera,* 1: 330–331.

[36]See the discussion in Arnaldo Morelli, "Nuovi documenti Frescobaldiani: i contratti per l'edizione del primo libro di *Toccate,*" *Studi musicali* 17 (1988): 255–265.

[37]I have taken the text and translation (with minor changes) from Massimo Ossi, "A Sample Problem in Seventeenth-Century *Imitatio:* Claudio Monteverdi, Francesco Turini, and Battista Guarini's 'Mentre vaga angioletta,'" in *Music in Renaissance Cities and Courts: Studies in Honor of Lewis Lockwood,* ed. Jessie Ann Owens and Anthony M. Cummings (Warren, Mich.: Harmonie Park Press, 1997), 253–269, at p. 256, which discusses it (and the settings by Francesco Turini and Monteverdi) in some detail.

[38]For Guarini, see the comments in Tim Carter, "New Songs for Old? Guarini and the Monody," in *Guarini: la musica, i musicisti,* ed. Angelo Pompilio, Connotazioni no. 3 (Lucca: Libreria Musicale Italiana, 1997), 61–75. I also intend to make this the subject of a future study. The contest between a singer and a nightingale in Canto VII of Giambattista Marino's *Adone* is the outstanding example.

[39]See Guarini's letter of 20 August 1581 to Duke Alfonso given in Ossi, "A Sample Problem in Seventeenth-Century *Imitatio,*" 253 (my translation differs slightly), after Newcomb, *The Madrigal at Ferrara, 1579–1597,* 1: 264: "Mando la Canzonetta, che mi fu da V. A. ordinata, nella quale mi sono ingegnato di descrivere lo sgorgheggiare et le tirate et i groppi, che si fan nella musica, cosa nuova et difficile assai et, per quel ch'i habbia fin qui veduto, da niun rimatore, nè tampoco da poeta greco, et tra' latini dal diviniss. Ariosto in una sua ode, et da Plinio, prosatore antico, solamente tentata. Nella qual credo che'l Musico troverà molta invenzione di farsi honore . . ." ("I am sending the Canzonetta which was

requested of me by Your Highness, in which I have striven to describe the *sgorgheggiare* and the *tirate* and *groppi* that are performed in music. This is a new and quite difficult undertaking, and, so far as I have seen until now, one not attempted by any other rhymster, nor even by a Greek poet, and among the Latins, only the most divine Ariosto in one of his odes, and Pliny, the ancient writer, have tried it. In it I believe that the Musician will find much invention through which to do himself honor . . .").

[40]The piece is edited in Claudio Monteverdi, *Tutte le opere,* ed. Gian Francesco Malipiero, 2nd ed., 17 vols. (Vienna: Universal Edition, 1954–1968), 8: 246–258, from which Ex. 1.2 is drawn (with editorial amendments).

[41]Compare Severo Bonini in his *Discorsi e regole sovra la musica* (c.1650, Florence, Biblioteca Riccardiana, MS 2218, f. 98[r]): "Dimandai ad uno Cantore . . . che per grazzia mi dichiarasse qual fusse lo Stile moderno, e quale l'antico del comporre Musica; rispondendomi trà li denti e vergognandosi, non intesi mai altro, che queste parole, Il Moderno Stile consiste TANT'E, non saprei dire. Soggiunsi forse è quello della Ciaccona? de passacagli? del recitativo? Di nuovo rispose non so bene esplicare" ("I asked a singer . . . that he might please explain to me what was the modern style and what the ancient in composing music. Of his muttered, blushing reply, I understood nothing but these words: 'The modern style consists of what it is, I don't know how to say.' I added: 'Perhaps it is that of the *ciaccona,* of *passacagli,* of the recitative?' Again he replied: 'I don't know how to explain it well'"). I am grateful to Andrew dell'Antonio for this reference.

[42]Caccini complained in the preface to *Le nuove musiche* that his songs had been circulating "tattered and torn" in versions distorted and appropriated by singers (Caccini, *Le nuove musiche (1602),* ed. Hitchcock, 43). See also the title-page of Francesco Lambardi's *Secondo libro de villanelle* (Naples: Giovanni Giacomo Carlino, 1614), which accuses Oratio Cataneo of publishing some of these pieces with different words in the (now lost) collection *Gli amori dolenti.* There are similar complaints of plagiarism in the sixteenth century: see Carter, *Music in Late Renaissance and Early Baroque Italy,* 43. Of course, this itself could be an advertising ploy.

CHAPTER 2

Elite Books, Popular Readers, and the Curious Hundred-Year History of the *Liber Usualis*

KATHERINE BERGERON

I remember the day I got my first *Liber Usualis*. It was an ordinary fall afternoon in Andover, Massachusetts, in 1981. I received a telephone call from a friend saying he could deliver what I had been waiting for. We arranged to meet. When he arrived with the package, looking both triumphant and a little sheepish, I learned that the book had been stolen, not by my friend but by an unidentified third party, a woman who had discovered a box of the precious *Libri* lying unattended in the basement of the church where she worked as organist. The anonymous thief, whom I would never be able to thank, managed to pilfer three of them before the authorities or her guilt caught up with her—I never knew which. I simply felt lucky to have benefited from her sin.

It was like no other music book I had ever owned. Both shorter and fatter than an ordinary hymnal, sprouting a half-dozen satin ribbons from its heavy binding, it contained over 1,500 pages of Gregorian chants and texts for the Roman Catholic Mass and Office, printed in tiny type. The sheer abundance of music made the book unique, a much coveted prize for anyone interested in the ancient chant of the Roman Church. But the volume of chant was unique in another sense. It had become, in effect, a "rare" book, having fallen out of circulation and out of print when the second Vatican Ecumenical Council called for revisions within the Roman Rite, a decree that had made portions of the printed text obsolete.[1] The copy I now possessed, an edition from 1956, had probably lain unopened for nearly two decades. Indeed, the book looked as if it had never been used.

The *Liber Usualis* could thus be counted among the many bibliographic casualties of Vatican II, like the pile of discarded Latin Missals I
remember from my childhood: beautiful books with soft leather bindings
and gilt edges that my mother kept in a chest of drawers, no doubt for
sentimental reasons. And yet the fate of the equally defunct book of
music was different, for despite its obsolescence it managed to maintain
a kind of status, and a function, as it began circulating among a new body
of readers whose interests lay outside the contemporary practices of
Roman Catholic worship. I, like many others, after all, had first encountered this unusual book not in church but in college, where it adorned the
reading lists of courses in music history. In such a context the old book of
chant, which we tended to call simply "The Liber," obviously retained
none of its original function, appearing instead as a quirky reference
work, a virtual encyclopedia of the Gregorian repertory. Professors for-
aged through its pages in search of the most interesting melodies; students learned to perform the unfamiliar square notation without ever
really learning the rituals with which the music was associated. If we
rarely paused over the psalm tones, we never bothered with the prayers
or rubrics, the countless columns of fine print.

This latter-day transformation of the *Liber Usualis* from ritual text
to reference tool is perhaps best glimpsed in a passing remark made by
Richard Hoppin in the course of his introduction to *Medieval Music,* one
of the standard music history texts published by W. W. Norton for use in
American colleges. "For a number of reasons," he says,

> all musical references in the following chapters will be to chants that
> appear in the *Liber Usualis* (LU): it is usually the most readily avail-
> able of the various chantbooks; in addition to chants for the Mass and
> daytime Offices, it contains some examples of the very important
> chants for Matins that do not appear in the *Antiphonary;* it provides
> more than enough material for an introductory survey of Gregorian
> chant.[2]

The list of practical virtues leaves no doubt about the value of the retired
chantbook for Hoppin's classroom enterprise. More telling, however, is
the subtle, parenthetical change that signals its new musicological function. In a single stroke, the intimidating Latin title becomes an acronym,
a bibliographic code, whose standardizing function ultimately reshapes
our perception of the music within. No longer to be identified by their
unique place within the Church calendar, the Gregorian melodies may

now assume a flatter, more certain identity, as a page number in a common source known as "LU."

What is the consequence of such appropriation? When consumed by the body of naive readers for whom Hoppin writes, the LU retains no trace of its former value as a ritual book, becoming just another anthology of medieval music in an introductory survey course. The new meanings produced through these altered conditions obviously reflect back on the book itself, to form a dimension of that paradoxical phenomenon Roger Chartier has called *l'ordre des livres*. As he explains, "a book changes by the fact that it does not change . . . when its mode of reading changes."[3] The 1956 edition of the *Liber Usualis* may indeed refer to a single material entity, but the historical meaning of that typographic production—however "stable in its letter and fixed in its form," to use Chartier's words—becomes unstable, varied, even contentious, the moment it is conceived as a phenomenon governed by its readers. Chartier envisions a history of the book informed by "a history of reading practices," a history "that would seek to identify the major oppositions that can give different meanings to the same text."[4] This essay is an attempt to realize Chartier's vision, to sketch a history of the book I first knew as "The Liber," by taking account of the multiple impressions left by its unusual music not just on a single generation of music students, but on a host of different readers over the course of a hundred years.

For that, of course, we need a different kind of music history, one that comprehends the chant of the *Liber Usualis* in terms of not only musical but bibliographic coherence, the specific, material forms in which the chant creates an impression on the page. Chartier, once again, reminds us of this distinction:

> We need to remember that there is no text apart from the physical support that offers it for reading (or hearing), hence there is no comprehension of any written piece that does not in part depend upon the forms in which it reaches its reader. This means that we need to make a distinction between two sets of mechanisms, the ones that are part of the strategies of writing and the author's intentions, and the ones that result from publishing decisions or the constraints of the print shop.[5]

The point is perhaps obvious. As musicologists, we are all too aware of the ways in which various kinds of physical documents—manuscripts, published scores, part books—can impinge on our "comprehension of any written piece." And yet in our discipline, the idea of this impact has traditionally centered on some notion of an authentic text, which the source in question may or may not accurately represent. Chartier's cautionary tale encourages us to expand our view of the text to reconsider its authority in terms of not only what but also *how* it represents—to think not of pure "readings" but of actual readers—and thus to account for the role played by the print medium itself in the reading process, the ways in which the physical text and its notation can enlarge our comprehension of "the music itself."[6]

Chartier's point is especially pertinent for readers of the *Liber Usualis,* whose odd collection of signs—the squares and diamonds, dots and slashes—may at first glance appear more like obstacles than paths to musical understanding. Like the letters of an unknown alphabet, the rare Gregorian notation ensures that readers will grasp the sheer difference of the music even before they have attempted to decipher a single melody. For evidence of this impression we must look only as far as the title page of Hoppin's aforementioned textbook, where a designer at W. W. Norton saw fit to include a string of these strange signs from an unidentified mode 1 chant, an excerpt that was reproduced directly, as it happens, from the pages of the Liber (Figure 2.1). Positioned beneath the title words, the fragment of Gregorian notation becomes, like an advertising logo, a symbol for all that the student will encounter in the ensuing chapters, the strange and exotic world of "Medieval Music."

This admittedly imaginative handling of the Liber's notation constitutes, I would contend, a kind of reading, one that moreover adds nothing to our comprehension of the pitch or rhythm of the Gregorian text. According to our unnamed designer, the little sequence of printed signs simply has "medieval music" written all over it, an impression of antiquity that issues not from the audible but the visible aspect of the melody, from the character of the typography: as if the obliqueness of the remote past were chiseled into the angled surfaces of the notes themselves.

Figure 2.1 Title words from *Medieval Music* by Richard Hoppin (Norton, 1977).

However fanciful this view "from the printshop," it cannot be easily dismissed, for it, too, has a history, indeed, one that is about as old as the Liber itself. A glance into this past will allow us to bring the original chantbook and its Gregorian types more clearly into view, and with it, the mixed impressions of its earliest readers.

THE STORY OF A SQUARE

We must look back, then, more than 150 years to a very different time and place—to France circa 1830—and to a generation of Romantics captivated with the idea of rescuing the postrevolutionary Catholic Church. Among the significant results of the Romantic mission was the reconstitution of the French Benedictine order, a feat realized almost singlehandedly in 1833 by a young cleric called Prosper Guéranger, at a priory in the tiny village of Solesmes.[7] Over the course of the next seventy years the community of monks he reestablished at Solesmes would devote their lives to restoring, both in practice and in print, the lost traditions of the Roman liturgy—including, of course, the tradition of chanting whose legacy had been documented in manuscripts as far back as Carolingian times. The modern editions of chant produced by the Benedictines during those years tell a story all their own, exposing a history of imaginative effort to reclaim that Gregorian legacy, to seize, by increasingly creative means, not just the letter but the spirit of the ancient sources.

The quest began in earnest in 1860. This was the year that the 25-year-old Joseph Pothier, having just taken vows to become a member of Guéranger's community, assumed charge of directing both the choir and the monastery's new scriptorium. The dual responsibility apparently inspired the new monk, who dreamed of one day producing at Solesmes a truer, more "medieval" book of chant. It had become clear that even the best edition in use at the monastery, a gradual originally published in 1856 for the dioceses of Reims and Cambrai, fell far short of the perfection—and charm—of the ancient sources he knew through the work of copying manuscripts. In 1873 Pothier made his first attempt to capture some of that missing beauty, reproducing by means of lithography a small, handwritten *Processional monastique* for the use of his fellow monks (Figure 2.2). A story told by Pothier's colleague Dom Guépin suggests that the effort had indeed been worthwhile. The meticulous details, meant to resemble those found in a medieval book of hours, produced nothing short of delight among the recipients. "What joy we felt," Guépin recalls, "when these books were distributed!"[8] The testimony reveals the extent to which Pothier's handiwork—with its utterly homespun

PROPRIUM
DE
TEMPORE

DOMINICA PRIMA ADVENTUS.

Figure 2.2 Page from *Processional monastique* designed by Pothier, 1873.
Courtesy of Abbaye Saint-Pierre, Solesmes, France. Authorization No. 105.

elegance—could transform the experience of the music for an unsuspecting community of singers.

The success of this private venture encouraged Pothier, with Guéranger's approval, to undertake the more ambitious, and more public, project of editing a new Benedictine gradual. Turning now to the manuscripts, Pothier set about improving the flawed Gregorian text of the Reims-Cambrai edition, revising it both in content and in form. If the melodies of this edition, like those of other nineteenth-century chantbooks, suffered by comparison to the sources, the notation fared even worse—the rudimentary square notes of most modern presses having almost nothing in common with the complex range of neumes employed by ancient scribes and printers. Pothier had already attempted, in a limited way, to rehabilitate this more nuanced notation in the lithographic plates of his monastic Processional. With his new gradual he hoped to make the traditional neumes even more widely available by recasting them in a font of Gregorian type.

He lacked only one thing: a printing press staffed with artists who could do the job. In 1873 his own monastery was hardly equipped to realize such a task. Nor, it seemed, were most of the liturgical presses currently doing business in France. This was a conclusion Pothier had reached already in 1864, the year he tried, and failed, to produce a satisfactory Gregorian type with the firm of Henri Vatar in Rennes.[9] Before too long he was ready to seek help beyond the border; and so in 1876, just a year after Guéranger's death, he travelled to Belgium to try his luck with a new printing establishment in Tournai. The press was the vision of Jules and Henri Desclée, two brothers well known to the Benedictines for having donated a large piece of land on which they would later build the opulent neo-Gothic Abbey of Maredsous. Understanding that the monks' work of liturgical reform required not just quality buildings but quality books, the brothers dedicated a press to the Benedictine cause, travelling as far as England to employ some of the best artisans of the printing industry. When Pothier learned that these craftsmen were prepared to deal with the special problems of printing music, he began negotiations with Desclée to publish what he believed would be the first truly authentic book of chant—a book that could offer, as he put it to one of his fellow monks, "the purest St. Gregory possible."[10]

The authenticity of this new and improved chantbook was to be confirmed by the most immediately visible aspect of the musical text: the typeface. Pothier himself supplied Desclée with the basic design, to ensure that the punches and matrices they eventually fashioned would reflect, as much as possible, the tradition emanating from the Gregorian sources. And yet the true face of this tradition, the image of a pure St. Gregory, remained elusive. The early Renaissance prints that Pothier admired offered a "classic" view of that tradition, with neumes created by some of the best Venetian typographers: squares, losenges, ligatures, ornaments and clefs, all of them geometrically perfect and elegantly arranged to produce a distinct harmony on the page. The older Gregorian manuscripts were quite another story. Products of a long scribal tradition, they revealed a wide range of writing styles, both legible and illegible, whose overriding impression was—especially by comparison to the Venetian imprints—more utilitarian than beautiful, more ascetic than aesthetic. The manuscripts, in other words, showed a notation born not of art but praxis, a functional writing filled with predictable flaws and variations. If the new Benedictine edition was somehow to bear the full weight of Gregorian history, then the task facing the Desclée typographers was to impress a sense of the whole notational tradition—from script to print—on every page.

This historic impression did indeed weigh heavily on Desclée's new Gregorian font, coming to rest on the only structual element that could bear the load, the little squares on which the traditional notation was built. From an evolutionary perspective it was the square, of course, that represented the natural end of the tradition, the point at which the Gregorian notation reached maturity. Emerging from centuries of development, the squares had arrived—or so the story could be told—to civilize the more barbaric cursive neumes, endowing them finally with the intelligence and grace they lacked. The end of the story came with the disappearance of these exquisite squares of chant from the face of music, one of the more egregious errors of history that now required undoing.

Pothier himself shared this deterministic view of Gregorian history, as can be seen in more than one argument of his *Mélodies grégoriennes,* the important treatise on chant he would publish with Desclée in 1880.[11] An early chapter of his treatise in fact went to some length to illustrate the point, including a series of paradigmatic tables that attempted to chart "the diverse phases of the neumes" in two-century intervals: from their scribbled, Carolingian origins to their ignoble modern end (Figure 2.3). The status of the next-to-last phase of development—the beautiful neumes of the high Middle Ages—became instantly clear in the context. For even in their squareness these more developed signs could be seen to maintain the essential character of the earlier ones, and thus to preserve their rich heritage, a precious deposit of something like five centuries of Gregorian tradition. There was only one detail of this graceful and intelligent notation—perhaps the most impressive—that would remain concealed from Pothier's readers: the fact that these exemplary neumes of the "XIVe et XVe siècles," as he labeled them, had actually been created by Desclée.

On closer inspection, the historical weight of these neumes could be seen in a feature of the quadratic design—the signature innovation of the Desclée font—that no Renaissance printer would ever have thought to include: a subtle and elegant curve.[12] This barely noticeable aspect of the note form had two related functions. Not only did the presence of the curve distinguish the Desclée squares from the perfectly faceless blocks—the graphic travesty Pothier disparagingly labeled "notes modernes"—that were the standard fare of modern liturgical presses. It was this same distinction, the odd little curve, that made the notation designed by Desclée capable of recalling the entire history of Gregorian writing that preceded it. For the deviation suggested the presence of some other force, the pressure of a pen, the movement of a hand—in short, the very element of human error that the perfectly rational (and perfectly geometric) types of the great Renaissance typographers could proudly leave behind. With Pothier's help Desclée had designed a Gregorian type that recuperated this human element in order to place itself behind the times, behind the coarse "modern notes" of contemporary chant books—a Gregorian type that had never before existed in any Gregorian manuscript or imprint. The new Desclée font was, in fact, a marvelous, modern hybrid, a notation that belonged to neither "the fourteenth or the fifteenth centuries," but somehow called back to both.

This powerful historic effect shone from the pages of the book for which the types had originally been intended, the Benedictine *Liber Gradualis* that Desclée finally brought out in 1883, three years after Pothier's *Mélodies grégoriennes.* Indeed, the opening page of this edition undertook to confirm the effect in pictures, including along its upper border an illustration that traced the pedigree of the music all the way back to its mythical origins (Figure 2.4). The medieval-style decoration took the form of a miniature triptych, the central frame showing an inspired Pope Gregory sitting with his scribe, the two surrounding panels bearing a hymn whose Latin text related the scene in music: "When the most Holy Gregory poured out prayers to the Lord that He might surrender to him from above a musical gift in song, then the Holy Spirit descended upon him in the form of a dove and enlightened his heart to such a degree that at last he began to sing, saying thus: 'Ad te levavi' . . ." The connection between Gregory's original inspiration and the chant

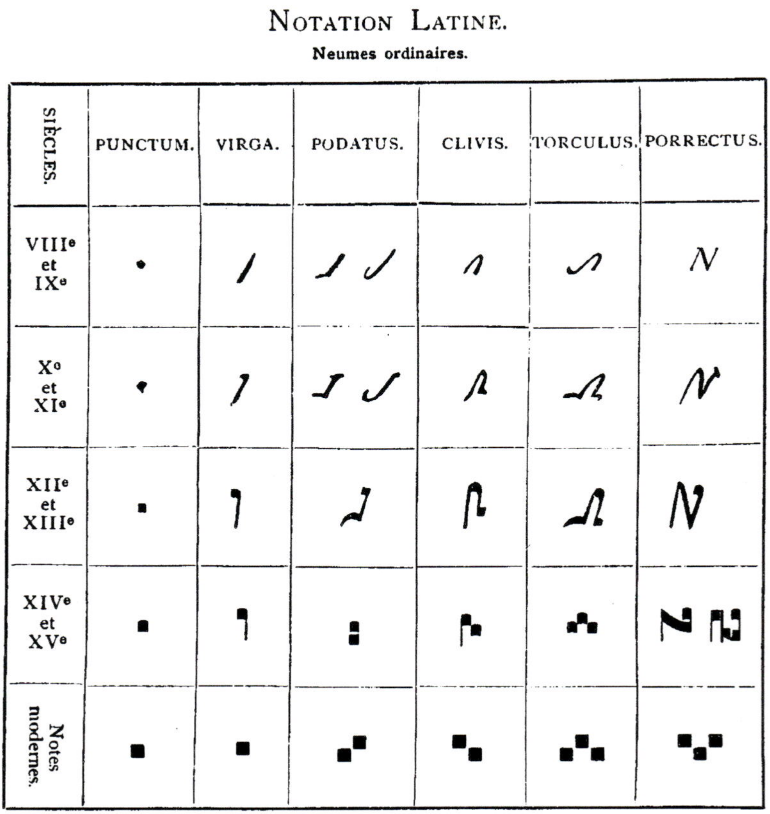

NOTATION LATINE.

Neumes ordinaires.

SIÈCLES.	PUNCTUM.	VIRGA.	PODATUS.	CLIVIS.	TORCULUS.	PORRECTUS.
VIIIᵉ et IXᵉ						
Xᵉ et XIᵉ						
XIIᵉ et XIIIᵉ						
XIVᵉ et XVᵉ						
Notes modernes.						

Figure 2.3 Table of neumes from Pothier's *Mélodies grégoriennes,* 1880.

presented within this modern edition was tellingly suggested by the ellipsis, which broke off right where Desclée's book would begin, with the chant that marked the beginning of the liturgical year, the Introit "Ad te levavi." The design thus reproduced the same evolutionary history told by Pothier's tables in a compact, visual narrative, beginning with the illegible scratches of the scribe's tablet, continuing in the cursive notes of the hymn, and ending, at the bottom of the page, with the perfect squares of Desclée's new Gregorian font. The iconography virtually ensured that readers of this new book would discover in its pages not just another version of the chant but exactly what Pothier himself had imagined: the superlative text of St. Gregory himself.

Figure 2.4 Opening page of *Liber Gradualis* published by Desclée (1883).

FORMS AND MEANINGS

If, to paraphrase Chartier, the form of a book must always serve to *in-form* the text carried on its pages, then the release of the Benedictine *Liber Gradualis* from the Desclée printshop, together with Pothier's influential treatise, had to mark significant moments in the history of Gregorian chant, for both books served immeasurably to alter the perception of this ancient music in the eyes of their nineteenth-century readers. The self-conscious antiquarianism of the Desclée neumes served in effect to historicize the repertory more completely than ever before, transporting it to a past both more remote and unfamiliar than that suggested by any contemporary chantbook. The sheer difference of the notation not only conferred mystery on the melodies; the chic curves and perfect proportions also lent an air of distinction and grace that, as Pothier was quick to point out, stood in stark contrast to the rough-hewn blocks of modern editions. Through the Desclée books the Gregorian repertory was accorded, in short, a different kind of status. Assuming a new place among the elite, the melodies came to be seen not merely as church music but as an ancient and venerable art—indeed, as one of the most important musical traditions in history.

This elite status was just as apparent in the editions produced by the Solesmes monks themselves. In the 1890s the monastery, which had managed in 1879 to set up a small print shop of its own, acquired enough financial stability to release two editions important to the Abbey's reputation: the first, a long awaited *Liber Antiphonarius,* completed in 1891, which contained the complete music for the monastic office; the second, a new edition of the *Liber Gradualis,* completed four years later. The publication of this second volume was to take the place of the now 12-year-old Desclée edition, which had sold out of the Belgian press. Both editions held to the high standard of typography previously set by Desclée (in fact, the Solesmes press, by arrangement with Belgium, had access to a complete range of the Pothier-inspired types). The only difference was in the size of the books: both were longer than Desclée's first efforts. The new antiphoner groaned with more than 1,000 pages of chant, the gradual with about half that amount, although the increase in length had in both cases as much to do with the requirements of typography as with the music, the editions featuring an increased proportion of white space in the design of the page. In the words of Alexandre Grospellier, who reviewed the publications for the Benedictine journal *Revue du chant grégorien,* the new gradual was for this reason "more accomodating," especially with respect to the Latin text, which appeared "less squeezed between the staff lines" than Desclée's and thus a good deal easier to read. Other design features (always "artistic and of the purest taste") proved the books to be, in Grospellier's words, "a great honor to the Solesmes presses."[13]

Such artistry did not, however, ensure a universal welcome for the Solesmes editions. For some religious reformers, the books were simply too "deluxe" to make sense in the humbler, diocesan parishes, with their amateur choirs and country priests. This was the view held, for example, by Jean Olive, editor of the monthly *Revue de musique religieuse et de chant grégorien* published by J. Mingardon in Marseille, a liturgical press also known for a line of chantbooks used in the dioceses of Digne and Dijon. In an editorial from 1896, Olive complained of the "fifteenth-century characters" employed in Dom Pothier's gradual, types that in his view made the books both "too voluminous and too expensive":

> We understand that had the edition in fifteenth-century characters not been made with a certain luxury, it would easily have become illegible. The consequences of employing such characters therefore makes it impossible ever to have cheap books. An artist, of course, would no more look at the price of a book than would a millionaire. But this is not the case among the ordinary faithful. Good value [*le bon-marché*] is an important factor in the diffusion of plainchant.[14]

The logic of the passage ultimately confirmed the superiority of the Benedictine editions; for it was precisely through their lack of "good value" that the Solesmes books could be said to have attained their uniquely elite status—the "real" value that placed them above the standard fare of the modern liturgical presses. Outclassing the competition by a significant margin, the historically informed types of the Benedictine editions lavished an unmistakable luxury on the chant, a quality that even if lost on the ordinary churchgoer was sure to be appreciated, as Olive reminds us, by "an artist or a millionaire."

Even so, the charge of elitism did not go entirely unnoticed. In 1896, as if in silent response to Olive's complaint, the Solesmes monks brought out on the heels of their hefty new gradual and antiphoner yet another edition whose purpose was to make the superior Benedictine chant available to a larger number of faithful, and at a significant reduction in cost. The edition represented an entirely new concept of liturgical book, a kind of hybrid that included text and music for both Mass and Vespers on

Sundays and double feasts, as well as the complete Office for the Holy
Week triduum and the Office for the Dead, music for Matins and Lauds
of Christmas, together with sundry pieces for other common rituals. The
result was something like a summary of four separate liturgical books—
a missal, gradual, kyriale, and antiphoner—bound in a single volume:
four books for the price of one. (Indeed, according to Grospellier, the
price of the book in 1896 came to just 4 fr 50, a mere 50 centimes more
than the price of one Benedictine antiphoner.) The compilation was
given the name *Paroissien romain,* a vernacular title invoking the common parishioner to whom it was addressed. In Latin, it would be known
as the *Liber Usualis.*

If the beauty of the previous Benedictine editions had worked to
change the image of the repertory, the utter practicality of this new "book
of common practice" would make an even bigger difference. The monk
standing behind this new creation was not Pothier but his protégé Dom
André Mocquereau, a Benedictine who in 1896 had been at Solesmes for
twenty years. Mocquereau's prior musical training had made him an immediate asset to the various Gregorian projects that were underway in
1875, the year he entered the order, and in no time he became involved
not only in work on the forthcoming gradual, but also in matters of performance. By 1889, just a decade after his ordination, he had taken over
Pothier's job as general director of choir. A few years later, after Pothier
had in fact left Solesmes to become abbot of Saint-Wandrille,[15] Mocquereau assumed responsibility for the Gregorian research as well,
bringing to Pothier's aesthetic concerns a new pedagogical focus. Under
Mocquereau's leadership there would emerge at Solesmes a new kind of
"practical school," as some liked to call it, aimed at increasing knowledge of the chant through general education both inside and outside the
monastery. Mocquereau's ultimate goal was to popularize the repertory
Pothier had worked so hard to aestheticize—to bring an understanding of
this beautiful, historical music to a larger number of faithful Catholics.
The *Liber Usualis* was his first significant attempt to realize that goal.

For one thing, the *Liber Usualis* offered all the refinement of the previous Desclée/Solesmes editions in a format that one might today call
"user friendly." In this way it represented a new kind of bibliographic
feat, for it managed, even with its substantial bulk, to maintain the distinct, historical face that was the mark of the Solesmes chant while dispensing with the more ostentatious aspects of book design that would
have made it too "deluxe." The effect of the book was thus at the same
time elegant and humble. The volume exuded a quiet grace without call-

ing attention to itself, an impression largely aided by the most surprising aspect of its form: it was small. This unexpected feature was significant enough for Grospellier to point out (at some length) in his 1896 review. As he explained, the use of a "very lightweight although not at all transparent paper" had allowed for a reduction of about three centimeters in a volume containing almost 1,250 pages. The remaining dimensions were even more significant. Measuring only 16 centimeters high and 11 centimeters across, the book represented, according to Grospellier, "in every sense of the word a manual—a manual ideal both for the liturgy and for the chant of the Church." Indeed, what better way to get the traditional melodies into the hands of more of the faithful than to shrink the book that contained them?

Grospellier failed to mention only one thing: that this newly downsized handbook made use of equally downsized characters. Yes, the perfect "fifteenth-century" types of the Desclée/Solesmes editions had been ingeniously reduced to a little less than half the size in the *Liber Usualis,* so that the little manual could carry at least twice the amount of music. Yet Grospellier perhaps knew better than to call attention to this feature, for in every other respect the Gregorian characters were identical. Readers of the *Liber* were, after all, not supposed to notice the reduced size of its Gregorian melodies because, even in their diminished state, they managed to carry the same historical clout.

This power can be proved—in a roundabout way—by turning to a curious little essay published in the Benedictine *Revue du chant grégorien* in 1898 and bearing the coy title "Comment, à Marseille, on écrit . . . Solesmes" ("In Marseille, this is how they write . . . Solesmes"). The essay offered a snide rebuttal to a certain Jean Dupoux of Mingardon and Co., who had attacked the chant of Solesmes the previous June in the same organ that had published Olive's complaints in 1896, Mingardon's house journal, the *Revue de musique religieuse et de chant grégorien.* The author of the rebuttal, who signed himself A. Dabin, focused his response on what he considered the most egregious aspect of the attack, a passage in which Dupoux had quoted an "alleluia" from the 1883 Desclée *Liber Gradualis* (Figure 2.5). In fact, Dabin took special care to reproduce the offensive passage note for note in order to expose the source of his consternation, which was simply this: the notation did not belong to Solesmes. Mingardon had had the audacity to attribute to Solesmes an "alleluia" printed in the ugly, modern characters Pothier had long ago rejected. "This must be some kind of joke," Dabin fumed, then, turning to the books he loved best, offered the *real* Solesmes "alleluia" on the

Figure 2.5 "Alleluia" printed by Mingardon.

facing page as proof (Figure 2.6), complete with page references from both the old *Liber Gradualis* and the brand new *Paroissien romain.*

One look at the diminutive neumes of the counter-example confirms that the types had been drawn, of course, not from the older Desclée edition but from the newest creation of Solesmes. Yet for Dabin it made no difference. Big or small, the importance of the so-called traditional notation remained the same, lending to the Solesmes "alleluia" an air of distinction that Mingardon's could never have:

> Nothing could be clearer, could it? Here, seventy-four clearly differentiated *signs,* easy to recognize, to spell like letters pulled from syllables, syllables from words, words from phrases—each one having its own particular name of *podatus, clivis, torculus, scandicus . . .* Over there, an ugly scrawl of two hundred seventeen *notes,* aligned, according to the old game, by *tails, squares, lozenges, maxims . . .* without design, without cohesion, without relief.[16]

Dabin likened the effect of Mingardon's simple geometric forms to that of reading a popular edition of a classical text that had been printed in Roman instead of Greek characters to facilitate comprehension. While

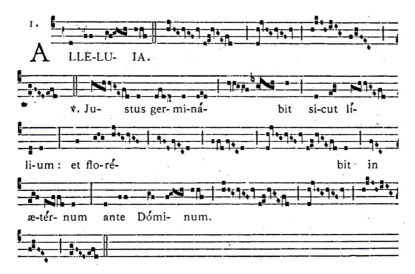

Figure 2.6 Same "Alleluia" as Fig. 2.5 published in the traditional Gregorian characters of the Solesmes editions.

the transliteration pretended to offer the reader the "real" Greek in a familiar, easy-to-read form, translating the sounds of one language into the forms of another, the result was more confusing than clear. The use of the Roman alphabet produced, in effect, a garbled version of the text, a foreign orthography that would inevitably render the meaning of certain words opaque.

As should by now be clear, the Solesmes books sought to eliminate all such confusion by presenting the melodies, even in an admittedly popular edition like the *Liber Usualis,* with their original Gregorian "spellings." The more exact orthography of the Benedictine editions thus carried an important dimension of musical meaning, through the presence of neumes whose precise melodic function was indicated by name: (*torculus*) "turning," (*clivis*) "sloping," (*podatus*) "stepping." These were characters with real character: that is, with a quality capable of impressing upon readers the genuinely Gregorian contours of the music. By comparison to the shorthand chant published in Mingardon's edition (mere "notes" in Dabin's view), these neumes offered observant Catholics a true "sign"—an authoritative demonstration (like an omen or a miracle) of the authentic Gregorian tradition. And now that these powerful signs had been reduced to half the size, this ancient truth could become more accessible than ever before.

That is certainly how Mocquereau perceived the benefits of the new *Liber*. In fact, shortly after the release of the first edition, he was hard at work on a second, which was to offer an even truer version of repertory, reflecting the recent advances made by his Gregorian workshop. A more extended study of the manuscripts (made possible by the use of photographic facsimiles) had led the Solesmes researchers to reconsider a number of the decisions made by Pothier, and to undertake a more or less complete revision of the melodies printed in the earlier Solesmes books.[17] Not only would the new *Liber Usualis* include numerous corrections to the musical text, it would also include a notational innovation, a set of signs designed to clarify a dimension of Gregorian performance that no previous edition had fully taken into account: its rhythm. Mocquereau set about designing a rhythmic notation to lay alongside the squares—a small collection of dots and slashes that were, in his view, just as "historical" as the Desclée/Solesmes neumes, as he like Pothier had adapted them from signs found in early Gregorian manuscripts.

But the purpose of the notation was more practical than historical, more prescriptive than aesthetic. For the supplementary marks were meant above all to serve as aids to performance, helping singers with the nuances that were the most critical (and most difficult) aspect of good chanting: the *ralentissements,* the swells, the subtle prolongations, the rests. The new notation, in short, was designed to improve the mode of reading—that is, of singing—in Gregorian choirs everywhere, to introduce a kind of standardization into their collective decipherment so as to ensure that more and more Gregorian readers would read the chant not only more proficiently but in more or less the same way: according to the method of Solesmes. The supplementary signs were introduced slowly, dot by slash, appearing initially (accompanied by ample instructions) in just a few pamphlets published by the Solesmes press between 1899 and 1901. The first *Liber Usualis* to be supplied with a full complement of the signs would not appear until 1903.

By that time, however, the Solesmes monks were no longer residing at Solesmes; they were not even in France. The passage of new, anti-clerical legislation in 1901, which in effect denied all religious orders the right to own property, forced countless communities to quit their abbeys and relocate beyond French borders. Most escaped to Belgium. The Solesmes monks set their sights on England, where they found hospitality on the Isle of Wight. The rapid exodus from their monastery required, of course, that the monks leave behind a good deal of their belongings, including many publications associated with their now lucrative print shop. Not least of these was the nearly complete second edition of the *Liber Usualis*. In order to save the work from oblivion—in fact, to prevent it from being seized by government liquidators—the Solesmes monks had no choice but to take the rash decision of selling their copyright to a reliable publisher outside France. And so they chose the only sensible option, returning once more to the company that had first established their Gregorian reputation, Desclée of Tournai.

Desclée obviously wasted no time in making good on the arrangement, taking just a little over a year to complete a book that in both content and form significantly departed from their first efforts with the 1883 *Liber Gradualis:* a book that represented almost two decades of Gregorian advances made by an entirely new generation of Solesmes monks. In the eyes of Mocquereau, this new and improved *Liber Usualis* got even closer to fulfilling Pothier's original goals (Figure 2.7). With its corrected melodies and simplified typography (whose only frills were a set of utterly practical performance marks), the book succeeded in putting into the hands—and mouths—of the faithful a truly "plain" plainchant, a

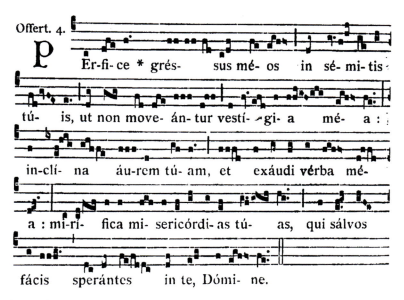

Figure 2.7 Page from *Liber Usualis* (1903) with rythmic signs, showing offertory "Perfice gressus." Courtesy of Abbaye Saint-Pierre, Solesmes, France. Authorization No. 105.

cleaned-up repertory that could now be called, even more accurately than before, the "purest St. Gregory possible."

The monks would have less than a year to wait before this view was seconded by an even higher authority. A newly elected Pope Pius X, inspired by the superior work produced at Solesmes, decided in 1904 to sponsor at the Vatican an official Gregorian edition for the use of the whole Church. In a *motu proprio* published in the same year (25 April 1904) he outlined his intentions to use the already published Solesmes editions as his model. But, as he explained, in order to ensure the unity of the new edition the text would be produced at home, at the Vatican Press, and then offered as an exemplar to all liturgical presses who would have equal right to reproduce it. This meant, of course, reproducing not just the notes of the chant but their exact material form. Evidently Pius X did not need a Roger Chartier to remind him that the official Gregorian "text" was inseparable from the characters in which it would be printed. The pontiff had his secretary of state inform Solesmes (which now meant Desclée) that they would have to turn over the copyright to all the Gregorian types currently used for their editions, with the exception of the rythmic notation, which His Holiness deemed inappropriate for use in a Vatican Urtext, and so the signs continued to remain in the monks' possession.[18]

This final legal transaction changed the meaning of the Solesmes chantbooks for all time. With the subsequent publication of the Vatican edition, the uniquely historical "face" of St. Gregory, once associated with an elite community of Benedictine monks, became the only face imaginable for the traditional music of the Church. The margin became the center; the unique, the norm. And the name of Solesmes, far from forgotten, would become even more firmly attached to those little rhythmic signs that continued to be disseminated through Desclée's most popular edition, the *Liber Usualis*. Over the next half century, in fact, Desclée would publish hundreds of thousands of these editions—until, that is, the decisions of another newly elected pope made them obsolete, taking them out of the hands of faithful Catholics so that they might one day end up in the libraries of musicologists.

THE RETURN OF THE REPRINT

Which brings us back to where our story began. Or almost. For it turns out that this out-of-print book has once again become available—and at a site whose promise of universal access suggests that the manual may enjoy an even broader community of readers than it apparently once did. I am not visiting a library or a dealer of rare books when I find it; no, I am surfing the net. My search delivers me to a press in Great Falls, Montana, called "St. Bonaventure Publications," whose homepage directs me to another site (http://www.libers.com) and to the main item of its modest catalogue: "The Liber Usualis: The Book of Gregorian Chant." In the center of the page, a scanned excerpt of the mode 8 Kyrie Rex splendens provides visual evidence, through the contours of its familiar face, that the book on offer is indeed "*The* Book." A list of features offers further bibliographic evidence, confirming that the text is a reprint, a copy of a *Liber Usualis* originally published by Desclée in 1953. The book apparently contains everything it should, including "all the Little Hours of the Divine Office," the "tone for the Gloria Patri and also the 8 [psalm] tones," as well as a few extras "such as [the] new text of Pope Pius XII for the Assumption, *Signum magnum.*" Even more telling is this account of the book's form:

- Hardbound, embossed "*Liber Usualis*" in gold leaf, red page edges
- Smyth (sewn) binding, 6 colored ribbon markers

The list of bibliographic details verifies, in other words, that the book has been remade to look exactly as it used to.

This likeness is proved, in fact, as we scroll further down the page, where we find a photo offering one of the newly reprinted specimens for examination (Figure 2.8). Opened invitingly on a lectern, the volume appears in soft focus, bathed in a warm light that reflects gently off two of its satin ribbons. The accompanying caption creates an appropriately spiritual atmosphere for the image, reminding us that "Mother Church has ever called this prayerful chant *her own Music,*" and ending with the historic words of Pope (now Saint) Pius X: "this form of music must be given back to the faithful." The caption introduces, that is, a telling conflation between Gregorian chant and its notation, between "this form of music" which according to the beatified Pius X "must be given back" and the form of one particular chantbook, now out of circulation for more than a quarter century. The misty internet photograph encourages us to view the reprinted *Liber Usualis* as a kind of messianic promise, a savior in a world bereft of spiritual music.

It is precisely because of its faithful resemblance to the rare 1953 original that the photographed book gives off such an unmistakable aura, an aura that proves the reprinted *Liber* can no longer hold the same

Mother Church has ever called this prayerful Chant *her own Music*; she has inseparably connected it with her Divine Worship; hence it will endure to the end of time, and will outlive every other form of music. This music rests on the rock-bottom foundation of *diatonic tone-succession* and on the natural rhythm of free text declamation: hence it is lifted far above the varying moods of convention and human passion. "This form of music," says Pope St. Pius X, "must be given back to the faithful." The study of chant presents itself, therefore, as a most sacred obligation.

Continue on for more Gregorian Chant

This site is under construction!

Figure 2.8 Page from St. Bonaventure Press website, 1998.

meaning it held for those historical readers who once sang from its pages. The book has profoundly changed, to quote Chartier once again, "by the fact that it has not changed." The binding, the embossing, the gold leaf, the tinted pages, the ribbon are all signs of that transformation: they are high-end frills in a world where hymnals often come in paperback, and the most commonly used parish missals—those conveniently disposable "missalettes" printed from month to month—have no covers at all. The price of the edition certainly reflects the high value attached to these specialty features, bibliographic details that were at one time, like the chant itself, more commonplace than unique. Indeed, these special books today apparently warrant special treatment, as the advertisement makes clear further down the page. We learn that, for a small additional charge, we may also purchase a custom-made leather case to protect our reprint from wear and tear, making the total cost of just one of these reproduced editions, complete with custom leather case, postage, and handling, about $140.00.

It is perhaps a modern-day irony that the new price tag should elevate the formerly practical book into the ranks of those deluxe, "elitist" editions for which it was originally proposed as an alternative. A book at one time thought to be "usual," a volume reflecting the common practice of the average parishioner, has now become the domain of special-interest publishing: a vintage edition created for cognoscenti in search of a chant they imagine to be lost, and for which they are willing to pay dearly. Incidentally, for those on a tighter budget and willing to sacrifice some amount of bibliographic luxury, St. Bonaventure offers other options, which can be found simply by pressing a button labeled "Used Libers." A window opens onto a new link offering a line of slightly imperfect reprints (marred by smudged notes or uneven embossing) for $85, as well as used originals in a variety of conditions, with prices ranging from $35 to $125. These flawed or damaged specimens are like "starter" volumes, to be used by would-be chanters until the time they can afford a perfect reprint of their own, for even in their diminished condition the used books imply a high-end market, pitched toward a body of consumers willing to get their hands on the chant at any cost. The whole phenomenon suggests, in an odd way, the kind of bibliographic culture long ago eclipsed by the advent of widespread literacy, a culture in which "the mere possession of a book signifie[d] cultural difference."[19] These modern-day owners of the *Liber,* in their very desire to possess "the book," do indeed appear to represent a culture apart, a rare and literate audience of chant connoisseurs.

A glance at another portion of the same web page encourages, however, a different view. In a section marked "Comments on The *Liber Usualis*" we find, for instance, the testimony of several customers whose expression of satisfaction makes them sound more like ordinary fans than experts: "We just received our Libers [sic] this past week and wanted you to know how pleased we are . . ." The comments give the impression—like the button marked "Used Libers"—of a far less specialist body of readers, who are probably not scholars, or, at least, are not fussy about their Latin plurals. According to Joanie M. Gillespie, the representative from St. Bonaventure Publications who very kindly answered a few of my questions, the readers in fact cover a broad spectrum, blurring boundaries defined by both education and religion: "Our clientele . . . rang[es] from people with a slight interest in Gregorian chant, to music scholars, to Anglicans, Episcopalians, and traditional Catholics." The tone of her account makes the reprint business sound less like a special-interest (or "niche") industry than like a philanthropic concern responding to a pressing social need: "Prior to our reprinting the Liber, one could purchase a tattered, torn, stained Liber that was in sad need of rebinding for around $110.00—if they could find one." Explaining that the St. Bonaventure reprints have been sold to customers "throughout the entire world," she confesses, "it is truly a joy to bring back to print a book of such longstanding beauty."

But it remains for us to ask why it is *this* book, in particular, that brings such joy. It is certainly worth pointing out that the world may not be quite so bereft of Gregorian music as the testimony of St. Bonaventure would suggest. After all, an extensive and relatively economical line of chantbooks—including graduals, psalters, antiphoners, and noted missals—has become increasingly available through the Solesmes monastery for the past twenty years,[20] books that not only conform to liturgical practice post Vatican II (unlike the out-of-print *Liber Usualis*), but also continue to uphold the high standard of printing long ago established at the Solesmes press. Although nothing like the unique hybrid format of the old *Liber* is currently in print, its absence is hardly a loss: a reader can have access to an even larger quantity of Gregorian chant for the Mass and Office simply by purchasing a collection of these books (for example, Missal, Gradual, Antiphoner) for about the same total cost as one reprinted *Liber.* And one needn't travel all the way to France to find them; the books are distributed widely through religious bookstores in Europe and North America. They are even accessible on the web, at a site (www.solesmes.com) that offers a complete catalogue including descriptions and prices. So what is it about the old *Liber Usualis* that continues to hold such a fascination for readers?

An answer is suggested by turning briefly to the other books available through St. Bonaventure Publications, books that contain no music but are nonetheless advertised right alongside the used and reprinted chantbooks. The first is, like the Liber itself, a remake of a superannuated edition called *The St. Andrew Daily Missal,* a book of roughly the same vintage as those old missals stored away in my mother's chest of drawers, coming from a time when Catholic families were often large and the Mass was always prayed in Latin. The missal dates from 1952, in fact, and among its many qualities is a "special section devoted to the Sacraments (in English with the Latin alongside)," providing comforting information about those acts of Christian faith whose traditional forms have been slowly eroded with the changes brought by Vatican II. The last and most surprising item of the St. Bonaventure catalogue reminds us even more poignantly of such dimly remembered values, these forms of a collective Christian past. It is not a prayerbook this time but a product for the young (or at least the young at heart), advertised simply as "St. Therese Coloring Book": a little book of pictures relating "the life of St. Therese . . . in traditional artwork."

These publications together form a collection whose common perspective may help us to glimpse the real meaning of the old Liber for its modern users. For what these reprints return, in every case, is not just a beautiful book but an equally beautiful memory, of a bygone era before that turbulent decade that gave us Vatican II, a time in which one imagines the chant sung effortlessly and willingly by countless choirs in countless countries. Indeed, the very fact that these book are known to be reprints ensures that they will evoke a memory. They are destined to remain in a second-order relation, haunted by the books they are meant to have replaced. In this sense the St. Bonaventure *Liber Usualis* could be said to enjoy two equally significant functions. The act of reprinting not only serves to return a beloved book to print, but, perhaps more importantly, it manages to recall, like a child's coloring book, the very thing modern-day Catholics will never be able to get back—which, of course, is their innocence.

NOTES

[1]See Henri Daniel-Rops, *The Second Vatican Council; The Story Behind the Ecumenical Council of Pope John XXIII,* trans. Alastair Guinan (New York: Hawthorn Books, [1962]); and *The Rites of the Catholic Church as Revised by Decree of the Second Vatican Ecumenical Council and Published by Authority of Pope Paul VI* (New York: Pueblo Publishing Company, 1983).

[2]Hoppin, *Medieval Music* (New York: W.W. Norton, 1977), 51.

[3]Chartier, *The Order of Books: Readers, Authors, and Libraries in Europe between the Fourteenth and Eighteenth Centuries,* trans. Lydia G. Cochrane (Stanford: Stanford University Press, 1994), 16.

[4]Ibid., 17.

[5]Ibid., 9. Chartier is expanding on a point made by Roger Stoddard in "Morphology and the Book from an American Perspective," *Printing History* 17 (1990).

[6]Jerome McGann argues for the role played by the print medium in the reception of literature in his *Black Riders: The Visible Language of Modernism* (Princeton: Princeton University Press, 1993).

[7]For a more detailed account of this history see my *Decadent Enchantments: The Revival of Gregorian Chant at Solesmes* (Berkeley and Los Angeles: University of California Press, 1998), Chap. 1. Much of the argument that follows is derived from Chapter 2.

[8]As reported in Dom Lucien David, *Dom Joseph Pothier: Abbé de St-Wandrille et la restauration grégorienne* (pamphlet, Abbaye de Saint-Wandrille: Saint-Wandrille, 1943).

[9]The story of this failure and the book for which it was designed can be found in my *Decadent Enchantments,* 40; also Dom Pierre Combes, *Histoire de la restauration du chant grégorien d'après les documents inédits* (Solesmes: Abbey of Solesmes, 1969).

[10]David, *Dom Joseph Pothier,* 19.

[11]After Guéranger's *Institutions liturgiques* (1840), Pothier's treatise was the most important nineteenth-century research to emerge from the Solesmes monastery.

[12]For examples of early Gregorian incunabula and of the types from which they were printed, see Mary Kay Duggan, *Italian Music Incunabula: Printers and Type* (Berkeley and Los Angeles: University of California Press, 1992).

[13]A. Grospellier, "Nouveaux livres de chant publiés à Solesmes," *Revue du chant grégorien* (15 June 1896): 166.

[14]Olive, "Ecriture de plain-chant," *Revue de musique religieuse et de chant grégorien* 5 (April 1896): 90.

[15]Pothier left Solesmes in 1893 first to assume the post as Prior at the nearby monastery of Ligugé. In 1894 he moved on to the recently reopened Abbey of Saint-Wandrille in Normandy. He was installed as abbott on Christmas day of that same year.

[16]A. Dabin, "Comment, à Marseille, on écrit . . . Solesmes," *Revue du chant gregorien* (15 July 1898): 195.

[17]For a discussion of the role of photography in turn-of-the-century Gregorian research, see my *Decadent Enchantments,* Chap. 3.

[18]The edition was not completed without difficulty. The story of the conflicts that arose between the Vatican Commission and Solesmes during the course of the book's publication, as well as the contestatory status of the Solesmes rhythmic notation, is told in my *Decadent Enchantments,* Chap. 5.

[19]Chartier, *The Order of Books,* 16.

[20]Among the relevant publications are the *Graduale triplex: seu Graduale Romanum Pauli PP. VI cura recognitum & rhythmicis signis a Solesmensibus*

monachis ornatum, neumis Laudunensibus (Paris: Abbaye Saint-Pierre de Solesmes & Desclée, 1979), at a cost of about $45; the *Psalterium cum canticis novi & veteris testamenti: iuxta regulam S.P.N. Benedicti & alia schemata liturgiae horarum monasticae cum cantu gregoriano* (Solesmes: Abbaye Saint-Pierre de Solesmes, 1981), for about $38; and *The Gregorian Missal for Sundays: Notated in Gregorian Chant by the Monks of Solesmes* (Solesmes: Abbaye Saint-Pierre, 1990), for about $25.

CHAPTER 3

Public Music in Private Spaces
Piano-Vocal Scores and the Domestication of Opera

THOMAS CHRISTENSEN

Books are amazing vehicles of intellectual transportation. Over vast distances of both space and time, they can vividly carry ideas and stories from author to reader. Even more, they can connect and meld otherwise disparate social spheres. For example, books can transform literature that is inherently private in origin—for example, diaries and correspondence—into "public" literature, just as "public" texts ranging from civic orations and Sunday sermons can be read at home as "private," even intimate literature when conveyed through the printed text. In short, the printed word acts as a kind of circulatory system in human society, connecting and penetrating multiple spheres of social activity.

Yet we also know that printed texts never convey ideas to a literate reading public innocently and transparently; the many forms that the printed word takes shape the content of what is being disseminated, and the routes and byways by which it arrives frame its reception and understanding by readers.[1] The precarious identity of the text is especially exacerbated in the domain of music, where the musical text can never be a fully stable and objective conveyor of its own content. After all, a "reading" of any musical text requires the mediation of a performer or group of performers (the piano sonata played by a recitalist or the symphony performed by an orchestra). And even the most ardent believer in "authentic" performance recognizes that the score can be only an imperfect representation of a piece, one whose activation by a performer (or performers) requires interpretation, discrimination, and imagination. To be sure, the audience and the "reader" can sometimes be the same, as when a pianist sits down to play music alone at home. But in either case, the score is always an object that needs some kind of activation and subjective interpretation.[2]

Matters are considerably more complex when we consider the question of arrangement and transcription. This is of course a phenomena in music history with a long pedigree. Whether it is an arrangement of a Haydn symphony for the piano, an adaptation of Bach's "Toccata and Fugue in D Minor" for marching band or a Beatles tune played by "101 Strings," transcription is one of the oldest and most venerable means by which musical works could be more widely disseminated and played. Needless to say, though, the transcription problematizes the ontological identity of the individual musical work beyond those issues related to performance and interpretation. Not only does the arrangement alter the *sonic* representation of the work it purports to convey, it can radically destabilize its reception by changing the space and context of its performance.

The transcriptional economy that I want to consider in the present essay concerns operatic music, and, more specifically, the many piano-vocal scores of this music printed since the late eighteenth century. These piano-vocal scores were published under various names—*partition pour piano et chant, Klavier-Auszug, Spartito (or Riduzione) per canto e pianoforte*—and are so familiar to most musicians today as to scarcely warrant any notice or thought. Yet the kind of reduction and representation these scores make of the operatic work is a peculiar one. To make the most obvious point first, an "opera" played on the keyboard sounds different than one performed with a full orchestra and cast of singers. Secondly, and perhaps no less obviously, though, its "performance" takes place in a radically different environment. Through the agency of the piano-vocal score, the "opera" can be transported from the public sphere of the large opera house to the private, intimate setting of the home parlor or drawing room.

This last point is worth dwelling upon because, historically, no musical genre was probably more tethered to a specific location for its performance than opera. A "performance" of an opera, after all, is more than singers accompanied by an orchestra; it also involves visual spectacle: scenery, machines, dances, costumes, and so forth, that have historically been so integral to the operatic "experience." And many social rituals structured attendance at the opera.[3] By bringing the public spectacle of the opera to the domestic space of the parlor as a piano reduction, then, the vocal score effects an ironic transformation of the genre; it shifts the aesthetic focus away from the visual to the aural, and implicitly alters the identity of the art work itself. As piano-vocal transcriptions became one of the key foundations of operatic literacy for many musicians before the age of the radio broadcast and phonograph, it is worth examining some of the complex aesthetic implications and social paradoxes of this print medium.

OPERA AS LITERATURE; OPERA AS SPECTACLE

When one spoke generally of "opera" in the eighteenth century, no matter which of its many diverse subgenres this might be—the *opera seria,* the *Singspiel,* the *tragédie en musique*—it was almost always in reference to the poetry and story presented on stage rather than the actual music to which it might be set. So a reference to, say, "Alessandro nell'Indie" in the eighteenth century was usually to Metastasio's *Alessandro nell'Indie*—the specific story and lyrics penned by the Venetian court poet—not to any one of its dozen or so musical settings to be found at the time. The text was the stable element of an opera, whereas the music was considered variable.[4] Not that this should be surprising. After all, since the birth of modern opera among the cabal of Florentine Platonists known as the Camerata in the late sixteenth century, the *dramma per musica* was considered first and foremost a genre of dramatic literature.[5] In a gendered metaphor that was aged even by the time Monteverdi invoked it, music was seen as the mistress of the text. This is not to say that music was unimportant. But it was only one of many elements to the drama, and by no means the most important. In the neo-Aristotelian poetics taken up by writers such as Metastasio, *musica* was considered one of the less important components ("parti di qualità") of tragedy, ranking below subject (*azione*), ethos (*costumi*), pathos (*sentenza*), diction (*discorso*), and sometimes even stage design (*decorazione*).[6] Beaumarchais may have best captured the prevailing sentiment of his contemporaries when he quipped maliciously that too often "there is too much music in music drama."[7] There were lots of things to observe at the opera, and sometimes there just was not enough time for the music.

When music was discussed by critics, for example as in the reviews and pamphlets produced during the Bouffon quarrel in the 1750s, facile characterizations of French and Italian styles might be bantered about, and the affective poignancy of a given air, or the realistic depiction of a storm or earthquake during some instrumental symphony could also earn attention. But rarely did critics ever discuss any specifics of a musical setting. In fact we have to look hard for any critical analysis of operatic music much before 1770 that engages in technical detail. One such discussion was that by Rameau and Rousseau over Armide's recitative from Lully's eponymous *tragédie en musique*.[8] But this was an exceptional argument made by two exceptional individuals colliding at the borders of poetics and music theory. Few of the other *philosophes*—let alone the reading public—possessed the musical literacy to follow Rameau's minute analysis of the music's harmony, modulation, chromaticism, and other elements of its *basse fondamentale*. It is telling, too, that the bulk of Rousseau's criticism in his pamphlet (it is from his infamous *Lettre sur la musique française*) deals with issues of language and expression, not the music itself. The kind of technical analysis cultivated by Rameau in his music theory was too rarified for most French readers of his day.

There was one very practical reason for the silence of most critics in the early eighteenth century concerning the details of operatic music: few of them had access to a score for consultation. In most cases, a printed *partition* of the music simply did not exist. Whether we speak of the Italian *opera seria* or the French *opéra comique,* virtually all opera scores circulated exclusively in manuscript, and even then, in a bewildering number of versions employing differing symphonies, arias, recitatives, and ensemble numbers. (This is not even to speak of the popular genre of the operatic "pasticcio"—a composite work of several composers.) In rare instances, "full" scores of certain classically certified composers were published with royal subvention for overtly nationalist reasons. Such were the motivations behind the "complete" editions of Lully's oeuvre in France and Handel's in England. But these were expensive and bulky editions meant to "monumentalize" the composer; they were hardly of use to the average opera spectator or critic.

What an opera connoisseur in the eighteenth century did have access to, though, was the libretto. Editions of the most popular opera librettos by notable authors such as Quinault, Houdar de la Motte, Zeno, and Metastasio were repeatedly printed in various collections and "complete" editions, some of them quite large and luxurious. More commonly, however, librettos were available as individual, rapidly produced booklets published for a given operatic run. These pocket *livrets* were in octavo size, and were typically sold at the opera on the night of performance, not unlike today. Besides the cast of characters and their performers, the libretto would include the text of all the recitatives, arias, and choruses, and sometimes brief synopses of the action and stage directions.[9] But it was also possible to purchase these librettos through booksellers and peddlers on the street. When an opera enjoyed particular popularity or notoriety—as during the Bouffon and Gluck quarrels—one could be sure to find a lively trade in pocket *livrets,* not surprisingly, often in multiple, pirated editions. For most enthusiasts in the eighteenth century, it was the libretto that constituted the printed representation of the opera outside of the opera house; it was the site of reference and memory for the operatic performance.

OPERA AND THE KEYBOARD

This is not to say that operatic music was entirely unavailable in some printed form to the musical public. On the contrary, excerpts of music from popular operas were repeatedly "arranged," "adapted," or otherwise "disposed" by eighteenth-century publishers for a multitude of musical ensembles. And by far the most favored medium of presentation was that of the keyboard arrangement, often with flute or violin obbligato. Throughout the eighteenth century, a torrent of such arrangements were issued by publishers, allowing a growing bourgeois clientele of opera enthusiasts the chance to play at home versions of their favorite operatic arias, overtures, dance numbers, and choruses in transcription. Oftentimes these arrangements were radically simplified; just as often, they might be augmented with elaborate embellishments and variations. But whether simplified or embellished, keyboard transcriptions of operatic music constituted one of the main staples of music publishers throughout the eighteenth—and well into the nineteenth—century (see Figure 3.1).[10]

Now the history of keyboard arrangements of vocal music is as old as the keyboard literature itself. (The very first surviving collections of organ music—such as the fifteenth-century "Buxheimer" organ book— contain adaptations of sacred and secular vocal works.) In the case of arrangements of music drawn specifically from opera, we could cite d'Anglebert's harpsichord arrangements of dance music by Lully published in the seventeenth century. But the real commerce in keyboard arrangements of operatic music began only in the early eighteenth century, one whose story is well illustrated with the case of Lully's music.

By the beginning of the eighteenth century, Lully's *tragédies en musique* had long since earned canonical status in France, enjoying as they were regular revival at the Opéra. Arguably, they were the first operatic works to have become truly canonical in both a commercial and an aesthetic sense. Not surprisingly, too, all of Lully's *partitions* were quickly codified in large, luxurious folios published in moveable type during his lifetime by the "official" music printer of France, Christophe

Figure 3.1 Example of nineteenth-century opera arrangements. From the private collection of the author.

Ballard. But Ballard's bulky folios were costly and of little practical value to amateur musicians. In the generations following Lully's death, Ballard's competitors surmised that there might be a lucrative market for more practical and cheaper editions of Lully's music, and this demand could be satisfied with the production of a *partition réduite*.[11]

Henri de Baussen was one of the first publishers to break the monopoly of Ballard by engraving eight of Lully's operas in such "short scores." The "partition réduite" or "partition en trio" was a reduced score in two (or sometimes three) parts, a form in which French operas were often published by 1715. It consisted of the continuo-bass score (usually in oblong format with quarto folding) bound with the two primary instrumental parts (the upper "dessus de violins" and the lower "basse de violin," both in upright formats, folio foldings). In such a score, the standard five-part orchestra and four-part chorus were reduced to the two outer voices (two staves), and any music in trio texture was given in full (three staves). All other inner parts of the full score were simply omitted, the reduction relying on the natural treble-bass polarity of the music for its effect. The single exception occurs at imitative entries (as during the overture) when the *dessus* or *basse* part could indicate differing voices through changes of clef.[12]

In fact, Baussen's first reduced score published in 1702 for Henri Foucault was not of Lully, but an engraved *partition réduite of* Theobaldo di Gatti's *Scylla*. Other French publishers soon followed suit, with Ribou, Boivin, LeClerc, and Leclair all producing short scores of current repertoire at the Paris Opéra.[13] These engraved scores were far cleaner looking than Ballard's antiquated moveable type, far more compact to read, and most importantly, far cheaper to produce. Recognizing the threat that engraved scores posed to his firm, Ballard sued to regain control of his printing monopoly in 1713. Although the verdict was not in his favor (Ballard was able to retain Royal protection only for scores set by the older method of moveable type), he remained undeterred in his quest to regain control of the Lully publishing trade. In 1715, he made this (slightly disingenuous) announcement:

> Now that I am the sole proprietor of all the works of Mons. Lully, I will attempt to make these incomparable works much more accessible than they have been until now . . . by publishing them in six different forms. . . . I believe that the variety of these editions will satisfy the different needs of all who would wish to make music [toutes les personnes qui musiquent].[14]

The six versions Ballard offered his readers were described and priced as follows:

La Partition [générale]	in-folio	16 livres
La Partition [réduite]	in-quarto	9 livres
La Basse-Continuë générale	in-folio	3 livres
Les Dessus de violins	in-folio	1 livre 10 s.
La Basse de violin	in-folio	1 livre 10 s.
Les airs détachez	in-douze	1 livre 10 s.

Ballard had capitulated. His *partiton réduite* was obviously an attempt to catch some of Foucault's success (just as the "airs détachez" may be read as Ballard's answer to English publishers who had long since pioneered the printing of individual "hit" arias from popular comic operas). As with Foucault, Ballard's reduced score was made up of three performing parts: the continuo, violin, and bass. The complete reduced score included both the instrumental dance music ("Airs à jouer") as well as all the vocal music ("Airs à chanter"). At just half the cost of the full score, the continuo score made playable the full corpus of Lully's *oeuvre* to any small group of music lovers.[15]

As already suggested above, the commercial advantage of publishing operatic music in reduced format had already been recognized in England. In 1706, the London music printer John Walsh issued his first engraved vocal score of opera songs (from Clayton's *Arsinoe*). But more typical were the selected "hits" that were printed in figured-bass arrangement, either separately or collected in anthologies by opera or composer. English publishers such as Thompson, Welcker, Bremner, Dale, and Fraser issued hundreds of scores consisting of "favourite songs" from popular operas arranged for "thru-bass" accompaniments. The preface to one English collection from 1725 is typical in sentiment (if not in syntax):

> The reducing a large Folio to a small pocket Octavo, still to retain all the advantages it had before as symphonies, legibility, etc. with that considerable additional one of portability, must among all lovers and real judges be looked upon as a work of some use as well as curiosity for the eye which in large ill disposed folios is dilated and fatigued, by this mathematical contraction being at the same time full as legible is much eased.[16]

But two points must be kept in mind concerning all these various arrangements and reductions. First, in most instances only excerpts were offered—not the complete opera. The countless transcriptions, intabulations, reductions, adaptations, variations, and collections of operatic music to be found throughout the first half of the eighteenth century made no claim to represent the drama itself. Second, the keyboardist was expected to possess the skill required to realize the figured bass—something fewer and fewer amateurs could do with any facility as the century progressed. (In numerous thorough-bass treatises in the latter half of the eighteenth century, authors would lament the decline of thorough-bass skills among keyboardists.) Most keyboard players would need the continuo part already "filled out," by which the orchestral accompaniment was rendered in an idiomatic keyboard style.

Thus, to make something like a complete piano-vocal score both conceptually meaningful and musically practical, a number of changes in the aesthetics and consumption of the opera needed to take place. And these changes can be identified and chronologically situated with surprising precision within the decade of the 1770s. At least four such changes can be identified.

To begin with, music needed to become more highly valued as a component of the operatic drama. That is, in order to make something like the vocal score in any sense a recognizable simulacrum of the opera, the opera itself needed to be reconceived as more of a musical genre than one that was primarily literary and spectacular. This obviously necessitated music's release from the fetters of classical mimetic theory. One of the central reforms of Gluck and Calzabigi was precisely to accord a greater role for music as an agent of expression in the drama. To be sure, there were numerous writers and composers who had adumbrated such an aesthetic of music earlier (particularly Algarotti). But it was Gluck and Calzabigi who in 1769 offered arguably the most powerful and widely advertised articulation of this doctrine in the preface to their first great success, *Alceste*.[17] Whether by direct influence or in tandem response, their aesthetic stance was almost immediately taken up and codified by a number of critics and philosophers writing in the same decade, including Morellet (1771), Beattie (1776), Heinse (1776), Chabanon (1779), and Boyé (1779).[18] Music in the 1770s was beginning to be accepted as a powerful autonomous force of emotional expression, one that endowed the opera with much of its visceral power.

Second, the full opera score itself needed to be stabilized. In other words, before an opera could be fixed in a printed score—whether it be the full partition or the piano-vocal arrangement—the habit of treating operatic numbers as so many interchangeable parts needed to be contested. This entailed another reconceptualization of opera in which the drama and music were seen to be fully integrated within the whole, and in which the overture and recitatives were as inseparable from the drama as the arias and duets. Once again, such a unifying concept of opera was not forcefully articulated until the reforms of Calzabigi and Gluck.[19] (It is not surprising, then, that Gluck's own works were among the first to be canonized in print in complete piano-vocal reductions.)

Third, there needed to be a practical medium by which the newly codified operatic score could be rendered. This was finally available— also in the decade of the 1770s—with improvements made to the forte-piano by John Broadwood and Johann Andreas Stein.[20] Unlike the harpsichord, the square fortepiano of the 1770s could effectively render contrasts of dynamics and textures in its accompaniments; and unlike the clavichord, the fortepiano offered a far more robust sound. All in all, the fortepiano proved to be the most gracious, flexible instrument to accompany the voice. By the last quarter of the eighteenth century, it had completely eclipsed the harpsichord in popularity, just as written-out keyboard accompaniments had eclipsed figured-bass scores. As a consequence, more and more operatic music became known to musicians through the filter of the fortepiano.[21]

Fourth and finally, there needed to be a commercial demand for the piano-vocal score. All the changes in the aesthetics of the opera or improvements to the fortepiano would have been without meaning to the economic viability of the printed vocal score were there not also a growing number of keyboardists who actually wanted to reproduce this music themselves. Such consumers first arose among those professional singers, conductors, directors, stage designers, and intendants who wanted them for rehearsing and learning parts of opera scores, especially as operas were produced beyond the major opera houses in smaller towns, provinces, and colonies. But the greatest demand came from the broader mass of amateur opera enthusiasts—the "dilettantes"—looking for a practical means of reproducing the music they may or may not have heard on the stage or in semi-private salon recitals—those, in the words of Ballard, who simply wished "to make music."

THE *KLAVIER-AUSZUG*

One of the first individuals to recognize—and capitalize upon—the need for such accessible piano arrangements for domestic use was the German composer and journalist, Johann Adam Hiller. As the self-proclaimed "inventor" of the piano-vocal score, Hiller arranged several oratorios,

cantatas, passions, and *opera seria* arias by Benda, Hasse, Graun, Per-
golesi, Handel, and Haydn in *Klavier-Auszüge*.[22] But the genre that most
interested Hiller as both composer and arranger was the *Singspiel*—the
German answer to Italian *opera buffa* and French *opéra comique*.[23] The
patriotic Hiller was eager to win the widest possible audience for his favorite operatic genre, and he believed that a score in which the full orchestral accompaniment was condensed in an easy keyboard version
without figured bass would serve this purpose.[24] It is true that many of
Hiller's transcriptions scarcely exceeded in complexity the two-voiced
scaffolding of the older continuo reductions. "I have felt free to change
significantly the exterior of this structure [the accompaniment]," Hiller
admitted, "sometimes even eliminating it entirely." But he felt such
changes were justified, as a skilled accompanist would be able to fill out
the harmonies with little effort.[25] To add more of the inner voices (which
in any case were rarely very complex in the *Singspiel*) would have made
the accompaniment more difficult for those amateurs to whom Hiller ap-
pealed and risked obscuring the vocal line. As it was, the simple keyboard renditions Hiller produced worked well either as solo keyboard
arrangements or as vocal accompaniments. Figure 3.2, from Hiller's
comic opera, *Lisuart und Dariolette* of 1768 is typical in this respect.
The keyboard reduction—mostly in two voices—can be read alone or as
an accompaniment to the voice. Hiller has indicated with smaller type
face (an innovation of Breitkopf) the modest obbligato part that would
otherwise be omitted when the keyboardist played the vocal line.[26]

Hiller's piano-vocal scores turned out to be one of Breitkopf's most
profitable wares and arguably one of the first great commercial "hits" in
the history of music publishing. According to Arthur Loesser, the piano-
vocal score of *Lottchen am Hofe,* to take one example, went through four
separate editions, amounting to a total run of 2,750 copies within fifteen
years—an astonishing number for the eighteenth century. Another *Singspiel* of Hiller's—*Die Jagd*—was evidently even more successful, eventually achieving a run of 4,000 copies.[27]

The commercial success enjoyed by Breitkopf was not lost upon
other publishers. By the turn of the century, few operas were henceforth
produced without piano-vocal scores in tow. As mentioned, all of Gluck's
operas came out in vocal score, as did those of Benda, Dalayrac, Ditters-
dorf, Paesiello, Salieri, Grétry, and of course Mozart. Indeed, the printing
of full orchestral scores was the exception. Save for some French publications, few publishers saw any need to engrave large, expensive full
scores. Only a handful of operas in the first half of the nineteenth century

Figure 3.2 Piano-vocal score of Hiller's comic opera, *Lisuart und Dariolette* (1768). Photo courtesy of the University of Iowa Music Library.

were ever published as such.[28] British publishers in particular made a cottage industry out of vocal scores of popular comic operas, musical romances, and farces.[29] In Figure 3.3, I have reproduced a publishing list of opera scores from the firm of Simrock in 1797, although most of these scores were not in fact published by Simrock himself, who was merely serving as a sales agent for other publishers. In any event, the list shows how quickly commerce in piano-vocal scores "im billigsten Preiss" had taken root.[30]

The solo piano arrangements of opera scores ("fürs Klavier ganze Auszüge") mentioned at the top of this list deserve some further explanation. Often called by English publishers "Cabinet operas," these scores were written as piano pieces without any vocal parts or text. Such a textless piano score allowed a "complete" opera to be played on the keyboard with all vocal parts enmeshed in the accompaniment reduction. Figure 3.4 offers a typical example. It is a page from a piano score to Rossini's *Ricciardo e Zoraide* (the duet of Agorante and Ricciardo "Donala a questo core" from Act 2). Here both vocal lines—including the virtuosic coloratura passage work—are subsumed within the piano part, thus transforming the dramatic duet into a lyrical piano arabesque. As peculiar as this may strike us today, it was in fact one of the most popular means of rendering opera scores in the nineteenth century.[31] And it was, of course, of no little influence upon the development of piano writing in the second quarter of the nineteenth century, with composers such as Field, Thalberg, and Chopin imitating Belliniesque *bel canto* melodies and Rossinian coloratura passagework in their lyrical piano pieces, not to mention heroic climaxes reminiscent of the chorus in grand opera.

And who arranged these operas as piano-vocal scores? Sometimes the composer himself, as in the case of Hiller or Carl Maria von Weber, though more commonly publishers hired hack arrangers for the job. Beethoven told his publisher that he had neither the time nor the patience to reduce *Fidelio* and was happy to turn the job over to Czerny.[32] (Certainly, though, he was interested in retaining the lucrative royalties its sale would generate!) When an opera became a hit, it was also common to find multiple, often unauthorized, arrangements in circulation. Mozart complained loudly about the appearance of his Singspiel, *Die Entführung aus dem Serail,* in unauthorized piano reductions by the Augsburg publisher Stage in 1785, and in Mainz by Schott the same year.[33] Obviously publishers and composers alike recognized in the genre a lucrative commodity.

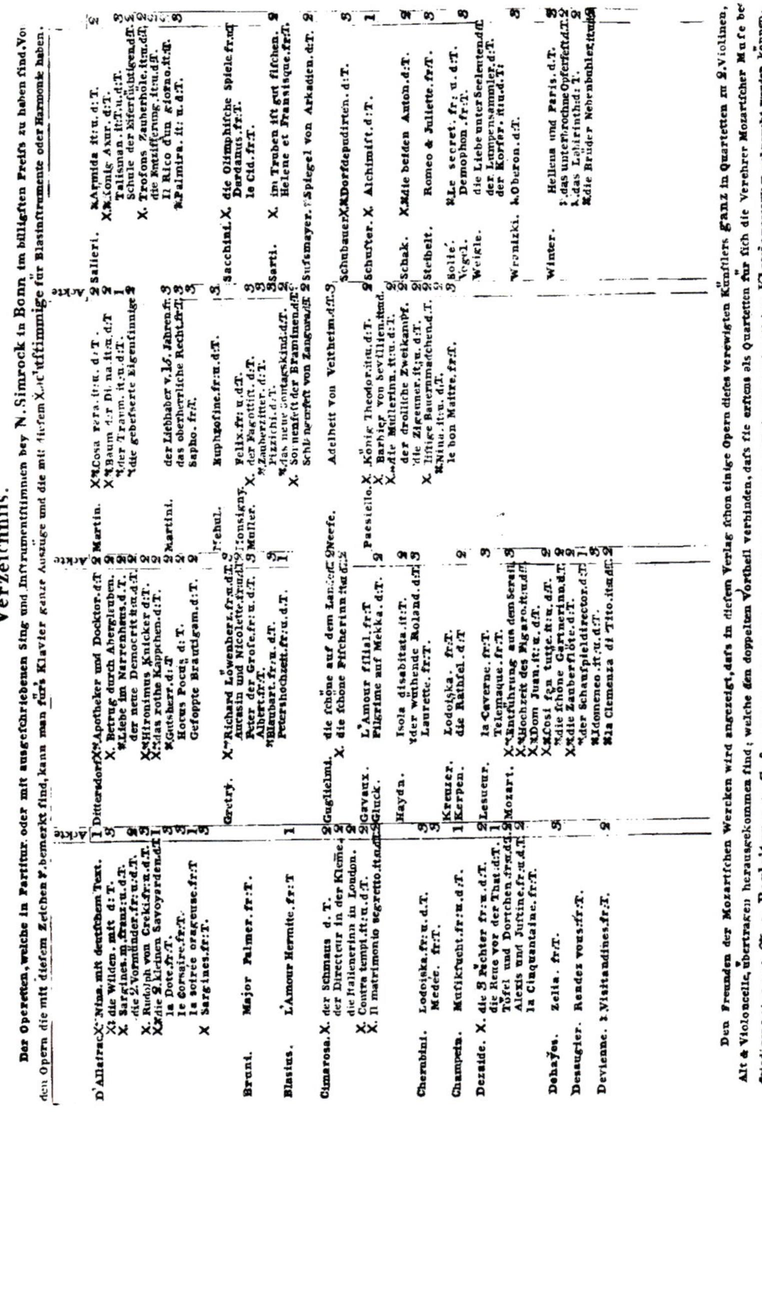

Figure 3.3 Opera scores available from Simrock in 1797. Photo courtesy of the University of Iowa Music Library.

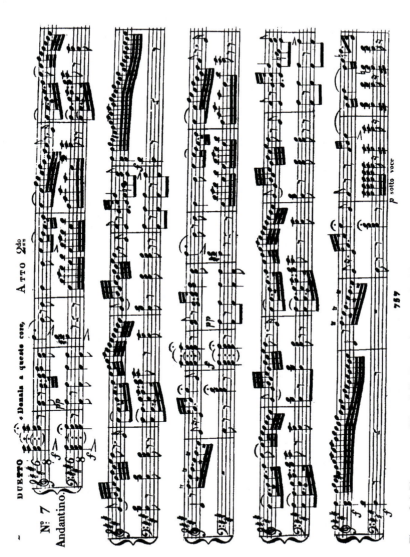

Figure 3.4 Piano score of Rossini's *Ricciardo e Zoraide* (Vienna: Pietro Mechetti, c. 1820). From the private collection of the author.

Alongside the piano-vocal scores, publishers in the early nineteenth century continued to issue prodigious quantities of free arrangements of operatic music—the endless stream of potpourris, variations, "reminiscences," "souvenirs," and fantasies on operatic themes composed by the likes of Daniel Steibelt, Louis Jardin, Josef Gelinek, and Carl Czerny and aimed primarily at amateur pianists (as opposed to the more notorious virtuosic transcriptions of Liszt and Thalberg). Although this topic lies beyond the scope of my present essay, it is amusing to note here the exasperated remarks of one Viennese critic of this transcription industry writing in 1847: "Far too many contemporary operas—or at least those originating from beyond the Rhine—die at the hands of piano arrangers before they even reach the Rubicon. Scarcely has such a poor child emerged from the head of the composer when it is sprung on the Parisian stage clad with tam-tam, triangle and the like—a leap that often turns into a somersault (*salto mortale*). Scarcely has its feeble germination begun than the transcription vampires immediately descend upon the sweet, defenseless body and begin to suck out with their gluttonous snouts the few inventive and fresh ideas offered by such products in order to send into the world etudes, quadrilles, transcriptions, souvenir themes, and *airs variés* arranged for ten, twenty, sixty, or more fingers of every kind of proficiency or lack thereof."[34] Some satirical couplets from 1823 also play upon the popularity of parlor opera extracts among music dealers:

The Miller: [Opera] excerpts are sold here? On what authority do you trade the products of the miller? That is against the law.
The Music Seller: Sir, we do not trade flour that is finely ground! It is only the threshed straw left over from the opera.[35]

Still, although individual arias, choruses, and instrumental pieces continued to be extracted for separate transcription, variation, and arrangement, reflecting the resilient habit of viewing the opera as a compilation of detachable elements, there was an emerging consensus that the opera constituted some kind of dramatic whole, and the piano-vocal score was the most efficacious means for conveying it.

SPACES OF PROJECTION AND RECEPTION

If the piano-vocal reduction was the primary medium by which the genre of opera could be optimally reproduced and circulated before the advent in our own century of the radio, phonograph, and CD player, then it was of course an imperfect, partial reproduction. Given his importance in its creation and promotion, Hiller was himself surprisingly dismissive of his own progeny. Piano reductions, he bemoaned, were ultimately "impoverished and confused" renditions, useful only for dilettantes who lacked the musical training to read the full score.[36] The problem was that the piano reduction omitted too many inner voices and washed out the contrasting timbres of the instruments. Consider the following criticism from one Austrian writer in 1841 who was uncompromising when it came to the deficiencies of piano reductions of operatic music:

> There are so many examples where the effect [of the music] can only be obtained by the instruments for which it was written, for example the trio in the fifth act of *Sibellinen,* where the clarinet alone works indescribable magic; or the original, if bizarre, C minor song of Marzell in the first act accompanied by piccolo, bassoon, and bass drum. How empty this would all sound on the piano. Consider, too, the oboe solo in Lindpaintner's overture to *Vampyr,* and the English horn solo in Rossini's *William Tell,* the frightening effect of the horns, tremolo violins and violas with pizzicato basses in the second act finale of Weber's *Der Freischütz,* not to mention those effects which the poor disappearing basset horn is capable of, and countless others.[37]

The piano-vocal score, Hiller ruefully had to admit, was akin to a black-and-white engraving of a painting; each was but a poor facsimile of some colored original. At least if one could read from the full *Partitur,* he thought, it would be possible to know all of the colors, textures, and lines intended by the composer. Ideally, piano-vocal scores should only be used as temporary crutches until a musician was competent enough to read through the full score.[38] The choice seemed self evident. "Who would rather ride a hobbyhorse when he could command a steed? Who would, when invited to a feast at a banquet table, prefer to eat gruel and potatoes in the kitchen?"[39] But Hiller's idealism was unrealistic. Increasingly in the nineteenth century, musical scores were getting too complex to sight-read, even for skilled keyboardists.[40] This is not to mention the ever-increasing price discrepancy between full scores and piano reductions. The need and desire to sound operatic music in the home demanded something like the practical, cheap piano-vocal score.

If we overlook for the moment its obvious deficiencies in acoustical reproduction, we can see that the piano-vocal score served an indispensable pedagogical role in the musical literacy of many bourgeois musicians. Through the modest piano-vocal score, the music of the opera house was heard by thousands of amateur musicians for the very first time. As the music critic Cramer noted in 1789, piano transcriptions of operas "have the real value of making widely known the greatest and most worthy compositions."[41] Over a hundred years later, George Bernard Shaw could confirm Cramer's prophecy. The piano—and, by implication, the piano-vocal score—had been the primary medium by which most musicians in the nineteenth century got to know their operas:

> . . . What is it that stands as the one indispensable external condition of
> my musical culture? Obviously, the pianoforte. Without it, no har-
> mony, no interweaving of rhythms and motives, no musical structure,
> and consequently no opera or music drama. But on the other hand,
> with it nothing else was needed except the printed score and a fore-
> knowledge of the power of music to bring romance and poetry to any
> enchanting intimacy of realization.[42]

Even as a professional music critic, Shaw had to depend upon the "pi-anette-Peters culture," since "nobody, not even a critic, can acquire more than a fragmentary musical culture from public performances alone."[43]

The importance of the piano-vocal score as the disseminator of musical literacy and ideology in the nineteenth century can scarcely be overestimated. It became the primary means by which most amateur musicians came to know, judge, and reproduce works they could experience—if they were lucky—only one or two times in live performance. For all that we speak of the growth of the opera in the nineteenth century, it must be recalled that most opera performances were still prohibitively expensive. The subscribers to the opera throughout the century remained heavily gentried.[44] Moreover, it was not always possible to hear diverse repertoire in any given opera house.

But a second, and perhaps more critical social element beyond the republicanization of opera was implicated by the piano-vocal transcription. By playing the overtly "public" music of the opera house at home in the private space of the parlor or drawing room, amateur pianists effected a radical dislocation in the genre's reception. If the symphony and opera house were the paradigmatic locations of musical publicity and spectacle in the eighteenth century, and conversely, the parlor piano the locus of private, bourgeois music-making, then the piano-vocal score served to break down the barriers of the musical landscape; it introduced into the private sphere of the parlor and drawing room the publicity-oriented rhetoric of the opera house.[45] Paradoxically, though, such domestication of the opera through the piano-vocal score made possible the reconfiguration of opera as an object of public criticism. In essence, the opera was able to expand beyond the economy of representative publicity to that of the "authentic" public sphere described by the German sociologist, Jürgen Habermas.[46]

It is worth pausing here to consider this important transformation for a moment. In his celebrated study, Habermas brilliantly outlined the emergence (and subsequent decline) of an "authentic" bourgeois public sphere in the eighteenth century, one that stood apart from the hitherto dominating *publicus* of the court, church, and state. The orientation of this latter sphere is perfectly emblematized in the seventeenth-century opera, where genres such as the Lullian *tragédie en musique* and the Venetian *opera seria* functioned as a kind of "representative publicity" of the court and state, respectively.[47] In essence, the opera represented and displayed *before* the subjects and citizens (much as did any architectural monument or civic ceremony) the imperial majesty and authority of the king, or perhaps the republican virtues of an affluent mercantile state. (It is also in this sense that we may understand the state-sponsored monumental editions of the works of Lully and Handel mentioned above.)

According to Habermas, the publicity-oriented sphere of the court and state began to be contested in the late seventeenth and early eighteenth centuries by the gradual emergence of an independent bourgeois public sphere. Catalyzed by a confluence of economic and social changes (particularly the growth of a literate middle class), members of an emerging bourgeois stratum would meet in various social settings (academies, coffeehouses, fraternal lodges, and salons) to discuss and debate current economic, political, and social issues of the day. For Habermas, this constituted the "authentic," democratic public sphere, one where "private people come together as a public to exercise their reason."[48] A paradoxical, though critical, aspect of Habermas's formulation is that this bourgeois public sphere is ultimately connected to the private sphere, and more specifically, that of the intimate sphere of the conjugal family. That is to say, the bourgeois public sphere is composed of individuals applying their notions of reason and reasonableness to public affairs derived from their personal experiences and values. At the same time, interior affections and sentiments inculcated in the private arena of the family could become objects of public identification and debate through their propagation in such widely circulated and discussed literary genres as the novel.

The evolution of themes treated in opera librettos in the eighteenth century offer a good marker of these changing values. We need only consider how widespread topics of bourgeois sentimentality became in operas during this period, ranging from Hiller's *Lottchen am Hofe,* Paisiello's *Nina,* and Mozart's *Così fan Tutte.* The moral and subjective topics treated in these operas are presented before an audience capable of identifying with them based on their own private experiences and values (Habermas's "audience-oriented subjectivity"). But it is not only a case of audience empathy. Through institutions such as the coffeehouse and salon, and published media like the newspaper and literary pamphlet (which were, of course, read and discussed in the coffeehouses and salons), a robust culture of criticism was developed by which topics of literature and art became subjects of public debate. The many operatic "pamphlet" wars of the eighteenth century are perfect examples of the bourgeois public sphere engaging in debates over issues of aesthetic and nationalist import.

It can be seen, I hope, how the piano-vocal score could play an important role in this process. Whereas previously the opera was represented and debated in the public sphere through the medium of the libretto, with the piano-vocal score, the music could now be taken into critical consideration. By allowing individuals to play and reproduce this music in the privacy of their homes (at least for individuals who were musically literate and had access to a keyboard), the piano-vocal score was paradoxically able to bring the music to a broader public sphere. It is not surprising, then, that much music criticism in the last quarter of the eighteenth century tended to be more oriented to the music. Journals such as the French *Journal de musique* (1773–), Johann Forkel's *Musikalisch-Kritische Bibliothek* (1778–), and the *Allgemeinen Musikalischen Zeitung* (1798–) included reviews of operas in which music was not only discussed in detail, but excerpted and published from the piano-vocal scores.[49] Music heard at the opera could now be played at home, and reintroduced back to a public sphere as an element of criticism and discussion.[50]

Not only did the piano-vocal score change the nature and focus of operatic criticism during the eighteenth century, we could even argue that it altered the reception of opera itself. By playing and singing operatic music at home, the genre could be opened up to a more intimate, internalized reception than was possible in the opera house, with all its distracting bustle and chatter. The parlor, after all, was the quintessential site of bourgeois domestic values, the nexus of familial activities, of personal letter-writing, reading, prayer, and intimate conversation.[51] The music of the Biedermeier parlor was associated with the qualities of sentiment and *Empfindsamkeit,* and identified musically with genres such as the Lied, the quartet, and the lyrical piano piece. We could go so far as to argue that in bringing operatic music into the home via the parlor piano, the opera itself took on a new meaning and was opened to new horizons of expectation, new modes of listening and response. Certainly, opera excerpts rendered on the fortepiano in the home constitute a dramatic transformation of genre; the intoxicating vocal music of the public opera house is reduced to instrumental *Hausmusik* of private, Biedermeier sobriety.[52] With typically jocular metaphor, Arthur Loesser has ventured that through such domesticated opera transcriptions, "Daughters and wives [belabored] with shavings from *William Tell, La Juive, Norma* and *Lucia di Lammermoor* were exhaling faint dilutions of the glorious vapor of Paris and thus were offering and taking holy communion with Louis XIV and James Rothschild."[53]

Yet with the piano-vocal score, such fumes could also be potent. There is evidence that the rapt absorption and attentiveness that opera goers evinced in the nineteenth century was reinforced, if not actually inculcated, in the home through the playing of operatic music on the piano.[54] It may well be that, contrary to James Johnson's recent argument, the many testimonies of emotional vertigo induced by operatic music in the nineteenth century were effusions reinforced at the piano with a piano-vocal score propped open on the music stand—not sentiments gained just from listening to the vocal pyrotechnics of Rossini's coloratura arias and feeling the galvanic energy of his ensemble numbers.[55] Such an argument finds support in a revealing "prospectus" prefacing a piano-vocal score of Rossini's *Tancrède* issued by the Parisian firm of Carli in 1821. "Until now," Carli tells us, "the admirers of the music of Rossini have had to be content with hearing [his music] in the theater and sung in public [en société] with the accompaniment of a piano." But such public presentations of Rossini's music clearly could not satisfy his "most passionate amateurs and principally the connoisseurs" who desired to "see by what means he has been able to convey such charms in his music, particularly in those passages where he is able to produce the most beautiful effects and where nonetheless the purists found mistakes." For most musicians of the nineteenth century, the most practical means "to judge these beauties" outside of the opera house and concert hall was to play the music at home on the piano in a keyboard reduction.[56]

To verify this proposition, to accurately gauge the aesthetic relation between the opera house and the parlor piano in the nineteenth century will naturally require further investigation, taking scholars to archives in order to study the surviving memoirs, diaries, and letters of countless amateur musicians in order to sketch out the worlds of bourgeois musical consumption; it will entail the detailed study of reviews in newspapers, accounts in novels, and reviews in professional journals by which we can better understand the conditions of musical literacy in the nineteenth century; it will also require distinguishing various national traditions of operatic genres and reception, as well as cultures of domestic music-making.[57] And even then, of course, there will be much we don't know. The vast majority of times we sit alone at the piano bench dreamily playing through our favorite music literature—whether transcribed or original, orchestral or operatic—goes unrecorded and unremarked upon. But just as surely, the piano-vocal score must have had *some* impact on the reception of opera, just as recordings and radio broadcasts have had in the twentieth century. As the primary medium connecting what are arguably two of the most important spaces of musical activity in the nineteenth century—the opera house and the parlor—the importance of the modest piano-vocal score is hard to exaggerate.

NOTES

[1]For an insightful expansion of this thesis in a seminal study, see Roger Chartier, *The Order of Books: Readers, Authors, and Libraries in Europe between the Fourteenth and Eighteenth Centuries,* trans. Lydia G. Cochrane (Stanford: Stanford University Press, 1994).

[2]I pass over the case of passive score study. While this kind of "silent reading" is not uncommon among trained musicians, it is in most all cases not the intended way in which the text is to be "read."

[3]A revealing portrait of the many elements of spectacle and publicity that have been historically integral to the opera—in this case, that of the Parisian experience—is found in James H. Johnson, *Listening in Paris: A Cultural History* (Berkeley and Los Angeles: University of California Press, 1995).

[4]Silke Leopold, "Von Pasteten und Don Giovannis Requiem: Opernbearbeitungen," in *Musikalische Metamorphosen: Formen und Geschichte der Bearbeitung,* ed. Silke Leopold (Kassel: Bärenreiter, 1992), 88–89.

[5]Reinhard Strohm, *Dramma per Musica: Italian Opera Seria of the Eighteenth Century* (New Haven: Yale University Press, 1998), 1.

[6]Ibid., 239.

[7]Preface to Antonio Salieri, *Tarare*. Chefs-d'oeuvre classiques de l'opéra francais no. 40 (reprint, New York: Broude Brothers, 1971), 3.

[8]A story well narrated by Cynthia Verba in *Music and the French Enlightenment* (Oxford: Clarendon Press, 1993), 8–50.

[9]Richard Macnutt, "Libretto (I)," in *The New Grove Dictionary of Opera*, 4 vols., ed. Stanley Sadie (London: Macmillan, 1992), 2: 1185.

[10]A fuller discussion of these popular transcriptions—which would arguably constitute the primary chapter in the history of music publishing in the eighteenth century—lies beyond the domain of my present essay. Some idea of its import, though, can be gleaned by consulting Maurice Hinson, *The Pianist's Guide to Transcriptions, Arrangements, and Paraphrases* (Bloomington: University of Indiana Press, 1990).

[11]Patricia M. Ranum, "'Mr de Lully en trio': Etienne Loulié, the Foucaults, and the Transcription of the Works of Jean-Baptiste Lully (1673–1702)," *Jean-Baptiste Lully Actes du colloque Saint-Germain-en-Laye—Heidelberg 1987*, ed. Jérôme de la Gorce and Herbert Schneider (Laaber: Laaber Verlag 1990), 309–330. Much of my discussion over the following paragraphs is indebted to Ranum's insightful article.

[12]My thanks to Lois Rosow for clarifying the function and format of these various scores to me in a private communication.

[13]Richard Macnutt, "Publishing," in *The New Grove Dictionary of Opera*, 3: 1158.

[14]Preface to *Proserpine: Tragédie en musique*, Troisiéme edition, de cinq manières différentes de la partition générale (Paris: Ballard, 1715), my translation.

[15]For a comprehensive history of Ballard's publishing empire and the saga of his many run-ins with competitors, see Anik Devriès, *Édition et commerce de la musique gravée à Paris dans la première motié du XVIIIe siècle: Les Boivin, Les Leclerc* (Geneva: Minkoff, 1976).

[16]*The Delightfull Musical Companion for Gentlemen and Ladies; Being a Choice Collection out of All the latest Operas composed by Mr. Handel, Sigr. Bononcini, Sigr. Attilio, etc.* (London: Peter Fraser [1725]), Preface.

[17]John Neubauer, *The Emancipation of Music from Language: Departure from Mimesis in Eighteenth-Century Aesthetics* (New Haven: Yale University Press, 1986), esp. 143–148.

[18]Edward Lippman, *A History of Western Musical Aesthetics* (Lincoln: University of Nebraska Press, 1992), 174 ff.

[19]For reasons of its own classicist pedigree, the French genre of the *tragédie en musique* was one of the few precursors of Gluck's to have been considered an integral, dramatic whole.

[20]Katalin Komlós, *Fortepianos and Their Music: Germany, Austria, and England, 1760–1800* (Oxford: Clarendon Press, 1995), 6–9.

[21]The same could be said for rendering instrumental and chamber music in transcription, particularly when arranged as a duet. But that is a different story, one chapter of which I have tried to narrate in my article "Four-Hand Piano Transcription and Geographies of Nineteenth-Century Musical Reception," *Journal of the American Musicological Society,* forthcoming 52 (1999).

[22]Marlise Hansemann, *Der Klavier-Auszug von den Anfangen bis Weber* (Leipzig: Helmut Meyen, 1943), 31 ff.

[23]Although properly speaking, the term "Singspiel" was not used by Hiller, who preferred the designation "Komische Oper." See Thomas Bauman, *Northern German Opera in the Age of Goethe* (Cambridge: Cambridge University Press, 1985), 9.

[24]The publishing house of Breitkopf evidently agreed, for among the first works that it produced with its innovative printing process was a reduced vocal score of Hiller's own comic opera, *Lisuart und Dariolette,* in 1768 (Hansemann, *Der Klavier-Auszug,* 30). To be more precise, though, the first proper "keyboard-vocal score" published by Breitkopf was actually a cantata by Hiller from 1765 entitled "Cantate auf die Ankunft der hohen Landesherrschaft."

[25]Forward to *Lottchen am Hofe* (Leipzig: Breitkopf, 1769), my translation. In another keyboard-vocal score, Hiller apologized: "The harmony is thus not as empty as the published score seems, since instruments fill out the gaps that I here and there seem to have allowed" (forward to *Der Dorfbalbier* [Leipzig: Breitkopf, 1771]).

[26]*Lisuart und Dariolette* (Leipzig: Breitkopf, 1768), 1.

[27]Arthur Loesser, *Men, Women, and Pianos: A Social History* (New York: Simon and Schuster, 1954), 153–154.

[28]Macnutt, "Publishing," 3: 1161. One example will suffice: Maurice Schlesinger's full score of Halvey's grand opera *La Juive* from 1835 would cost a purchaser 250 francs compared to some 15 francs for the piano-vocal score. Even when an opera might be printed in full score, some publishers included a piano reduction at the bottom, presumably to make reading the score easier for amateurs. See, for example, the editions of Giovanni Mayr's operas published by Ricordi and reprinted in *Italian Opera 1810–1840,* ed. Philip Gossett (New York: Garland Publishing, 1991), vol. 11.

[29]Jane Girdham, *English Opera in Late Eighteenth-Century London: Stephen Storace at Drury Lane* (Oxford: Clarendon Press, 1997), 83–84.

[30]The designation "Partitur" in this advertisement—as with many in the eighteenth century—is deceptive, in that no full orchestral score was necessarily

ever published. Here Simrock simply was referring to a score containing all the vocal parts in separate staves with a piano reduction of the orchestral accompaniment. A solo piano reduction of all the parts was issued for about one third of the operas, while it was also possible to buy some of these operas arranged for combinations of wind and string instruments, as the rubrics indicate. Such arrangements, the advertisement informs us at the bottom of the page, will be a double pleasure for lovers of Mozart, as "first, they can be performed as a quartet for those disciples of the Mozartian muse, but also secondly as an accompaniment to the voice without [full] instrumental accompaniment, either alone or with the use of the piano score" (my translation).

[31]Many reviewers in the nineteenth century were particularly dismissive of such piano arrangements. One critic writing in 1842 suggested that all texts to vocal works should at least be printed above the music so that the pianists would know what dramatic situation or affect they should be attempting to project in performance (*Allgemeine Musikalische Zeitung* 42 [1842]: 1048).

[32]Hansemann, *Der Klavier-Auszug,* 108–109.

[33]Mozart's irritation was no doubt exacerbated because he was already working on his own piano arrangement of the score for Torricella (Mozart's Viennese publisher). See the letter dated Dec. 28, 1782, written to his father (*The Letters of Mozart and His Family,* trans. Emily Anderson, 3 vols. [London: Macmillan, 1938], 3: 1242). It seems, though, that it was Wolfgang's father who had arranged these German publications unbeknownst to his son.

[34]*Allgemeine Wiener Musik-Zeitung* 108 (1847): 435.

[35]Ibid. (1823): 455; cited in Hansemann, *Der Klavier-Auszug,* 106.

[36]Quoted in Hansemann, *Der Klavier-Auszug,* 31.

[37]*Allgemeine Wiener Musik-Zeitung* 97 (1841): 411.

[38]Typical were these sentiments expressed by a critic in 1825: "One is put in a certain predicament when having to review a major vocal or instrumental work using a piano reduction. . . . It would be as inappropriate as the critic trying to appraise the artistic content and merit of Raphael's 'Transfiguration' by studying an engraving rather than the original painting, or the work of a poet by consulting a mere chrestomathy." *Cäcilia* 3 (1825), 23 (my translation).

[39]Preface to *Meisterstücke des Italienischen Gesanges* (Leipzig: Breitkopf, 1791); quoted in Hansemann, *Der Klavier-Auszug,* 30.

[40]This is why transcriptions for four hands became so popular in the nineteenth century. Aside from the pleasures such duets afforded in mutual music-making, they were far more effective in capturing the range and textures of orchestral music than any solo piano transcription was.

[41]Quoted in Hansemann, *Der Klavier-Auszug,* 74.

[42]George Bernard Shaw, "The Religion of the Pianoforte" [1894], in *Complete Musical Criticism,* 3 vols., ed. Daniel Lawrence (New York: Dodd, Mead and Co., 1981), 3: 111–113.

[43]George Bernard Shaw, "Music in London, 1890–94" in *The Collected Works of Bernard Shaw,* 30 vols., ed. Ayot St. Lawrence (New York: Wm. H. Wise, 1931), 27: 147. For more on the critical role of the piano as a medium of musical literacy for bourgeois families in the nineteenth century, see Leon Plantinga, "The Piano and the Nineteenth Century," in *Nineteenth-Century Piano Music,* ed. R. Larry Todd (New York: Schirmer, 1991), 1–15.

[44]William Weber, *Music and the Middle Class: The Social Structure of Concert Life in London, Paris and Vienna* (London: Croom Helm, 1975), 16 ff.

[45]Again, the same point could be made for transcriptions of instrumental music, though I will confine my remarks in the following pages to consideration of operatic transcriptions.

[46]Jürgen Habermas, *The Structural Transformation of the Public Sphere,* trans. Thomas Burger with Frederick Lawrence (Cambridge, Mass.: MIT Press, 1989), 43 ff.

[47]Ibid., 7. Ellen Rosand, *Opera in Seventeenth-Century Venice: The Creation of a Genre* (Berkeley and Los Angeles: University of California Press, 1991); Robert Isherwood, *Music in the Service of the King: France in the Seventeenth Century* (Ithaca: Cornell University Press, 1973).

[48]Habermas, *The Structural Transformation of the Public Sphere,* 27.

[49]Other interesting evidence of this shift in critical focus can be found in pamphlets from the "Gluck-Piccini" skirmish. In one such pamphlet entitled "Entretiens sur l'état actuel de l'opéra de Paris" from 1779, Claude-Philibert Coquéau recorded a fictive dialogue between two antagonists of Italian and French operatic styles sitting at a keyboard and playing through a piano-vocal score of Gluck's *Armide.* Through this literary device, Coquéau was able to offer an analysis of each movement of the opera, with commentary on everything from the meter and key selected by the composer to specific instances of dissonance, orchestration, and rhythmic phrasing. Coquéau's pamphlet is reprinted in *Querelle des Gluckistes et des Piccinnistes: Textes des pamphlets,* ed. François Lesure, 2 vols. (Geneva: Minkoff, 1984), 2: 367–540.

[50]There was another interesting way in which the private "experience" of the piano-vocal score could be made an element of public participation and identification: namely, printed subscriber's lists. By prefacing a given publication with a list of patrons and sponsors (and this applies, of course, not just to musical scores, but any kind of literature), the publisher implicitly defines a common public who presumably can share in the sentiments and values of the music or literature presented, while at the same time advertising their own pedigree of tastes

and education. Hence, the title page to Stephen Storace's last opera is dedicated to "The Public Patrons and Private Friends of Worth and Genius" whose 350 or so names preface the vocal-score: *Mahmoud and the Iron Chest. Adopted for the Piano Forte or Harpsichord by Joseph Mazzinghi* (London: Widow of Stephen Storace, 1797).

[51]Michelle Perrot, "At Home," in *From the Fires of Revolution to the Great War,* vol. 4 of *A History of Private Life,* ed. Philippe Ariès and Georges Duby (Cambridge, Mass.: Harvard University Press, 1990), 341–357.

[52]There was another popular version of opera transcription for piano produced in the nineteenth century that deserves mention here, though I will not analyze it in any detail. This is, of course, the virtuosic opera paraphrase or potpourri. Needless to say, works like Liszt's *Réminiscences de Don Juan* or Thalberg's *Variations on Themes from Norma* do not represent themselves as facsimiles of the operas of Mozart and Bellini. They are explicitly subjective, impressionistic interpretations. (In this sense, Liszt's transcriptions of Wagner were more "faithful" renditions.) More significantly, though, these paraphrases were not intended as intimate, parlor music for domestic consumption by amateurs. They were ferociously "public" pieces intended for concert recitals or the salon (itself a semi-public space of performance). In both aesthetic character and function, they were as radically different from a performance using the modest piano-vocal score as they were from a staged performance of the opera.

[53]Arthur Loesser, *Men, Women and Pianos,* 362.

[54]So, for example, when the celebrated soprano Giuditta Pasta revived the role of Medea in Giovanni Mayr's *Medea in Corinto* in 1823, any enthusiastic Parisian would not have been able to peruse the music with a full score, since it was not yet published. But they could buy a piano-vocal score that was brought out in the same year by Carli. Obviously, Carli was savvy enough to capitalize on Pasta's fame. For the facsimile of the piano-vocal score, see Gossett, ed., *Italian Opera 1810–1840,* vol. 12.

[55]Johnson, *Listening in Paris,* esp. 206–227.

[56]*Partition de Tancrède de Rossini* (Paris: Carli, 1821), "Prospectus."

[57]Some model studies that have already done so are Ruth Solie, "The Schubert Circle and the Culture of Domesticity," unpublished typescript; James Parakilas, "The Power of Domestication in the Lives of Musical Canons," *repercussions* 4 (1995): 5–25; and Nicolai Petrat, *Hausmusik des Biedermeier im Blickpunkt der zeitgenössischen musikalischen Fachpresse (1815–1848)* (Hamburg: Karl Dieter Wagner, 1986).

CHAPTER 4

Alban Berg Remembers Emil Hertzka
Composer and Publisher between Real and Ideal

ROBERT R. HOLZER

On 9 May 1932 Emil Hertzka, Vice-President and Managing Director of Universal Edition, died in Vienna of a heart attack. He was sixty-two. The next day the city's paper of record, the *Neue freie Presse,* reported:

> Although he himself was not a professional musician, he had a fine understanding for many significant and pathbreaking ones, such as Gustav Mahler, Schoenberg, Schreker, Marx, Alban Berg, and Wellesz. Emil Hertzka was himself a characteristic figure in international musical life; his kindness, his devotion to work, his tireless efforts hastened his end, which his friends lament.[1]

The death notice his colleagues placed in the same issue was still more effusive. "His life's work," they proclaimed, "has built him a lasting monument in the history of contemporary music."[2]

For once, partisan claims trumped journalistic detachment. Universal's catalog included far more than the Austrian composers, great and small, named in the *Neue freie Presse:* in the quarter century Hertzka had guided the firm it grew to include works by nearly every major composer alive in Europe; for many of them, Universal was the first to publish their music.[3]

To honor further its late director, Universal established a memorial foundation in his name, which was to award prizes annually to promising young composers.[4] In its first public act, however, the *Emil Hertzka Gedächtnisstiftung* presented a concert on 20 June 1932, during the tenth festival of the International Society for Contemporary Music.[5] The noontime program of works by Anton Bruckner, Gustav Mahler, and Arnold Schoenberg—Universal composers all—called upon the best talents available. The Kolisch Quartet, augmented by an unnamed violist, opened the concert with the first movement of Bruckner's String Quintet. The contralto Enid Szánthó, a soloist with the Vienna State Opera, performed three Mahler songs, "Nicht wiedersehen!," "Wo die schönen Trompeten blasen," and "Ich bin der Welt abhanden gekommen."[6] The Kolisch Quartet closed the program with the Adagio from Schoenberg's First String Quartet.

Listeners in the Kleiner Musikvereinsaal that afternoon were also presented a work of a different sort by another composer in the Universal list. Between the performance of the quintet and the songs, Alban Berg delivered a brief address in Hertzka's memory. Barely five pages of typescript, his *Gedenkrede* touched upon a variety of topics, among them the relation of composer and publisher, of art and commerce, and the course of recent music history.[7] In so doing, Berg offers us a glimpse of his own thoughts during his last years.

In the *Gedenkrede* Berg deployed, at times in rather obvious ways, ideas with which he was long familiar. Such is hardly surprising, given the haste in which he wrote. The composer had left Vienna for the countryside in mid-May; as he admitted to his friend Soma Morgenstern in a letter of 3 June 1932:

> I would already have long since written you, if I were not so—diligent. But since my work [on Act II of *Lulu*] is going well, I am stingy with every minute. Indeed, in fourteen days I must of necessity interrupt it (the work) again (I tremble at the thought of Vienna), and must in the meantime also compose a talk for the Hertzka memorial celebration on 20 June.[8]

Some of these ideas came from Berg's "household gods," as Morgenstern christened them, Karl Kraus and Arnold Schoenberg; others echo Berg's own praise of Hertzka and Universal from years past.[9] His exordium, for example, is thoroughly Krausian. "Of the many enemies that the living composer has, one is the publisher": even casual readers of *Die Fackel* knew the gusto with which Kraus, Austria's tireless literary scold, blasted publishers of all sorts, from press lords to the editors of small magazines.[10] At the time of the *Gedenkrede,* moreover, Berg was much taken with this side of Kraus's activity. In January 1932 the first issue of *23: Eine Wiener Musikzeitschrift* appeared, for which the composer himself helped write the programmatic statement.[11] A kind of musical *Fackel* run by the Bergian partisans Willi Reich, Ernst Krenek, and Rudolf Ploderer, the journal satirized the failings of Austrian press criticism; Berg himself played a role in the contents of early issues.[12] Finally, and in part thanks to Kraus, Berg was long familiar with another withering portrait of a publisher. *Pandora's Box,* the second of Frank Wedekind's Lulu plays, opens with a prologue set in a bookshop.[13] Four characters hold forth: The Normal Reader, The Enterprising Publisher, The Shy Author, and The Public Prosecutor. The Publisher is by far the oiliest, befriending The Author only because the scandal surrounding his work will improve sales. Like the others, moreover, he is to be played by an actor who impersonates another character in the drama proper: for him Wedekind chose the white-slaver Marquis Casti-Piani.[14]

Called upon to praise rather than bury a publisher, though, Berg let his last words revise his first: "Of the few friends that we living composers have, this was one, our publisher Emil Hertzka."[15] Such a reversal, though, was also typical of Kraus, and was a device the composer himself had put to good use before.[16] In 1920 he entitled his demolition of Hans Pfitzner's *New Aesthetic of Musical Impotence* "The Musical Impotence of Hans Pfitzner's *New Aesthetic*."[17] Ten years later it was Hugo Riemann's turn: his words were amended to make Schoenberg the equal of J. S. Bach. As Bryan R. Simms explains, Berg first quoted the musicologist

> [on Bach's] pivotal position between modal and tonal composition and between the ages of counterpoint and homophony, then re[wrote] passages placing Schoenberg in the same position of importance between diatonic and chromatic composition and between the ages of homophony and the new counterpoint.[18]

As the body of the *Gedenkrede* makes clear, Hertzka's uniqueness occasioned the revisionist wordplay. Other publishers, bowing to the market, were hostile to modern composers ("I must say that it is a tall order for a businessman—and a publisher has to be that—to dispose of a product that the consumer has rejected as unpalatable").[19] Not so Hertzka, a singularity Berg explained as follows:

> I have no other answer—and for us musicians there is no other explanation—than: it was the power of the idea! The idea that was brought into the world with the "musical movement" that I was speaking of

earlier; the idea from which the whole spiritual debit and credit of this publishing house derives, even the material success which in the end was not lacking, even the real power that went out from this publishing house, and the leading position that it occupies today.[20]

The "musical movement" was, of course, that of Schoenberg and his followers, "a movement that would last for twenty-five years, and remains today the only movement of which one can say that it is still a movement."[21] "The power of the idea" was a similarly Schoenbergian conceit. Adapted from Schopenhauer, it placed thought beyond world and time, at once the core of valid art and the goad to human endeavor.[22] Berg's mentor, moreover, had himself invoked the latter concept to praise Hertzka. For the twenty-fifth anniversary of Universal on 25 January 1926, Schoenberg, Webern, and Berg sent Hertzka dedication copies of their recent music.[23] Schoenberg contributed *Unentrinnbar,* the first of his Four Pieces for Mixed Chorus, op. 27; its text, the composer's own, begins "Brave are those who accomplish deeds to which their courage is not equal. They possess only the strength to conceive their task and the character not to be able to reject it."[24] Berg had also been reminded of the notion more recently, when he read the libretto of Schoenberg's *Moses und Aron* in December 1931: in Act I, scene iv, Moses assures the priests "In the desert the purity of thinking will nurture, maintain, and develop you."[25]

Finally, Berg reworked ideas he himself had used for Universal's silver jubilee. In the *Gedenkrede* he reminded his audience that despite rejection, great music's time eventually came: "Bruckner, Mahler and Schoenberg united in a single concert. To us today that seems quite natural; in those days [when Universal was founded] it was daring to perform even one work by one of them."[26] Berg had already made the point in an essay for the volume *25 Jahre neue Musik: Jahrbuch 1926 der Universal-Edition.*[27] Asked by the editors "to give the prospects for the coming twenty-five years," Berg confessed he could do no more than assure them of Schoenberg's leading role.[28] He then showed the ease with which contemporaries and near contemporaries mistook greatness in their midst, citing jokes about Beethoven's Ninth Symphony from 1847 and Mahler's Eighth from 1910.[29]

Honor as he might the Schoenbergian spirit, Berg contradicted the letter of his mentor's situation. Well did he know that Schoenberg had published nothing new with Universal since 1929, when the Orchestra Variations, op. 31, the Piano Piece, op. 33a, and an arrangement of J. S. Bach's Prelude and Fugue in E-flat, BWV 552, had appeared.[30] Dissatisfaction with Universal's offer for *Von heute auf morgen* precipitated the break, whereupon Schoenberg published the opera at his own expense; the following year he entrusted *Begleitungsmusik zu einer Lichtspielszene,* op. 34, and Six Pieces for Men's Choir, op. 35, to publishers in Germany.[31]

Schoenberg was more clear-eyed about this reality than was his former pupil. His own memorial for Hertzka portrays something other than a divinely inspired publisher squaring the circle of commercial and artistic interests:

> Emil Hertzka was my publisher for twenty years. And if I must state the main reason why he is no longer so, I believe I have to say because lately he was no longer *my* publisher. I believe that the business arrangements that he was perhaps forced to make, whether I agreed or not, divided us. Perhaps one can build up a publishing house in no other way. But here Hertzka's merit became an obstacle: his nature obliged him to base all business dealings on friendship. But publisher and author can not in the long run be friends. And so Hertzka the publisher was again and again forced to take what Hertzka the friend had given. And Hertzka the friend could give: he never saw the needs of his authors without acting. If it was ever possible for him, he helped, he did not leave one in the lurch.[32]

Berg did not need to know this piece, which Schoenberg never published, in order to know the clash of spiritual and temporal it described. In 1928 Schoenberg and Franz Schreker, worried that Hertzka would soon retire and mistrustful of possible successors (and eager in either case to improve their financial arrangements), sought to found an association of Universal authors.[33] Berg declined to join, explaining to Schoenberg on 10 April:

> At the moment I cannot take the risk that Hertzka—in reaction to this project—might take a businessman's attitude and suspend or reduce my monthly 600 schillings, an annuity representing my sole income (the few student fees don't count), for which the current returns from my works are no equivalent. (Already I owe—even if only on paper and not morally—about 6,000 schillings on this annuity, which has only been running for 2¼ years.) . . . I, with my two dozen *Wozzeck* performances and the prospect (not even assured) of another acceptance

in — — Oldenburg, depend on Hertzka's personal goodwill if I am
not to endanger the continuation of my full annuity for the next few
years (until I finish another opera). For my contract, which runs until
1932, doesn't offer the slightest security in this regard.[34]

Hertzka remained, of course, and Berg soon became a star of the
Universal list: the Oldenburg *Wozzeck* came off in March 1929, and the
next two seasons saw the opera's triumphant march through German theaters, along with performances in Vienna and Philadelphia.[35] At the end
of the second season, in a letter of 7 June 1931, Berg could tell his erstwhile pupil Theodor Adorno: "at the moment [Hertzka] sets greater store
by me than any of his authors."[36] Yet Berg's success only made him more
aware of the tensions Schoenberg described. In the same letter, for example, he could not guarantee that his recommendation would help Adorno
break into print with Universal:

> Things at the moment are such that U.E. (and I also believe no pub-
> lisher [Bote & Bock, for example, has recently cut back enormously!])
> can not think, *may* not think (it is under bank supervision: highest dis-
> cretion!!!) to undertake something that costs money which does not
> earn *with certainty* and soon. Where this is guaranteed, it publishes of
> its own accord (for example *Der Wein,* whose score, without my slight-
> est involvement, on account of American prospects, etc., it suddenly
> had printed); where that certainty is not guaranteed, no encouragement
> is of use—no coaxing, no assuring.
>
> Nevertheless I consider it important and right (for you, for our
> music*, indeed for the publisher) that you "appear" in U.E. as soon as
> possible. Are you ready to bear the costs? thus to do, what we all did
> (be it directly or through a patron: Schoenberg's opp. 1–3, op. 10,
> Berg's opp. 1, 2, 3, 4 [*recte* 5], and 7, Webern's large orchestra pieces,
> etc., etc., etc.)?
>
> *that means for *the* music that began with Schoenberg.[37]

When he wrote the *Gedenkrede,* then, Berg knew as well as anyone
that economic realities could hinder Hertzka's spreading of the true faith;
as the letter to Adorno shows, he had known so for a long time. In 1910
the composer himself had paid the engraving and printing costs of his
Piano Sonata, op. 1, and Four Songs, op. 2, and had done so again in
1920 for the String Quartet, op. 3, and the Four Clarinet Pieces, op. 5.[38]

In none of these cases was the publisher Universal, whose list Berg was not to enter until 1923 when he sold the firm the rights to *Wozzeck* and the Three Orchestra Pieces, op. 6.[39] Thus, Berg lamented to Schoenberg on 14 August 1920: "I don't believe Hertzka will publish anything of mine any time soon, having neglected to do so for 10 years, despite your frequent advocacy to the point of quarreling with him, and even though at one time I offered to assume the engraving costs (of the sonata) myself and he has since then published *every* other Viennese beginner, be he ever so untalented and immature."[40]

But if in those days Hertzka could not see a return on even so modest an investment as four chamber works, he was glad to have Berg work on projects that he guessed—rightly, as it turned out—would earn money. In 1911 Berg prepared the bulk of the piano reduction of Franz Schreker's opera *Der ferne Klang,* a huge success upon its premiere the following year.[41] He did the same for Schoenberg's *Gurrelieder,* which had its triumphant premiere in 1913.[42]

The Hertzka that appears in Berg's correspondence with Schoenberg from this time was not even a friendly collaborator constrained by the market, but a businessman at once bumbling and hypocritical. On 11 January 1912, the day after delivering his *Gurrelieder* reduction to Hertzka and signing a contract for it, he wrote:

> Considering how long it takes to publish a work long after it has been completed, one cannot be too insistent, especially with a publishing house and a director as disorganized as U.E. and Hertzka. (His desk even looks like a Viennese dung collector's cart. Right down to the bell! Ancient memoranda and rubbish are piled in confused layers and the only thing missing is a prod to poke around with, to see if there's something useful there after all. And just as dung collectors aren't connoisseurs of art, he generally hits on the wrong things, too, e.g., symphonies by [Karl] Weigl, [Robert] Konta, etc. — —)[43]

Hertzka's contemporaneous decision not to publish Schoenberg's Five Orchestra Pieces, op. 16, called forth equal sarcasm, despite his having been the first to print any of the composer's atonal or orchestral works.[44] When Schoenberg sold the pieces to C. F. Peters in January 1912, Berg found it "delightful to observe Hertzka's reaction (for whom, of course, it is the greatest embarrassment)."[45] Hertzka only feigned happiness at having released the Five Pieces back to Schoenberg:

intending thereby to serve you and get your work out, as well as to see
you promoted by this publisher (Peters) (since he was, *nota bene,* not
able to publish the work at the moment!). Instead of saying straight
out: "I am no artist and don't understand Schönberg, [and] can therefore be of no service to him. But I'm not a good businessman either,
which is why I undermine my own publishing house!!" One should
tear the bearded mask off the face of this old prattler! Then the whole
world would know what we have known all along![46]

Hertzka's direct action on behalf of Schoenberg also earned disapproval. The publisher helped establish a subscription to sell tickets for
the *Gurrelieder* premiere. Berg wrote on 12 April 1912: "Again Hertzka
set himself up as your most enthusiastic admirer and patron and I could
only think of the 'fog' of which you speak in the Gutmann calendar."[47]
His reference is to Schoenberg's recently published essay *"Parsifal* and
Copyright." Only "publishers, theater-directors, etc.," he wrote, "stand to
gain when genuinely artistic and moral questions become befogged, for
then they can advance their business interests."[48]

Berg wrote these early attacks while acting as Schoenberg's agent in
Vienna; some were no doubt conditioned by his erstwhile teacher, most
of whose relationships were shot through with suspicion and hostility.[49]
His other activity for Universal, however, that of musical publicist, was
tinged with a rancor unmistakably his own. Having published his analytic guides to Schoenberg's *Gurrelieder, Pelleas und Melisande,* and the
Chamber Symphony, Hertzka hired him in 1920 to edit Universal's new
journal, *Musikblätter der Anbruch.*[50] In the same letter to Schoenberg of
14 August 1920 cited before, he observed:

> For Hertzka the only reason to publish something after all could be if
> he wanted to take advantage of me in some other way, for example, if I
> were to come to him after a probationary period at *Anbruch* with the
> demand for a salary increase he could say, "I can't do that, for I can't
> increase the already high costs of *Anbruch,* which brings in no profits,
> but I will publish something of yours, for the time being as a supple-
> ment in *Anbruch,* [the journalist Hugo Robert] Fleischmann will write
> about it, and you and your name would be better served than if I raised
> your salary from 500 to 550 kronen."[51]

The *Gedenkrede,* then, does not square with the reality of Berg's experiences with his publisher. Of course, even a man far less gracious than

Alban Berg, whose material success was owed in large part to Universal, would not have used a memorial speech to dredge up ancient unpleasantries. But if Berg distorted the truth by casting his praise in Schoenbergese (just as he had his early blame) he knew the language well enough—haste or no—to speak it with subtlety. Towards the end of the talk he remarked:

> If I have hitherto hardly spoken about the man who was—I can find no more honorable description—the bearer, the agent, the custodian of that "idea," I have refrained because it would have meant lapsing from the general onto the personal level. And if I were to do that, if I were to speak of what is close to my own heart, then I would become too personal. My speech—which is supposed to be filled with the radiant recognition of that "idea"—would then bear a dark tone of profound sadness, which I wanted to avoid.[52]

Berg eschewed sadness for joy by celebrating the idea rather than mourning the man. In so doing, he also avoided the need to offer a sanitized account of an often problematic relationship, one marked to the very end by disagreements. As the editors of *23* noted in their otherwise appreciative obituary, Hertzka had opposed Berg's latest pet project: "We were not close to him personally and knew only that he took the appearance of our journal with mixed feelings and in particular expressed himself rather unfavorably to friends about the first issue."[53]

In his characteristically gentle way, though, Berg was also quite harsh with Hertzka.[54] By calling him an "agent" of the idea, he reminded everyone that the canny businessman with a sixth sense for spotting talent had in fact been seized by an idea not his own. Even Schoenberg had been more generous to his publisher: *Unentrinnbar* opens with a plural ("Brave are those . . .") that can include a Hertzka as well as a Schoenberg.

In similar fashion Berg also deflected attention from Universal. After listing some of its economic virtues he declared:

> All these [successful business] matters seem to me to be the private concern of the authors—and stockholders. But what has been written down in the course of this quarter century on five-line paper is no private concern, but the concern of the history of music. And it is alive, just as it was twenty-five years ago, because it serves the idea of that

> great musical movement—and in the end it must be right, for this spir-
> itual capital is perhaps the only kind of capital that is not subject to the
> risk of crisis. It cannot be devalued.[55]

Once again, apparent praise brought its object up short. By ending his
discussion so abruptly, Berg suppressed more thoroughly what he had
told Adorno confidentially the year before, that Universal was in financial trouble.[56] Yet by remarking on the immunity of "spiritual" capital
from crisis, he elevated idea above publishing house, placing it beyond
the reach of the Great Depression.[57]

Berg's Krausian reversal also hinted at deeper troubles with
Hertzka. True, by transforming the publisher from one of a composer's
many enemies to one of his few friends, he turned on himself a polemical
device usually reserved for others. Yet jokes at his own expense were second nature to Berg: Willi Reich wrote of his "highly developed ironic
awareness of himself coupled with benevolent good humor toward others," while Adorno noted that "he did not hesitate to apply irony to his
own assessment of himself or a certain skepticism, which in the form of
patient self-criticism, became so extremely fruitful in his creative
work."[58] Self-irony, in turn, could signal deeper pain. As we have seen,
Berg excused himself with Soma Morgenstern for having been too "diligent" to write. His crack, part of a running joke between the two about
who was the lazier, also registers unease at having to interrupt work on
Lulu, whose lengthy gestation displeased his publisher.[59] As Berg wrote
to Schoenberg on 6 August 1931, after completing Act I:

> I think I succeeded [in the difficult task of shaping text and music] and
> that will have to console me for my slow progress. After all, I can't
> simply treat the whole thing as a rush job for Philadelphia, which is
> what U.E. and Stokowski would like! For now I have given both of
> them hopes for a "world premiere" in the 1932/33 season.[60]

Berg's unease at the social conditions in which composers and publishers found themselves also underscores his explanation for his opening statement in the *Gedenkrede:*

> On the one hand there is the artist, whose activity—if he is concerned
> with matters proper to his art—is directed towards the spiritual, and on
> the other hand there is the business man, whose activity—if he is con-
> cerned with matters proper to his business—is directed toward the ma-
> terial. I would not dare pronounce this commonplace about the gulf

between artist and dealer, between idealism and realism, if we were not living in a time when this realization is hardly a commonplace any more—indeed, today the opposite tends to be considered obvious: the artist has to be "matter-of-fact" [*sachlich*] . . . since in any case . . . the dealer is "inspired" [*genial*].

So if I am to persist in my view of the ideal artist who stands in contrast to the realities of the world, I will have to cast my glance back— and this quarter century of Universal Edition makes it possible for me to do so—to a time when this view was not yet antiquated, and when this contrast was considered a sheer and unbridgeable gulf.[61]

Berg, then, described a dilemma that his concluding revision could not resolve. Had businessmen and artists stayed within their respective realms, modern music would have remained obscure. Yet the alternative offended Berg still more. As we have seen, the publisher who confused "artistic and moral questions" was just the sort Schoenberg had denounced in his *Parsifal* essay, and it was there that Berg found an apt characterization of Hertzka. Their combined attack, moreover, shows that Berg did not consider the *genial* businessman a recent phenomenon, but one present since the start of Universal's activity.[62]

In the same way, disdain as he might the *sachlich* artist, Berg himself could be obliged to act like one. Just two months earlier, on 5 April 1932, he wrote a scolding letter to Clemens Krauss, music director of the Vienna State Opera. Though pleased that a special performance of the work for which he was most famous, *Wozzeck,* had been planned for the upcoming ISCM Festival—the same one at which he delivered the Hertzka address—he was unhappy that the *Staatsoper* had not produced the work during its 1931–1932 season. To show Krauss his folly, Berg insisted on the work's popularity, citing box office receipts from the previous two seasons to prove his point: the five performances of 1930 netted an average of 10,700 shillings apiece, and the six in 1930–1931 each yielded 8,000.[63] Anxious lest he seem too interested in money, Berg concluded by contrasting his popular success with that of his rivals:

I hope that you, Herr Direktor, do not misunderstand this letter of mine, meaning that you do not construe it as the act of a performance- and royalty-hungry author. The fact is that in the last two, three seasons hardly a week passed in which *Wozzeck* was not on the program somewhere, and there were sometimes weeks with two, three performances . . . and also the fact that this year this opera, besides German provincial towns, had first performances in capitals such as Zurich,

Brussels, and New York (to illustrate what was said before of Viennese musical life: *not one* Viennese newspaper took the slightest notice of this New York premiere. One can imagine what would have happened in our Piffl-Korngold region if, were the unimaginable case encountered that an opera by [Max] Springer or [Erich Wolfgang Korngold's *Das Wunder der*] *Heliane* were performed at the Metropolitan!) and finally is put on at the Vienna Music Festival. These facts defend me from the imputation of such ambitious and greedy motives.[64]

Not the vulgar crowd, then, but such well-placed reactionaries as the archbishop of Vienna and the music critic of the *Neue freie Presse* kept *Wozzeck* from the *Staatsoper* stage.[65] But if Berg the moneywise populist does not sit well with Adorno's famous pronouncement ("Schoenberg envied Berg his successes, while Berg envied Schoenberg his failures"), he was likewise at odds with his own background.[66] Like so many who came of age during the decline of Austrian liberalism, he found commerce irredeemably philistine.[67] Writing in July 1910 to his future father-in-law, the young composer defended his desire to marry Helene Nahowski by comparing himself to her sister's fiancé, Arthur Lebert. The latter was trained to manufacture emery boards; Berg's whimsical missive drips with contempt for industry. Lebert would earn well,

but *only when* the factory exists, *when* it *is* put in operation. Thus, hardly less "music of the future" than *my* music! Accordingly, no greater risk in considering *me* as fiancé (since, as mentioned, we have also been so wise as to wait). Because as I have proved to you, Herr Nahowski, *I have as much a so-called secure background as Herr Lebert, as much the prospect (through our exceptional backgrounds in our respective fields) of a respectable, perhaps even brilliant income at hand,* and in order to create this income for me, one need not *build* me a factory, because I have my own with all the newest equipment and greatest productive capacity *in my head!* And should this thought factory of mine in fact yield less monetary earning than the emery board factory of the brothers Lebert, so may it console you, Herr Nahowski, "we can make do!"[68]

In the same way, the public whom Berg would one day invoke in his defense had not always been the object of his affection. The aesthetic elitist whose *Altenberg Lieder* were shouted down in 1913 had little use for the average concert-goer.[69] As he wrote to his wife on the last day of

1914, the war, horrible as it was, had "the task to make *pure!*"[70] The rot he hoped it would abolish included "philistinism" and "business spirit," and Berg grimly joked that operetta composers would soon treat their enthusiastic audiences to jingoist tunes.[71]

Finally, despite what he told Nahowski senior, Berg did not see compostion as a way to earn money. In the same letter to Schoenberg of 14 August 1920 cited earlier, he declared his preference for "a retiring life dedicated to composition and to writing about your works and on your behalf."[72] Straitened circumstances after World War I forced him to do otherwise:

> I have now thrown myself into the arms of the public and must seek there what is known by that revolting term, "a career" (synonymous with the *living* one earns in this way), and cannot afford to pass up any opportunity promoting such a "career." Since I also appear in my capacity as composer, that requires *compositions*. And these have wider significance only when they are performed and otherwise available. *You,* dear friend, have seen to a number of performances these past 2 years. So it remains to make these compositions available to those who are interested, who wish to orient themselves and possibly to perform something.
>
> This *possibility* has not existed—outside my immediate sphere of activity—until now. (And the fact that a sonata of mine is "generally" known and doesn't displease people doesn't change anything.) But if I now pursue that possibility and publish something of my own, it is not due to ambition, but solely because I regard that as one way effectively to establish my public standing, which I have resolved to do, though again not for reasons of ambition.[73]

At the very moment he wrote these words, moreover, Berg was composing his distaste of commerce into *Wozzeck*. In Act II, scene i, written in the summer of 1920, Wozzeck takes leave of Marie at mm. 116–124. Berg later explained that "Wozzeck's words 'Here is the money, Marie. My wages from the Captain and the Doctor' are sung to a held C major triad. . . . could the objectivity of money and what it represents be expressed more clearly!"[74]

Yet it was the completion of *Wozzeck* a year and a half later that sealed Berg's transformation into a successful Universal composer. Such was not easy—Schoenberg's recommendation of the opera to Hertzka in October 1921 went unheeded, and it took Alma Mahler's help in 1922 to get the vocal score printed privately, an edition that Universal (saving it-self the engraving costs) then took over the next year.[75] Berg's persis-tence in the face of such obstacles, though, bears witness to a new (or newly professed) willingness to enter the market. In letters to his wife of March and April 1923, he eagerly described acts he once would have found unedifying.[76] In the "tricky business" of signing his first contract, the composer evaluated rival offers from Schirmer, listed precise figures, and considered possibilities for first performances.

After his opera's publication, Berg became a good soldier in its pro-motion. To make concert performance possible, he took Hermann Scherchen's advice and prepared a suite; *Three Excerpts from Wozzeck* were premiered and published in 1924. When the complete work began its stage life in 1925, Berg traveled as far afield as the Soviet Union to oversee the various productions. And finally, when *Wozzeck* became a repertory staple at the end of the decade, the composer prepared a lecture for delivery before each new production.[77]

Yet Berg's transformation, real or apparent, did not negate all his youth-ful beliefs. Other artists of the time, among them those most important to the Schoenberg circle, sought to take by force the very public that so often disgusted them. Peter Franklin has noted this tendency in Gustav Mahler, whose double career as composer and conductor was a monu-ment to mixed motives.[78] Likewise, the great Germanist Ladislao Mitt-ner suggested for Stefan George the motto "Odi profanum vulgus et coerceo" ("I hate the profane crowd and I coerce it"), a revision of Hor-ace's dismissive "Odi profanum vulgus et arceo" (. . . and I keep it dis-tant").[79] In the case of George, said coercion was achieved in large part through print, as limited editions destined for acolytes were then repub-lished for the world at large.[80]

Berg's role as propagandist, first for Schoenberg, then for himself, was likewise made possible by print, and by the formidable public rela-tions apparatus of Universal Edition. Yet in realizing one artistic ideal, the composer acted contrary to those he described in the *Gedenkrede*. But if external necessity occasioned the distance between what was said and what was done, the unsaid hinted at this deeper conflict. As men-tioned, the composer drew on a repertory of familiar notions to fashion the *Gedenkrede*. One, however, which he had used to praise Hertzka be-fore, is conspicuously absent. In 1926 Berg dedicated old and new set-tings of "Schließe mir die Augen beide" to his publisher:

> Twenty-five years of Universal Edition matching the enormous dis-
> tance covered as music has gone from tonal composition to the "method
> of composing with twelve Tones related only with one another," from
> the C-major triad to the "Mutterakkord" [Note: the 12–note chord dis-
> covered by Fritz Heinrich Klein; it also contains all twelve intervals]. It
> is the imperishable achievement of Emil Hertzka to have been the only
> publisher who covered the distance from the very start.[81]

Though he published this endorsement of musical progress in February
1930, the composer avoided such talk in the memorial address.[82] Instead,
as we have seen, he spoke in general terms of a "musical movement" that
had unfolded in the previous quarter century.

In so doing, Berg made his own thought conform more closely to
Schoenberg's. Though the older composer often spoke of necessity and
inevitability, he did not conceive progress in stylistic terms, for such
would deny the Idea its leading role.[83] Indeed, in his other contribution to
the Universal silver jubilee, an essay for the publisher's 1926 *Jahrbuch,*
Schoenberg dismissed the rival claims of tonality and atonality: "He who
can do something pure may make it tonal or atonal; but those who think
impurely, namely those who do what anyone can, may quietly form tonal
or atonal parties or else make noise about it."[84] More recently, Berg himself had downplayed considerations of style. In 1928 he averred that only
isolated masterpieces advanced operatic history; by contrast "the use of
'contemporary' means—such as cinema, revue, loudspeakers, jazz—
guarantees only that such a work is contemporary."[85]

Berg's omission in the *Gedenkrede,* however, complements developments in his late music. *Der Wein,* which had its Viennese premiere the
day after his talk, was not the work of a composer who believed that history progressed from the C-major triad to the all-interval row: scale segments and arpeggi form its basic series, recondite manipulations of
which yield tonal progressions and parodies of jazz.[86] Nor was *Lulu,*
whose juxtapositions of old and new are still more stunning, as echoes of
Mahler take their place in the sound world forged in the concert aria.[87]

But if Berg did not speak here of musical history as progress, neither
did he articulate his own vision of the past twenty-five years: to do so
would have sounded the "dark tone of profound sadness" he aimed to
avoid. As Robert P. Morgan argues, the growing incorporation of "historically distant moment[s]" in the composer's late work betrays a belief in
the doctrine of eternal return.[88] But unlike other Bergian manifestations

of Nietzsche's bracing conceit—retrogrades and circular forms—this last also points once more to Schopenhauer.[89] The philosopher, who rejected any attempt "to comprehend the history of the world as a planned whole, or, as [Hegelians] call it, 'to construct it organically,'" proclaimed that "constructive histories [are] guided by a shallow optimism."[90] By contrast, the world-weary thinker could not but see "the same thing in all history, just as at every turn of the kaleidoscope we always see the same things under different configurations."[91] As Adorno recalled, Berg could make "a word such as 'secession' sound contemporary when he said it."[92] Yet unlike Webern, who at this very moment spoke publicly of modern music's endless ascent, Berg kept his syncretism to himself.[93]

Cryptic autobiographer that he was, Alban Berg softened public sadness with a text that hints of private unhappiness. Yet just as grace and good humor keep sentimentality at bay, another gesture signals acceptance of the very unpleasantries the composer sought to hide. Berg cast the *Gedenkrede* itself in circular form: his revisionary last sentence leads back to the first. As Morgan argues, the form reflects the composer's view of existence, acceptance of which he saw "as a necessary condition of life."[94] In the *Gedenkrede* Berg tells us that the Idea can thrive even as one comes quietly to terms with material demands. That he was not wrong is shown by the extraordinary achievements of his final years, the difficult time after the passing of his publisher, Emil Hertzka.

NOTES

[1]"Obwohl selbst kein Musiker von Beruf, hatte er doch ein feines Verständnis für manches Bedeutende und Bahnbrechende, wie für Gustav Mahler, Schönberg, Schreker, Marx, Alban Berg, Wellesz. Emil Hertzka selbst war eine charakteristische Figur im internationalen Musikleben, seine Güte, seine Hingebung an die Arbeit, seine rastlosen Bemühungen haben sein Ende beschleunigt, das seine Freunde betrauern." *Neue freie Presse,* 10 May 1932, p. 5. For a list of obituaries in musical journals, see *Jahrbuch der Musikbibliothek Peters für 1932* 39 (1933): 72.

[2]"Sein Lebenswerk hat ihm ein dauerndes Monument in der Geschichte der zeitgenössischen Musik gesetzt." *Neuefreie Presse,* 10 May 1932, 13. A notice from Hertzka's widow Yella also appears on the same page.

[3]For a summary of Hertzka's tenure see Ernst Hilmar, "75 Jahre Universal Edition," *Österreichische Musikzeitschrift* 31 (1976), 661–664. For a list of composers published by the firm through 1925, see *25 Jahre neue Musik: Jahrbuch*

1926 der Universal-Edition, ed. Hans Heinsheimer and Paul Stefan (Vienna: Universal Edition, n.d.), 9–20. Further details can be found at the firm's website, http://www.uemusic.co.at/history.html. For more on Hertzka himself, see Hans W. Heinsheimer, *Menagerie in F sharp* (Garden City, N.Y.: Doubleday, 1947), 43–60, and *Best Regards to Aida: The Defeats and Victories of a Music Man on Two Continents* (New York: Alfred A. Knopf, 1968), 10–12.

[4]See "Aufruf zu einer Emil Hertzka-Gedächtnis-Stiftung (1932)," quoted in Ernst Hilmar, ed., *75 Jahre Universal Edition: Katalog zur Ausstellung der Wiener Stadt- und Landesbibliothek im Historischen Museum der Stadt Wien Dezember 1976/Jänner 1977* (Vienna: Universal Edition, 1976), 52.

[5]This was the first time the festival was held in Vienna. The complete program, which ran from 16 to 22 June, is found in *Anbruch: Monatsschrift für moderne Musik* 14 (1932): 113–118. For a review, see Paul Stefan, "Vienna Welcomes International Music Festival," *Musical America* 52, no. 12 (July 1932): 13.

[6]She was accompanied by pianist Paul Ulanowsky. For more on Szánthó, see the article by Elizabeth Forbes in *The New Grove Dictionary of Opera,* ed. Stanley Sadie, 4 vols. (London: Macmillan, 1992), 4: 621.

[7]The typescript is found in A Wn, F 21 Berg 110/II. The text was first published in Willi Reich, *Alban Berg: Mit Bergs eigenen Schriften und Beiträgen von Th. Wiesengrund-Adorno und Ernst Krenek* (Vienna: Herbert Reichner, 1937), 197–201 under the title "Gedenkrede auf Emil Hertzka." Unless otherwise noted, citations here are from "Commemorative Address for Emil Hertzka," in Willi Reich, *Alban Berg,* trans. Cornelius Cardew (London, 1963; reprint, New York: Vienna House, 1974), 84–89.

[8]"Ich hätte Dir längst schon geschrieben, wenn ich nicht so—fleißig wäre. Aber da mir die Arbeit gut von der Hand geht, geize ich mit jeder Minute. Muß ich sie (die Arbeit) ja in 14 Tagen wieder gehörig unterbrechen (:Mir graut vor Wien) und muß ich zwischendurch auch noch eine Rede verfassen für die Hertzka-Gedächtnisfeier am 20.VI." Quoted in Soma Morgenstern, *Alban Berg und seine Idole: Erinnerungen und Briefe,* ed. Ingolf Schulte (Lüneburg: zu Klampen, 1995), 245. For more on the friendship of Morgenstern and Berg, see Joan Allen Smith, "Berg's Character Remembered," in *The Berg Companion,* ed. Douglas Jarman (Boston: Northeastern University Press, 1990), 13–32. For the notations in Berg's *Tagebuch* that place him in the country, see Patricia Hall, *A View of Berg's "Lulu" through the Autograph Sources* (Berkeley and Los Angeles: University of California Press, 1996), 52.

[9]Morgenstern listed Berg's "Hausgötter" in "Im Trauerhaus," *23: Eine Wiener Musikzeitschrift,* 24–25 *Alban Berg zum Gedenken* (1 February 1936): 16; the others were Peter Altenberg, Adolf Loos, and Gustav Mahler.

[10]Berg, "Commemorative Address," 84. For a summary of Kraus's attacks on the press see Harold B. Segel, *The Vienna Coffeehouse Wits 1890–1938* (West Lafayette, Ind.: Purdue University Press, 1993), 59–60.

[11]See Reich, *Alban Berg,* trans. Cardew, 81–83.

[12]See John L. Stewart, *Ernst Krenek: The Man and His Music* (Berkeley and Los Angeles: University of California Press, 1991), 151. Reich, *Alban Berg,* trans. Cardew, 82–83, claimed that Berg was involved in every issue of the magazine.

[13]Berg first saw the play in a private production sponsored by Kraus on 29 May 1905. See George Perle, *The Operas of Alban Berg,* vol. 2, *"Lulu"* (Berkeley and Los Angeles: University of California Press, 1985), 38; the seating plan of the invited audience is reproduced as Plate 5.

[14]See Frank Wedekind, *The Lulu Plays and Other Sex Tragedies,* trans. Stephen Spender (New York: Riverrun Press, 1978), 107–110. Though Berg eliminated this section from *Lulu,* it may have inspired his own use of multiple roles. For different views on Berg's precise intentions in this regard compare Hall, *A View of Berg's "Lulu,"* 72 and Perle, *The Operas of Alban Berg,* 2: 60–65. Berg's Krausian disdain for newspapermen probably helps explain as well his enthusiasm for Hermann Broch's *The Sleepwalkers,* which he read later in the summer of 1932. He particularly commended the final volume of the trilogy, the story of a World War I deserter who transforms himself into the publisher of a provincial newspaper, later advancing to murder and rape. For Berg's letter to his erstwhile schoolmate of 25 August 1932, see Paul Michael Lützeler, *Hermann Broch: A Biography,* trans. Janice Furness (London: Quartet Books, 1987), 85–86.

[15]Berg, "Commemorative Address," 89.

[16]For Kraus's use of the device and its echoes in Berg, see Susanne Rode, *Alban Berg und Karl Kraus: Zur geistigen Biographie des Komponisten der "Lulu"* (Frankfurt: Peter Lang, 1988), 179–183.

[17]For the complete text in English, see Reich, *Alban Berg,* trans. Cardew, 205–218.

[18]Bryan R. Simms, *Alban Berg: A Guide to Research* (New York: Garland Publishing, 1996), 37. The essay, "Credo," which first appeared in the journal *Die Musik* in 1930, was reprinted in Reich, *Alban Berg: Mit Bergs eigenen Schriften,* 161.

[19]Berg, "Commemorative Address," 85. I render Berg's *"Ware"* as "product"; Cardew preferred "ware."

[20]Ibid., 87.

[21]Ibid., 86.

[22]For the relation between composer and philosopher on this point see Pamela C. White, "Schoenberg and Schopenhauer," *Journal of the Arnold Schoenberg Institute* 8 (1984): 45–47. For further philosophical explication see Bryan

Magee, *The Philosophy of Schopenhauer,* 2d ed. (Oxford: Clarendon Press, 1997), 148–149, 165–169; and Dale Jacquette, "Schopenhauer's Metaphysics of Appearance and Will in the Philosophy of Art," in *Schopenhauer, Philosophy, and the Arts,* ed. Jacquette (Cambridge: Cambridge University Press, 1996), 8–18. Berg, it should be noted, used the more aptly philosophical *Idee;* Schoenberg favored *Gedanke.* For the relation of these terms see the introduction by Patricia Carpenter and Severine Neff to their edition of Arnold Schoenberg, *The Musical Idea and the Logic, Technique, and Art of Its Presentation* (New York: Columbia University Press, 1995), 15–21.

[23]Hertzka's letter of thanks is printed in Arnold Schoenberg, *Sämtliche Werke,* vol. 18/2, series B, *Chorwerk I: Kritischer Bericht,* ed. Tadeusz Okuljar and Dorothee Schubel (Mainz: Schott, 1996), xxii; for details of Schoenberg's manuscript see p. 15.

[24]"Tapfere sind solche, die Taten vollbringen, an die ihr Mut nicht heranreicht. Sie besitzen nur die Kraft, den Auftrag zu konzipieren und den Charakter, ihn nicht abweisen zu können."

[25]"In der Wüste wird euch die Reinheit des Denkens nähren, erhalten, und entwickeln." For more on the related concept of the unrepresentability of god, see Pamela C. White, *Schoenberg and the God-Idea: The Opera "Moses und Aron"* (Ann Arbor, Mich.: UMI Research Press, 1985), 73–76. For Berg's response to the libretto, see his letter to Schoenberg of 23 December 1931 in *The Berg-Schoenberg Correspondence: Selected Letters,* ed. Juliane Brand, Christopher Hailey, and Donald Harris (New York: W.W. Norton, 1987), 426.

[26]Berg, "Commemorative Address," 84.

[27]See n. 3 for full citation. Berg's "Verbindliche Antwort auf eine unverblindliche Rundfrage" appears on pp. 220–225.

[28]"Einen Ausblick auf die kommenden fünfundzwanzig Jahre zu geben." Ibid., 220.

[29]Ibid., 223–225.

[30]The Variations were published on 4 June (score) and 30 September (parts), the Piano Piece on 31 July (in vol. 6 of *Musik der Zeit;* a separate edition, dated 1929, appeared on 1 March 1930), and the Bach arrangement on 20 November (score; parts were issued between then and January 1930). See the following volumes of series B, *Kritischer Bericht,* of Arnold Schoenberg, *Sämtliche Werke:* vol. 13, *Orchesterwerke II,* ed. Nikos Kokkinis and Jürgen Thym (1993), 20, 30; vol. 4, *Werke für Klavier zu zwei Hände,* ed. Reinhold Brinkmann (1975), 41; and vols. 25–26, *Bearbeitungen I/II,* ed. Rudolf Stephan and Tadeusz Okuljar (1988), 35, 44–45. In addition, the parts to Schoenberg's Third String Quartet, op. 30, published in score in 1927, appeared on 4 April 1929; see vol. 21, *Streichquartette II, Streichtrio,* ed. Christian Martin Schmidt (1984), 7–9.

[31]For the break with Universal and its consequences, see H. H. Stuckenschmidt, *Schoenberg: His Life, World, and Work,* trans. Humphrey Searle (New York: Schirmer Books, 1977), 326–328. On the publication of the opera, see Arnold Schoenberg, *Sämtliche Werke,* vol. 7/2, series B, *Von heute auf morgen, Oper in einem Akt, op. 32: Kritischer Bericht,* ed. Gösta Neuwirth and Tadeusz Okuljar (1974), 14–15. Heinrichshofen issued the *Begleitungsmusik;* Bote & Bock issued the Six Pieces. See Schoenberg, *Sämtliche Werke,* vol. 18/2, series B, *Chorwerk I: Kritischer Bericht,* 223. Universal later issued *Von heute auf morgen* under its own imprint (plate number 10545); see "Verzeichnis der Werke von Arnold Schönberg," in *Arnold Schönberg zum 60. Geburtstag: 13. September 1934* (Vienna: Universal Edition, 1934), 74. It did the same with his *Concerto for Violoncello after Monn* (plate number 10818); see Jan Maegaard, *Studien zur Entwicklung des dodekaphonen Satzes bei Arnold Schönberg,* vol. 1, *Chronologischer Teil* (Copenhagen: Wilhelm Hansen, 1972), 139.

[32]"Zwanzig Jahre lang war Emil Hertzka mein Verleger. Und wenn ich den Hauptgrund sagen sollte, warum er es nicht mehr ist, so glaube ich sagen zu müssen: weil er in der letzten Zeit eben nicht mehr *mein* Verleger. Ich glaube, getrennt haben uns: Geschäfte, die er vielleicht machen mußte, gleichviel: ob ich das einsehe oder nicht. Man kann vielleicht einen Verlag nicht anders aufbauen. Aber hier wurde Hertzkas Vorzug zum Hindernis: Seine Natur zwang ihn, alle geschäftlichen Verhältnisse auf Freundschaft zu begründen. Aber Verleger und Autor können auf die Dauer nicht Freunde sein. Und so war Hertzka, der Verleger, immer wieder gezwungen, zu nehmen, was Hertzka, der Freund gegeben hatte. Und Hertzka, der Freund, konnte geben: niemals hat er der Not seiner Autoren untätig zugesehen. Wenn es ihm irgend möglich war, hat er geholfen, hat einen nicht im Stich gelassen." Arnold Schoenberg, *Versuch eines Nachrufs für Hertzka,* quoted in Nuria Nono-Schoenberg, ed., *Arnold Schönberg 1874–1951: Lebensgeschichte in Begegnungen* (Klagenfurt: Ritter, 1992), 286.

[33]See Christopher Hailey, *Franz Schreker, 1878–1934: A Cultural Biography* (Cambridge: Cambridge University Press, 1993), 220–221.

[34]*The Berg-Schoenberg Correspondence,* 367–368.

[35]For a list of premieres in those seasons see Ernst Hilmar, *Wozzeck von Alban Berg: Entstehung—erste Erfolge—Repressionen (1914–1935)* (Vienna: Universal Edition, 1975), 89–91, and Konrad Vogelsang, *Dokumentation zur Opera "Wozzeck" von Alban Berg* (Laaber: Laaber-Verlag, 1977), 37–92.

[36]"Er augenblicklich auf keinen seiner Autoren mehr gibt als auf mich." Theodor W. Adorno, *Briefe und Briefwechsel,* vol. 2, *Theodor W. Adorno Alban Berg Briefwechsel 1925–1935,* ed. Henri Lonitz (Frankfurt: Suhrkamp, 1997), 260.

[37]Die Verhältnisse sind dzt. solche, daß die U.E. (u. ich glaube auch sonst kein Verlag [Bote & Bock z. Bsp. hat in letzter Zeit kolossal gebremst!]) nicht daran denken kann, denken *darf* [sie ist unter Bankaufsicht: höchste Diskre-

tion!!!] etwas zu unternehmen, was Geld kostet, das nicht *mit Sicherheit* und bald hereinkommt. Dort wo *dieses* gewährleistet ist, verlegt sie von selbst (z. Bsp. bei der Weinarie, deren Partitur sie ohne mein geringstes Hinzutun, rein wegen der amerikanischen Aussichten etc. plötzlich drucken läßt), dort wo jene Sicherheit nicht gewährleistet ist, nützt keine Anregung, kein Zureden, kein Sich verbürgen.

Trotzdem halt[e] ich es für wichtig u. richtig (für Sie, für unsere Musik*, ja für den Verlag) daß Sie möglichst in der U.E. »erscheinen«. Sind sie bereit, die Kosten selbst zu tragen? Also das zu tun, was wir selbst alle getan haben (sei's direkt oder durch einen Mäcen: Schönbergs op 1–3, op 10 Bergs op 1, 2, 3, 4 u 7, Weberns große Orchesterstücke etc.—Etc etc . . .)?

*das heißt für *die* Musik die mit Schönberg beginnt." Adorno, *Briefe und Briefwechsel,* 2: 259–60. As it happened, Adorno did not publish his music with Universal. See Rainer Riehn, "Werkverzeichnis," *Musik-Konzepte 63/64: Theodor W. Adorno der Komponist* (January 1989): 144–146. Universal, which had published the vocal score of *Der Wein* on 31 May 1930, issued a limited facsimile edition of the full score the following year; Berg sent a copy to Schoenberg as a Christmas present. See the letters of 19 January and 16 February 1932 in *The Berg-Schoenberg Correspondence,* 429–431. For more on the publication history of the work, see Klaus Schweizer's introduction to Alban Berg, *Sämtliche Werke,* vol. 6, *Orchestergesänge* (Vienna: Universal Edition, 1997), xxv–xxvi.

[38]See Rosemary Hilmar, *Alban Berg: Leben und Wirken bis zu seinen ersten Erfolgen als Komponist* (Vienna: Hermann Böhlaus, 1978), 48, 162.

[39]The text of the contract, dated 13 April, is published in Hilmar, *Wozzeck von Alban Berg,* 88.

[40]*The Berg-Schoenberg Correspondence,* 285.

[41]For Berg's work on the reduction, see Hailey, *Franz Schreker,* 67, 69.

[42]For Berg's work on the reduction, see Hilmar, *Alban Berg: Leben und Wirken,* 57–58.

[43]*The Berg-Schoenberg Correspondence,* 64. The text of Berg's contract is printed in Hilmar, *Alban Berg: Leben und Wirken,* 183.

[44]Universal published the Three Piano Pieces, op. 11 in October 1910, *Pelleas und Melisande* in October 1911. See Schoenberg, *Sämtliche Werke,* vol. 4, ed. Brinkmann, 4; and Jan Maegaard, *Studien zur Entwicklung des dodekaphonen Satzes bei Arnold Schönberg,* vol. 1, *Chronologischer Teil* (Copenhagen: Wilhelm Hansen, 1972), 36.

[45]*The Berg-Schoenberg Correspondence,* 67. The editors date the letter "c. 26 January 1912."

[46]Ibid., 67–68.

[47]Ibid., 83. Berg continued by pointing up a howler: "He's also publishing the George Songs now ('granted, only the piano reduction,' as he said)." *The Book of the Hanging Gardens,* of course, is for piano and voice.

[48]Schoenberg, *"Parsifal* and Copyright," in *Style and Idea,* 491.

[49]Even death could not guarantee one freedom from Schoenberg's wrath. When the composer failed to come to terms with Oxford University Press for his Concerto for String Quartet after Handel, he wrote Berg on 17 September 1933 that "the incompetence of those people as demonstrated on this occasion was enough to place a Hertzka in the most shining light." *The Berg-Schoenberg Correspondence,* 445.

[50]The text of the contract, dated 24 June, is published in Hilmar, *Alban Berg: Leben und Wirken,* 187. After a serious illness in the Fall of 1920, Berg resigned his position with *Anbruch.* For details of the Schoenberg guides, see Simms, *Alban Berg: A Guide to Research,* 27–28, 30.

[51]*The Berg-Schoenberg Correspondence,* 285.

[52]Berg, "Commemorative Address," 88–89.

[53]"Wir standen ihm persönlich ferne und wußten nur, daß er das Erscheinen unserer Zeitschrift mit gemischten Gefühlen aufnahm und sich besonders über die erste Nummer Freunden gegenüber recht ungünstig aussprach." "Kleine Chronik," *23: Eine Wiener Musikzeitschrift* 5 (1 July 1932): 16.

[54]Elias Canetti, who knew Berg in his last years, described a harshness born of kindness: "Having come to him as a total stranger, I also sensed his love of people, which was so strong that his only defense against it was his inclination to satire. His lips and eyes never lost their look of mockery, and he could easily have used his irony as a defense against his warmheartedness. He preferred to make use of the great satirists, to whom he remained devoted as long as he lived." Elias Canetti, *The Play of the Eyes,* trans. Ralph Manheim (New York: Farrar, Straus & Giroux, 1986), 233.

[55]Berg, "Commemorative Address," 88.

[56]Nor was this the first time that the firm had seen rough times. When Berg first signed with Universal in 1923, it was on the edge of bankruptcy. See Rosemary Hilmar, "'. . . nach den hinterlassenen endgültigen Korrekturen des Komponisten revidiert': Eine Studie zur Drucklegung von Musikalien im 20. Jahrhundert, dargestellt am Beispiel der Oper *Wozzeck* von Alban Berg," *Gutenberg-Jahrbuch* 58 (1983): 112.

[57]For the havoc the crisis wreaked on the Austrian economy in this period see Charles A. Gulick, *Austria from Habsburg to Hitler,* 2 vols. (Berkeley and Los Angeles: University of California Press, 1948), 2: 922–951. See also Barbara Jelavich, *Modern Austria: Empire and Republic, 1815–1986* (Cambridge: Cambridge University Press, 1987), 185–186.

[58]The quotes are found in Reich, *Alban Berg,* trans. Cardew, 71, and Theodor W. Adorno, *Alban Berg: Master of the Smallest Link,* trans. Juliane Brand and Christopher Hailey (Cambridge: Cambridge University Press, 1991), 10.

[59]On this aspect of their relationship see Smith, "Berg's Character Remembered," 15. On p. 30 n. 6, Smith dates a letter from Berg about completing *Lulu* by the end of the century as 13 September 1931; it is assigned to 1930 in Morgenstern, *Alban Berg und seine Idole: Erinnerungen und Briefe,* 240.

[60]*The Berg-Schoenberg Correspondence,* 414. For more on this moment in the genesis of the opera see Hall, *A View of Berg's "Lulu,"* 49.

[61]Berg, "Commemorative Address," 84.

[62]This is not the only spot in the *Gedenkrede* where Berg described a change that had not occurred. To find it "natural" that Bruckner, Mahler, and Schoenberg were performed together was to "overstat[e] the case; the works of Schoenberg had never reached the point of being considered 'safe' in the same way as those of Bruckner or Mahler." Karen Monson, *Alban Berg* (Boston: Houghton Mifflin, 1979), 304–305.

[63]See Rosemary Hilmar, *Katalog der Schriftstücke von der Hand Alban Bergs,* Alban Berg Studien no. 1/2 (Vienna: Universal Edition, 1985), 120. The shilling was then worth about $0.14; see *The Berg-Schoenberg Correspondence,* xxvii.

[64]"Ich hoffe, daß Sie, Herr Direktor, diesen meinen Brief nicht mißverstehen, das heißt, ihn nicht als eine Aktion eines Aufführungs- und Tantiemenhungrigen Autors auffassen: Die Tatsache, daß in den letzten zwei, drei Saisons kaum einen Woche verging, in der nicht *irgendwo* der "Wozzeck" am Spielplan stand, und es sogar Wochen mit 2, 3 Aufführungen gab . . . und auch die Tatsache, daß diese Oper heuer—außer in deutschen Provinzstädten—auch in Haupstädten wie Zürich, Brüssel und New-York [Zur Illustrierung des eben über das Wiener Musikleben Gesagten: Von dieser New-Yorker Erstaufführung hat *nicht eine* Wiener Zeitung auch nur die kleinste Notiz genommen. Man stelle sich vor, was sich in unserer Piffl-Korngold-Region ereignet hätte, wenn der, allerdings unvorstellbare Fall eingetreten wäre, daß eine Oper von Springer oder die "Heliane" in der Metropolitan aufgeführt worden wäre!] zur Erstaufführung kam und schließlich beim Internationalen Musikfest in Wien angesetzt ist, diese Tatsachen dürften mich wohl vor der Imputation solcher ehrgeizigen und habsüchtigen Beweggründe bewahren." Quoted in Hilmar, *Katalog der Schriftstücke von der Hand Alban Bergs,* 120–121.

[65]For more on Cardinal Friedrich Gustav Piffl, whose *Zu sozialen und kulturellen Fragen* was published in 1932, see Gulick, *Austria from Habsburg to Hitler,* 1: 610–611. Julius Korngold's opinion of *Wozzeck* is summarized in Douglas Jarman, *Alban Berg: Wozzeck* (Cambridge: Cambridge University Press, 1989), 77. For more on *Wozzeck* in Vienna, see Walter Pass, "Für und Wider im Streit um die Wiener Erstaufführung des *Wozzeck*," in *50 Jahre "Wozzeck" von Alban Berg: Vorgeschichte und Auswirkungen in der Opernästhetik,* ed. Otto

Kolleritsch, Studien zur Wertungsforschung no. 10 (Graz: Institut für Wertungs-forschung, 1978), 92–124.

[66]Adorno, *Alban Berg,* 29. On this topic see also Christopher Hailey, "Be-tween Instinct and Reflection: Berg and the Viennese Dichotomy," in *The Berg Companion,* 226–227. Consistent with this populist turn is Reich's report that after the Austrian state tobacco monopoly named an expensive cigarette *Heliane,* Berg attempted to have a cheap one named *Wozzeck; see* Reich, *Alban Berg,* trans. Cardew, 75–76.

[67]For the change in attitudes between Berg's generation and the previous, see Carl E. Schorske, "Politics in a New Key: An Austrian Trio" and "Gustav Klimt: Painting and the Crisis of the Liberal Ego," in *Fin-de-siècle Vienna: Poli-tics and Culture* (New York: Vintage Books, 1981), 116–180, 208–278. For a sur-vey of the political transformation, see John W. Boyer, *Political Radicalism in Late Imperial Vienna: Origins of the Christian Social Movement 1848–1897* (Chicago: The University of Chicago Press, 1981); and idem, *Culture and Politi-cal Crisis in Vienna: Christian Socialism in Power, 1897–1918* (Chicago: The University of Chicago Press, 1995).

[68]"Aber doch auch *erst dann, wenn* die Fabrik steht, *wenn* sie in Betrieb gesetzt *wird.* Also auch nicht viel weniger 'Zukunktsmusik' als *meine* Musik! Dementsprechend kein viel größeres Risiko, *mich* als Bräutigam zu betrachten (nachdem wir, wie gesagt, noch außerdem so klug sind zuzuwarten). Denn wie ich Ihnen, Herr Nahowski, bewiesen habe, ist ebenso *wie bei Herrn Lebert auch bei mir der sogenannte sichere Hintergrund, die durch unsere exzeptionellen Fähigkeiten in unserem jeweiligen Fache begründete Aussicht eines respek-tablen, vielleicht auch glänzenden Einkommens vorhanden,* und zu alldem braucht man mir, um mir dieses Einkommen zu schaffen, nicht einmal eine Fa-brik zu *bauen,* denn ich habe meine mit den neuesten Errungenschaften und der größten Leistungsfähigkeit versehene Fabrik *in meinem Kopf!* Und sollte tatsäch-lich diese meine Gedankenfabrik weniger pekuniären Gewinn abwerfen als die Schmirgelscheibenfabrik der Gebrüder Lebert, so sei Ihnen, Herr Nahowski, der Trost: 'Wir sind bescheiden geworden!'" Alban Berg, *Briefe an seine Frau* (Mu-nich-Vienna: Albert Langen-Georg Müller, 1965), 165–166. Bernard Grun's translation in Alban Berg, *Letters to His Wife* (New York: St. Martin's Press, 1971), 109 omits several sentences. The letter is also discussed in Perle, *The Op-eras of Alban Berg,* 2: 39.

[69]For a summary of the *Skandalkonzert,* see Reich, *Alban Berg,* trans. Cardew, 39–41.

[70]"Die Aufgabe, *rein* zu machen." Berg, *Briefe an seine Frau,* 281. For a dif-ferent translation, see Berg, *Letters to His Wife,* 177.

[71]Berg, *Letters to His Wife,* 177.

[72]*The Berg-Schoenberg Correspondence,* 284.

[73]Ibid. Berg expressed similar sentiments in a letter to Webern written the same day. See Willi Reich, "Aus unbekannten Briefen von Alban Berg an Anton Webern," *Schweizerische Musikzeitung* 93 (1953): 51. On performances of Berg's Piano Sonata in 1919, see Volker Scherliess, "Zur Rezeption der *Klavier-sonate* op. 1," in *Alban Berg Symposion Wien 1980: Tagungsbericht,* ed. Rudolf Klein, Alban Berg Studien no. 2 (Vienna: Universal Edition, 1981), 232–244.

[74]Alban Berg, "A Lecture on *Wozzeck,*" in Jarman, *Alban Berg: Wozzeck,* 163. Adorno would later parrot this interpretation; see Theodor W. Adorno, *Philosophy of Modern Music,* trans. Anne G. Mitchell and Wesley V. Blomster (New York: The Seabury Press, 1973), 58 n. 18.

[75]See Hilmar, *Wozzeck von Alban Berg,* 26–31. Universal practiced a similar economy with the Three Orchestra Pieces, op. 6, reproducing the work photographically.

[76]See Berg, *Letters to His Wife,* 307–318.

[77]For more on Berg's activities on behalf of *Wozzeck,* see George Perle, *The Operas of Alban Berg,* vol. 1, *"Wozzeck"* (Berkeley and Los Angeles: University of California Press, 1980), 195–201.

[78]See Peter Franklin, *The Life of Mahler* (Cambridge: Cambridge University Press, 1997), 54–55, who quotes a letter from early 1883 in which the young conductor speaks of his "enthusiasm" at trying to "sweep [his public] along"; just a few lines later he referred to "these poor wretches' souls."

[79]Ladislao Mittner, *Storia della letteratura tedesca,* vol. 3, *Dal realismo alla sperimentazione (1820–1970)* (Turin: Einaudi, 1971), 951, 954–955. The Horatian verse is *Odes* 3.1.1.

[80]See Mittner, *Storia della letteratura tedesca,* 3: 951.

[81]Alban Berg, *Zwei Lieder (Theodor Storm),* trans. Eric Smith (Vienna: Universal Edition, 1955). On the role of Klein, see Arved Ashby, "Of *Modell-Typen* and *Reihenformen:* Berg, Schoenberg, F. H. Klein, and the Concept of Row Derivation," *Journal of the American Musicological Association* 48 (1995): 67–105. For further thoughts on the topic, see Neil Boynton, "Compositional Technique 1923–6: The Chamber Concerto and the Lyric Suite," in *The Cambridge Companion to Berg,* ed. Anthony Pople (Cambridge: Cambridge University Press, 1997), 189–194.

[82]It appeared as a supplement to the journal *Die Musik.* For small differences in wording between the dedication copy and the published version see Joan Allen Smith, "Some Sources for Berg's 'Schliesse mir die Augen beide' II," *The International Alban Berg Society Newsletter* 6 (June 1978): 12 n. 12.

[83]The concept appears most famously in Arnold Schoenberg, "New Music, Outmoded Music, Style and Idea," in *Style and Idea: Selected Writings,* 2d ed.,

ed. Leonard Stein, trans. Leo Black (New York, 1975; reprint, Berkeley and Los Angeles: University of California Press, 1984), 113–124. Schoenberg first delivered the text as a lecture in Prague in 1930. Berg heard it in Vienna, in February 1933, during his final meeting with his mentor. See *The Berg-Schoenberg Correspondence,* 440 n. 2.

[84]"Wer Reines kann, wird es tonal oder atonal können; die aber unrein denken, die nämlich, die tun, was man kann, die mögen ruhig tonale oder atonale Parteien bilden, oder auch dabei Lärm machen." Arnold Schoenberg, "Gesinnung oder Erkenntnis," in *25 Jahre neue Musik,* 30. For a different translation, see Schoenberg, "Opinion or Insight," in *Style and Idea,* 264.

[85]Alban Berg, "The 'Problem of Opera,'" in Reich, *Alban Berg,* trans. Cardew, 63. For the history of this text, see Simms, *Alban Berg: A Guide to Research,* 33–34.

[86]The concert, led by Anton Webern, was reviewed in the *Neue freie Presse* on 26 June 1932. Excerpts are quoted in Rosemary Hilmar and Günter Brosche, *Alban Berg 1885–1935: Ausstellung der Österreichischen Nationalbibliothek Prunksaal 23. Mai bis 20. Oktober 1985* (Vienna: Österreichische Nationalbibliothek-Universal Edition, 1985), 151. Berg's own analysis of *Der Wein* is summarized in Reich, *Alban Berg,* trans. Cardew, 153–155. For more on the row manipulations see Herwig Knaus, "Alban Bergs Skizzen und Vorarbeiten zur Konzertarie *Der Wein,*" in *Festschrift Othmar Wessely zum 60. Geburtstag,* ed. Manfred Angerer et al. (Tutzing: Hans Schneider, 1982), 355–379, and Dave Headlam, *The Music of Alban Berg* (New Haven: Yale University Press, 1996), 289–300.

[87]On echoes of Mahler's Tenth Symphony in *Lulu,* see Claudio Spies, "Review of Gustav Mahler, Tenth Symphony, ed. Deryck Cooke," *Notes* 39 (1982–1983): 201–204.

[88]Robert P. Morgan, "The Eternal Return: Retrograde and Circular Form in Berg," in *Alban Berg: Historical and Analytical Perspectives,* ed. David Gable and Robert P. Morgan (Oxford: Clarendon Press, 1991), 148.

[89]It is probably no coincidence that in his first work after signing with Universal, Berg indulged his love of retrograde as never before. In 1926 he instructed the engraver of the piano reduction of his Chamber Concerto for Piano, Violin, and Thirteen Winds to arrange the central palindrome (mm. 357–364) such that "the symmetry of the two four-bar units (mirror image!) is plainly visible." Quoted in Brenda Dalen, "'Freundschaft, Liebe, und Welt': The Secret Programme of the Chamber Concerto," in *The Berg Companion,* 153.

[90]Arthur Schopenhauer, *The World as Will and Representation,* trans. E. F. J. Payne (1958; reprint, New York: Dover, 1969), 2: 442. The quote is from vol. 2, Chap. 38, "On History."

[91]Arthur Schopenhauer, *Parerga and Paralipomena: Short Philosophical Essays,* trans. E. F. J. Payne (Oxford: Clarendon Press, 1974), 2: 445. The quote is from vol. 2, Chap. 19, "On the Metaphysics of the Beautiful and Aesthetics." For Schoenberg's careful reading of this chapter see Robert R. Holzer, "Schoenberg Sets Petrarch: Schopenhauer, Mahler, and the Poetics of Resignation," in *Schoenberg and Words: The Modernist Years,* ed. Charlotte Cross and Russell Berman (New York: Garland Publishing, 2000).

[92]Adorno, *Alban Berg,* 19. In the same passage Adorno remarked on "the *Jugendstil* element in [Berg's] life, the *fin-de-siècle* that remained in his oeuvre to the very end and was so magnificently thematicized in *Lulu.*"

[93]For Webern's lectures of 1932 and 1933 see Anton Webern, *The Path to New Music,* trans. Leo Black (Bryn Mawr, Pa.: Theodore Presser, 1963).

[94]Morgan, "The Eternal Return," 149.

PART II

Authors and Entrepreneurs

CHAPTER 5

Orlando di Lasso, Composer and Print Entrepreneur

JAMES HAAR

Samuel van Quickelberg, whose entry in a biographical dictionary published in 1566 is the earliest source for our knowledge of Orlando di
Lasso's life, has this to say about the publication of the composer's
music:

> Although compositions by Lasso are indeed to be found in great abun-
> dance everywhere in the world, there are nonetheless many more
> which are at present held apart by his prince, who does not in the least
> want to share them with the vulgar crowd. There are so many works of
> his composition, including various motets for four, six, eight, and more
> voices, that it seems superfluous to list them here in order, especially
> since his books, published in Nuremberg, Munich, Venice, Florence,
> Naples, Antwerp, Lyons, and Paris, will be able to supply such a list. In
> 1565 I saw and heard with great pleasure this very Orlando singing and
> directing everything in the palace chapel of Munich, where he to this
> day is active, and where he presently invents worthy new things, to
> great praise.[1]

Quickelberg, who contributed several articles on important Munich figures to Pantaleon's enterprise, knew Lasso in person, as he says.[2] He
must have been extraordinarily impressed by the composer—or urged on
by Lasso's ducal employer Albrecht V—for Lasso is the only musician to
have an entry in the *Prosopographia*.[3] The composer doubtless gave
Quickelberg an account of his early life as well as some idea of how
much music he had written by 1566. That some works were withheld

from publication at ducal request is something we know to be true; the *Prophetiae Sibyllarum,* written about 1560 but not published until 1600, is an example.[4] The list of places where Lasso's music had been published, at first sight a rather odd bibliographical detail, must also have been supplied by the composer, who was clearly keeping track of his music in print and thought it important to do so.

This list is not quite complete nor quite accurate (see Appendix I, entries through 1566). As Horst Leuchtmann points out, neither Naples or Lyons is known as a place of publication for Lasso's work; to these he might have added Florence.[5] And Quickelberg does not mention either Louvain or Rome, cities where Lasso's work had appeared in print.[6] There might of course have been music by Lasso in volumes, now lost, printed in Naples and Lyons, but Florence had no music printer at this time, so here Quickelberg was really mistaken. The omission of Rome is curious; perhaps Lasso did not approve of the way his music had been handled by Roman printers (on which, see below).

Lasso probably continued to keep a close eye on the publication of his music, and on several occasions, as we shall see, he even took active steps to further it. But he could hardly have kept count of the numerous reprints of volumes devoted to his music, let alone the many anthologies in which his name figured. Appendix I contains 275 volumes devoted completely or largely to Lasso's compositions; adding reprints and significant anthologies, Leuchtmann counts more than 450, speculating that something like 100 more, now lost, should be added to the list. Not a year passed, after his "Opus 1" of 1555, without something—usually many things—appearing; thus the list of places of publication grew far longer than that supplied by Quickelberg, and posthumous volumes, including the enormous motet collection *Magnum opus musicum* (1604) and the collected Magnificats of 1619, appeared after his death in 1594. According to Leuchtmann's estimates, something approaching half of all the music prints of the second half of the sixteenth century contained work by Lasso.[7]

In number of publications Lasso is clearly exceptional for his time. The geographical spread of these publications is also unusual, numbering fourteen cities in Italy, France, Germany, Austria, the Netherlands, Switzerland, and England. His fame exceeded that of any other sixteenth-century composer except perhaps Josquin des Prez, and his music was surely known to more people than that of Josquin. He was published and republished because of his reputation. That this reputation was based on the variety and quality of his music hardly needs stressing; what should be emphasized here is that it was through the medium of print that his international fame was circulated and increased. As Elizabeth Eisenstein points out,

> [Early printers] also extended their new promotional techniques [title pages, books lists, circulars, broadsides] to the authors and artists whose work they published, thus contributing to the celebration of lay culture-heroes and to their achievement of personal celebrity and eponymous fame.[8]

How this extraordinary run of publications developed and what role the composer himself played in shaping it will be the subject of this essay. First, a brief sketch of sixteenth-century music printing up to the time of Lasso's first publication in 1555 seems useful if we are to realize the blend of conventional and novel elements that made up his publishing career.

MUSIC PRINTING, 1500–1550

In 1498 Ottaviano de' Petrucci obtained a Venetian privilege for the publication of polyphonic music. Petrucci, unlike most of the printers in late fifteenth-century Italy who were transplanted Germans, was a native Italian. His *Odhecaton A,* a small oblong choirbook-format volume of chansons, appeared in Venice in 1501, marking the beginning of commercial printing of part music.[9] The beauty and accuracy of Petrucci's books, produced by a demanding multiple-impression process in which staves and notes were separately printed, have been much admired. Here, only a few features of his activity call for comment. One is the repertory he printed: on the one hand, sacred music (chiefly Masses and motets) and chansons of "international" character, on the whole—and especially in his early years—music ten to twenty years old and the work of Northern musicans, some but not all resident in Italy; and on the other hand, a large body (eleven volumes) of North Italian frottolas. He also printed a few books of lute songs combining mensural notation with tablature as well as volumes completely in tablature. Where did he get this music? The immediate source was his friend and editor the Venetian Petrus Castellanus (Pietro da Castello); yet how and from what manuscript sources all this music was collected we do not yet fully know.[10]

Most of Petrucci's volumes were anthologies, but a few books were devoted to the music of single composers, beginning with the *Misse*

Josquin (the first of three books) in 1502. These, along with motet collections beginning in 1504, were issued in separate partbooks. This may have been convenient, as it solved the problem of coordinating long-note tenors with the other voices, but it seems odd; Masses could hardly have been intended primarily for solo singers, and as the century went on, Masses were often printed in single-folio choirbook volumes (as Le Roy and Ballard were to do with Lasso's Masses).[11] Chansons and frottolas as printed by Petrucci appeared in single volumes even though this repertory was well suited to partbook format; not until the end of his career did Petrucci print secular music in partbooks.[12] This, as much as Petrucci's somewhat old-fashioned treatment of text underlay, makes one wonder if his books, rather expensive and printed in small editions, were intended for direct practical use rather than serving, in the way most manuscript collections had, as repertorial collections from which music could be copied (and arranged) for performance.[13]

Petrucci, although he printed little other than volumes of music, was emphatically a book-man in the Venice of Aldus Manutius. He obviously took pride in the beauty and accuracy of his presswork (perhaps a bit less so after his removal from Venice to Fossombrone in 1511), and designed title pages and colophons as badges of his membership in the fraternity of book publishers.[14]

Multiple-impression printing was too cumbersome and too chancy to last, though it was used by early music printers elsewhere in Italy and in Germany. An alternative method, printing from woodcut blocks, was used by Andrea Antico, active in Rome and Venice from c.1510 to the late 1530s. Antico, who began by publishing repertory similar to that of Petrucci and ended by producing woodcuts for a Venetian edition of the madrigals of Verdelot, did beautiful work; but this method was even less suited than that of Petrucci to the development of music printing as a commercially viable enterprise.[15]

A solution to the problem was found in the 1520s with the introduction of single-impression printing, produced by a type font that featured notes fixed on staff segments, which were expensive to create initially but easy to use once problems of vertical registration were overcome. The first music printer to make sustained use of this new method was Pierre Attaingnant in Paris, whose first volume of mensural music appeared in 1528.[16] Attaingnant received a royal privilege and by 1537 was named royal printer of music. His close ties to the court of Francis I are evident in a number of ways, above all by the repertory he printed; in contrast to the rather international scope of Petrucci and other early music publishers, Attaingnant produced an overwhelmingly French list, much of it devoted to music by composers close to the court. Using part-books, two-book sets, and choirbooks (small quarto for chansons, a large folio with specially designed type for a volume of Masses), Attaingnant printed some volumes devoted to single composers but many more an-thologies, sacred, and above all secular music. With him the central posi-tion of the French chanson in French music printing was established.

Single-impression printing soon spread, to Lyons, to Germany and the Netherlands, to Naples, Rome, and above all to Venice, where the presses of Antonio Gardane and Girolamo Scotto put Italian music print-ing on a solid commercial basis. The Italian publishers ranged fairly widely in their choice of sacred music, whereas for secular music they concentrated on the madrigal. Beginning with Gardane's issue of four volumes (each in partbook format, standard for the madrigal throughout the century) of the madrigals of Arcadelt in 1538(?)–1539, the madrigal flowed in increasingly large numbers from Italian, mostly Venetian, presses, and Venetian publishers were as closely identified with it as Parisian printers were with the chanson.[17]

In the Netherlands, where the manuscript tradition was strong and where the books of foreign publishers were readily available in a port city such as Antwerp, music printing was late to begin. The first im-portant figure in the business was the composer and wind player Til-man Susato, who obtained a privilege in 1543 and began several series of volumes of sacred and secular music, most of it the work of Neth-erlandish composers. He was followed by Pierre Phalèse in Louvain and by Laet and Waelrant in Antwerp. German music printers fa-vored local composers where they could, but on the whole published an international repertory, much of it "borrowed" from foreign printers' work.[18]

An extraordinary feature of Lasso's career in print was the control he seems to have exercised, or at least tried to exercise, over it. As we have seen, printers tended to concentrate on music produced in their own linguistic and regional areas; but as Henri Vanhulst has pointed out, Lasso—born in the Netherlands, trained in Italy, employed in Ger-many—was the first composer to adopt as a principle the publication of his music, which was varied in genre and text language, by territorial re-gions.[19] This unusual procedure was in part accidental, the result of Lasso's international career. It was also the product of an entrepreneurial urge unusual among composers at such an early date. The discussion that follows will be organized by regions in order to illustrate this.

LASSO AND PRINTING IN THE LOW COUNTRIES

Lasso (b. 1530, or more probably, 1532) surely began to compose actively while he was in his teens. But by the time he left Italy (June, 1554), arriving in Antwerp in the fall of that year, none of his work had yet appeared in print. This was quickly to change; in 1555 a volume of his madrigals appeared in Venice, one of *villanelle* in Rome, and his familiarly nicknamed "Opus 1," a mixed volume of sacred and secular music, was published in Antwerp. This last book, whether or not it preceded the Italian prints, will be discussed first, as Lasso's first active engagement with printers dates from his residence in Antwerp.

If Lasso accompanied Giulio Cesare Brancaccio on the latter's brief and unsuccessful visit to the English court in the summer of 1554 he may have been with Brancaccio when the latter arrived at Calais in September of that year. The young composer seems to have acted fast.[20] Quickelberg says that Lasso visited his birthplace, Mons, only to find that his parents had died; but he must then have gone quickly to Antwerp. How he established himself with the printer Tilman Susato is not known, but he persuaded Susato to publish a volume of his works, an undertaking that disrupted the printer's schedule and involved him in printing unfamiliar music by a composer as yet unknown in the Netherlands. This book, tacked somewhat incongruously onto a series of chanson volumes, appeared with the title *Le quatoirsiesme livre a quatre parties contenant dishuyct chansons italiennes, six chansons francoises, & six motetz faictz (a la nouvelle composition d'aucuns d'Italie) par Rolando di Lassus*. It was soon reissued by Susato as *D'Orlando di Lassus il primo libro doversi contengono madrigali, villanesche, canzoni francesi & motetti a quattro voci*, with a dedication, dated 13 May 1555, to the Genoese banker Stefano Gentile, resident in Antwerp.[21]

This book, reprinted by Susato c.1558 and again in 1560, has attracted attention as Lasso's first publication and as an unusual collection of sacred and secular, Latin-, French-, and Italian-texted works.[22] Lasso may indeed have brought a good deal of its contents with him from Italy, as the title page suggests, although other pieces might have been newly composed. As a kind of guarantee of the advertised "nouvelle composition d'aucuns d'Italie" a motet by Cipriano de Rore, daringly chromatic for Netherlandish taste, was included in the volume.[23] Lasso's volume was not unique in mixing secular and sacred contents, as a few such prints had appeared in Rome and Venice in the 1520s. Moreover, a book with very mixed contents published by Melchior Kriesstein in 1540,

Selectissimae necnon familiarissime cantiones, described as in "varie id-
iomate" or "mancherley Sprachen," might have afforded Susato a precedent.[24] But Kriesstein's print is an anthology of the work of more than
forty authors, an altogether different thing from Susato's Lasso print.

Did the composer not have enough pieces in any one genre to fill up
the volume? He had certainly written enough madrigals to have done so,
as a whole book of five-voice madrigals was published by Gardane in
Venice in 1555. Lasso probably did not have these pieces in his possession when he left Italy; indeed Gardane may have obtained them from a
Roman agent. But this is probably not the point; the fact that the composer had a whole volume of motets ready for an Antwerp publisher in
1556 shows that he was not short of music or slow to compose it. The
"Opus 1" volume looks as if Lasso meant to advertise his versatility,
proudly displaying his wares for buyers and for putative patrons, of
whom Stefano Gentile may have been the first. That he was able to persuade Susato to issue such a volume suggests that the young Lasso already had a shrewd sense of self-promotion and an early command of the
personal charm he was later to display toward his Wittelsbach employers
in Munich.

Lasso may have acted as Susato's editor for the 1555 print.[25] Its reis-
sue with the Italian title, whether his idea or that of Susato, was surely
designed for appeal to an Italian market—the Italian "nation" in Antwerp
and possibly Italy itself. The print did achieve international circulation;
in 1556 it was sent to Spain, along with other Susato volumes in a packet
with a Spanish title page.[26] Susato, who published rather small editions,
reprinted the volume in about 1558.[27] A 1560 reprint (with the French
title) may have been done at the behest of the Fugger family and aimed at
South-German circulation;[28] it is easy to believe that Lasso, now in Munich, may have encouraged this reprint.

Lasso may have worked for Susato; at the same time he attracted the
notice of prominent residents of the Low Countries. His *Primo libro de
motetti a 5 et 6,* published in 1556 by Jan Laet in Antwerp, is dedicated to
Antoine Perrenot de Granvelle, advisor to Charles V and at the time re-
gent of the Netherlands in all but name. Lasso seems really to have
known Granvelle, and the latter took an interest in the career of the
young composer.[29] Hans Jakob Fugger, of the great Augsburg family, and
Dr. Georg Seld, agent for Albrecht V of Bavaria at the imperial court,
also knew Lasso and doubtless saw the Antwerp prints of his music. It
was through them that the composer was engaged by the ducal court at
Munich.[30]

In 1560 Lasso visited the Netherlands in an unsuccessful search for singers for Duke Albrecht's chapel.[31] In this same year Pierre Phalèse published a volume of Lasso chansons in Louvain, and Susato reprinted the motet volume Laet had issued in 1556. As Vanhulst observes, these initiatives suggest further direct connections between the composer and Netherlandish printers.[32] In 1564 Phalèse printed another chanson collection, and in the same year Susato's son Jacob issued a set of Lasso chansons.[33] After this, however, Netherlandish printers did rather little with Lasso's music, ceding priority to Parisian publishers for chansons and to German ones for motets. Disturbed political conditions in the Netherlands had an adverse effect on the printing business, no doubt; yet it also seems clear that Lasso had nearly ended his entrepreneurial efforts in this part of Europe.[34] The place of Netherlandish publishers in the composer's career in print is nonetheless an important one, for it was in Antwerp that Lasso was first able to further his bid for fame through a deliberately controlled use of the musical press.

ITALY

When Lasso left Italy in June, 1554, none of his music had yet been printed there. In the next year two collections of his work appeared. One, Gardane's print of Lasso's *Primo libro di madrigali a 5,* was to become one of the composer's most popular books, with more than a dozen reprints issued by various Venetian publishers. Gardane's first edition, referring to the composer as "Orlando di Lassus," the form of the name used in Susato's Italian "Opus 1," has no dedication, and there is nothing to indicate that Lasso had anything to do with this print. Its contents must date from the composer's years in Rome (1552–1554), if not in part even earlier. The Venetian publisher doubtless had Roman contacts, and it is possible that he may have obtained, perhaps bought, the music directly from the composer before the latter's departure, although there is no direct evidence for this.[35] Italian publishers were to print and reprint most of Lasso's madrigal output, even when, in the 1580s, the composer gave new works to German firms. There is evidence (see below) to suggest nevertheless that in the earlier part of his career Lasso had less direct influence on Italian publishers than he did with printers in the Netherlands, France, or, later, Germany.

The other Italian print of 1555 featuring Lasso was the Roman publisher Valerio Dorico's *Villanelle d'Orlando di Lassus e d'altri eccellenti musici libro secondo.*[36] Dorico's volume, which does not survive complete, "features" Lasso on its title page; but for only one of its twenty-one three-voice pieces is there any evidence for his authorship.[37] Lasso's *villanelle*, which survive in other sources, were probably written partly in Naples (where he lived from 1548 through 1551) and partly in Rome.[38] Donna Cardamone suggests that Lasso was at the center of a group of "transplanted Neapolitans" who entertained Roman audiences with performances of *villanelle*.[39] Lasso had clearly established himself as a composer in Roman circles for Dorico to give him such prominence in the 1555 print. In 1560 Dorico printed his *Libro primo a 4,* a madrigal volume published the same year, with slightly altered contents, by Gardane in Venice. And the Roman composer-printer Antonio Barrè included works by Lasso in two of his books of four-voice *madrigali ariosi*.[40] These volumes are part of a larger series of *libri delle Muse,* one of which is devoted chiefly to Lasso (*Secondo libro delle muse a 5 voci, madrigali d'Orlando di Lassus,* 1557). In the dedication to this volume it is said that Lasso's madrigals were found "per aventura" in Spoleto; evidently the composer had no direct role in the publication of this second book of five-voice madrigals (it was reprinted by Gardane in 1559).[41] Even the third madrigal book, published by Barrè in 1563, was said by the printer in a dedicatory letter to have been collected as the result of a "diligent search" for more madrigals by Lasso; again there is no suggestion of collaboration with the composer.[42] Perhaps these publishers gave Lasso good reason to omit Rome from Quickelberg's list of places his music had been published.

In keeping with general trends linking publishing ventures with "national" genres, Italian printers were never interested in Lasso's chansons; they left the field to Netherlandish printers and especially to the Parisian firm of Le Roy and Ballard.[43] In the 1560s they began instead to issue motet collections by Lasso, starting with Gardane's reprint of a 1562 German imprint and continuing with Venetian publications of four more volumes in series.[44] At the same time, reprints of the first three five-voice madrigal books and the single four-voice book were issued in some number; Lasso had become an established figure in Italian music printing. This prepared the way for another madrigal print, the *Libro quarto de madrigali a 5,* published by Gardane in 1567. Gardane obtained a special privilege for this volume, asking for a ten-year protection so that "others might not enjoy the fruits of his labors and expenses"—a statement that rings rather hollow when one thinks of the cavalier attitude Italian publishers had taken toward earlier madrigal volumes by Lasso.[45] The composer took special care over this fourth book, going to Venice to supervise its editing and writing his own letter of dedication, to Duke Alfonso II of Ferrara. Whether or not he was contemplating a move to Italy, Lasso clearly wanted to assert his stature as a composer of madrigals, perhaps in competition with Giaches de Wert, whose own *Libro quarto a 5* was published by Gardane in 1567.[46]

FRANCE

Lasso's longest and perhaps closest relationship with any printer was to the Parisian firm of Le Roy and Ballard. Though he never held a working appointment in France, Lasso did visit there; French was his native language, and from an early period he was aware of French music. All the chansons in his Antwerp "Opus 1" were settings of texts appearing in chanson prints of Pierre Attaingnant, French royal printer active from 1528 until his death in 1551–1552.[47] The first French book to contain music by Lasso, Nicolas Du Chemin's *Second livre de chansons a 4v* of 1557, contains two chansons taken from Susato's 1555 volume; thus, Lasso connected himself with the French tradition at an early point.[48]

In August 1551 Adrian Le Roy and his cousin Robert Ballard received a privilege from Henry II to print and sell music. Two years later, Attaingnant having died, they were accorded the title of royal printers of music. This was the firm for Lasso to attach himself to, and he soon did so. Le Roy and Ballard at first featured the chansons of Jacques Arcadelt in their anthologies; their *Livre de meslanges* of 1560 contains a preface by Ronsard extolling Arcadelt.[49] But Lasso, a few of whose chansons were included in Le Roy and Ballard books appearing in 1559, had eight in the 1560 volume, and in 1561 the publishers issued a *Douziesme livre de chansons . . . par Orlande de Lassus & autres autheurs,* with twelve works by Lasso and only two by Arcadelt.[50] By the end of this decade Lasso was established for the publishers as *the* chanson composer, a position he was to hold until the late 1580s when the work of Claude Le Jeune began to replace his as his had replaced the chansons of Arcadelt.

A special relationship between Lasso and the French court, doubtless stimulated by the publishers, developed early. In 1560 the composer, who as yet had had only a few chansons published in France, received a sizeable pension from the king, suggesting that a good deal of the music that was soon to be published in Paris was already known at court. The early Netherlandish and Italian prints of his music could of course have reached France before this time, but Le Roy was surely instrumental in bringing Lasso's music to royal ears.[51]

During the reign of Charles IX (1560–1574) Lasso's reputation in France continued to grow as Le Roy and Ballard issued volumes of chansons and of motets and other sacred music. For much of this period the firm was the composer's principal publisher. Several volumes were dedicated to the king, and one included an ode to Charles IX signed by Lasso himself.[52] In January of 1574 Le Roy, who seems to have been a personal friend of the composer, wrote to Lasso telling him that he had been granted a large pension (the 1560 pension must have lapsed) and that the king, for whom Le Roy had recently had performed chansons and the first of the *Prophetiae Sibyllarum*,[53] wanted more than ever for Lasso to take up residence at the court ("le Roy est en plus grande ardeur de vous pouvoir avoyr quil ne fut onques").[54] In the words of a court chaplain,

> The king loved music; heavens, how he loved it, whether that for instruments or that for voices! And above all he was pleased with the music of Orlande, one of the most distinguished musicians of our times, in the service of the Duke of Bavaria. He liked this music so much that he could hardly enjoy that of any other composer.[55]

It is worth emphasizing that the royal love for Lasso's work was created and fostered by a publisher. How interested the composer was in a possible move to France we do not know, although rumors about it were strong enough to disturb the Bavarian ducal house.[56] The death of Charles IX in May of 1574 surely ended prospects for a move; Lasso did not visit France at this time, nor is he known to have done so later.

His one documented visit to France, in 1571, was the occasion for one of the most remarkable events in Lasso's career in print. He received by royal decree a personal privilege to have printed, by whatever firm he chose, all his music—that already composed and that to come. This privilege, confirmed in 1575 and renewed in 1582, was of ten years' duration for each volume published.[57] In effect the privilege, tacitly good only in France, was accorded to Le Roy and Ballard as well, as they were Lasso's nearly exclusive printers there.[58] Nonetheless, it is an extraordinary document, as no composer before Lasso had ever obtained this kind of personal privilege in France. It must have been Lasso himself who asked for it, although given his close relationship with Le Roy he might have wanted to benefit the printer as well. In any event this, along with the imperial privilege he was to get ten years later (discussed later in this essay) marks Lasso not only as a composer of great stature but as an active entrepreneur bent on protecting his music from pirated printing. He did not necessarily or even probably stand to derive financial benefit from the privilege, but he could exercise control over what was published and possibly over the quality of the editions. Lasso entertained Charles IX on this 1571 visit; on his return to Munich he was given a raise in salary, perhaps as an effort to discourage his thinking too favorably about life in France.[59] He was never to move to France, but Le Roy and Ballard remained among the most important printers of his music for the rest of his life.

EXCURSUS: *ORLANDI LAUDES*

Composers began to receive written accolades, in manuscript and printed treatises, in the late fifteenth century; these were sincere if brief, like the words of the theorist-composer Johannes Tinctoris in praise of Dufay, Ockeghem, and a few of their contemporaries. The first composer to receive extended praise in print was Josquin des Prez, notably in the *Dodecachordon* (printed in 1547, but begun a good deal earlier) of Heinrich Glareanus, but elsewhere as well. For Gioseffo Zarlino (*Istitutioni harmoniche*, 1558) Adrian Willaert was the composer who could not be too highly lauded.[60] Music printers saw this sort of praise, however sincerely intended, as useful promotion for their books; Arcadelt was "divino," Willaert "musicorum omnium . . . sine controversie principis celeberrimi, & in presenti Ill. Reipublice venetiarum in ede Divi Marci Capelle Rectoris eminentissimi" in title pages and dedications of Antonio Gardane's publication of their music.[61]

Poems in praise of literary figures were very common features in sixteenth-century books. Many of these are humanistic exercises, opportunities to display learning and verbal dexterity in addition to, often rather than, sincere praise. The same thing is of course true of poetical effusions about musicians; but it is an important feature of music prints that they should contain them at all. Their appearance is testimony that composers, their work far more widely circulated than it had been before the advent of printed music, were now being regarded as artists, the equals of painters and poets, not mere craftsmen who put harmonic science into practice like builders putting architectural programs into tactile form. Musical rhetoric was now regarded, in other words, as just as much a liberal art as verbal rhetoric. This shift, marking a renaissance in music, had a variety of causes; its success was made possible by the power of the musical press, which could help to create reputations even as it celebrated them.

Lasso came in for a very full share of adulation. The earliest instance is to be found in a poem "ad librum Orlandi Lassi artis musices peritissimi" by the Munich singer and chapel copyist Johannes Pollet in the first German publication of Lasso's music, a motet collection issued by Montanus and Neuber in Nuremberg in 1562.[62] Most of the testimonials to the composer are in French sources; Le Roy and Ballard were particularly given to their inclusion. Lasso's praises increased as his fame grew, and as he became the most celebrated musician in all of Europe the praise grew ever more extravagant. At first, as in the poem (1562) of Pollet mentioned above, he was simply known and admired in Italy, Germany, France, and Brabant.[63] Then his power of matching words and music with unrivalled aptness was extolled; in the words of Quickelberg, Lasso was able to express the affective nature of the text so well that in hearing his music it was "as if the affective object itself were placed before one's eyes."[64]

The names of heroes of ancient musical myth are often cited in these poetic tributes: Orpheus taming beasts, Amphion moving stones, Arion riding the dolphin are there, along with many others. In Le Roy and Ballard's *Mellange d'Orlande de Lassus* of 1570, a large chanson collection, a poem by Jacques Gohory accompanying a portrait of the composer introduces Orpheus and Hercules along with the medieval hero Roland, to whom "Rollandus Lassus" is favorably compared.[65] This strain is exhaustively cultivated in a *chapitre* by Etienne Jodelle in the same volume.[66] It is heard again in a poem *De Cantionibus Orlandi Lassi, Musicorum nostri seculi facile Regis* [On the songs of Orlandus Lassus, easily king of musicians in our time] by Paul Schede Melissus in a Parisian motet print of 1572.[67] In 1584 the poet Mégnier went still further; writing first of Arion and his "daufin," Timotheus and "roy" Alexander, Amphion and his "pierres," and Orpheus and "enfer," he concludes with this:

Mais ce que de l'esprit d'un seul ORLANDE part,
Avec plus de pouvoir, de grace, d'heur, & d'art,
Tire, émeut, amollit, flechit par gran trophée
Les daufins, & les rois, les pierres, les enfers,
Par ses chants, ses accords, ses tons, ses sons divers,
Qu'Arion, Timothée, Amphion, ni Orphée.[68]

[But the talent that comes forth from a single Roland draws out, moves, softens, conquers by its great glory dolphins [dauphins], kings, stones, hell, through its melodies, harmonies, modes, diverse sounds, with more strength, grace, fortune, and art than Arion, Timotheus, Amphion, or Orpheus.]

Less learned but with a telling contemporary slant are poems comparing Lasso to other sixteenth-century musicians. Nicodemus Frischlin in a poem of 1575 ranks Lasso with Clemens non Papa and "der alte Josquin."[69] A sonnet by Mégnier (1586) carries this further; after praising "Le bon père Josquin," "Le grave doux Willaert," and "L'inventif Cyprian [de Rore]," the poet concludes by awarding prizes:

Josquin aura la Palme ayant esté premier:
Willaert la Myrte aura: Cyprian le Laurier:
Orlando emportera les trois comme le maistre.[70]

[Josquin will take the palm, being the oldest; Willaert will win the myrtle, Cipriano the laurel. Orlando will carry off all three of them as the master.]

The praise of other musicians was perhaps most important of all. The *avertissement* in a *Traicte de musique* published by Le Roy and Ballard in 1583 speaks of new rules used by contemporary musicians, notably "Orlande, ce grand maistre et Supreme Ouvrier," whose excellence in every fact of music "pourroit seule servir de loy et reigle a la Musique."[71] Le Roy himself, in a lute tutor published in 1567, spoke, in a preface written by Jacques Gohory, of Lasso:

Here then will I end, after I have advertised you that all the examples of this booke be taken and chosen out of Orland de Lassus . . . esteemed the most excellent Musitian of this time, as well in grave matters, as meane and more pleasaunt, a thing given from above to fewe other, in the which he hath attayned not only the perfection of melodie, but also a certaine grace of sound beyond all other such as Appelles did accompt of Venus portrature. . . . And if it be permitted to very good care to judge somewhat of Musick, as by Cicero it was permitted to the people to judge of painting in which they have no skill: I do protest unto you that if the songes of other Musitians do delight mee, those of Orland do ravish me [there follows a comparison of Lasso's variety of sound and texture with Vergil and Cicero].[72]

Comparison of "Orlande" [or Roland] to the chivalric hero, seen in several of these poems, suggests that Lasso was fortunate in his given name. His surname also offered possibilities; Lasso himself often punned on his name, in letters to his ducal employer and in dedicatory poems; and he may have preferred the Italian version of it so as to have the chance, rarely if ever missed, to set the Italian text syllables 'las-so' to the solmization syllables *la-sol*. Other writers also punned on his name, in Latin and in French. Here are a few examples. An ode addressed by Le Roy and Ballard to Charles IX says

> *Votre France n'a pas affaire*
> *De notre musique vulgaire*
> *Affin de la remettre sus*
> *Il faut, pour amollir l'audace*
> *De ce facheux tems, que la grace*
> *Et l'accord, vienne de LASSUS.*[73]

> [Your France has no business with our base music; in order to raise it up it is necessary—to soften the harshness of this unhappy time—that the grace and harmony come from on high {=Lasso}.]

A Latin poem by Albrecht V's agent in Venice, Nicolaus Stopius, uses the composer's surname thirteen times, in every singular and plural case; I will spare the reader its text.[74] Lasso himself addressed a poem to the Flemish humanist Charles Utenhove, ending "Par moy, Orlando de Lassus, Pour vous servir sous et dessus."[75] An anagram on the composer's name [Orlandus de Lassus = SOLUS LAUREA DONANDUS ES (you alone deserve the [Apollonian] laurel; there are a few extra letters)] is prefaced by some lines pointing out the intimate connection between Lasso's name and his art.[76]

Indeed Orlando di Lasso was lucky in his name (and characteristically made the most of it). The worthy imperial choirmaster Jakob Vaet, a contemporary of Lasso, was not his equal in talent and certainly not in name. A remark cited by Jacques Barzun seems appropriate here:

> There is a harmony . . . between men's lives and their names: a poetic justice. . . . Hector Berlioz could not have pursued his high-fevered career under the name of Georges Jourdain.[77]

GERMANY

Lasso's first publishers were, as we have seen, Netherlandish and Italian music printers. In the early 1560s his work began to appear in substantial quantities in France, and at the same time he also started to turn to

German publishers. Nuremberg was an established center of music printing, and it was to its leading firm, Montanus and Neuber, that Lasso gave his *Sacrae cantiones a 5v,* a motet collection that was soon reprinted by Gardane in Venice and thereafter often reissued in Germany and Italy.[78] Montanus [= Johann Berg] died in 1563, and shortly thereafter his widow Catharina married (and outlived) Dietrich Gerlach. The Gerlach firm printed and reprinted (not always to Lasso's satisfaction, as discussed later) collections of his motets and other sacred music, and in the 1580s the composer even turned away from Italy and to them for two madrigal collections.[79] Lasso seems to have maintained good relations with Catharina Gerlach. He supported her in a suit brought against her in 1582 by the Munich printer Adam Berg over a collection of Lasso motets she said were "sold to her by the composer himself" even though some of them had previously been printed by Berg.[80]

The chief German printer of Lasso's work, as important to him as Le Roy and Ballard were in France, was this very Adam Berg (no relation to Johann Berg/Montanus) of Munich. Berg began printing music in 1564; three years later he issued Lasso's first published collection of German songs, thus rounding off the composer's "territorial" approach in publishing his music. After this Berg printed and reprinted some two dozen Lasso books; after 1600 Lasso's sons replaced him with the firm of Berg's son-in-law Nikolaus Henricus, who likewise replaced Berg as court printer.[81]

With ducal support Berg undertook the most ambitious edition of Lasso's music to be done during the composer's lifetime, devoting seven volumes of his *Patrocinium musices* (1573–1576) to the composer. These large choirbook volumes, for which new type had to be cast, contained motets, Masses, Offices, Passions, and Magnificats in sumptuous format.[82] A few years earlier Albrecht V had commissioned superb manuscript collections of Lasso's music, illuminated by the court painter Hans Mielich; now his son Wilhelm evidently decided to make a public gesture, celebrating the magnificence of the Munich court in the published work of its chapelmaster and world-famed composer.[83] These books could hardly have been affordable by many people (some of them were reprinted by Phalèse in modest partbook format); but they must have made impressive ducal gifts.

In 1580–1581 Lasso asked for and obtained from Emperor Rudolf II a personal privilege for the printing and reprinting of past, present, and future compositions within imperial territories. This repetition of the French privilege he had received ten years earlier is additional proof of

Lasso's concern over the publication of his music. In this case we know more: Lasso's letter of application to the emperor (along with a letter of support from the new Bavarian duke Wilhelm V) survives, and from it we can see something of the composer's motives.[84] Lasso began by pointing out how necessary it is to make sure that printers do careful work and how difficult it is to identify and correct musical errors (in partbook format the difficulty is especially great). His own compositions, he proceeds, have been published in many countries and languages, and he has tried to insure, on behalf of the public and of his own reputation, that the editions be as accurate as possible. He realizes that German printers in order to safeguard their own interests have obtained imperial privileges to prevent the pirating of their books. In this way, they are protected, but he, the composer, is not. First editions tend to be accurate, but reprints are often so full of errors that the composer can hardly recognize his own work (here Lasso employs a bit of the rhetorical vividness for which his music was celebrated). To protect his work, in which he has invested his life's blood ("quibus vitam studiumque omne impendo") he asks that instead of granting further privileges to printers who handle his work, he, the composer, be granted the privilege, on the basis of which he can then choose publishers and thus control the printing and reprinting of his music.

Leuchtmann speculates that Lasso was particularly annoyed over recent German reprints—actually the work of the Gerlach firm—of his motets.[85] This may be true; but it was a good time for the composer to make his request because he could count on the support of Duke Wilhelm V, friendlier to and more supportive of the composer than his father had been at the end of his life. In any event, the privilege was granted; whether or not it was effective, Lasso had made his point.

Individual privileges were not unheard of in the sixteenth century. In Venice Cipriano de Rore and Perissone Cambio each got one (1544, 1545) for the printing of a single volume, by Antonio Gardane and Girolamo Scotto respectively (Italian music printers got privileges, chiefly from Venice and/or the papal court, for single volumes).[86] Lasso himself got one of these, for his fourth madrigal book of 1567, as we have seen. Imperial privileges were granted to a small number of German musicians, beginning with Arnold Schick in 1511, for single works or projected groups of volumes, some of which came to nothing.[87] Two more far-reaching privileges deserve mention here, both Venetian. In 1521 Bartolomeo Tromboncino, one of Petrucci's most prolific suppliers of music for frottola books up to 1520, received a privilege for "molti Canti

de Canzone madrigali, soneti, Capitoli et stramboti, Versi latini et ode la-
tine, et volgar barzelete frotole et dialogi"—this list comprising all the
genres in which he had already published music along with madrigals,
which he is not known to have composed—as well as a fifteen-year privilege for "tuti altri canti esso supplicante componesse."[88] This apparently
came to nothing; Tromboncino was still alive in 1535, but no music written after the issuance of this privilege is known to exist. In 1538 the papal
singer Costanzo Festa received a ten-year privilege for "all the works
which he might choose to publish."[89] Festa, whose surviving work was
published chiefly in anthologies, tried as early as 1536 to find a publisher
to print all his music, an edition like that of the madrigals of Verdelot
(1533–1537) and Arcadelt (1538–1544).[90] One book, a *Libro primo* of
madrigals issued by an unidentified printer in 1538, did appear, but there
is nothing more extant.[91]

    This rather scant list is all that exists, or is known to me, by way of
precedent for Lasso's privileges; its contents make the latter all the more
extraordinary by contrast. It seems fair to say that Lasso was the first
composer to pursue an active international publishing career and to win
wide recognition, at the highest official levels, for his efforts. Because of
the breadth and evident intensity of his dealings with publishers, Lasso's
career in print has been compared with that of Beethoven. This strikes
me as more than faintly absurd, if only because it ignores some noteworthy publication histories of composers such as Haydn; but Lasso was certainly unique in his own time. He was concerned about the fate of his
music—for the sake of the public, as he says, but also, and perhaps more,
for his present and future reputation as an artist. He would doubtless
have been concerned as well about making money from his music, apart
from the sums, probably small, he got for selling it to publishers. The
days when there was money to be made for composers from publishing
music—if they ever fully arrived—were as yet far off.

    Lasso worked primarily to please his ducal patrons in Munich. He
took this obligation very seriously to the end of his life, as a touching interview with the theorist Lodovico Zacconi makes clear.[92] He was a *bon
bourgeois* (certainly not a Beethovenesque figure!), acquiring goods and
property along with a coat of arms and a membership in a papal order,
and raising a family which included two sons who were musicians and
faithful custodians of their father's music. His published compositions
were designed (apart from the splendid *Patrocinium musices* series) to
have broad appeal at modest cost, and in this he was surely successful,
not only contributing decisively to the success of the music printing busi-

ness but setting a standard of excellence in serious and popular genres that raised the general level of musical achievement in his time and, thanks to the new-found power of the musical press, spread music of the highest quality to an unprecedented number of consumers. In the words of a tribute accompanying a portrait made in the last year of his life,

> *Hic ille Orlandus qui Lassum recreat orbem*
> *Discordemque sua copulat harmonia.*[93]

[Here is that Orlandus who revivifies a fallen world and unites a discordant [world] with his harmony.]

NOTES

[1]"Tametsi verò Orlandinae cantiones ubique terrarum extant maxima copia, sunt tamen adhuc plura, qua subinde principi suo separatim custodiunt, quae is vulgari minimè permittet. Extant tamen eius compositionis plurimae conciones cum variis mutetis quatuor, sex, octo, & plurium vocum quae hic ordine enumerare supervacaneum videtur, cum hoc eius publicati libri Norimbergae, Monachij, Venetijs, Florentiae, Napoli, Antwerpiae, Lugduni, & Parisiis, sunt suggessuri. Hunc Orlandum Monachij in arcis sacello canentem, & omnia digerentem ipse 1565 vidi, & magna voluptate audivi, ubi is etiamnum pergit, & subinde aliquid novi in sua arte magna laude excogitat." Samuel van Quickelberg, "Orlandus de Lassus Musicus," in Heinrich Pantaleon, *Prosopographia heroum atque illustrium virorum totius Germaniae* (Basel: Nicolai Brylingeri, 1565–1566), 3: 541–542; German version in *Teutscher Nation Heldenbuch* (Basel: Onstein, 1578), 507–508. Given in facsimile in Horst Leuchtmann, *Orlando di Lasso,* 2 vols. (Wiesbaden: Breitkopf und Härtel, 1976–1977), 1: 298–301.

[2]On Quickelberg (1529–1567) see Fernand Donnet in *Biographie nationale publiée par l'Académie des sciences, des lettres et des beaux-arts de Belgique,* 44 vols. (Brussels: Bruylant-Christophe, 1866–1986), 17: cols. 499–501. A Flemish scholar who studied at Basel, Quickelberg was recommended to Albrecht V of Bavaria by the Fugger family; he arrived at Munich in 1553 and remained there until his death. He wrote the commentary for Munich, Bay. Staatsbibl. Mus. Ms. A, an illuminated manuscript containing Lasso's *Penitential Psalms*. See *Bayerische Staatsbibliothek. Katalog der Musikhandschriften,* vol. 1, *Chorbücher und Handschriften* (Munich: Henle, 1989), 54–56.

[3]Leuchtmann, *Orlando di Lasso,* 1: 22.

[4]On the history of the *Prophetiae Sibyllarum* and of the *Penitential Psalms,* written about the same time as the former but published only in 1584, after the

death of Albrecht V, see Leuchtmann, *Orlando di Lasso,* 1: 124–134. Both collections are edited in Lasso, *Sämtliche Werke. Neue Reihe,* ed. Wolfgang Boetticher, Siegfried Hermelink et al., 26 vols. (Kassel: Bärenreiter, 1956–1995), vols. 21 and 26.

[5]Leuchtmann, *Orlando di Lasso,* 1: 28–29. Quickelberg may have named these cities simply because of their fame. Naples and Lyons had a history of music printing in the sixteenth century; Florence (in 1565) did not.

[6]Loc. cit. Leuchtmann thinks that Quickelberg may have misheard Lasso and written "Lugduni" (Lyons) for "Lovani" (Louvain).

[7]Leuchtmann, *Orlando di Lasso,* 1: 44. The twenty-two pages devoted to Lasso in *Einzeldrucke vor 1800 [Repertoire international des sources musicales A/I = RISM A],* 13 vols. to date (Kassel: Bärenreiter, 1971), 5: 232–254, are out of all proportion to space given any other sixteenth-century composer, even so prolific a one as Philippe de Monte.

[8]Elizabeth Eisenstein, *The Printing Press as an Agent of Change: Communications and Cultural Transformations in Early-Modern Europe,* 2 vols. (Cambridge: Cambridge University Press, 1979), 1: 59. Lasso's music is not widely preserved in manuscripts; these are mostly restricted to sources emanating from the Munich court and its sphere of cultural influence.

[9]On Petrucci see Claudio Sartori, *Bibliografia delle opere musicali stampate da Ottaviano Petrucci* (Florence: Leo S. Olschki, 1948); Stanley Boorman, "The First Edition of the *Odhecaton A,*" *Journal of the American Musicological Society* 30 (1977): 183–207; idem, "Petrucci's Typesetters and the Process of Stemmatics," in *Formen und Probleme der Ueberlieferung mehrstimmigen Musik im Zeitalter Josquins Deprez* (Munich: Kraus, 1981), 245–280.

[10]Bonnie J. Blackburn "Petrucci's Venetian Editor: Petrus Castellanus and his Musical Garden," *Musica Disciplina,* 49 (1995; publ. 1998): 15–45, has convincingly identified Petrus as Pietro da Castello, a Dominican attached during the early years of Petrucci's career to the church of San Giovanni e Paolo in Venice, *maestro di cappella* there in 1505, a singer of polyphony who travelled a good deal and was in touch with music lovers such as Girolamo Donato, a known collector. Much of the music he edited for Petrucci must also have been gathered by him.

[11]Andrea Antico's anthology *Liber quindecim missarum . . . per excellentissimos musicos compositae fuerunt* (Rome, 1516) *(Recueils imprimés xvie–xviie siècles* [= RISM], [Munich: Henle, 1960], 1516[1]) is an early example of a printed folio choirbook. The masses of Morales and Palestrina among others were published as choirbook volumes.

[12]The *Musica . . . sopra le canzone del petrarcha* (Fossombrone, 1520) of Pisano was published by Petrucci in partbooks, not all of which survive.

[13]See Mary S. Lewis, *Antonio Gardano, Venetian Music Printer, 1538–1569,* 2 vols. to date (New York: Garland Publishing, 1988), 1: 5. On the use of Petrucci's prints by music theorists as sources for examples, obtained by reading straight through the books, see Cristle Collins Judd, "Reading Aron Reading Petrucci: The Music Examples of the *Trattato della natura et cognitione di tutti gli tuoni (1525),*" *Early Music History* 14 (1995): 125–152.

[14]The importance of title pages in early printing (contrasted with their absence in most manuscripts) is stressed by Eisenstein, *The Printing Press.*

[15]On Antico see Catherine W. Chapman, "Andrea Antico" (Ph.D. diss., Harvard University, 1964); Martin Picker, ed., *The Motet Books of Andrea Antico* (Chicago: The University of Chicago Press, 1987), 1–8.

[16]Daniel Heartz, *Pierre Attaingnant, Royal Printer of Music. A Historical Study and Bibliographical Catalogue* (Berkeley and Los Angeles: University of California Press, 1969), 43–60.

[17]On this see Lewis, *Antonio Gardano,*1: 95; Iain Fenlon and James Haar, *The Italian Madrigal in the Early Sixteenth Century: Sources and Interpretation* (Cambridge: Cambridge University Press, 1988), 47–86. The rise of a new generation of music publishers in Venice was part of a general expansion of the Venetian printing industry in the 1530s. See Brian Richardson, *Print Culture in Renaissance Italy. The Editor and the Vernacular Text, 1470–1640* (Cambridge: Cambridge University Press, 1994), 90–91.

[18]On Susato see Ute Meissner, *Der Antwerper Notendrucker Tylman Susato* (Berlin: Merseburger, 1967); Kristine K. Forney, "Tilman Susato, Sixteenth-Century Music Printer: An Archival and Typographical Investigation" (Ph.D. diss., University of Kentucky, 1978). For Phalèse see Henri Vanhulst, *Catalogue des éditions de musique publiées à Louvain par Pierre Phalèse et ses fils, 1545–1578* (Brussels: Palais des Académies, 1990); on Laet see Robert Lee Weaver, *A Descriptive Bibliographical Catalogue of the Music Printed by Hubert Waelrant and Jan de Laet* (Warren, Mich.: Harmonie Park Press, 1994). There is no modern general study of German music printing in the sixteenth century; there is information in Josef Benzing, *Die Buchdrucker des 16. und 17. Jahrhunderts im deutschen Sprachgebiet* (Wiesbaden: Harrassowitz, 1953). For Nuremberg printers see Paul Cohen, *Musikdrucke und -Drucker zu Nürnberg im sechzehnten Jahrhundert* (Nuremberg: Zierfuss, 1927); Susan Jackson, "Music Printing in 16th-Century Nürnberg: Berg and Neuber" (Ph.D. diss., City University of New York, 1998).

[19]Henri Vanhulst, "Lassus et ses éditeurs. Remarques à propos de deux lettres peu connues," *Revue belge de musicologie* 39–40 (1985–1986): 80–100, 87. Lasso's relationships with printers are compared to those of Beethoven in Hansjörg Pohlmann, *Die Frühgeschichte des musikalischen Urheberrechts (ca. 1400–1800)* (Kassel: Bärenreiter, 1962), 147.

[20]On this part of Lasso's early career see Donna G. Cardamone, "Orlando di Lasso and Pro-French Factions in Rome," in *Orlandus Lassus and His Time,* ed. Ignace Bossuyt, Eugeen Schreurs, and Annelies Wouters (Peer: Alamire, 1995), 23–47, esp. pp. 41–44; Kristine K. Forney, "Orlando di Lasso's 'Opus 1': The Making and Marketing of a Renaissance Music Book," *Revue belge de musicologie* 39–40 (1985–1986): 33–60, esp. pp. 35–37.

[21]On Stefano Gentile see Forney, "Orlando di Lasso's 'Opus 1,'" 37–38. Forney demonstrates conclusively (p. 33) that the French-title version is the first issue of the print. Dedications in Lasso prints are reproduced in Lassus, *Sämtliche Werke,* ed. F. X. Haberl and Adolf Sandberger, 21 vols. (Leipzig: Breitkopf und Härtel, 1894–1926); they are also included in Lassus, *Sämtliche Werke,* 2d ed., ed. Horst Leuchtmann (Wiesbaden: Breitkopf und Härtel, 1968) and in the *Neue Reihe* of Lasso's works (see above, n. 4).

[22]See Forney, "Orlando di Lasso's 'Opus 1,'" 47 for the 1557–1558 reprint, not listed in RISM.

[23]On this motet, *Calami sonum ferentes,* see Alfred Einstein, *The Italian Madrigal,* trans. Alexander Krappe, Roger Sessions, and Oliver Strunk, 3 vols. (Princeton: Princeton University Press, 1949), 1: 411, 414–415. Einstein speculates that Rore might have given this piece to Lasso, but this seems improbable. The piece is edited in Rore, *Opera Omnia,* ed. Bernhard Meier, 8 vols. (American Institute of Musicology, 1959–1977), 6: 108.

[24]RISM 1540[7.] On Susato's relationship with Kriesstein see Forney, "Orlando di Lasso's 'Opus 1,'" 43.

[25]Susato had not, for one thing, printed any Italian-texted music before this. The composer Claude Goudimel may have done some editing for Nicolas du Chemin in 1551–1555; see François Lesure and Geneviève Thibault, "Bibliographie des éditions musicales publiées par Nicolas du Chemin (1549–1576)," *Annales musicologiques* 1 (1953): 269–373, pp. 274–277.

[26]Forney, "Orlando di Lasso's 'Opus 1,'" 51–52. The 1555 print also found its way to France; two chansons from it were printed by Du Chemin in 1557 (RISM 1557[10]). See Lesure and Thibault, "Bibliographie des éditions," 324.

[27]See above, n. 22.

[28]Forney, "Orlando di Lasso's 'Opus 1,'" 54.

[29]See Ignace Bossuyt, "Lassos erste Jahre in München (1556–1559): eine 'Cosa non riuscita'? Neue Materialen aufgrund unveröffenticher Briefe von Johann Jakob Fugger, Antoine Perrenot de Granvelle und Orlando di Lasso," in *Festschrift für Horst Leuchtmann zum 65. Geburtstag,* ed. Stephan Hörner and Bernhold Schmid (Tutzing: Hans Schneider, 1993), 55–67.

[30]Leuchtmann, *Orlando di Lasso,* 1: 99–100.

[31]Ibid., 1:116.

[32]App. 5.1, 1560b. See Vanhulst, "Lassus et ses éditeurs," 89.

[33]App. 5.1, 1564d, 1564c. Susato's print is dedicated to Melchior Linck of Augsburg.

[34]A few new pieces reached Phalèse and were included in his various reprints of Lasso collections. See Vanhulst, "Lassus et ses éditeurs," 80. His volume of masses of 1570 (RISM 1570[1]) contains three new works by Lasso. The composer visited the Netherlands in 1572 and could have met with Phalèse then; see Leuchtmann, *Orlando di Lasso,* 1: 51.

[35]It was usual for publishers to buy individual pieces or whole collections from composers. For an example, Du Chemin's purchase of four collections from Nicole Regner in 1548, see Lesure and Thibault, "Bibliographie des éditions," 274–277.

[36]RISM 1555[30,] reprinted by Dorico in 1558[10.] Neither edition survives complete. The *Libro primo* is not extant.

[37]See Donna G. Cardamone, *Orlando di Lasso et al., Canzoni Villanesche and Villanelle* (Madison: A-R Editions, 1991), xliv; Wolfgang Boetticher, *Orlando di Lasso und seine Zeit (1532–1594)* (Kassel: Bärenreiter, 1958), 42.

[38]Cardamone, *Orlando di Lasso et al., Canzoni Villanesche,* xix. Lasso's four-voice *villanelle* were published by Le Roy and Ballard in 1581, reprinted by Phalèse and Bellère in Antwerp in 1582; see App. 5.1, 1581g, 1582g.

[39]Cardamone, "Orlando di Lasso and Pro-French Factions," 40.

[40]RISM 1558[12,] 1562[7]. On the *madrigale arioso* see James Haar, "The 'madrigale arioso': A Mid-Century Development in the Cinquecento Madrigal," *Studi musicali* 12 (1983): 203–219.

[41]Maureen Buja, "Antonio Barrè and Music Printing in Mid-Sixteenth Century Rome" (Ph.D. diss., University of North Carolina at Chapel Hill, 1996), 88–91, 308–316; cf. James Haar, "The Early Madrigals of Lassus," *Revue belge de musicologie* 39–40 (1985–1986): 17–32.

[42]Buja, "Antonio Barrè," 98–100, 359–366. Barrè's letter begins "Cognoscendo io quanto le compositioni di Orlando di Lassus siano a Musici & a tutti grati ho con molta diligentia cercato haver delle sue opere: & havendone io di quelle raccolto tante, che suppliranno a fare il Terzo suo libro di Madrigali a cinque, ho voluto mandarle in luce . . ."

[43]According to Frank Dobbins, "Textual Sources and Compositional Techniques in the French Chansons of Orlando di Lassus," in *Orlandus Lassus and his Time,* 139–161, p. 151, only one French chanson of Lasso was printed in Italy, in Barrè's edition of the *Terzo libro a 5v* (1563c).

[44]See App. 5.1, 1562a, 1565c, 1566d, 1566e, 1568d.

[45]The privilege is given in Richard J. Agee, "The Privilege and Venetian Music Printing in the Sixteenth Century" (Ph.D. diss., Princeton University, 1982), 264–265.

[46]See James Haar, "*Le Muse in Germania:* Lasso's Fourth Book of Madrigals," *Orlandus Lassus and His Time,* 49–72. Wert at this time had entered the service of the duke of Mantua.

[47]Dobbins, "Textual Sources," 140.

[48]See above, n. 26.

[49]François and Geneviève Thibault, *Bibliographie des éditions d'Adrian Le Roy et Robert Ballard (1551–1598)* (Paris: Société Française de Musicologie, 1955), 91; cf. Kate van Orden, "Vernacular Culture and the Chanson in Paris, 1570–80" (Ph.D. diss., University of Chicago, 1996), 176. See also Charles Jacobs, ed., *Le Roy and Ballard's 1572 Mellange de chansons* (University Park, Pa.: Pennsylvania State University, 1988), 12–14. In the 1572 reprint of the *Mellange* Ronsard's preface mentions Arcadelt as one of many; he singles out "le plus que divin Orlande qui comme une mouche à miel a cueilly toutes les plus belles fleurs des antiens, & outre semble avoir seul derobé l'harmonie des cieux pour nous en resjouir en la terre surpassant les autres, & se faisant la seule merveille de notre temps."

[50]Lesure and Thibault, *Bibliographie,* 97–98.

[51]The pension of 1560 is mentioned first by François Lesure, "Les premiers rapports de Roland de Lassus avec la France," *Revue belge de musicologie* 3 (1949): 242; see also Leuchtmann, *Orlando di Lasso,* 1: 118–119.

[52]For this poem, ending with the lines "Comme tu es a Orlande / Le Mecenas de son chantz," see Leuchtmann, *Orlando di Lasso,* 1: 279–280.

[53]The *Prophetiae* were as yet unpublished; Lasso must have given a manuscript copy to Le Roy.

[54]The letter is reprinted by a number of scholars; see Leuchtmann, *Orlando di Lasso,*1: 167–168; the best version is given by Leuchtmann, 1: 311–312.

[55]"Le Roy [Charles IX] aime la musique. DIEU, qu'il amoit la Musique, fust aux instruments, ou aux voix humains! Et sur tout luy estoit aggreable la Musique, principalement celle d'un de plus rare Musiciens de ce temps, nommé Orlande, serviteur au Duc de Bavières: de qui la Musique luy plaisoit si très-tant, qu'a peine en pouvoit il gouster d'autre." *Histoire contenant un abregé de la vie . . . du Roy Tres-Chrestien & debonnaire Charles IX . . . par A[rnaud] Sorbin* (Paris: Chaudiere, 1574), 59.

[56]A letter from Renata of Lorraine to her husband Wilhelm, heir of Albrecht V, finds it "fort estrange" that Lasso should think of leaving when he had promised not to "servir aultre prince que vous et de ne vous abandonner." Leuchtmann, *Orlando di Lasso,* 1: 166.

[57]See Lesure and Thibault, *Bibliographie,* 12; Pohlmann, *Die Frühgeschichte,* 203.

[58]The volumes of Lasso's motets issued by the Huguenot printer Pierre Haultin in La Rochelle are an exception; see App. 5.1, 1575f and five subsequent books (he printed eight in all).

[59]Leuchtmann, *Orlando di Lasso,* 1: 155–157.

[60]For a survey of this aspect of sixteenth-century musical historiography see Jessie Ann Owens, "Music Historiography and the Definition of 'Renaissance,'" *Music Library Association Notes* 40 (1990): 305–330.

[61]See Lewis, *Antonio Gardano,* 1: 183, 343. In this connection it might be noted that Dante's *Commedia* was first labelled "divina" in an edition of 1555 (Venice: Giolito). See Carlo Dionisotti, "Lodovico Dolce," *Enciclopedia Dantesca,* 5 vols. (Rome: Istituto della Enciclopedia Italiana, 1970–1976), 2: 533–535.

[62]App. 5.1, 1562a. Leuchtmann, *Orlando di Lasso,* 1: 267–296 has assembled a number of tributes and dedicatory poems from prints of Lasso's music.

[63]Leuchtmann, *Orlando di Lasso,* 1: 267.

[64]Ibid., 265. This is from the commentary to the splendid manuscript copy of Lasso's *Penitential Psalms* (see above, n. 2).

[65]App. 5.1, 1570d. For Gohory's poem see Leuchtmann, *Orlando di Lasso,* 1: 270. Comparisons of Lasso to "Roland" are always to the chivalric hero of French legend, never to the more vexed figure of Ariosto's Orlando.

[66]Leuchtmann, op. cit., 1: 272–278, one of the more tiresome of these poetic tributes. After token praise of Lasso in stanzas two-three (the French poem is written in the terza rima of an Italian *capitolo*) there follow fifty-four stanzas of classical, chiefly Orphic myth. Jodelle (1532–1573), a poet and playwright listed as a member of the Pléiade by Ronsard, was apparently of a quarrelsome and envious nature. He would have liked to have his verse set by Lasso; see the sonnet addressed to a musician friend, Loyse L'Archer, in his *Oeuvres complètes,* ed. Enea Balmas, 2 vols. (Paris: Gallimard, 1965–1968), 1: 46.

[67]App. 5.1, 1572a; for the text see Leuchtmann, *Orlando di Lasso,* 1: 281. Melissus was an acquaintance of Jodelle; but in any event these poets read each others' work and freely imitated it.

[68]App. 5.1, 1584f; Leuchtmann, op. cit., 1: 287. The same sentiments are repeated, in Latin paraphrase, in a five-line set of Latin hexameters by Melissus, in 1586g (Leuchtmann, op. cit., 1: 289). I have not been able to determine whether Mégnier was a member of the group of poets who wrote many of these tributes (Gohory [see above, n. 65] was also a friend of Jodelle).

[69]Leuchtmann, op. cit., 1: 284, citing a contemporary German translation of Frischlin's Latin poem.

[70]App. 5.1, 1586g; Leuchtmann, op. cit., 1: 288.

[71]Cited in Lesure and Thibault, *Bibliographie*, 45.

[72]Lesure and Thibault, *Bibliographie*, 34–35, from a 1574 English translation of Le Roy's now lost French edition.

[73]App. 5.1, 1565d; Leuchtmann, *Orlando di Lasso*, 1: 269.

[74]It is given in Leuchtmann, op. cit., 1: 269–270.

[75]Boetticher, *Orlando di Lasso*, 165.

[76]App. 5.1, 1577a, a Le Roy and Ballard Mass print. The anagram and short accompanying poem, by "Io. Auratus Poeta Regius" [= Jean Dorat], begins "Qui norit artem, norit & nomen simul (Orlande de Lassus) tuum"; see Leuchtmann, *Orlando di Lasso*, 1: 286.

[77]Jacques Barzun, *Berlioz and the Romantic Century*, 2 vols. (Boston: Little, Brown, 1950), 1: 23, citing Thomas Burke, who is not further identified.

[78]App. 5.1, 1562a. On Montanus see Marie-Louise Göllner in *The New Grove Dictionary of Music and Musicians*, ed. Stanley Sadie, 20 vols. (London: Macmillan, 1980), 2: 539–540.

[79]App. 5.1, 1585e and 1587k. On Gerlach see Göllner in *New Grove Dictionary*, 3: 755–759; Susan Jackson, "Who is Katherine? The Women of the Berg and Neuber-Gerlach-Kauffmann Printing Dynasty," paper read at the 16th International Congress of the International Musicological Society, London, 18 August 1997.

[80]App. 5.1, 1582e. On Berg's suit see Pohlmann, *Die Frühgeschichte*, 164, 167.

[81]On Berg and Henricus (Heinrich) see Göllner in *New Grove Dictionary*, 2: 524; 7: 484.

[82]App. 5.1, 1573a, 1574b, 1575a, 1576a, 1587c, 1589a. On the *Patrocinium* series in general see Nanette C. McGuiness, "Orlando di Lasso's Motets in the *Patrocinium Musices*, vol. 1 (1573)" (Ph.D. diss., University of California, Berkeley, 1990), Chap. 1.

[83]An earlier publication celebrating the Munich court, Massimo Troiano's account of the festivities for the wedding of Wilhelm in 1568, was issued by Berg in 1568 and, altered and expanded, reprinted in Venice (by Bolognino Zalatieri) in 1569. See Horst Leuchtmann, *Die Münchner Fürstenhochzeit von 1568: Massimo Troiano, Dialogi* (Munich: Katzbichler, 1980).

[84]For Lasso's letter see Horst Leuchtmann, "Ein neugefundener Lasso-Brief," in *Festschrift Rudolf Elvers zum 60. Geburtstag*, ed. Ernst Herttrich and Hans Schneider (Tutzing: Hans Schneider, 1985), 349–357. Wilhelm's supporting letter is given in Vanhulst, "Lasso et ses éditeurs," 94. The privilege, in German and in Latin, is given (after prints of Gerlach and Berg) in Pohlmann, *Die Frühgeschichte*, 271.

[85]"Ein neugefundener Lasso-Brief," 353.

[86]Agee, "The Privilege," 93–94, 96, 214–215.

[87]See Pohlmann, *Die Frühgeschichte,* 198–203. Lasso's French and German privileges are discussed on pp. 203–206.

[88]Agee, "The Privilege," 44–45. The privilege is discussed and printed in Knud Jeppesen, *The Frottola,* 3 vols. (Copenhagen: Munksgaard, 1968–1970), 1: 147–148.

[89]Agee, "The Privilege," 76–78.

[90]See Richard J. Agee, "Filippo Strozzi and the Early Madrigal," *Journal of the American Musicological Society* 38 (1985): 227–37, pp. 233–34.

[91]James Haar, "The *Libro primo* of Costanzo Festa," *Acta Musicologica* 52 (1980), 147–155.

[92]Lasso, near the end of his life, told Zacconi that he composed something every day, if only an exercise, to keep himself ready should his ducal patron ask for some music. See James Haar, "A Sixteenth-Century Attempt at Music Criticism," *Journal of the American Musicological Society* 36 (1983): 196–99.

[93]See Leuchtmann, *Orlando di Lasso,* 1: 291, Tafel 39.

Appendix 5.1: Short-Title List of Lasso Prints

The following list contains (1) dates with identifying letters, taken from RISM A (see n. 7); (2) places of publication in separate columns, with publishers' names entered in them.

	Antwerp	Louvain	Venice	Rome	Paris	Nuremberg
1555a/b Le quatoirsiesme livre/ Il primo libro (repr., 1558, 1560 (Susato)	Susato					
1555c 1° di madrigali a 5 (13 repr., up to 1586, by various Venetian publishers)			Gardane			
1556a 1° motetti a 5 & 6 (repr. 1560 Susato)		Laet				
1557b 2° delle Muse a 5 (repr. 14 times, up to 1586, by various Venetian printers)				Barrè		
1560b Tiers livre des chansons a 4, 5, 6 (4 repr. by Phalèse)		Phalèse				
1560[18] 1° de madr. a 4 (repr. 13 times, up to 1592, by various Venetian printers)				Dorico		

	Antwerp	Louvain	Venice	Rome	Paris	Nuremberg
1562a Sacrae cantiones, 5v (repr. 13 times, with Nuremberg [Montanus, Gerlach] and Venetian printers alternating)						Montanus & Neuber
1563c 3° di madrigali a 5 (repr. 7 times, up to 1586, by Venetian printers)				Barrè		
1564b Primus liber conc. sacr. a 5 & 6					Le Roy	
1564c 1er de chansons a 4 (1 repr. [Laet])	Susato					
1564d 4me des chansons a 4, 5 (2 repr. by Phalèse)		Phalèse				
1565a Modulorum 4 … 10v					Le Roy	
1565c 5 & 6v sacr. cant. lib. secundus (3 repr. [Gardane])			Scotto			

Appendix 5.1 (*continued*)

	Antwerp	Louvain	Venice	Rome	Paris	Nuremberg	Munich
1565d Novem quir. div. Job, 4v (7 repr., by Gardane, Gerlach, Phalèse, Le Roy, Haultin)					Le Roy		
1565f 18me livre de chansons a 4 & 5 (5 repr. [Le Roy] up to 1581)					Le Roy		
1566d Sacr. cant. 5 & 6v, Lib. Tertius (5 repr., all Gardane, up to 1599)			Gardane				
1566e Sacr. cant. 6 & 8v, Lib. Quartus (3 repr., all Gardane, to 1593)			Gardane				
1567b Magnificat 6, 5, & 4v (2 repr. [Gerlach])						Gerlach	
1567c 4me de chansons 4, 5, 6v (1 repr., Phalèse)		Phalèse					
1567d 16me de chansons 4, 5v (1 repr., Le Roy)					Le Roy		

	Antwerp	Louvain	Venice	Paris	Nuremberg	Munich
1567e 17me de chansons 4, 5v (2 repr. by Le Roy)				Le Roy		
1567k 4° de madr. a 5 (3 repr., to 1593 [Gardane])			Gardane			
1567l Neue teutsche Liedlein 5v (3 repr. by Berg)						Berg
1568a Select. cant. 6+v					Gerlach	
1568b Select. cant. 5, 4v					Gerlach	
1568d 5us lib. conc. sacr. 5, 6, 8v (2 repr., Gardane)			Gardane			
1569a Cant. aliquot 5v (2 repr. [Merulo in Venice, Berg])						Berg
1579a 5 Missae, 5, 4v (lib. 2us) (repr. by Tini in Milan, 1588)			Merulo			
1570c Select. cant. sacr. 6, 8v						Berg

Appendix 5.1 (*continued*)

	Antwerp	Louvain	Venice	Paris	Nuremberg	Munich	London
1570d Mellange de chans. 4, 5, 6, 8, 10v				Le Roy			
1570e Recueil du mellange 4, 5v							Vautrouller
1571a Moduli 5v (2 repr. [Phalèse, Berg])				Le Roy			
1571c 1us mod. 5v (1 repr. [Phalèse])				Le Roy			
1571e 2us mod. 5v				Le Roy			
1571f Livre de chans. nouv. a 5 (3 repr. [Phalèse, Le Roy])				Le Roy			
1572a Moduli 4, 8v				Le Roy			
1572g Ander Theil Lieder 5v (2 repr., Berg)						Berg	
1573a Patrocinium musices 1a pars (1 repr. [Phalèse])						Berg	
1573b Mod. 6, 7, 12v				Le Roy			

		Paris	Munich	La Rochelle	Geneva
1573c	3us mod. 5v	Le Roy			
1573d	6 Cant. lat., 6 lieder, 6 chans., 6 madr., 4., 8v		Berg		
1573g	13me livre de chans. 4v	Le Roy			
1574b	Patr. mus. 2^a pars (repr. Phalèse)		Berg		
1574c	Patr. mus. 3^a pars (3 repr. [Phalèse, Bergl])		Berg		
1575a	Patr. mus. 4^a pars (2 repr. [Berg, Phalèse])		Berg		
1575b	Lib. mot 3v (4 repr. [Phalèse, Berg, Gardane])		Berg		
1575f	Mellange de chans. spirituelles, 4v			Haultin	
1576c	Patr. mus 5^{a}pars (1 repr.,Berg)		Berg		
1576e	Mod. 4, 8v			Haultin	
1576f	Mod. 5v			Haultin	
1576g	Mod. 5, 10v			Haultin	
1576h	Mod. 6, 7, 12v			Haultin	
1576i	Meslanges, 4, 5, 6, 8, 10v	Le Roy			
1576k	Mellange 5, 8v (ch. spirituelles)			Haultin	
1576l	Thresor de musique, 4, 5, 6v				Goulart

Appendix 5.1 (*continued*)

	Venice	Paris	Nuremberg	Munich	Strasbourg
1576n 17ᵐᵉ livre de chans. 4, 5v (4 repr., Ballard)		Le Roy			
1576r Der dritte Theil Lieder 5v				Berg	
1577a Missae, Magnificat		Le Roy			
1577c Novae 2v Cant. (8 repr., to 1610, by French, Italian, and English printers)				Berg	
1577d Liber motettorum 3v (1 repr. [Berg])				Berg	
1578f Lib. 7ᵘˢ mot. 5v (1 repr. [Gardane])	Gardane				
1578g Magnificat 5v		Le Roy			
1578h 20ᵐᵉ livre de chans. 4, 5v		Le Roy			
1579a Select. cant. 6+v			Gerlach		
1579b Altera pars select. cant. 5, 4v			Gerlach		
1580b 6v Cantiones					Wyriot
1581a Liber Missarum 4, 5v			Gerlach		

	Venice	Paris	Nuremberg	Munich	Geneva
1581c 8 Magnificant		Le Roy			
1581d 8 Magn., 1 Mass		Le Roy			
1581g Lib. de villanelle (1 repr., Phalèse)		Le Roy			
1582a Missa quand'io		Le Roy			
1582b Missa ad imit. moduli		Le Roy			
1582c Fasciculi sacr. cant. 4, 5, 6, 8v			Gerlach		
1582d Sacrae cant. 5v				Berg	
1582e Motetta 6v				Berg	
1582f Lectiones Job 4v				Berg	
1582h Thresor, 2d ed.					Goulart
1582l Etlicher liedlein 4v				Berg	
1583a Neue teutsche lieder (1 repr., Gerlach)			Gerlach		
1584d Sacr. cant. 6v, Liber 8us	Gardane				
1584e Psalmi Davidis				Berg	
1584f Continuation du mellange (1 repr., Le Roy)		Le Roy			
1585a Sacr. cant. 4v				Berg	

Appendix 5.1 (*continued*)

		Venice	Paris	Nuremberg	Munich
1585b	Sacr. cant. 6, 8v				Berg
1585d	Hieremiae proph. lament.				Berg
1585e	Madrigali, 5v			Gerlach	
1586d	Sacr. cant. 5v, Lib. 6us	Gardane			
1586e	Ieremiae proph. lam., Passion		Le Roy		
1586f	B.V.M. 8 Cantica (1 repr., Le Roy)		Le Roy		
1586g	Meslanges a 4, 5, 6, 8, 10v (1 repr., Le Roy)		Le Roy		
1587a	Missa Beatus qui		Le Roy		
1587b	Missa Locutus sum		Le Roy		
1587c	Patr. mus. Magnificat 4, 5, 6v				Berg
1587d	Sacr. cant. 4v		Le Roy		
1587h	Novem quir. div. Job		Le Roy		
1587i	8 cantica B.V.M. (1 repr., Vincenti in Venice)		Le Roy		
1587k	Madr. a 4, 5, 6v			Gerlach	
1587l	5° di madr. a 5	Gardane			

		Antwerp	Venice	Paris	Munich	Graz
1588a	Misse 10		Gardane			
1588c	Mod., 4, 8v			Le Roy		
1588d	Mod., 5v			Le Roy		
1588e	Mod., 6c			Le Roy		
1589a	Patr. mus. Missae 5v				Berg	
1589d	Cantica B.V.M. 4, 5v		Gardane			
1590b	Neue teutsche Gesang, 6v				Berg	
1591a	Misse 5, 6v		Gardane			
1591c	14me livre, 4, 5, 6v			Le Roy		
1592b	La fleur des chans., 4, 5, 6, 8v (4 repr., all Phalèse)	Phalèse & Bellère				
1594a	Cant. sacr. 6v					Widmanstetter

		Antwerp	Venice	Munich	Cologny
1594b	Le thresor, 3d ed.				Marceau
1595a	Lagrime di San Pietro			Berg	
1600a	Prophetiae Sibyllarum			Heinrich	

Appendix 5.1 (*continued*)

		Antwerp	Paris	Munich	Würzburg
1604a	Magnum opus musicum			Heinrich	
1607a	Missa dixit Joseph		Le Roy		
1607b	Missa in die tribulationis		Le Roy		
1608a	Missa credidi		Le Roy		
1610a	Missae posth.			Heinrich	
1613a	Missa in te Domine		Le Roy		
1613b	Cant. sacr. 3v	Phalèse			
1614a	Missa douce memoire		Le Roy		
1614b	Missa sydus ex claro		Le Roy		
1619a	Iubilus. B.V. 100 Magnificat			Heinrich	
1625a	In Magnum opus musicum Bassus ad organum				Volmar
1687a	Missa Iager		C. Ballard		

CHAPTER 6

Authors and Anonyms
Recovering the Anonymous Subject
in *Cinquecento* Vernacular Objects*

MARTHA FELDMAN

> *"What matter who's speaking,"* someone said,
> *"what matter who's speaking."* [1]

The line is Beckett's, but the more familiar voice Foucault's. Invoked in the now notorious "What Is an Author?," Beckett's line points to a tension that sat uneasily amid the postwar scholars and critics targeted by Foucault's essay: between a hard-nosed postromantic mood that claimed to revere the author for his textual objects and objective facts alone and a romantic quest to crystallize the authorial mystique, which died hard amid canons of greatness, individuality, and originality. Foucault's aim probably seems milder and plainer now than it did when he voiced it in 1969. In the briefest possible synopsis, he tried to refocus questions that had long centered around who wrote particular works—and by extension and implication how original, valuable, and revealing of the author those works are—to questions about the ways in which discursive formations thrive, where they come from, how they circulate, and what positions they allow various subjects. This, of course, is a gloss on the famous ending of Foucault's essay and the foundation for his bid to replace the transcendant "author" with the more heuristic concept of the "author-function."

My interest here is not in questions about how musical works mark out authorial identity per se, nor specifically in how Foucault's philosophy of the author might help explain that. Rather, it concerns how his focus on prevailing concepts of authorship, and specifically the relations commonly thought to exist between authors and texts, can be reconsidered against one of the timeworn pursuits of Renaissance musicology, namely attribution scholarship. More expressly, it concerns how we have interpreted *sixteenth-century* attribution practices—those to which we are heir—in light of our own understanding of what authorship tells us.

In an attempt to situate issues of authorship in early modern musical print and allow them to follow their larger cultural ramifications, we might shift the author/text polarity around which Foucault defined his argument to one of the subject/object relations toward which his essay arguably pointed, but failed to pause—a polarity recently clarified by the essays collected by De Grazia, Quilligan, and Stallybrass between the covers of *Subject and Object in Renaissance Culture*.[2] For where questions of authorial function are at issue, the notion of "object" as distinct from "text" helps stress the material status that music acquired as authors' names circulated in the mass reproduction and trade of sixteenth-century vernacular music. This distinction is especially apt for the years starting shortly before 1530, when single-impression printing techniques increased the volume of music publication dramatically. It was around that time, too, that a highly repetitive set of poetic and musical tropes served as textual "rudiments" in a veritable imitative fury whereby objects circulated to wide and diversified audiences in the new form of commodities—printed objects dispersed in complex networks of exchange, often far removed from their producers, and traded among subjects for value pressed into the abstract form of money. Here, the notion of "subject" underscores the personal, social, and professional identities that generated musical works and marked their identities in circulation, even when their object forms were more apparent than their subjective signs. Thus, most importantly for my purposes, the subject/object distinction recognizes at once the material character of what circulates and the personae that hovered (however tacitly) behind circulating commodities, both named and nameless, through various reified codes visible to the buyer's eye and the listener's ear.[3]

In this essay I mainly take stock of how and why music circulated *without* authorial attribution, anonymously, and in ways that therefore must have placed its sheer materiality in high relief. In this sense, this essay looks for a typological subject, reducible enough to be packaged up, represented, and—at least in the present analytic—typified within print media and still discernible today. Such a view would eventually lead back to some of the same attribution questions that were among the major preoccupations of musicology in the last fifty years and struck the heart of its various postwar philological and bibliographical pursuits.

Musicology, after all, had produced its own virulent strain of anti-romanticism in those years, which gave the prospect of resolving attribution questions a special kind of allure—the allure of fixing the vagaries of elusive histories and erratic filiations in hard facts—not least those of early music, whose attribution problems are endless and baffling. Typically, though, anonymity interested musicology mainly in its inverse prospect, as a negative to be turned positive, a problem to be solved. In wanting to name the anonymous, it hoped to link it to a particular subject, of whom questions could then be asked about "the-man-and-his-work," around whom studies of manuscripts, printers, institutions, geographies, and genres could be built, and for whom bibliographies, stylistic profiles, and musical genealogies could be made or improved. Without slighting such projects, we might well find new ways to confront anonymous production that take our scrutinies beyond facts of attribution per se to the logics of early modern attribution practices, the special conditions of anonymous production, and the nature of authorial identity for sixteenth-century producers and publics.[4] So doing, the same issues of identity and subjectivity now warmly debated by so-called postmodern thinkers might be illuminated by reorienting the cool documentary concerns of a pre-postmodern method.

In order to localize my remarks within particular modes of production and circulation and the material cultures in which they participate, I focus in what follows on printed repertories, mainly of Italian vernacular music of the mid-sixteenth century and mainly as found in anthologies. This is the print repertory I know best, but it is also one of those in which anonymity, along with a welter of other attribution questions, proliferates.[5] Anonymity in the *cinquecento* vernacular tradition takes two interrelated forms, both familiar to musicologists and both worthy of attention: that of unidentified musical works and that of unidenti*fiable* verse in musical sources (bearing in mind that texts in musical sources were almost never attributed explicitly to their poets). Most anonymous printed music of the *cinquecento* is found in anthologies, which routinely by 1530 (and quite often beforehand) collected works of one particular genre—frottole, madrigals, villanelle, and so forth. (As we will see, printers also fleshed out single-author prints with settings by authors other than the principal one, but in those prints supplementary authors were more often named than anonymous.) To review the state of bibliographic affairs: such musical anthologies have been serviceably inventoried for over fifty years, since the time when Alfred Einstein catalogued all the extant vernacular anthologies as an appendage to Emil Vogel's bibliography of sixteenth- and seventeenth-century single-author prints, the *Bibliothek der gedruckten weltlichen Vocalmusik Italiens,* itself first published in 1892.[6] *Cinquecento* poetry, on the other hand, was given little bibliographic control until recent years. Later a computer database known as the Berkeley Italian Renaissance Project, created by Louise George Clubb, William G. Clubb, Michael Keller, and Anthony Newcomb in the 1980s, made possible extensive bibliographic control of *cinquecento* vernacular poetry. One result of their project is that in most cases where poems set to music exist in contemporaneous editions of printed poetry—whether single-poet *canzonieri* or anthologies—their authors could be identified using the Berkeley database.[7]

During my struggles with attribution questions surrounding mid-sixteenth-century madrigal production—overwhelmingly a printed repertory—two related points became increasingly clear, one concerning attributions of music, the other the implicitly "attributable" character of texts (as it might have been imputed by sixteenth-century musicians). First, contrary to the prevailing assumption among many musicologists in years past that anonymity was a mere byproduct of printers' inability to identify given works,[8] anonymous music often appears to have circulated for reasons that were far less serendipitous; ignorance about who composed a work was surely only one reason music went unattributed, and not necessarily the most frequent one. Second, much sung verse that begins to seem permanently unattributable by scholars of our time was probably never widely identifiable by sixteenth-century musicians and music-lovers, even the many who knew vernacular verse as well as they knew music. Admittedly, verse poses an inherently more elusive problem, not only because texts were rarely attributed to their poets in music prints, but also because we have little positive evidence about how readily much verse could have been identified by print audiences of the time. Nevertheless the level of bibliographical control over *cinquecento* lyrics that has recently become possible shows that verse anthologies and madrigal collections often formed virtually parallel corpuses—not in the sense that their poetic contents were literally identical (verse anthologies usually contained many, many more lyrics than their musical counterparts in any case) but in the sense that contributors were often drawn from overlapping social and/or academic circles and shared a common cache of poetic tropes, a common repertory of poetic forms, and arguably a common sense of lyric register and tone. Such parallelism was evidently pronounced in centers of printing like Venice, where poetic and musical anthologies emerged in close proximity and circulated among overlapping sets of users and buyers.[9] It gives us at least some means of control and some purchase on the possible reception of these corpuses, which we would otherwise lack.

If anonymity did indeed have a logic, a character, and particular conditions of existence, as I suggest, then we should ask what the sets of signatures are that could help reveal these. Here I can only offer some proposals of a general nature, based on a particular case of music print. I hope these will nevertheless suffice to buttress my contention that much bibliographical evidence within printed production needs to be understood in the broadest sense to ask not just who wrote what and why, but how practices of naming functioned in the context of mass circulation and what tendencies and tensions were introduced into naming practices by the accelerated commerce of sixteenth-century Italy.

We can probably assume that both composers and printers generally preferred non-anonymous works, even in the mid-sixteenth century, because they helped composers' careers to advance and were more commercially viable for printers.[10] Nevertheless in the early years of printing, whole corpuses attributed to authors were rarities—books like the *Laude libro primo* of Innocentius Dammonis printed by Petrucci in 1507 and Bernardo Pisano's *Musica . . . sopra le Canzone del petrarcha* (also Petrucci) of 1520. After mass production got underway, however, with moveable type and single-impression printing in the late 1520s and 1530s and the explosion of the printing industry in Venice, single-author corpuses became more normative. But printers still took many liberties in naming authors—especially in anthologies—sometimes barely hiding the fact.[11] Moreover, they quickly began to advance claims of authenticity, often competing ones. Hence, in 1546 a print could boast the addition of new madrigals "posto li suoi nomi veri di autori nelli madrigali dove erano stati posti altri nomi per errore" (under the real names of the madrigals' authors where other names had been placed erroneously).[12] Such claims of authenticity speak to the fact that names carried capital in a way that is not merely modern (or perhaps we should say, in a way that is also protomodern). Nevertheless, in a world with no copyright laws and with only limited use of the printing privilege within a restricted number of publishing centers, the bases of these authenticity claims, like sixteenth-century practices of attribution all told, were highly unstable.[13]

The notion that printers generally *wanted* to assign names, usually by printing what could legitimately pass as nameable, is borne out by the fact that when publishing an anthologized series, printers often used up available pieces by authors whose identities they presumably knew (or works to which they could creditably make attributions) before they began printing unnamed ones. An early example is that of Ottaviano de' Petrucci's eleven-volume series of frottola anthologies published in Venice and Fossombrone between 1504 and 1514. In the first volume of the series Petrucci assigned a composer to every single frottola he included. By the second, third, and fourth books, which followed in later 1504 and in 1505, he left about a third of the frottole unattributed; and by the fifth and sixth books of 1505 he printed about two-thirds of the frottole anonymously.

The Petrucci case is not unique. A somewhat analogous situation exists for the chanson anthologies brought out by the French royal court printer Pierre Attaingnant. The first one, issued in 1528 (Heartz, *Pierre Attaingnant,* Bibliographical Catalogue, no. 2), attributed twenty-four of its total of thirty-one chansons; the next, in 1529, attributed only eleven of thirty-four chansons (Heartz, no. 5); the next three chanson volumes (Heartz, nos. 6, 7, and 8—all undated but all presumably from 1529) did not attribute a single piece.[14]

Printers could import pieces into anthologies from general circulation in order to flesh out their repertories or simply fill the empty portions of gatherings. Some of the pieces that fulfilled these functions were thus pre-existent, having reached printers anonymously. But it seems evident that as presses cranked up production volume, publishers and editors needed to generate new works in order to print oblong octavo partbooks of standard length, without risking any wasted space. By the early 1540s they had begun devising copious anthologies, or—even more frequently—prints supposedly devoted to single authors with added pieces by "altri autori." Such prints were fed by much the same spirit of editorial entrepreneurism that engendered a new breed of polygraphs, and with them a new journalistic spirit, inspiring a multitude of vernacular publications of familiar letters, poetic anthologies, handbooks on geography, grammar, and morals, dialogues on love and beauty, and much else of a similar ilk.[15] To help with obtaining the large amounts of music that publishers now sought out, the wider system of print required middlemen, men who could fulfill a range of functions connected with obtaining and producing new music, but who might also write new pieces themselves when needed.

This is just one factor which throws light on a surprising aspect of mid-sixteenth-century music publishing: namely, that even if printers preferred non-anonymous production, all things being equal, they seem nevertheless to have regarded certain *pieces,* certain *kinds* of pieces, and most likely pieces by certain kinds of *authors* as being categorically "anonymous" in character. Among these were probably the pieces supplied by musicians working for—or collaterally, along with—presses on an ad hoc basis. Such arrangements became increasingly important as the interpersonal and business connections demanded by music printing became more competitive and at the same time more complex and diversified, encompassing musicians as composers, suppliers, editors, proofreaders, and independent entrepreneurs. In the course of the mid-sixteenth century, two different freelance musicians come to mind who functioned in some of these multiple roles, both connected with Girolamo Scotto: Paolo Vergelli and Giulio Bonagiunta. Much like many music printers (Scotto and Gardane included),[16] musicians who supplied music written by others could surely do rudimentary composing themselves; Bonagiunta certainly did.[17] And rudimentary is exactly what many unattributed works are. They could easily have been knocked out by minor entrepreneurs in the printing business or by composer-editors who were commissioned to furnish music on a piecemeal basis for a mass popular market. James Haar has speculated (in the absence of evidence to the contrary) that Jhan Gero may have been a house editor, and thus supplier of filler music, as well as composer—though if so, we would have to grant that he was doing this work at an order notable enough to warrant the use of his name in publications. At Scotto's behest, or by virtue of his commission ("a mia instantia"), Gero wrote a large volume of madrigal and chanson duos—an arrangement with immense popularity in the amateur and pedagogical music market.[18] It also seems possible that a composer like Gero could have commissioned (or sub-commissioned) anonymous pieces for anthologies from hack composers whom he knew were able and willing to produce fast work for cheap fees—minor chapel singers, for instance, or even instrumentalists, moonlighting for extra income.

Regardless, two seemingly contradictory conditions of music publishing need not be considered incompatible, practically or ideologically: on the one hand the fact that printers favored non-anonymous pieces, but on the other that they regarded certain works and authors as unsuitable in kind for attribution.

This suggests that once publishing became a boom industry in Venice, publishers gained an authoritative, quasi-authorial power in fashioning and broadcasting the composer's voice. That power could be made truly effective, however, only through the intricate networks within which tasks were designated, objects solicited, composers, bookmen, and underwriters influenced, and property then acquired.[19] This was particularly true within the highly commercial process that produced anthologies, for which publishers functioned as de facto master-authors. The black-note madrigals produced by Antonio Gardane and Girolamo Scotto in the 1540s provide a famous instance of the central role that publishers and editors assumed in conceiving, assembling, and marketing anthologies.[20] Indeed in this case, publishers virtually invented the genre itself—a genre of and for print.

Black-note madrigals were so-called because they utilized faster note-values than ordinary madrigals—hence their blacker-looking notation—and were consequently also marked by the wider range of declamatory rhythms they exploited.[21] They became identified with a heightened expressivity, and one of a flashier and perhaps more commercial type, at a time and place in which polyphony for singing high lyric poetry was mostly quite restrained. Both Gardane and Scotto participated in this, and Gardane used them to help build up a new business, first issuing an anthology of black-note madrigals when he was still a fledgling publisher in Venice, just beginning to gain good access to coveted repertories.[22] Only a few black-note pieces had previously appeared when Gardane brought out the *Primo libro d'i madrigali a misura di breve* in 1542, and his fostering and fashioning of the genre thus helped further him as well.

Black-note anthologies contain a number of unattributed works, some of which circulated with single or multiple attributions elsewhere—generally later—others not. Gardane only gradually, in his quasi-authorial role in promoting the genre, seems to have attracted "name" composers to it. The numbers of unattributed black-note madrigals diminished somewhat as volumes subsequent to the first two were issued: there were four of them in the *Primo libro* of 1542 and seven in the *Secondo libro* of 1543, plus numerous attributions that we would now regard as problematic—pieces that appeared without attribution or with different attributions elsewhere, or that mysteriously received attribution in only one or two of Gardane's partbooks. By 1549 only three unattributed works appeared in Scotto's *Terzo libro* of 1549 and only two in Gardane's so-called *Vero terzo libro* of the same year.[23] Unlike in the cases of Petrucci's frottole or Attaingnant's chansons, the markets plied by Gardane and Scotto now placed higher value on signed pieces, even as composers' names entered into newly complicated relations to markets as a result.

Two traits of anonymous madrigals in black-note anthologies speak pointedly to their particular form of material capital. First, they include a number of *ottave rime,* a musico-poetic form that circulated copiously in the unwritten tradition as the basis for oral (often improvisatory) recitation. Within that tradition, tunes—or more properly "tune types"—traveled in much the same way they do throughout parts of Asia and the Middle East, as formulas used as bases for improvisations or for newly composed variations on preexistent structural material.[24] Second, they include a number of pieces that reinforce the picture of fast house production I described for them above. Anonymous black-note madrigals were often very short, many setting tiny texts to produce madrigals of as little as forty-nine measures.[25] Anonymous works in other venues were often short as well; two of the three in the *Secondo libro a 5* of Cipriano de Rore printed by Gardane in 1544 set texts of six and nine poetic lines each.

Many such pieces were inserted as fillers. Unlike in manuscripts that were used for performance or preservation, to which new pieces were added over a period of time, printers producing music partbooks in standard oblong formats did not leave blank any significant portions of the pages that made up gatherings.[26] A good example of how pages were filled can be seen in the anonymous setting of Petrarch's sestina stanza *Consumando mi vo,* for which the cantus part appears as Figure 6.1.

Gardane clearly had to do something with the space left over by the previous piece, which ends on the top of the same page. The same thing happened with an anonymous setting printed in Cipriano de Rore's *Secondo libro a 5* (Venice: Gardane, 1544), which similarly fills up the space that would otherwise have been left blank after only one system.[27] It is telling that this little piece may not have been all Gardane wished for, with its clumsy text repetitions, four-square rhythms, and perfunctory expression—not to mention various parallel octaves and fifths between tenor and bassus. Yet it fit perfectly well into the volume all the same, and not just as filler that enabled the book to be brought to light sooner rather than later, but because the book was really an anthology anyway (cf. pp. 179–185), in which the piece kept company with a number of others of like kind.

The phenomenon of musical (and, as we will see, poetic) anonymity is linked not only to short settings, but to settings for fewer voices: four voices or less more commonly than five or more. The anthologized series of madrigals "delle muse" printed by another composer-publisher, Antonio Barrè, in Rome (and subsequently imitated by Gardane in Venice) makes this clear. Between 1551 and 1561 first Barrè and then Gardane

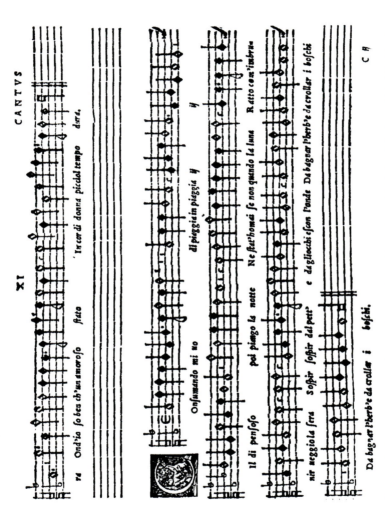

Figure 6.1 Anon., *Consumando mi vo di piaggia in piaggia* (poet: Petrarch, sestina, no. 237, 4th stanza); from *Il secondo libro de li madrigali … a misura di breve a quatro voci* (Venice: Gardane, 1543), soprano partbook, p. 11. Used with kind permission of Herzog August Bibliothek Wolfenbüttel (2.73.1 Musica).

published by turns three *five*-voice books under the "delle muse" rubric. Only one madrigal in all three books was printed anonymously. Barrè inaugurated the four-voice series in 1555 under the same title but with the added genre rubric of *madrigali ariosi,* publishing books two and three of the series in 1558 and 1562. By comparison with those in the five-voice series, no less than fourteen of the madrigals in the four-voice series were given anonymously.[28]

I would like to propose that a meaningful relationship exists between this density of anonymous works and the fact that many of them evoked the songlike, and purportedly more indigenous, side of Italian music by utilizing—or imitating—melodic formulas and bass patterns that formed common property among aria singers in the unwritten tradition. Barrè's *madrigale arioso* volumes a *quattro* were undoubtedly so-named because their aria-like qualities of simple, flexible declamation and formulaic melodies were used for oral recitation of epic stanzas, notably from Ariosto's *Orlando furioso.*[29] Accordingly, the volumes are dominated by *ottava rima,* especially the first volume, which Howard Mayer Brown has called the most "ideological" in appropriating and textualizing materials from the unwritten tradition.[30] Brown's work on the harmonic nature of these pieces shows that *ottava* settings in a shared tonal type (or at least sharing final and signature, as with his example of *ottava* settings using g-mollis) articulate the *ottava* structure using chordal progressions and melodic gestures common to all exemplars of that type (see Example 6.1).

It seems to me that we might therefore associate the prevalence of anonymity among the four-voice *madrigali ariosi* with their affinities for radically dispersed song; the dual presence of song types that traditionally circulated as musico-poetic formulas, on the one hand, and anonymous dissemination, on the other, might well be taken as aspects of an interrelated cultural practice. Tune types or standard modes of recitation circulated as shared materials of accompanied song; anonymous polyphony disseminated this common storehouse in a new, shared form of tangible property. Put differently, in *madrigali ariosi* both borrowed tunes and invented tune types traveled as material identities, much as they did in monodic song. Furthermore, authors' names may have seemed more dispensable—less needed for autho*rizing*—when it came to exemplars in a given corpus of traditional tune types and bass patterns than they did when it came to brand-new pieces more thoroughly differentiated in kind.[31] Let us recall, too, that unlike five-voice works, the four-voice polyphony of *madrigali ariosi* served as common fare for

Example 6.1   Antonio Barrè, *Non è pena maggior, cortesi' amanti* (poet: anon.);
from *Primo libro delle muse a quattro voci / Madrigali ariosi di Ant. Barre et
altri diversi autori* . . . (Rome: Barrè, 1555).

amateur madrigal singers of relatively modest skill. Haste and brevity were less problematic in such collections than in five- and six-voice ones, whose cachet depended on a complex poetic discourse, a contrapuntal intricacy to go with it, and often a more sophisticated skill in singing "on the book."[32]

We encounter, then, a series of links. Like all secular genres, but even more so than most, *ottave* found a happy habitat in the mid-century anthology. These anthologies contain many anonyms, which in turn find continuities with the manuscript tradition in which many *ottave* were originally transmitted as lyric *strambotte* and with the oral tradition in which, by the early sixteenth century, they were transmitted as epic stanzas.[33] Often anonymous, stanzas in *ottava* form collapse alleged differences between high and low cultures.

Such a collapse accompanied the huge ascendancy of Ariosto's *Orlando furioso*, which was abundantly recited to melodic formulas in both the elite courts of sixteenth-century Italy and its open town squares.[34] Ariosto's epic kicked up a storm of controversy over the issue of whether a single work could legitimately hold equal appeal for plebians and patricians.[35] Not just that, but critics of the epic deemed the narrator's voice too omnipresent, wishing that (like Aeneas to Dido) its characters would narrate their own deeds without having them constantly be envoiced by the poet. And this was something that epic stanzas, once pressed into musical form, easily got around.

Three of the phenomena that mark the circulation and character of *ottave*—their patterns of material dispersion, their work of bridging oral and written traditions, and something of their poet-centered narrative voice—are consistent with the proliferation of anonyms that they carried with them.[36] Moreover, it seems to have been precisely their promiscuous appeal that raised tensions, if less directly, around the marketing of anthologies, making hierarchies among composers glaringly obvious, but also equalizing the buying public to an unprecedented—and for some—uncomfortable degree.[37]

Franco Piperno's studies of the madrigal anthology over the course of the whole century illuminate further the specific relationship of the miscellany to secular music.[38] In their more humble mid-sixteenth-century guise, anthologies, he notes, point to real uses, to occasions in the profane world; they were not merely assembled for the sake of vanity (at least not that of any one author), nor to preserve and codify their authors' works.[39] At first, though, the anthology was marketed as aesthetically lower than the "monograph." One of several external markers of that inferior status was the almost total lack of dedications attached to madrigal anthologies in the period from 1530 to 1555.[40] Another indication, for Piperno, is that anthologies exalt music over text during the same period when monographs begin to vaunt their parity. And finally, there is the fact that anthologies, with their more commercial origins and more explicit and single-minded interests in commercial prospects, make rampant reprints, substitutions, and alterations that cause changes of authorial paternity to proliferate—partly, at least, to give one printer (most strikingly, Gardane or Scotto) an edge over the other.[41]

Correlated with these shifts is the glut of anonymous pieces in pre-1555–1560 anthologies (again continuous with the manuscript tradition), by contrast with later anthologies in which naming became more valued—more a matter of course and therefore more expected. The trend toward more frequent attribution signalled a sharpening dichotomy between authors and audiences: as print proliferated and mass reproduction was naturalized in an early modern world, printers pitted authors against an increasingly anonymous public, names against the nameless.[42]

At the axis of this shift, the history of the anthology takes a still more ironic turn (at least if we extend Piperno's thinking to its inevitable conclusion). For in 1555, beginning with Barrè, the anthology won a more lustrous place in the vanguard only by turning itself paradoxically into a more antiquated object of exchange: no longer, as had been the case from 1530, could anthologies form the ultimate sign of print's modernity—the sign, that is, of the *commodity*[43]; after 1555 they acquired the premodern currency of the *gift*. That was the year when anthologies first became regular objects of dedication.[44]

Dedications were indeed survivors of an old gift economy, presentation devices in the circulation of objects; but that economy did not simply flourish in archaic times, when authors and their names generally mattered less, only to fade from view when they came to matter more. On the contrary, the dedication (whether to prince, cardinal, merchant, or count)—as the most striking remnant of a gift-based logic—served increasingly as a tool of authors' efforts to exploit new markets of print. Thus, it was only once print made music securely part of a market logic that an older strategy of patronage was adapted to it, helping to turn music prints into commodities while preserving or even enhancing their attributes as gifts. Among the prominent strategies signalling a regard for musical objects as gifts—objects to be transacted in intersubjective exchange—were those dedications that claimed to bring the dedicatees honor in a wider world. The book, such objects often claimed, owed its

existence to its dedicatee, whom (as Roger Chartier has shown) it represented as its true "author" in a rhetorical bid for a dedicatee's loyalty,
protection, and material support.[45] Chartier cites a most striking case of
this hybridity in a 1605 print of *Don Quixote,* which bore emblazoned on
its title page (beneath its author's name) "Dirigido al Duque de Beiar,
Marques de Gibraleon, Conde de Benalcaçar, y Bañares, Vizconde de la
Puebla de Alcazar, Señoe de la villas de Capilla, Curiel, y Burguillos,"[46]
insisting with iconic clarity that old strategies of marketing were wholly
compatible with new modes of production and new strategies of marketing technology.

We should therefore bear in mind what Piperno's analysis fails to
note: that not only are the economies of gift and commodity not mutually
exclusive, they may well be reciprocally determining; and that, moreover, in the case of mid-*cinquecento* music printing, gift and commodity
are not just bilateral forms of exchange—coextensive with one another
but unrelated—but rather evince a highly characteristic moment in the
global history of their entanglements, a moment of mutual interchange-
ability that emerges just as the commodity makes a decisive bid to usurp
the gift.[47] Thus the inescapably obvious fact that books had indeed *become* commodities showed its ugly face in renewed attempts to purvey
them as if they were gifts.

It was natural that when the most entrepreneurial, commodity-
minded actors in the new Italian world of high-volume music print—
namely, printer/editor/musicians like Barrè (or before him, in 1542,
Gardane)—came almost to function as would-be "authors" by "composing" their own anthologies for print, they called on dedications to grease
the wheels of technologically driven markets.[48] Bonagiunta, too, in the
eighteen known prints he issued between 1565 and 1568, was an entrepreneur par excellence at the same time as he was a musician himself,
and he made much by exploiting the combined potential of anthologies
and dedications. In dedicating a book of Lasso's motets in 1565 he
claimed its contents as "gifts" to himself and in the same year claimed
in his dedication that Rore had "given" him "beautiful madrigals for
four and five voices" in order to keep them from falling into other
people's hands.[49] Yet these "gifts" clearly formed part of larger systems
of exchange whereby things "given" were reciprocated (not necessarily
directly) with other things and/or with acts—rewards, favors, connections, further obligations, additional gifts, further reciprocations. At
the same time it is also clear that such gifts never lay far from a fast-
developing consciousness of commodities—hence Giulio Ongaro's point

that commissioning music was doubtless part of how Bonagiunta assembled anthologies,[50] and also how he developed strategies for marketing anthologies *as* commodities in ways that were fundamental to their creation and perpetuation. Bearing this in mind, it seems that anonymous presentation of pieces within collections assembled by these printers may have been of little consequence, as the collection had its meta-author in the form of the printer and that "author" had his patron.[51] More salient, though, is the shift around 1555 to a new concept of authorship within anthologies, wherein (as Ongaro has pointed out) the anthology often assumes a more exalted role, endowed with historical consciousness in the form of great retrospective collections like Zantani's *La eletta*—not unlike the poetic anthologies with titles beginning *"Tempio,"* which were collected to sacralize an honored personage during the same time.[52] In anthologies like those, the anonym *does* fall largely out of view, for in such a context, it is the ability of authors to confer fame, to construct fame for another, that counts; or, in the case of a poetic *Tempio,* to exchange fame through panegyrics, *sonetti-risposti,* capitoli, and other forms of praise and dialogue.

Consistent with this new strategizing of fame, authorship had already gained clearer definition in print markets as early as the late 1540s through the sharpened wordings used on title pages both in miscellanies and monographs, in turn clarifying differences between the two. As Piperno has shown, it was in the late 1540s that production of Italian anthologies proper intensified. Concomitantly, monographs that were not exclusively composed of works by a single author came to be more clearly marked as hybrids—part monograph, part anthology—with the presence on their title pages of an "aggiunta," no longer signalled merely as "altri autori" but as a "nova gionta di madrigali" or a portion of compositions "aggiuntovi."[53]

With due caution we might extend aspects of the bifurcation between simpler anonymous music and more intricate non-anonymous music that I have just drawn for music to aspects of poetry that was set to music. As I noted already, no dichotomy with respect to attribution can be distilled from poetry in music prints, as no standard practices of naming poets existed that could provide prima facie evidence nowadays of exactly if and (if so) how such a dichotomy operated.[54] All the same, I believe we can discern certain patterns between what *could* have been attributed by a given performer or "reader" and what could not, which kinds of poems are at issue and which not, and who set each sort to music. Notwithstanding the lack of *direct* evidence, it is more scrupulous to heed those patterns than to ignore them.

As a first example, let me return to the so-called *Secondo libro a 5* of Cipriano de Rore brought out by Gardane in 1544, a book that reveals much about interests in profit-making, habits of naming, and authorial subjectivity in *cinquecento* vernacular production, and one that is rife with bibliographical complexities.[55] First of all, the book is Rore's in name only, as nineteen of the twenty-seven numbers in it are not his, and the core of Rore's contributions had just been published that same year in an expanded reprint of Rore's first book, the *Madrigali a 5* printed by Scotto, who had issued the original edition two years earlier.[56] Driven by commercial interests, this *Secondo libro* was undoubtedly merchandised as a single-author print to make it more saleable (which Rore's name could well do), even though it bears the physiognomy of an anthology.[57] Among other composers in it are Willaert—still the most venerated madrigalist at mid-century—with three settings, plus a number of Willaert's students, including Perissone Cambio and Girolamo Parabosco, and several composers with Roman ties: Hubert Naich, who has only one madrigal less than Rore, Ferrabosco, and Arcadelt (the last two with one madrigal each). Three of the madrigals in the book are anonymous.[58]

In keeping with this fragmentary and patently commercializing character, not a single poem in the entire corpus of twenty-seven can yet be attributed to a poet save six that are Petrarch's.[59] This surprising split between Petrarchan poetry and poetry that remains unattributable seems to be peculiar to the book's actual, though occult, status as an anthology—a print genre often dominated by texts whose poets cannot be identified.[60]

An analogous situation is concealed throughout Willaert's entire, much dispersed oeuvre, all of it scattered through anthologies save one great exception. That exception, the famed collection of madrigals and motets published in 1559 as *Musica nova,* dramatizes something of the same phenomenon, as every one of Willaert's settings of Petrarch's sonnets (twenty-four of them, mostly for five and six voices) appeared there and only there, near the end of his life.[61] Of his thirty other madrigals, dispersed throughout numerous anthologies (mostly four- and five-voice) over thirty years of publishing, an astonishing twenty-five texts remain anonymous, notwithstanding the best labors of many scholars.[62]

Important to bear in mind here is that at mid-century, Italian poetry set to music tended to draw poems from a large and diverse corpus, which followed an indefinite literary hierarchy cascading downwards from the Parnassus of Petrarch's *Canzoniere.* At the tier beneath Petrarch

were classic modern *canzonieri* by Bembo, Sannazaro, and Ariosto, and
beneath theirs, poems "canonized" in newly published, serialized anthologies of "diversi,"[63] as well as single-author collections of poetic
madrigals and stanzas by lesser lights such as Lodovico Martelli, Girolamo Parabosco, and Luigi Cassola. This hierarchy did not prevail everywhere, nor was it absolute. Yet I would argue that in those circles where it
did prevail, most of the poetry that remains unattributable today was con-
signed to subcanonic rungs of the aesthetic ladder, or fell off the canonic
ladder altogether.

This chasm between sovereign authorship and seeming authorless-
ness sharply divides the body of eight poems in settings attributed to
Rore in the *Secondo libro:* the four settings from Petrarch's *Canzoniere*
are all sonnets and all were positioned contiguously in mid-volume as
nos. 15 through 18. The four other works attributed to Rore are settings
of anonymous texts scattered throughout the book as nos. 1, 3, 14, and
27. By giving the Petrarchan sonnets weighty contrapuntal settings,
Rore's music locates them in the probing and timeless aesthetic of sacred
motets. Petrarch is the book's only poet of historical stature, and thus
stands both as a symbol of eternal recognition and as a sign of a composer's means of acquiring it. In the dichotomized scheme I have drawn
up here, the subjective status of anonymous poets, by contrast, represents
virtually the opposite: worldliness, simplicity, and anonymity, typical of
the transient imitators who proliferated in the sixteenth century, borrow-
ing Petrarch's amorous tropes for avowedly mundane ends.

Let me attempt to describe four hypothetical positions (among numerous possible ones) occupied by anonymous poets whose poems
circulated in prints of vernacular music. The first is that of the commissioned poet, prevalent in the worldly presentation of occasional verse
that dominates Rore's Second Book. Three of Rore's four unattributed
settings in Book 2 are occasional, all of them celebratory—two wedding
sonnets (nos. 1 and 14) and an encomium of a woman named Isabella of
Cremona (no. 3). Celebratory verse like this was much at home in anthologies, as both occasional verse and anthologies were explicitly generated out of processes of commodification with an ear to easy appeal
and a public persona that helped make them good capital. Music printers
typically placed settings of commissioned occasional verse at the heads
of books to commemorate specific events, specific dedicatees, or both.[64]

Hack lyric imitators, who worked as literary "artisans" and moon-
lighted for patrons and presses, represent yet another position for these
poets. An anonymous poet who glossed Petrarch's sonnet *Hor che 'l ciel*

et la terra e 'l vento tace to write *Hor che l'aria e la terra* filled such a role. His relation to Petrarch is staged in Rore's First Book of 1542, as is the general relationship of both settings to the contrast I have been drawing between Rore's Petrarchan settings and his settings of anonymous verse. *Hor che l'aria e la terra* is one of only two of the book's poems that remains unidentified. It loosely imitates Petrarch's *Hor che 'l ciel,* also included in Rore's First Book. Moreover, the two settings occupy inverse positions in the book, the Petrarch setting falling second and the setting of its anonymous imitation falling second to last. For the anonymous poem Rore used a light cantabile style and modest elocution, whereas for Petrarch's text his idiom is much weightier and more highly wrought.

This contrast is evident in Rore's exordia, as seen in Examples 6.2a and 6.2b.

The respective passages are similar in declamatory rhythms through the first eight syllables, but *Hor che 'l ciel* appeals to a more complex musical rhetoric, pitting a syncopated quintus against unsyncopated entrances in the other voices and varying the main motive with dotted rhythms (mm. 3–4) that make the whole metric edifice more complex and irregular from the outset. By comparison, the exordial rhythms of *Hor che l'aria* are completely uniform until irregularities crop up in bassus and quintus at m. 6; but this happens only after each voice has already given a rhythmically exact statement of the opening motive. The tonal sphere, moreover, is marked by an analogous contrast, as Rore saturated the opening measures of *Hor che 'l ciel* with semitone inflections (D-Eb, G-F#, B-C), but left the exordium of *Hor che l'aria* completely diatonic.

The connection between *Hor che 'l ciel* and *Hor che l'aria* raises a larger question regarding intersections between imitation, authorship, and circulation. Many of the materials that proliferated in vernacular imitations were drawn from Petrarch's *rime,* which came to be treated as a fetishized source of booty. Musical gestures conventionally used to set these vernacular imitations tended to function much the same way. Both "stockpiled figures and images," "accumulating and banking" them in "cultural storehouses." In characterizing them thus, I am glossing Stephen Greenblatt's *Marvelous Possessions,* where the three-pronged phenomenon I discuss—technology, imitation, circulation—is distilled in the phrase "mimetic machinery."[65] So doing, Greenblatt's analysis relates "social relations of production" to exploration narratives; but his identification of how imitations were continually reproduced there as

Examples 6.2a and 6.2b Cipriano de Rore, *Hor che 'l ciel e la terra e 'l vento
tace* (poet: Petrarch, sonnet, no. 164) and *Hor che l' aria e la terra* (poet: anon.);
from *Di Cipriano Rore i madrigali a cinque voci . . .* (Venice: Scotto, 1542),
nos. 2 and 19.

Example 6.2b

forms of mimetic capital meshes with the mass marketing of Petrarch's tropes in *cinquecento* vernacular production.[66]

This brings me from occasional poets to other sorts of pointedly realist poets. As the century wore on, and especially by the late 1530s and 1540s, Italian cities were saturated with poets writing in a realist vein who turned Petrarch's internal, self-reflexive poetics inside out, externalizing them satirically in interactive, often comic plays on real-life lovers. Verse of this kind, which embodies this externalizing strategy at its most extreme, can rarely be found at one and the same time in both a given musical setting and a contemporaneous literary source. Its anonymous appearance in music prints could, of course, serve to shield inversions of Petrarch's tropes at their most transgressive.[67] One of Willaert's three contributions to Rore's Second Book is a lengthy invective ballata-madrigal couched in the voice of a woman called "Chiara" who rails against the folly of a noble lover.

> *Sciocco fu 'l tuo desire*
> *veramente pensando ch'a miei danni*
> *teco n'entrassi a gli amorosi affanni.*
> *Mi maraviglio, quando*
> *non anchor chiaro sei del foll' errore,*   5
> *e come desiando*
> *l'amor mio ne perdest' i giorni e l'hore.*
>   *Donna cortes' e humana*
> *con vil amante certo mal s'accorda.*
> *Non mi conosci, o cieca mente insana*   10
> *di bastardo, nè vo' che per me leggi*
> *el suon di privileggi*
> *tuoi ch'ogni orecchia assorda.*
>   *Hor tienti al mio consiglio:*
> *pon giù, se puoi, l'insania e cangia l'ire,*   15
> *ch'assembr' al vespertil e non al giglio.*
>   *Chiara son io, qual fui, nè mi scompiglio*
> *a fart' il vero udire:*
> *Se di te mai pensai, poss'io morire.*

[Foolish was your desire in truly imagining that at my expense I should enter into amorous troubles with you. I wonder that you are not yet certain of the foolish error, and how you lost days and hours in craving my love. A courteous, humane woman with a vile lover surely is badly matched. You do not know me, o blind twisted mind of a bastard, nor do I want you to read me the sound of your titles, which deafen every ear. Now take my advice: Set aside, if you can, your madness and change your wrath, which resembles bats, not lilies. I am Chiara, as I was, nor do I trouble myself to make you hear the truth: If I ever thought about you, would that I might die.]

Sciocco fu turns on its head the notion that Venetian polyphonists adhered strictly to canonic literary norms. Its sardonic, chiseled diction replaces Petrarch's lyric meditations with the direct discourse not just of a real-life lover but a female one no less, and grounds her speech in vituperative secular protestations of class. Chiara's low-styled cannonade on her lover's high-born vice thus foregrounds the matter of social rank at the same time as it inverts it; her titled lover sinks low while she holds her head up high. Even the familiar Petrarchan turn to dying for her final rhetorical point does not assert a *Petrarchan* love-death—a love that ambiguously relishes love pangs as a welcome form of death—but rather hints at Petrarch's paradox only to reject it.

Madrigal prints that purportedly traded in more canonical texts than this one often contain a surprising number of poems like "Chiara's" that end up inverting the norms of gender or class and the delicacies of Petrarchan love. Chiara's invective serves to remind us that class registered in part through gender and gender through class. Gender had to have organized much of how identity was structured in sixteenth-century print, as access to print belonged more to men than to women. Compounding this, however, the texts that perpetuated vernacular musical prints were also (or especially) fueled by class: those who had insufficient notoriety could potentially mobilize their professional situations to increase their fame through print. Venice, as the hub of print culture, republican government, Petrarchan imitation, and the commercialization of music and letters with which these ambiguously intersected, forms the paradigmatic locus for such professional mobilizations.

Of course, the pursuit of fame had contrary effects too, increasing the stock of middle-class professionals while potentially decreasing the reputations of established aristocrats. But to say so is only to point out that once mechanical reproduction put fame within faster and easier reach, it also came to operate in a greater tension with obscurity. This phenomenon has considerable implications for aristocratic literary production, the fourth and last kind of authorial position that I wish to take up here. Just as anonymity could shield transgressive verse, it could likewise mask the activities of the elite. Whereas many aristocratic poems survive *only* in the sheltered pages of poetic manuscripts, others were scattered in a few printed verse anthologies or circulated anonymously in music prints. The Venetian patricians Domenico Venier and Girolamo Molino, and Florentines like Filippo Strozzi and Giovanni Battista Strozzi il vecchio, all had considerable amounts of lyrics set to music—as always without ascriptions—but had little or nothing published in poetic editions except posthumously.[68]

A musical counterpart to this situation exists in the biography of Guglielmo Gonzaga Duke of Mantua, one of the few wealthy aristocrats of the *cinquecento* who seriously devoted himself to composing music and had it published. In 1586 Antonio Gardane's son Angelo wrote the composer Giaches de Wert to discuss the sale of the Duke's anonymously printed madrigals and motets.[69] Gardane protested that a certain bookseller in Brescia, in writing the Duke's counselors, had inflated the number of his compositions that he had sold. "Without any doubt, if [the Duke's] name had appeared on the print, then a larger number of them would have been sold than was the case. But . . . it pleased his highness that his name should not be on them."[70]

How could the Duke have let Gardane publish music under his name while still avoiding the mien of self-promoting courtier, courting public grace? From such a lofty realm as his, approbation and appropriation formed a perilous kinship. Paradoxically, fame in print could easily cause a loss of public stature through a seeming loss of the private self—admitting the stares of an overly curious public by admitting to one's wish to curry its favor. It is no surprise, then, that the lyrics most easily identifiable by *cinquecento* buyers in commercial markets were mainly those written by professionally mobile poets of the middle class.

In sum, all of the vastly different cultural types we might link with anonymous dissemination—from artisan poets engaged for occasional and encomiastic commissions and hack musicians hired to knock out anthologies, to outspoken females or aloof aristocrats hiding from public view—were deeply implicated in productive pressures over consumerism and commercialization. Whether unnamed as composers or simply unnameable as poets, authors who were unidentified, unsigned, and unidentifiable confirm collectively that far from eliminating the phenomenon of anonymity, high-volume print consolidated it within the new physical conventions of print and its modes of circulation.[71] Thus, in various ways all authors, anonymous and not, exploited the new possibilities of print that allowed works to be endlessly reconstituted for commercial dissemination.

We should remember, finally, that a primary vehicle for this reconstitution was the repertory of tropes in Petrarch's vernacular *rime* and, in music, the figures used to set them. Petrarch's tropes in this era were everyone's master-tropes. And since the process of troping, once initiated, appeared in increasingly dispersed forms that cut through social registers and generic boundaries, the dispersion and repetition of Petrarchan tropes bears directly on an investigation of anonymous subjectivity. Composers who set anonymous lyrics entered the public domain with texts shorn of the subjective associations they could otherwise have carried. Nothing of poetic identity remained but a material one, grafted on to that of the composer. As the poet, as knowable subject, was lost, a material object was gained. Having slipped from the subject, in other words, its identity was displaced onto the object itself—the materiality of the text or the song.

It is an irony in the history of radical appropriations that took place in the sixteenth century that this sameness of material identity should nevertheless mark the difference of subjective identity that I propose we bear in mind.

NOTES

*A brief version of this essay was given orally at the session "Early Modern Objects as Historians' Subjects," which I co-organized with Gary Tomlinson for the Annual Conference of the Renaissance Society of America, Kansas City, 15–17 April 1993. I am grateful to participants in the seminar on "Print Culture in the Early Modern City," Newberry Library, Center for Renaissance Studies, April–June 1995, for stimulating discussions that helped reformulate the essay. A very special thanks to Jane A. Bernstein for sharing portions of her catalogue of Girolamo Scotto's publications before its appearance in print and for giving me copious, invaluable feedback on an earlier version of this essay. If my own views have not always been compatible with hers, I have nonetheless benefited greatly from her insights and her vast knowledge of sixteenth-century music printing.

[1]Beckett, *Texts for Nothing,* trans. Beckett (London: Caldar & Boyars, 1974), 16, quoted in Foucault, "What Is an Author?" Reprinted in trans. in *Language, Countermemory, Practice: Selected Essays and Interviews by Michel Foucault,* ed. with intro. by Donald F. Bouchard, trans. Bouchard and Sherry Simon (Ithaca: Cornell University Press, 1977), 115 n. 5. Orig. publ. in French as

"Qu'est-ce qu'un auteur?" *Bulletin de la Société française de Philosophie* 44 (July–September 1969): 73–104.

²Margreta De Grazia's essay, "The Ideology of Superfluous Things: *King Lear* as Period Piece," in *Subject and Object in Renaissance Culture,* ed. Margreta De Grazia, Maureen Quilligan, and Peter Stallybrass (Cambridge: Cambridge University Press, 1996), 17–42, is particularly astute in clarifying the turn from an early modern world in which subjects were indivisibly entwined with and constituted by their objects to a romantic ideology (exemplified at opposite poles by Marx and Burkhardt), which held that the ideal subject could only be fully realized through its transcendance of the objects around it. In the end, of course, the objects by which subjects are constituted are always also constituted by them. It is precisely this dialectical operation on which *Subject and Object in Renaissance Culture* tries to insist. An astute anthropological exploration of subject/object relations, approached from the perspective of autobiography, is that of Janet Hoskins, *Biographical Objects: How Things Tell the Stories of People's Lives* (New York: Routledge, 1998).

For another shift in emphasis toward an object-centered history, albeit more synthetic and derivative in kind, see Lisa Jardine's *Worldly Goods: A New History of the Renaissance* (New York: Nan A. Talese, 1996), esp. Chap. 3, "The Triumph of the Book," and Chap. 6, "A Culture of Commodities." In contrast to De Grazia's account (and those in *Subject and Object in Renaissance Culture* as a whole), Jardine's tends to focus singlemindedly on the newly accelerated culture of commodities, thus reducing its subjects to their interests in things and cash.

³An excellent preamble to the historiography of print, with attention to related issues of books, textuality, etc., is Sandra L. Hindman's Introduction to *Printing the Written Word: The Social History of Books, Circa 1450–1520* (Ithaca: Cornell University Press, 1991).

⁴Archer Taylor and Frederic J. Mosher, *The Bibliographical History of Anonyma and Pseudonyma* (Chicago: The University of Chicago Press for the Newberry Library, 1951), chronicles the history of anonyms and pseudonyms as used by scholarly authors. The documentation is fascinating, but their account largely assumes that authors' intentions are involved, leaving out cases in which scribes or publishers simply failed to attribute works to authors (as so often happened in musical sources).

⁵This, of course, is also true in the French and Franco-Flemish secular repertories of the same time period and the decades preceding it.

⁶Emil Vogel's *Bibliothek der gedruckten weltlichen Vocalmusik Italiens, aus den Jahren 1500–1700* (Berlin, 1892; reprint, Hildesheim: Georg Olms, 1962) was published in revised and enlarged form by Alfred Einstein in 1962 as *Bibliography of Italian Secular Vocal Music.* Einstein's primary contribution (first

brought out in installments in *Music Library Association Notes* between 1945 and 1948) consists of an addendum containing all the printed anthologies, which had been omitted from Vogel's catalogue; it was then reproduced as an appendix to Einstein's rev. ed. of Vogel of 1962. A third edition of Vogel's work was published by François Lesure and Claudio Sartori as *Bibliografia della musica italiana profana, nuova ed. interamente rifatta e aumentata con gli indici dei musicisti, poeti, cantanti, dedicatari e dei capoversi dei testi letterari. [= Il Nuovo Vogel.]*, 3 vols. (Pomezia: Staderini-Minkoff, 1977) with the addition of numerous indices but omission of the anthologies. For other additions and corrections to Vogel (and Einstein) prior to 1977 see Lesure and Sartori, 1: v–vi, and for their justification for not including anthologies, 1: xii.

[7]I am most thankful to the creators of the project, especially Michael Keller and Anthony Newcomb, as well as to Shuli Roth, a computer specialist on staff at the University of California, Berkeley, for their help in using the database from afar and for sharing materials in hardcopy while I worked on-site at Berkeley. I am equally grateful to Lorenzo Bianconi and Antonio Vassalli, who gave me access to a parallel project that they headed up in Italy (and started before the proliferation of computer technology), and especially to the latter for access in 1982 to all of their card files, then maintained at his hospitable farm in Impruneta.

[8]See, for example, the catalogue note of Alfred Einstein, who tended to assume that printers made ascriptions in later editions when the truth of a composer's identity came to light: "Some numbers, anonymous in 1542[2], are here ascribed to *the composers* [emphasis mine]" (Vogel/Einstein, *Music Library Association Notes* 3/1 [1945]: 51; Vogel/Einstein, *Bibliography,* 633).

[9]The work of Carlo Dionisotti, *Geografia e storia della letteratura italiana* (Turin: Einaudi, 1967), remains indispensible in understanding the poetic anthologies and their itineraries among audiences. Important on the major mid-century series of poetic anthologies, known generically as the *Rime diverse* (or *Rime di diversi*) series, is the essay by Louise George Clubb and William G. Clubb, "Building a Lyric Canon: Gabriel Giolito and the Rival Anthologists. Part 1," *Italica* 68 (1991): 332–344, which deals with how printing practices were instrumental in the formation of a modern lyric canon. All of the large poetic anthologies that comprise the series, together with various re-editions, have been entered into the Berkeley database.

[10]This has been the argument of Jane A. Bernstein, for instance. See her "Financial Arrangements and the Role of Printer and Composer in Sixteenth-Century Italian Music Printing," *Acta musicologica* 62 (1990): 39–56, and idem, *Music Printing in Renaissance Venice: The Scotto Press (1539–72)* (New York and Oxford: Oxford University Press, 1998), esp. Chap. 6. On "the importance of

being printed" as it pertains to literary authors, see Anthony Grafton's essay so titled, *Journal of Interdisciplinary History* 11/2 (1980): 265–286.

[11]Thus, for instance, Antonio Gardane printed Arcadelt's second book, entitled *Il vero secondo libro di madrigali d' Archadelt novamente stampato,* with the following statement in his dedicatory letter to one M. Nicolo Alberto: "La malitia de gli impressori . . . per acconsentire al'utile del guadagno, non cura ale volte dar fuori la vilta de le opre altrui sotto il titolo de i degni autori" (quoted in Mary S. Lewis, *Antonio Gardano, Venetian Music Printer, 1538–1569: A Descriptive Bibliography and Historical Study. Vol. 1, 1538–49* [New York: Garland Publishing, 1988], 208, and Iain Fenlon and James Haar, *The Italian Madrigal in the Early Sixteenth Century: Sources and Interpretation* [Cambridge: Cambridge University Press, 1988], 250; the latter speculate that the book may have been in fact the fourth or fifth in the Arcadelt series, rather than the second). We should also note that many discrepancies appear between the table of contents in a given partbook and the table of contents in another partbook of the same set; or between a given table of contents and the headers within the same partbook. Furthermore, Stanley Boorman argues persuasively that the intended attributions of printers cannot always be interpreted straightforwardly on the basis of their physical placements of composers' names in the headers of printed leaves ("Some Non-Conflicting Attributions, and Some Newly Anonymous Compositions," *Early Music History* 6 [1986]: 109–157).

[12]RISM 1546[15], *Il primo libro d'i madrigali de diversi autori a misura di breve novamente ristampata. Aggiontovi ancora alcuni madrigali novi et posto li suoi nomi veri di autori nelli madrigali dove erano stati posti altri nomi per errore a quatro voci* (Venice: Gardane, 1546).

[13]See Richard J. Agee, "Filippo Strozzi and the Early Madrigal," *Journal of the American Musicological Society* 38 (1985): 227–237; and Daniel Heartz, *Pierre Attaingnant, Royal Printer of Music* (Berkeley and Los Angeles: University of California Press, 1969).

[14]See Heartz, *Pierre Attaingnant,* 210ff. The pattern changed somewhat after that, especially once Attaingnant acquired additional chansons (or so it seems) by Claudin de Sermisy, who was royal court composer and the most prolific and prestigious source of Attaingnant's chansons (cf. Heartz catalogue nos. 9 and 14). However, Attaingnant's shop never showed a *sustained* return to the overall level of attribution found in the first book.

[15]See Paul F. Grendler, *Critics of the Italian World, 1530–1560: Anton Francesco Doni, Nicolò Franco, & Ortensio Landi* (Madison: University of Wisconsin Press, 1969); idem, "Form and Function in Italian Renaissance Popular Books," *Renaissance Quarterly* 46 (1993): 451–485; and Brian Richardson, *Print Culture in Renaissance Italy: The Editor and the Vernacular Text, 1470–1600* (Cambridge: Cambridge University Press, 1994).

[16]Gardane was known as a musician in southern France before arriving in Italy. A Mass of his was published in Lyon in 1532. Scotto published many of his own madrigals (a number of them so-called parodies of earlier settings), including the single-authored *Madrigali a quattro voci* of 1542, which includes a few black-note madrigals and madrigals *a voci pari*.

[17]Bonagiunta was a singer at St. Mark's who composed both madrigals and *canzoni villanesche alla napolitana*. Giulio Ongaro has clarified the way in which Bonagiunta not only edited and proofread music, but generally provided new music as well and evidently put up some money in the capacity of underwriter in order to have it printed (Giulio M. Ongaro, "Venetian Printed Anthologies of Music in the 1560s and the Role of the Editor," in *The Dissemination of Music: Studies in the History of Music Publishing,* ed. Hans Lenneberg (Lausanne: Gordon and Breach, 1994), 47–57. Bonagiunta worked mostly with Scotto as printer and with another bookman as publisher; Bernstein has identified at least three publishers with whom Bonagiunta had these kinds of complex arrangements (*Music Printing in Renaissance Venice,* Chap. 6). The possibility cannot be excluded that he was a house editor as well as working independently as an entrepreneur in editing and music printing (see Bernstein, *Music Printing in Renaissance Venice,* 143, and Ongaro, "Venetian Printed Anthologies of Music in the 1560s," 54). Whatever the case, however, he clearly was much more than a house editor during his fertile years from 1565 through 1568 when he published numerous prints of music through cooperative arrangements with printers.

[18]Scotto had enormous success with the volume as well as with a volume of his own duos and (somewhat less so) another volume of his own trios. See Bernstein and Haar, eds., *Ihan Gero, Il primo libro de' madrigali italiani et canzoni francese a due voci,* Masters and Monuments of the Renaissance no. 1 (New York: Broude Brothers, 1980), xvii–xxi and passim, and Bernstein, *Music Printing in Renaissance Venice.* The only real position Gero is known to have held was as composer for the establishment of Pietro Antonio Sanseverino, prince of Bisignano. Bernstein and Haar note that Gero was maestro of the establishment during some period before 1555 (whether in residence or not) and add that he also "could have" supported himself as a "staff composer" (xviii–xix). It seems possible that Gero's work for music printers had a longer life than his residence as "maestro" of the prince's chapel, as a number of prints from 1540 onwards signal his collaboration with printers. These include, in addition to the duos, the numerous three-voice madrigals that Gardane appended to his pseudo-Festa edition (RISM 1541[13]; see n. 57 below), the nine pieces by him that fill out Gardane's *Madrigali a tre voci de diversi eccellentissimi autori* (RISM 1551[10]), and the fourteen that fill out his *Secondo libro de li madrigali . . . a misura di breve . . . a quattro voci* (1543[18]). It should be noted that the biographical evidence adduced by Remo Giazotto (and cited in Bernstein and Haar, xx–xxi)

cannot be substantiated and must therefore be bracketed pending further corroboration.

[19]See Jane A. Bernstein, "The Burning Salamander: Assigning a Printer to Some Sixteenth-Century Music Prints," *Music Library Association Notes* 42 (1985–1986): 483–501," and idem, *Printing in Renaissance Venice,* 111ff.

[20]For a comprehensive study and critical edition see Don Harrán, ed., *The Anthologies of Black-Note Madrigals,* 5 vols, Corpus mensurabilis musicae no. 73 (Neuhausen-Stuttgart: American Institute of Musicology, 1978).

[21]See James Haar, "The *Note nere* Madrigal," *Journal of the American Musicological Society* 18 (1965): 22–41; Don Harrán, "Rore and the *Madrigale Cromatico,*" *Music Review* 34 (1973): 66–81; and Harrán, ed., *The Anthologies of Black-Note Madrigals.*

[22]On this process see Lewis, "Antonio Gardane's Early Connections with the Willaert Circle," in *Music in Medieval and Early Modern Europe: Patronage, Sources, and Texts,* ed. Iain Fenlon (Cambridge: Cambridge University Press, 1981), 209–226.

[23]Of course we cannot discount the possibility that, unlike in the cases of Petrucci's frottole or Attaingnant's chansons, Gardane and Scotto were working a market that was increasingly disinclined toward unattributed pieces.

[24]This formed a part of lectures given at the University of Chicago in the spring of 1993 by Harold S. Powers under the title "Do Tune Types Travel with their Titles? Excursions in Melodic Geography."

[25]See especially the *Secondo libro,* with three madrigals of 49, 53, and 59 semibreves, respectively (nos. 8, 14, and 20), and note Harrán's remarks on pp. ix–x, which mention (without further comment) that the group of short madrigals is all anonymous. No. 8 may be the work of Paolo Aretino and no. 20 of Francesco Layolle. See also nos. 26 and 29 in Scotto's *Libro terzo* and no. 26 in Gardane's *Vero terzo libro.* Gero's contributions to the last of these tend to be tiny, too, and it seems reasonable to connect the nature of Gero's production to the kind of high-volume vernacular print that was quickly put together for quasi-popular markets.

[26]The great majority of pieces were typeset in such a way as to take up one page. Each page generally began with a new piece, headed by its initial. Given the even-paced declamatory style that prevailed between 1530 and 1560, typesetters could more or less predict that *ottava* stanzas, octaves and sestets of sonnets (respectively), poetic madrigals, and sestina stanzas would each take up a single page. The problem was what to do with remaining space when this did not happen, as with longer poetic madrigals, *ballate,* and canzone stanzas.

[27]The piece is the anonymously printed *Aprimi, amor, le labbia* (poet also anonymous), from *Di Cipriano il secondo libro dei madregali a cinque voci in-*

sieme alcuni di M. Adriano et altri autori a misura comune novamente posti in luce (Venice: Gardane, 1544), p. xxxiiii in all partbooks.

[28]See James Haar, "Arie per cantar stanze ariotesche," in *L'Ariosto: la musica, i musicisti,* ed. Maria Antonella Balsano (Florence: Leo S. Olschki, 1981), 31–46; idem, "The '*Madrigale Arioso*': A Mid-Century Development in the Cinquecento Madrigal," *Studi musicali* 12 (1983): 203–219; Howard Mayer Brown, "Verso una definizione dell'armonia nel sedicesimo secolo: sui 'madrigali ariosi' di Antonio Barrè," *Rivista italiana di musicologia* 25 (1990): 18–60; and the editions of Barrè's *Madrigali ariosi* by the late Howard Mayer Brown and John Steele, in preparation. All eighteen of the madrigals in Barrè's *Secondo libro delle muse a* 3 were anonymous.

[29]See Haar, "Arie per cantar stanze ariotesche."

[30]For bibliography on the *aria* phenomenon see Brown, "Verso una definizione," 301 n. 21.

[31]At the broadest level of identification they might be compared in this sense with the dissemination of ancient romances, myths, tragedies, and so on in the Middle Ages, when, as pointed out by Foucault, "anonymity was ignored because . . . age was a sufficient guarantee of . . . authenticity" ("What Is an Author?" 125). Cf. also Roger Chartier's analysis of Foucault's thesis in *The Order of Books: Readers, Authors, and Libraries in Europe between the Fourteenth and Eighteenth Centuries,* trans. Lydia G. Cochrane (Stanford: Stanford University Press, 1994), 31.

[32]This is how I read the request that a Florentine employee of the elitist Strozzi clan wrote from Venice to Lyons when asking to have a text set *a quattro* or—better yet, as he said—*a cinque* (see Agee, "Filippo Strozzi," 236–237 nn. 37–38). Presumably the more elaborate five-voice setting was classier, but perhaps also costlier and surely more time-consuming for the composer. Thus, for its patron it meant a longer wait, as it required more skill and time on the part of the composer. The Venice-based Strozzi employee, writing on 26 April 1539 just when five-voice pieces were gaining favor over four-voice ones, may have been emulating the Florentine fervor for novelty, as well as satisfying the pride that the Strozzi circle in Venice took in their performing skills.

[33]See James Haar, *Italian Poetry and Music in the Renaissance, 1350–1600* (Berkeley and Los Angeles: University of California Press, 1986), Chap. 2; and Giuseppina La Face Bianconi, *Gli strambotti del codice estense* α *.F.9.9.* (Florence: Leo S. Olschki, 1990).

[34]On this phenomenon see especially Haar, "Arie per cantar stanze ariotesche," and idem, "The *Capriccio* of Giachet Berchem: A Study in Modal Organization," *Musica disciplina* (1988): 129–156. A new recording entitled *Jacquet de Berchem: La favola di Orlando* by Ensemble Daedalus, directed by

Roberto Festa (Accent 95112 D), attempts to recreate the spirit of Ariostian epic recitation through alternating sung and spoken stanzas; for the former they use Berchem's three books of madrigal cycles, the *Capricci,* which were published by Gardane in 1561; for the latter they draw on the recitational tradition of the *cuntastorie* and puppeteers of present-day Sicily. As Festa writes in the liner-note booklet, "The *cuntastorie* improvise a text in Sicilian dialect, syncopating the delivery, brightening the words, shaping the phrases, seeking to recreate the rhythm and pathos of the story" (liner notes, [6]). This practice complements the observation of Montaigne, who claimed that everywhere in Italy he met "peasants with a lute in their hands and the pastorales of Ariosto on their lips" (*Journal de Voyage,* ed. Francois Rigolot [Paris: Presses Universitaires de France, 1992], 188: "contadini il liuto in mano, e fin alle pastorelle l'Ariosto in bocca. Questo si vede per tutta l'Italia."). For further allusions from the sixteenth century (by the literary critic Girolamo Ruscelli, Ariosto's biographer G. B. Pigna, the music theorist Gioseffo Zarlino, and the seventeenth-century music critic G. B. Doni) to the orally transmitted practice of reciting Ariosto's stanzas—widespread among commoners as well as the elite—see Haar, *Essays on Italian Poetry and Music,* 94, nn. 64–66, and idem "Ariosto," *The New Grove Dictionary of Music and Musicians,* ed. Stanley Sadie, 20 vols. (London: Macmillan, 1980), 1: 585.

[35]Daniel Javitch, *Proclaiming a Classic: The Canonization of 'Orlando furioso'* (Princeton: Princeton University Press, 1991), 14–20, 31ff.

[36]In this respect it resembled a genre across the seas, the English broadside ballad. Though the vagrant ballad-seller and balladeer traded in print, he relied for interested audiences and hence sales on the presumptions, performing strategies, and knowledge of an audience steeped in oral/aural skills. See Tessa Watt, *Cheap Print and Popular Piety, 1550–1640* (Cambridge and New York: Cambridge University Press, 1991), Chap. 1.

[37]I thus disagree with Franco Piperno's analysis of the anthology (see note 38) as a newly "democratizing" print form (following Dionisotti, *Storia e geografia*) in which nobles, theorists, peripheral composers, etc., all rubbed shoulders as equals (see *Gli "eccellentissimi musici della città di Bologna"*). This insistence on democratization and symmetry minimizes the reality that the entire enterprise of the early- to mid-sixteenth-century anthology was problematically undertaken against and within possibilities for social mobility that could result from increasing one's fame. Those took place against a prevailing background structure of hierarchical class relations in which composers' different positions and reputations were implicated, however ambiguously. Composers were awarded more distinguished positions in some anthologies than others, either through their placement in the book or the way they were signalled on the title page, precisely because contemporaries were mindful of these differences. Such

distinctions often bore no relation to the amount of music they contributed, and we would be hard-pressed to chalk all such distinctions up to quality, or some absolute inherent value in their music. I elaborate upon the example of Rore's *Secondo libro* in *City Culture and the Madrigal at Venice* (Berkeley and Los Angeles: University of California Press, 1995), 297–310, but many other examples could be adduced as well.

[38]Franco Piperno, "Musicisti e mercato editoriale nel '500: le antologie d'ambiente di polifonia profana," *Musica/realta* 15 (1984): 129–151, and idem, *Gli "eccellentissimi musici della città di Bologna" : con uno studio sull'antologia madrigalistica del Cinquecento,* "Historiae Musicae Cultores" Biblioteca no. 39 (Florence: Leo S. Olschki, 1985).

[39]Cf. also Ongaro, "Venetian Printed Anthologies of Music in the 1560s."

[40]For the only two exceptions to this among books of madrigals—both printed by Gardane and both from 1542—see n. 48 below and Piperno, *Gli "eccellentissimi musici della città di Bologna,"* 9 n. 19. Apart from these, there were a few prints from the 1530s and 1540s *not* of madrigal anthologies that included printers' dedications, although they, too, are relatively rare: Scotto's publications of two books of motets by Jacquet of Mantua, a book of Gombert's motets for four voices, and the third of Arcadelt's madrigal books, all from 1539; and Gardane's publication of the *Venticinque canzoni francese* from 1538 (1538[19]). A greater quantity of anthologies issued from the north during the 1530s and 1540s seems to have included printers' dedications: for example, Attaingnant's *Primus liber viginti missarum* of 1532 (RISM 1532[1], dedicated to Francis, Cardinal of Tournon), Susato's *Vingt et six chansons* of 1543 (dedicated to Queen Mary of Hungary), his *Cinquiesme livre* of 1544 (dedicated to Gaspar Duchi Conseillier de la Maieste Imperiale), etc.

[41]A recent trend in print studies of sixteenth-century music has moved away from the view that Gardane and Scotto were predominantly rivals; yet even Bernstein, who adds her erudition to the view that their relationship was largely cooperative, concedes rivalry between them in Gardane's early years in the late 1530s and early 1540s. See in particular her discussion of the Arcadelt four-voice madrigal series, *Music Printing in Renaissance Venice,* 167–170.

[42]For a skillful treatment of this paradox, situated in sixteenth-century France, see Natalie Zemon Davis, "Printing and the People," in *Society and Culture in Early Modern France* (Stanford: Stanford University Press, 1975), 216–220.

[43]Even if it still resembled manuscript compilation.

[44]For a summary of dedication types, their authors and recipients, see Bernstein, *Music Printing in Renaissance Venice,* 144–150 and passim.

[45]On the interrelationship between dedications and the independence of authors see Chartier, *The Order of Books,* Chap. 2, esp. 46–47; and idem, *Forms*

and Meanings: Texts, Performances, and Audiences from Codex to Computer (Princeton: Princeton University Press, 1995), Chap. 2.

[46]See Chartier, *The Order of Books*, 44–47 and first plate. A copy of the print survives in the Newberry Library, Chicago.

[47]I have benefited in this from Valerio Valeri's account of exchange and bridewealth in *Blood and Money: Being and Giving among the Huaulu of the Moluccas* (typescript in preparation for posthumous publication), which offers a reassessment of anthropological theories concerning relationships between gifts and commodities and the types of economies which embed them.

[48]Two of Gardane's anthologies of madrigals from 1542 affix dedications. One of those, the *Primo libro d'i madrigali di diversi eccelentissimi autori a cinque voci* (RISM 1542[16]), was dedicated to an eight-year-old Bolognese boy named Carlo Saraceno (see the dedication in Lewis, *Antonio Gardano, 348*); the other, the *Primo libro d'i madrigali de diversi eccellentissimi autori a misura di breve* (RISM 1542[17]), was dedicated to his father Ambrosio Saraceno (Lewis, *Antonio Gardano, 352*). The father was evidently a middle-class music-lover who helped subsidize the publications (as Gardane said of the latter book, "senza lei non havria possuto illuminarla"), in exchange for which Gardane publicized the virtues of father and son.

[49]Respectively, *Orlandi Lassi . . . quinque et sex vocibus . . . sacrae cantiones* (RISM L 786), and *Le vive fiamme de' vaghi et dilettevoli madrigali dell'eccell. Musico Cipriano Rore, a quattro et cinque voci* (RISM 1565[18]).

[50]"Venetian Printed Anthologies of Music in the 1560s," esp. 55–56.

[51]A good example of the process whereby the printer functioned as "master-author" is that of Antonio Zantani's anthology *La eletta di tutta la musica intitolata corona di diversi,* printed in 1558 and issued only in 1569 (on which see Feldman, *City Culture,* 63–81, and Bernstein, *Music Printing in Renaissance Venice,* 187–196).

[52]See Ongaro, "Venetian Printed Anthologies of Music in the 1560s," 59 n. 9.

[53]See Piperno, *Gli "eccellentissimi musici della città di Bologna,"* 7, with the example of Constanzo Festa: *Il vero libro di madrigali a tre voci di Constantio Festa novamente raccolti et con una nova gionta di madrigali di Jacomo Fogliano, & de altri autori nuovamente stampati, & corretti* (Venice, 1547). Before that time, the same volume could even be marketed in one printing as a monograph and in another as an anthology. An example is Scotto's publication *Le dotte et eccellente compositioni de i madrigali a cinque voci . . . da diversi perfettissimi musici fatte. Novamente raccolte, & con ogni diligentia stampate. Auttori. Di Adriano Vuillaert, & di Leonardo Barri suo discipulo. Di Verdelotto. Di Constantio Festa. Di Archadelt. Di Corteggia. Di Iachet Berchem. De Ivo, & di Nolet . . .* (RISM 1540[18]), which listed nine composers on its title page. It was

reprinted a year later by Gardane as *Le dotte, et eccellente compositioni de i madrigali di Verdelot, a cinque voci, & da diversi perfettissimi musici fatte. Novamente ristampate, & con ogni diligentia correte . . .* (RISM 1541[17]) (cf. Lewis, *Antonio Gardano,* 301–302, and Bernstein, *Music Printing in Renaissance Venice,* 162). Such instances highlight how unstable the book's status was in the sixteenth century—a topic I cannot delve into here but which is beautifully dealt with by Nancy J. Vickers, "The Unauthored 1539 Volume in Which Is Printed the *Hecatomphile, The Flowers of French Poetry,* and *Other Soothing Things,*" in *Subject and Object in Renaissance Culture,* 166–188, who treats a literary/visual case from Paris during the same period.

[54]There were some prints over the course of the century—few and far between—that devoted their contents to canonizing a single poet: Bernardo Pisano's settings of canzoni by Petrarch (1520); Giaches da Ponte's book setting fifty stanze by Bembo (1545); Salvadore di Cataldo's book setting all forty-six opening stanzas from Ariosto's *Orlando furioso* (1559); Berchem's so-called *Capricci,* all of it setting stanzas from the *Orlando furioso* (1561) (cf. n. 34 above); Lambertin's book setting Bernardo Tasso (1565); and Nicolao Dorati's *Stanze della signora Vittoria Colonna* (1570). One print named every poet included in it, Giovantommaso Cimello's *Libro primo di Canti a quattro voci sopra madriali & altri Rime con li nomi delli authori volgari* of 1548 (see Haar, *Italian Poetry and Music,* 131), but it appears to be unique in this.

[55]On the printing history, see Bernstein, *Music Printing in Renaissance Venice,* 162, and catalogue entries 28 and 46 (pp. 280–282 and 316–318), and Lewis, *Antonio Gardano,* catalogue entry 58 (pp. 435–440). While dividing the contents of Scotto's 1544 reprint of Rore's first book, the *Madrigali a 5,* into two books, called *primo* and *secondo,* Gardane also emphasized a distinction between them by contrasting the term "madrigali cromatici" (i.e., black-note madrigals) of the first book with the term "a misura comune" (i.e. in standard notation) for the second.

[56]I elaborate on what follows in *City Culture,* 297–310.

[57]In this respect it resembles other pseudo-monographic prints of the 1540s. A notable example, as Piperno points out (*Gli "eccellentissimi musici della città di Bologna,"* 5), is the so-called first book of Maistre Jhan, printed by Gardane in 1541 under the title *Il primo libro de i madrigali, di Maistre Jhan, maestro di capella, dello eccellentissimo Signor Ercole duca di Ferrara, & de altri eccellentissimi auttori. Novamente posto in luce* (RISM 1541[15]). The book opens with two of Maistre Jhan's madrigals but prints only five of his altogether, whereas it includes seven each by Arcadelt and Constanzo Festa, four by Corteccia (one of which closes the volume), and a smattering of others by Tudual, Matthias, Layolle, Yvo, and Verdelot. Both the title page and dedicatory letter from Gardane to

one Signor Girolamo Bustrone make much of Maistre Jhan's position as head of the Duke's chapel—perhaps an excuse for the book's title, though the book is in reality an anthology all the same. For catalogue information on it, see Lewis, *Antonio Gardano*, 276–279, and Fenlon and Haar, *The Italian Madrigal*, 277–281.

A still more bizarre case is Gardane's edition of Constanzo Festa's so-called *Primo libro a 3*, a reprint dated 1541 for which no original edition has been found: *Di Constantio Festa il primo libro de madrigali a tre voci, con la gionta de quaranta madrigali di Ihan Gero novamente ristampato, & da molti errori emendato. Aggiuntovi similmente trenta canzoni francese di Ianequin* (RISM 1541[13]). As Lewis writes: "only one of the madrigals, *Afflitti spirti miei*, appears to be by Festa. All the rest are attributed in later editions to Jan Gero. The wording of the title is ambiguous, so perhaps Gardane was referring only to Gero's madrigals as being reprinted and corrected; thirty-two of them were printed in the same year by Petreius (1541[2]), but there is no solid evidence at this time as to whose edition appeared first. All the pieces in this collection except *Afflitti spirti miei* and *Ben madonna* were republished in 1543[23]; that edition omits Festa's name from its title and instead claims to contain *Quaranta Madrigali di Ihan Gero insieme trenta Canzoni francese di Clement Ianequin*. The attributions of these thirty chansons to Janequin is doubtful. The majority had been published in the 1530s by Attaingnant and Moderne with ascriptions to a variety of composers—Heurteur, Claudin, Gosse, and Gascogne. Eighteen of the thirty can be found in Attaingnant's *Trente et une chansons musicales . . .* of 1535" (ibid., 321; cf. also Fenlon and Haar, *The Italian Madrigal*, 231–233). Important to note is that of the seventy-two numbers in the print, the only ones given *any* attributions whatsoever are those to Parabosco (with one only) plus the chansons (falsely ascribed) to Janequin. Thus, all a consumer would have seen was a thoroughly ambiguous title page and many unattributed madrigals to which to attach the names given on it of Festa and Gero.

[58]For a complete table see *City Culture*, 299–301.

[59]I have searched the Berkeley database for all of these texts.

[60]Another example is the pseudo-anthology for three voices titled with the names of Festa et al. (= RISM 1541[13]; cf. 16 above), for which *Il Nuovo Vogel* (1: 631–632) lists six poets only, corrected to five by Fenlon and Haar (*The Italian Madrigal*, 232–233 and n. *a*).

[61]Of the total of twenty-five madrigals in the *Musica nova*, nine are for five voices, eight for six voices, and four each for four and seven voices, respectively. See my *City Culture*, 224–259, and the copious secondary literature cited there.

[62]Ibid., 201–202.

[63]Cf. n. 9 above.

[64]In Feldman, *City Culture,* 390–404, I discuss the striking example of Donato's first book of madrigals of 1548. Numerous others exist from the mid-sixteenth-century Venetian context as well.

[65]Greenblatt, *Marvelous Possessions: The Wonder of the New World* (Oxford and New York: Clarendon Press, 1991).

[66]I am much in debt to Nancy J. Vickers for many stimulating conversations on this problem, and to her essay "Vital Signs: Petrarch and Popular Culture," *Romanic Review* 79 (1988): 184–195, which shrewdly demonstrates how forms of mimetic capital assumed by Petrarchan tropes in the first explosion of mass printing during the sixteenth century resonate with the circulation of rock lyrics in our own "age of mechanical reproduction" (cf. Walter Benjamin, "The Work of Art in the Age of Mechanical Reproduction," in *Illuminations,* ed. Hannah Arendt, trans. Harry Zohn [New York: Schocken Books, 1969], 217–251).

[67]Marcy L. North shows how anonymity sprang from similar motives in Elizabethan England; see North, "Authoring Anonymity in Renaissance England," Ph.D. diss, University of Michigan, 1994; and idem, "Ignoto in the Age of Print: The Manipulation of Anonymity in Early Modern England," *Studies in Philology* 91 (1994): 390–416.

[68]On this see my *City Culture,* Chaps. 2 and 4 and pp. 159–160, and the important article by Lorenzo Bianconi and Antonio Vassalli, "Circolazione letteraria e circolazione musicale del madrigale: il caso G. B. Strozzi," in *Il madrigale tra cinque e seicento,* ed. Paolo Fabbri (Bologna: Il Mulino, 1988), 123–138.

[69]The exchange was uncovered by Richard Sherr, who elaborates on it in "The Publications of Guglielmo Gonzaga," *Journal of the American Musicological Society* 31 (1978): 118–125.

[70]Ibid., 123.

[71]Cf. North, "Ignoto in the Age of Print": "The task I have set myself here is to establish the continued usefulness of anonymity and name suppression and to suggest some of the possibilities for the manipulation of these conventions within the printed book trade of the sixteenth and early seventeenth centuries, that is, within the very environment which is said to have made anonymity archaic" (391).

CHAPTER 7

Enterprise and Identity
Black Music, Theater, and Print Culture in Turn-of-the-Century Chicago

THOMAS BAUMAN

At the turn of the twentieth century roughly ninety percent of African Americans still lived in the South. Historians assign the most dramatic change in this distribution to the Great Migration, which began in 1915 in response to the northern demand for industrial labor created by the First World War. This demographic watershed seems all the more important in light of its cultural repercussions—the emergence of early jazz in the North and the flowering of the Harlem Renaissance. But in the two decades preceding the Migration, a steady if less spectacular northward stream of black migrants had already begun to transform the "race question" from a regional to a national issue. Rather than merely adumbrating later developments, however, this earlier influx set in play a racial dynamic that molded a distinctive turn-of-the-century ideology within northern black enclaves.

Although the situation of southern blacks at the time has to be considered one of the sorriest in the nation's history, many African Americans in the urban North clung to the hope that white racism could eventually be overcome or at least attenuated through constructive measures. Historians tend to construe the choice facing those in a position to undertake such measures in terms of the programs espoused at the time by Booker T. Washington and W. E. B. Du Bois. But the question of how the battle was to be joined—through economic self-help or through agitation for political and social equality—misses the deeper, more divisive, and more lasting issue concerning the scope and form that black racial identity was to take in the new century. Washington, whatever his private convictions may have been, maintained in public a pragmatics of deference that evoked a familiar and reassuring cultural image of blacks based in nineteenth-century southern paternalism. The northerner Du Bois, on the other hand, embodied in his famous concept of double consciousness a more complex and combative vision of blackness in modern America as an inassimilable essence with its own historical mission. Du Bois's ideas, along with the blues, black spirituals, and jazz, were tributary to the "New Negro" and later discourses on black subjectivity that aimed to aestheticize a distinctive vernacular subculture. Washington's appropriation of the mask of minstrelsy, on the other hand, complemented an array of black cultural moves undertaken with an eye to clearing a space for advancement within the realities of turn-of-the-century white hegemonic practices.

The implications of both strategies for black self-representation are especially marked in the case of a unique entrepreneurial venture begun on Chicago's South Side in 1904, the Pekin Theater, the nation's first wholly black-owned stage. Rooted in Washingtonian economic separatism, yet catering to an élite, mixed-race spectatorship, the theater had to enact several different roles: as a successful black enterprise it sought to affirm an ideology of racial uplift; as an elegant, well-regulated social institution it both acknowledged and exploited divisions within the black community it served; and as the home of an all-black stock company it provided a potentially counterhegemonic space for expressing racial identity.

This essay explores the difficulties that the task of balancing these three roles entailed, and in particular how the theater enlisted an array of print media in articulating a public image of itself as a locus of enterprise, class dynamics, and racial identity. The media themselves were those already in general use—the program book, the newspaper review, the advertisement, and sheet music. Yet, just as black class structure did not simply mirror white divisions but developed as a distinctive cultural formation, black print culture used the familiar machinery of its white counterpart to set in circulation its own far more ambiguous discourse, one that echoed the unsettled and unsettling racial images and ideologies striating the urban North during the Progressive Era.

In 1905 the New York philanthropic journal *Charities* devoted its October number to the growing problems faced by blacks in the "cities of the North." Implicitly or explicitly, all the contributions stress two features of northern ethnic assimilation—that its economic, political, and social dimensions were inseparable, and that the way assimilation worked for

Washington himself looked with deep misgiving on emigration from his native South to the cities of the North. "Those of you who would help my race," he told an approving, mostly white audience at Chicago's Auditorium in 1903, "use your influence to keep it on the soil. On the soil the negro is found at his best. He is found at his worst when in contact with the temptations of city life."[7] As a social prescription, Washington's southern rural ideal partook of the same nostalgia that suffused the idyllic plantation scenes in contemporary extravaganzas, minstrel shows, and stage productions of *Uncle Tom's Cabin*. Newer forms of black theatrical entertainment, notably the musical comedies and vaudeville sketches that flourished on northern stages in the early 1900s, ironized these romantic images of black docility in an idealized South,[8] projecting them either explicitly or implicitly against the world familiar to their ever more urban and heterogeneous audiences.

For blacks as well as other immigrant groups, this world was disproportionately one of young, unattached working males.[9] Echoing the gentle ethnic humor of journalists like Finley Peter Dunne, George Ade, and Ring Lardner,[10] black comedians and vaudevillians—who either singly or in pairs formed the mainstay of "colored shows"—wreathed an aura of good-natured risibility around the figure of the countrified newcomer trying to cope with the strange and confusing urban environment that northern cities offered him. An especially apt mechanism for this portrayal lay at hand in the modern-day descendants of two celebrated caricatures from the earliest days of blackface minstrelsy, Jim Crow and Zip Coon. The comedy team of Bert Williams and George Walker brought this tradition to its zenith at the turn of the century. Northern audiences entered freely into sympathetic engagement with the slow-witted, luckless southern bumpkin perfected by Williams, ever the victim of the stratagems hatched by Walker as the slick, dandified, streetwise con man.

The cultural reassurance these intraracial interactions provided in a world of rapid ethnic and social reconfiguration offered a comforting counterexample to the contemporaneous racist scare tactics peddled by the novelist Thomas Dixon in *The Leopard's Spots* (1902) and *The Clansman* (1905). In order to discredit the caricatures of black sexual aggression served up not only in this strain of popular fiction but also in the yellow journalism of the day, black performers made virtual taboos of both romantic passion and sexual innuendo in all of their stage representations. Their counterstrategy was to pilot the old stereotypes toward the havens of either unstudied innocence or hyperrefined elegance. When

H. G. Wells attended a vaudeville show in Chicago's Black Belt in 1906, he took these stage images as a direct reflection of the social bearing of African Americans:

> I watched keenly, and I could detect nothing of that trail of base suggestion one would find as a matter of course in a music-hall in such English towns as Brighton and Portsmouth. What one heard of kissing and love-making was quite artless and simple indeed. The Negro, it seemed to me, did this sort of thing with a better grace and a better temper than a Londoner, and shows, I think, a finer self-respect. He thinks more of deportment, he bears himself more elegantly by far than the white at the same social level. The audience reminded me of the sort of gathering one would find in a theatre in Camden Town or Hoxton. There were a number of family groups, the girls brightly dressed, and young couples quite of the London music-hall type. Clothing ran "smart," but not smarter than it would be among fairly prosperous north London Jews. There was no gallery—socially—no collection of orange-eating, interrupting hooligans at all. Nobody seemed cross, nobody seemed present for vicious purposes, and everybody was sober.[11]

Although Wells's discursive elision of performance and audience is racially marked (these are not just performers but black performers, and not just an audience but a black audience), its aim tends in quite a different direction—not only to displace popular prejudices about public gatherings of blacks as loud, vulgar, and intemperate onto their white counterparts in the English music hall, but also to rebuke white America's racial hypocrisy both inside and outside the theater. Just as the minstrel translation of black subjectivity into the lost world of the plantation myth jarred with the lynchings and Jim Crow tactics then escalating in the South, Wells's praise for the black vaudevillians and their audience cast a glaring light on the physical and social segregation with which the North was fashioning its own solution to "the race question."

The rebuke was no doubt lost on white audiences, for whom the combination of artlessness and elegance praised by Wells carried a different and more reassuring message—that acts of self-representation on the black stage were being scripted not by a restive racial consciousness but by an affirmation of traditional typologies that seemed to promise a modicum of social, economic, and political stability amid the disruptive trials of urbanization. As long as this message remained clear, even those far less progressive-minded than Wells could afford to be generous toward black theatrical achievement. "'Artist' is a large word to apply to any worker—a word of honor which, despite its careless use, means much—but it is a word which is merited by Bert Williams," declared the *Chicago Tribune,* a paper notorious for its hostility toward blacks.[12] And the fashionable New York magazine *Theatre* drew a provocative parallel between Williams and the representative of his race most universally admired among white Americans:

> Despite our twentieth-century enlightenment, probably we should never accept seriously a negro tragedian, but those who know what Mr. Williams can do are convinced that in a part combining comedy and pathos this colored thespian would score a great triumph and soon attain as prominent a place on the dramatic stage as Booker Washington has attained in politics.[13]

A comforting comparison, this, and also an apt one, for Williams practiced the same philosophy of social deference and accommodation that Washington preached. When he joined Florenz Ziegfeld's *Follies* in 1910, Williams himself asked for a clause in his contract stipulating that he was at no time to appear on stage with any of the impresario's bevy of white seductresses.[14]

Washington's lifelong mantra that economic advancement was best achieved through resources and institutions separate from those of the white world urged a virtue that already wore the vesture of necessity in America's theaters and vaudeville houses, where a sharply etched color line prevented blacks from either managing or financing the shows in which they appeared. The proscription had less to do with the character of the stage representations involved than with market control, at the time heavily concentrated in the hands of Eastern theatrical owners, managers, and financiers. In 1897 the black comedy team of Billy Johnson and Bob Cole had attempted to buck the system by financing and producing their own show. The musical comedy in question, *A Trip to Coontown,* represented no very marked departure from prevailing norms: its most severe deviation was the omission of a cakewalk. Nonetheless, the syndicate of theatrical managers in New York "passed the word that any performer who signed up with the show would be boycotted for life." And once it had reached the tryout stage, they let it be known that "any house booking *A Trip to Coontown* could not expect any other colored show."[15]

It was, in fact, a black businessman unconnected with eastern theatrical management who discerned that the key to black theatrical empowerment lay in ownership of the means of production. In 1904 Robert T. Motts, a saloon keeper, gambling lord, and political leader on Chicago's South Side, converted his saloon in the middle of the Black Belt into the Pekin Temple of Music, a stylish cabaret offering high-class vaudeville. The business flourished to the point that a year later he took out the cabaret tables and rebuilt the interior with a new stage, theater-style seating, and amenities that put the Pekin on a par with the most elegant downtown houses. This was the theater Wells attended on his visit to Chicago in 1906.

That same year Motts assembled a standing, all-black stock company that began replacing the theater's vaudeville fare with newly composed musical comedies written by a staff of house composers. Although the Pekin Stock Company left Chicago only once for a brief appearance in New York in August 1907, it captured national attention among African Americans. No matter that few of them had ever actually attended one of the troupe's performances, for in their eyes the theater was as much an entrepreneurial victory as an artistic success story, the first real crack in the monolithic wall of white theatrical ownership, management, and control. "I have never felt so proud of being a colored man as Friday afternoon, November 23, 1906," wrote the actor Sherman H. Dudley on his first visit to Motts's theater, "when it was my pleasure to sit in the only recognized Negro theater in the world." And, he added, "Let us hope that in the near future every city will have its Pekin."[16] Dudley's wish was prophetic. By early 1909, there were thirty-three black theaters across the country that bore the name Pekin in honor of Motts's pioneering enterprise.[17]

Motts himself had formulated his agenda with deceptive simplicity—to make his new theater "a playhouse worthy of the name and a credit to the Negro race."[18] Yet almost immediately he found himself caught up in the same crosscurrents that had buffeted Fannie Barrier Williams. With ticket prices higher than those at other South Side houses of entertainment, the Pekin offered itself as a stylish showplace to an élite stratum of Chicago's black community already dubious not only of Motts's own background but also of the Washingtonian strategy of independent self-help on which the theater was founded.[19] The civil rights leader Ida Wells-Barnett played a critical role in legitimating the Pekin as an emacipatory endeavor among Chicago's black aristocracy, some of whom had objected to supporting a theater run by a former gambling lord:

I said that now Mr. Motts was engaged in a venture of a constructive nature, I thought it our duty to forget the past and help him; that if he was willing to invest his money in something uplifting for the race we all ought to help. I described the beautiful little gem of a theater which he had created; told of the stock company of colored actors he had gathered together; of the Negro orchestra composed entirely of our own musicians, and how all employees from the young man in the box office were members of our race, and how proud I was to see a payroll upward of a hundred persons by him.[20]

Some of the groundwork for the community support that the Pekin eventually won had already been laid. During the Gilded Age northern theaters were one of a series of arenas (housing, health care, social clubs, unions, secret societies, and mortuary services were others) that carried out a systematic pattern of de facto racial segregation. In April 1904, a Chicago jury awarded $100 damages each to two African American women who, having bought orchestra seats at the Columbus Theater, had been told either to sit in the balcony or to have their money refunded.[21] As early as 1901 leaders of black society in Chicago, irked by such exclusionary practices, had investigated the possibility of starting "a colored theatre . . . controlled by colored people and catering only to colored patronage."[22] Four years later, the Pekin arose as the fulfillment of this wish. In lobbying in behalf of the theater in 1906, Ida Wells-Barnett admonished Chicago's black leadership that, in addition to supporting its economic agenda, they owed Motts a considerable debt "for giving us a theater in which we could sit anywhere we chose without any restrictions."[23]

And yet to sit where one chose among one's own was not enough. Sensing the abiding assimilative aspirations of his black patrons, Motts did not let his economic policy of hiring only black employees stint his theater's role as an emblem of black participation in the civilized pleasures on which the dominant culture based its social distinctions. Although in its early cabaret days the Pekin had catered to a largely black clientèle, once its role as a haven for the city's black élite was firmly established, Motts began actively soliciting white patronage.[24] On a visit to the Pekin in late 1905, the journalist Dan Riley already noticed "a very liberal sprinkling of white people who have heard of this curious little theater, and who, if the truth were known, come to leer, but who remain to split their sides with laughter and their gloves with honest applause."[25] Soon the sixteen boxes at the front of the balcony were set aside for the white parties who regularly attended the theater. In 1908 Motts opened a second theater, the Columbia, at State and Division on Chicago's North Side, and formed a second all-black company that played there to mostly white audiences. His increasing efforts to cultivate white patronage acknowledged the importance of white culture in conferring status on his enterprise. Even so outspoken and racially conscious a critic as Sylvester Russell admitted as much when, in summarizing the history of the Pekin in 1911, he defined its shining hour as the day when the undisputed empress of Chicago high society, Mrs. Potter Palmer, bought out the theater "in order that her friends might get a fair chance to see an all Negro stock company perform in a colored theater."[26]

Through the revolution it worked on black theatergoing and entrepreneurship, the Pekin amply fulfilled Motts's twin goals of providing "a playhouse worthy of the name and a credit to the Negro race." Far more troubling for modern sensibilities are the racial images projected by the stage representations of its stock company. With only slight modification, they embraced the typologies that black actors and entertainers had been serving up on America's white-controlled stages for decades. The problem did not lie in an absence of serious works by black playwrights dealing with racial themes. Charles S. Sager had fêted black society at Chicago's Institutional Church in 1901 with a production of his uplifting "spectacular melodrama" *Darkness and Dawn.* Its three acts and accompanying tableaux offered a panorama of black progress illustrated by scenes of life under slavery on a Louisiana plantation, followed by a post-emancipation essay in colonization and self-government in Abyssinia, and ending with a session of a social club in contemporary Chicago.[27] In 1905 Motts had hired Sager as stage manager at the Pekin, and when the stock company was formed in 1906 the theater announced that its inaugural show was to be "A Beautiful Spectacular Musical Comedy" by Sager dealing with "The Negro of the 50th Century."[28] But in the event the company opened with a traditional comedy about the misfortunes of a shiftless ne'er-do-well, with both book and lyrics supplied by local white authors.

What was going on? Why would a theater that aimed to be "a credit to the Negro race" traffic in stereotypes that critical hindsight anathematizes as demeaning caricatures of racial inferiority? And how could its black patrons have greeted them night after night, show after show, with gales of laughter? The white theatrical critic Lucie France Pierce, who visited the Pekin in late 1907, interpeted the theater's fare as an instance of in-group humor: "Many a satirical thrust, intolerable from a white man," she noted, "is met with indulgent shrieks when delivered by their own comedians." Pierce reveals the power over white America of Washington's message of independent self-help in assigning a corporate, meliorative purpose to these comedic practices: "It is evident they understand their own weaknesses and limitations, and the satire of their theatre is an evidence of their sincere efforts to rise above them."[29]

By conflating the ideology of uplift with the classic Horatian prescription for theatrical representations (*ridendo corrigere mores*), Pierce located the Pekin on a trajectory that implicitly took her own culture's practices and values as its telos. Yet the trappings associated with the practices of white culture served the Pekin not as a model but as a medium through which status, identity, and community could be rethought and enacted within a multilayered black world. The ability to sit anywhere one chose, for example, carried for black patrons the collateral freedom to decide for themselves whether to reproduce the comportment of white auditors or to invent their own theatergoing practices. Similarly, Motts's blacks-only hiring policy did not merely generate employment for members of his race, it incorporated and dignified the nature of black labor. No position, no matter how lowly, carried racial associations anymore. Deference had been transferred from something implicitly owed by a black person to a white person to a social transaction that could take place within a racially unmarked space—one that effaced racial difference even as it affirmed class divisions within Chicago's black community.

Something of the same logic—and something much deeper than the pat notion of in-group humor—carried over to the theater's stage representations. When the stock company's chief comedian, Harrison Stewart, blackened his face with burnt cork, exaggerated his mouth with white greasepaint, and launched into a series of minstrel grotesqueries on the Pekin's stage, it was no longer a caricature of a black man that he portrayed but a familiar stage type that African Americans suddenly found themselves able to invest with their own social associations and meanings, separate from the racial Other he represented for white audiences at the downtown theaters.

The play of similarity and difference at the Pekin left its mark on the way contemporaneous print media were adapted to the theater's entrepreneurial and expressive needs. To a much greater degree than in white culture, print was a message as much as a medium in turn-of-the-century black culture. The rest of this essay will explore three vehicles in particular whose very use served to legitimate the theater, its mission, and its representations: newspaper criticism, the program book, and sheet music.

Absent from this list, tellingly, is the playbook. Black musical comedy of the day was deeply embedded in the spontaneous world of orality, for which print offered but a feeble channel of communication. It is not that the texts of these shows were insignificant; rather, they were inherently unstable or, better, labile. The "legitimate" stage did exert a certain influence on the company's chief stage director, J. Ed. Green, but his efforts to elevate the Pekin's offerings centered not on texts but on technique, on showing that a black troupe need yield nothing to its white counterpart in skill and professionalism. He showed no interest whatsoever in dramatic productions by black authors with pretensions to literary status as an avenue to this end, but rather appropriated stylish works already established on the white stage, such as C. Haddon Chambers's four-act comedy-drama *Captain Swift* (29 November 1907, with Green himself in the title role), Bronson Howard's *The Young Mrs. Winthrop* (31 January 1908), and a series of English and French farces given (without music) in early 1909.

All but ignoring these efforts, the theater's home-grown fare of traditional black musical comedies relied largely on the inventive and improvisatory. The absolute necessity of being there, of seeing as well as hearing, is conveyed by a rare instance of transcribed dialogue that Mollie Morris, a theatrical critic for the *Daily News,* published in 1908. The play under review, called *Honolulu,* was nothing new. It had been making the rounds since at least 1904, when the traveling troupe known as The Smart Set performed an edition under the title *Southern Enchantment.*[30] At the Pekin, the stock company had presented a shortened version (together with a vaudeville olio) in July 1906. This was later expanded into the full-length musical comedy *Honolulu* in February 1907. In all its various incarnations the story provided in its eccentric protagonist, George Washington Bullion, a vehicle for the leading comedians of the black stage. Harrison Stewart's success in the role was such that *Honolulu* was chosen to open Motts's North Side theater, the Columbia, in February of 1908. In the scene that caught Morris's fancy in this production, Stewart is preparing to fight a duel:

> It is the last act. George has been "resulted" ["insulted"] not once, but twice, and declares his intention to fight. He is seen on the road to the forest. There is a mysterious bulkiness to his person not hitherto noticeable and Cain [a wealthy plantation owner] as his "second" makes

inquiries. A long tan overcoat is buttoned tightly over George's chest and a broad leather belt is strapped about his waist.

"Are you prepared to fight?" Cain asks.

"Sure, I got a gun an' a razor."

Both weapons are confiscated, much to his dismay.

"What's the mattah with you back?" asks Cain, as George turns a bumpy broadside to the audience. The pillow is removed, not, however, without protest from George. "Wha' you do dat for? How you spose I's goin' to fall on de ha'd groun'?"

The investigation continues.

"George, what you got under dat coat?"

"I ain' got nothin' but me under dat coat."

"Sho, let me see what you got. Open dat coat."

"Dis coat don' belong open. It's one o' dem button-up overcoats."

"Go 'long, now, what you got?"

"I can't unfasten it, I tole you. Dat's de last word my tailor say to me. He say, 'Keep dat coat buttoned.'"

The overcoat is finally thrown open only to disclose a bullet protector in the shape of a large-size corset.

George is overpowered with terror when he faces the other duelist. He makes it plain that he would rather fight with almost anything than guns. Neither the minister's benediction nor the visit from the two women in widow's weeds tends to cheer him. Matters are hastily straightened out when Did-He Ketchum [a detective] appears on the scene with the missing heiress and George announces his immediate return to the land of watermelons and sweet 'taters.[31]

Why did Morris decide to reproduce this exchange in such literal detail? In order to convey the sense of the scene she could easily have paraphrased the lines spoken by George and Cain. By transcribing their dialect exactly she may have intended to mark the show's humor as distinctively black, to be framed and relished by her white readership within a tradition of racial paternalism. George's malapropisms ("resulted" for "insulted," and elsewhere "defective" for "detective") signal verbally the same cultural overreaching of the subaltern laid bare by his efforts to wriggle out of the duel in which he has entangled himself. For Morris, George is simply running true to type—and not to a stage type or personality type but to the "regulation down-south colored man, ignorant, trustful, happy-go-lucky." Although a millionaire, George proves to be as inept with money as he is with language and comportment: "It is evident

he doesn't know one denomination from another. Slipping off two or
three bills, he announces 75 cents, two more, $1.25; a few more, $3.98; a
handful more, $100." Here George dispenses the same reassurance that
whites heard in Washington's rhetoric about black independent economic betterment, a reassurance that even in the contemporary climate
of rapid social transformation prevailing boundaries of caste and race
were being maintained.

The differences between black weekly newspapers and the white
dailies of the age has frequently been remarked, particularly the tendency of the former to see almost all issues from a racialized perspective.
Theatrical notices of black performances present an exception to this
rule of thumb. A typical example is offered by the notice printed in *The
Broad Ax,* Chicago's most outspoken black weekly, describing the original production of *Honolulu* at the Pekin in February 1907:

> "Honolulu," the new production at the Pekin Theater which opened
> last Monday night, promises to be one of the most popular and suc-
> cessful of any of the musical comedies staged at this theater. The situa-
> tions are mirth-provoking and are led up to in a natural manner. Every
> line is alive and the music original and tuneful.
>
> Harrison Stewart, the Pekin comedian, follows a long line of prede-
> cessors in the principal role, "George Washington Bullion," and it may
> be said with truth that in many ways his interpretation of this part is far
> superior to anything yet seen in this city.[32]

This told Pekin regulars all they needed to know: another well-con-
structed, well-acted, musically gratifying production. The title role,
thrice familiar by now, needed no special comment. Indeed, the part had
grown so canonic among black companies that what invited notice was
how well Stewart acquitted himself in the succession of its interpreters,
much as one might judge an actor's Falstaff or Figaro today. In other
words, George Washington Bullion was emphatically an established, accepted stage type when acted at the Pekin—not the stereotype drawn
from life that Morris was to describe in her review when Stewart enacted
the same role a year later at the Columbia Theater.

The Pekin aligned itself even more decisively with the social practices of white culture through the elegant program books issued to its patrons. They are all but indistinguishable from those printed for the
downtown houses. The first thing a patron saw on receiving a copy of the
book from the usher was an idealized white female figure on the cover. A

stock feature of all the Pekin program books, this was not the imposition of a white publisher but had been supplied by another black enterprise, The Pony Press, located four blocks north of the Pekin on State Street. Next came the notices to patrons, which signaled clearly the class of clientèle and kind of deportment expected at the theater. Reservations were required for all seats, with mail and telephone orders accepted. Patrons were urged to "report to the management instances of inattention, misdemeanor or incivility on the part of any attache of the theatre as well as any demand for tips," and physicians and others who might be paged during the performance were aked to leave their seat numbers with the box office. The notices also pointed out the availability of a ladies' dressing room, a maid charged with attending to coats, a lost and found, a café, and a public telephone for both local and long-distance calls. Perhaps the clearest indicators of the audience's tastes and pedigree were the advertisements carried in the program book. They included several downtown banks, a photographer, tailors, cafés, cigar makers, and a supplier of high grade furnishing goods who claims "I treat everybody white"—the only reference to color in any of the advertisements.[33]

Motts's original name for his venture—the Pekin Temple of Music—had signaled from the start the domain that was to share equal honors with its stage representations in showcasing black performers. Himself an ardent admirer of black musicians,[34] Motts spared no expense in establishing the theater's all-black band as its centerpiece. During the Pekin's initial period as a cabaret, the group consisted of thirty musicians.[35] In addition to playing in the theater, it gave nightly open-air concerts, which placed it in a clear line of descent from the large bands that accompanied circuses and other itinerant companies of entertainers, parading through town and giving outdoor concerts in order to stir up interest in the evening performance. When in 1905 the Pekin was made over into a vaudeville house, a theater orchestra provided the music: for four-and-a-half hours every night, plus a matinee on Sunday, this group set the brisk pace that filled the little theater to capacity at each performance. A reporter for the *Inter Ocean* who visited the theater in late 1905 sang its praises:

> There is something doing at the Pekin from the time the colored orchestra of ten pieces tunes up for the opening overture until the lights go out at somewhere around 1 o'clock in the morning. And, by the way, this same orchestra, composed entirely of colored men, is a genuine

novelty in itself. The members are equally at home in rag time or grand opera—and it is surprising with what facility they adapt themselves to either of the musical extremes.[36]

From its inception the band's guiding light was young Joe Jordan, a versatile pianist, conductor, arranger, and composer. Jordan, whose real estate dealings were to make him one of the richest blacks in America by 1915, set up an ancillary venture with Motts, the Pekin Publishing Company, almost as soon as the theater was founded. The firm lasted only a few years and remained modest in its scope, but it commands interest not only as one of the first black-owned music publishing houses, but also as a window on the relationship of black popular culture to the medium of print.

The company's first publication was a march that Jordan had written in honor of the cabaret, "Pekin Rag: Intermezzo." Whereas its title indicates the number's affiliations with contemporaneous ragtime music, its brassy repeated-note upbeat beginning (something of a rarity in that repertoire) alludes directly to the world of the marching band (Example 7.1). This ceremonial exordium, when combined with the explicit ragtime syncopations that follow, summons up an aural image of the distinctively African American marching style that Paul Laurence Dunbar celebrated in his dialect poem, "The Colored Band":

> You kin hyeah a fine perfo' mance w' en de white ban' s serenade,
>   An' dey play dey high-toned music mighty sweet,
>   But hit' s Sousa played in rag-time, an' hit' s Rastus on Parade,
>   W' en de colo' ed ban' come ma' chin' down de street.[37]

The house band itself appears prominently in the large photograph of the interior of the Pekin that adorned the cover of Jordan's march (Figure 7.1). The photograph also shows the theater's fashionable black clientèle and, of course, the interior of the theater itself in its cabaret configuration (including the Chinese decorations that presumably inspired its whimsical name). No doubt intended as a handsome souvenir for the parlors of visitors to the new theater, this inaugural print of the new publishing company encapsulated in a single visual image the preeminence of black music and musicians at the Pekin, the thriving business it did as an elegant, black-owned enterprise, and the unquestioned status of its patrons as lords of the house.

Like the theater itself, the sheet music edition of Jordan's "Pekin Rag" projected a double image of racial identity, the one embodied in the

Example 7.1 "Pekin Rag: Intermezzo." Used with permission of the William Ransom Hogan Jazz Archive, Tulane University.

Not too fast

sociabilities of theatergoing as depicted on its cover, the other carried by the ragtime strains on the inside. Opinions about ragtime's origins, aesthetic value, and moral effects varied widely across and within different classes and ethnicities, as well as among musicians and critics.[38] Early on, disapproval inside the ranks of upper-class blacks stemmed both from the genre's unwholesome connections with saloons, honky-tonks, and brothels and from its lowly aesthetic pedigree, far beneath the high cultural forms that defined white gentility. In 1901 the Ohio Federation of Colored Women's Clubs passed a resolution denouncing ragtime for its tendency "to lower the natural taste of colored people for music and deprive the race of one of its most promising tendencies toward culture."[39] By 1908, however, Professor Kelly Miller of Howard University was celebrating ragtime as the first truly urban category of black music.

Figure 7.1 Cover of "Pekin Rag: Intermezzo." Used with permission of the William Ransom Hogan Jazz Archive, Tulane University.

He was also able to discern its importance as a commercial emblem of race progress:

> The Negro's chief musical distinction, up to the rise of rag-time, rested upon rendition, rather than upon composition. For the past few years, however, music sheets by Negro authors have been flying from the press as thick as the traditional autumn leaves. There has scarcely been a musical collection, so the critics tell us, during that interval that has not contained songs by Negro authors. Colored troupes in the rôles of Negro authorship or improvisation have crowded the largest theaters in all parts of the land. Several such troupes have undertaken European tours with marked success. There is a group of Negro composers in New York whose works bear the imprint of the best-known publishing houses. Some of them have accumulated fortunes from their composition and performance.[40]

Miller's mélange of music, theater, and commerce defines black artistic success through institutional channels controlled by the dominant culture—"the largest theaters," "the best-known publishing houses." At the same time, he seems undecided about the relative contributions of composition and performance toward the success accorded blacks in this world. In transplanting black artistry from its marked role in a white-owned world to intraracial soil, the Pekin and its publishing company remained similarly ambivalent.

Following the formation of the new stock company in 1906, the Pekin Publishing Company turned from instrumental music to the most popular songs included in the musical comedies written for the troupe. Given the nature of the plots and characters in their productions, most of these songs carried lyrics in some form of black dialect. (This little-studied category of popular song[41] is not to be confused with the "coon song," a tawdry form of racial caricature that by 1905 had already fallen into disrepute.[42]) To say that the dialect songs published by Motts and Jordan were written "for the Pekin" requires qualification. Like the contemporaneous vaudeville stage, the Pekin represented in most cases a vehicle for popularizing tunes that were conceived first of all with a broad commercial market in mind. A major point of interest, therefore, is not their relevance to plot or character, but their connection with efforts by blacks to penetrate a white-dominated national market as authors, publishers, or in some cases both. Did Motts and Jordan have such a market in view when they formed the Pekin Publishing Company?

At the time the firm was created, entry into the sheet music business was not a particularly expensive proposition, but the ruinous costs of promoting a popular song had already begun to depress the national market. "The actual cost of printing and getting out sheet music is very small," explained *The Music Leader* in 1901, "compared with the cost, either real or assumed, of 'publishing' or distributing it, i.e. 'booming' it."[43] By mid-1906 the trade journal *Presto* was complaining that the ruthless pricing policies of the large "10–cent scores and the department store counters are cutting the life out of the business until the sale of popular music is about ruined."[44]

An alternative to competing in this broad, cut-throat market lay in a substantial and loyal local market. Practically speaking, this is precisely what Washington and his National Negro Business League were urging on black consumers and entrepreneurs. Yet even modest black-owned enterprises such as Howard's Music Store, which had opened its doors four blocks south of the Pekin in 1904 under the management of the attorney C. Eugene Howard, sensed the limitations of such local, race-based commerce. Howard's developed in its own modest way a national sense of scope that later distinguished such emblems of black entrepreneurship in Chicago as the *Defender, Ebony,* and *Jet.* Although the store advertised itself as "A Race Enterprise That is a Credit to Chicago," it refused to limit itself either to cultivating a strictly local market or to promoting the works of black composers alone. "So well has this store become known," reported a black business annual in 1905, "that scarcely a day passes that they do not receive mail orders from all over the country and Canada. The music writers of our race recognize this place as one place where their songs are displayed as well as the other fellow's."[45]

The national market was a much more daunting challenge for the Pekin Publishing Company. Certainly the firm did not lack for first-rate material. During the stock company's first year Motts assembled an impressive team of black composers with national reputations to contribute to the new shows. Jordan and J. Tim Brymn proved the mainstays, and two conservatory-trained musicians had briefer tenures. The temperamental Will Marion Cook came for a few months in late 1906 with his wife, the actress Abbie Mitchell, and H. Lawrence Freeman contributed ensemble music to some of the most ambitious shows of 1907.

All of these composers actively pursued—and achieved—national recognition for their compositions, but the Pekin Publishing Company did not figure in these efforts. Even Jordan placed some of his songs, including those introduced in Pekin productions, with other publishers in both Chicago and New York. During his brief tenure at the Pekin, Will Marion Cook chose to self-publish a Chicago edition of one of his finest creations, "Wid de Moon, Moon, Moon," rather than throw in with Motts and Jordan. The song figured as part of the Pekin production *In Zululand,* which opened on 7 January 1907, but Cook had in all likelihood not written it with this show in mind. The words were the confection of a local black judge, W. H. A. Moore, otherwise unconnected with the production, and in the show this "little romance," as the Chicago *Broad Ax* called it in singling Cook's song out for special praise,[46] was assigned to the U. S. Consul to Zululand—scarcely a personage one would expect to break into a balmy love song in southern dialect.[47] Probably much more decisive in bringing about its interpolation was the fact that it provided a high-class vehicle for the company's skilled baritone J. Francis Mores. The Chicago edition of the song makes no mention of its connections with the Pekin, but instead bruits its association with the popular white vaudeville singer Marie Cahill.

As soon as he returned to New York, Cook took steps to bring this and other numbers connected with the Pekin to national attention. At the Pekin Cook had contributed the words to a delightful number by Jordan, "Sweetie Dear," which the Pekin Publishing Company issued in late 1906.[48] In 1907 Cook acquired the copyright and placed "Sweetie Dear" with a white-owned New York firm, Barron & Thompson. He also made them the sole agents of his self-published Chicago print of "Wid de Moon" and soon after that was able to sell its rights to the prestigious firm of G. Schirmer, who issued a handsome new edition later that year. These two cases, together with the scarcity of the Chicago editions of both "Wid de Moon" and "Sweetie Dear," illustrate the economic constraints placed on black publishing ventures by their lack of ready access to the machinery of national distribution and promotion.

The Pekin Publishing Company does not seem to have lasted beyond 1908, when Jordan left Motts's theater to pursue an independent career. Other black publishing houses issuing sheet music during this period had even shorter lifespans. Another Chicago firm had been founded toward the end of 1903 by J. Berni Barbour, a singer and songwriter, and N. Clark Smith, a respected choral conductor (who subsequently moved to Tuskegee to direct musical activities there). Their brief partnership appears to have been limited to bringing out Barbour's song, "Baby, I'm Learning to Love You," written for the Meredith Sisters, in early 1904.[49] At about the same time the Liberty Music Company opened for business in Pittsburgh. It lasted only long enough to issue a sacred song, "Only a

Dream of the Beautiful City," by W. A. Kelley, a waltz song by Robert A. Lewis, "Jane, Sweet Jane," and some instrumental waltzes.[50]

The year 1904 also saw the founding of the most important black music-publishing venture of the era, the Attucks Music Publishing Company, which opened an office on Broadway in August under the management of the songwriter Shephard N. Edmonds. Its name, which invoked the memory of Crispus Attucks, the slave who had been the first casualty in the Boston Massacre of 1770, reflected the firm's Washingtonian aim of promoting the work of black composers and lyricists among black consumers. Almost at once Edmonds formed a staff comprising some of the best talent in New York: Tom Lemonier, Alex Rogers, Tim Brymn, Williams and Walker, Richard C. McPherson (who wrote lyrics under the pseudonym Cecil Mack), and Jesse A. Shipp. A year later, in mid-1905, the company merged with another fledgling New York house, the Gotham Publishing Company, which had been started by McPherson and Cook.

Much more explicitly than the other institutions already discussed, Gotham-Attucks was ideologically committed not only to black ownership, management, and artistic promotion, but also to directing this agglomeration of racial enterprise and creativity toward a burgeoning market of eastern middle- and upper-class blacks. To this end it instituted as one of its first ventures a circulating library, allowing the works of race composers to be "introduced into the homes of colored people, so they will know who they are."[51] Like the Pekin Publishing Company, Gotham-Attucks could not compete nationally with the leading white houses. As mentioned earlier, Cook chose not to place either "Wid de Moon" or "Sweetie Dear" with the firm when he returned to New York in early 1907, even though he was one of its owners. What seems to have distinguished Gotham-Attucks from the Chicago company was its commitment to instilling a sense of racial identification with black creative accomplishment in a consumership habituated to fashioning its cultural practices and tastes after those of white society.

Although both these firms were intimately connected with the black theater, they took up different niches on the continuum extending from the public presentation of race in the theater to the private cultivation of racial identity inside the homes of the black bourgeoisie. Through their music, texts, and visual images, the sheet music editions published by these two firms both mediated and mirrored the complex and sometimes conflicting needs of these public and private spheres.

Cook's "Wid De Moon, Moon, Moon" stood near one extreme along this continuum. In spite of its early association with the Pekin, in both of its sheet music editions it adopted the demeanor of the domestic art song. One way it did so was by enforcing the kind of textual integrity and stability associated with Cook's own honorific, "masterpiece." The two successive editions of the song are identical in both their musical and poetic texts. Structurally, "Wid de Moon" consists of two verse-chorus pairs (the building block of nearly all popular songs of the day) with identical music. Yet the words appear successively, each supplied with its own musical notation, rather than one stanza beneath its twin. Not only does this lend the song physical spaciousness, it also implies a stronger and more carefully crafted relationship between music and poetry. Further, as was the norm with art songs (but never with popular music), both editions offer the song in different keys to accommodate high and low voices. They also present themselves to the eye through dignified cover designs, one with no graphic images at all (Cook's Chicago print) and the other with an "artistic" nature scene including moon, trees, and birds on the wing (G. Schirmer's edition).

A different story is told by two sheet music editions of "Take Your Time," a number added by Jordan to the 1907 revival of the Pekin's inaugural show, *The Man From 'Bam*. It appears there at the end of the first act of the comedy when Sam Peabody, the title character played by Harrison Stewart, pauses to share with his valet a bit of his philosophy of life:

[Verse 1]
I don't believe in rushing through this world at no time,
I may be somewhat foolish but dat is a rule of mine.
When folks rush up to you and say what dey want you to do,
Just think it over before you speak, it may mean trouble for you.

Although Jordan and Stewart (who supplied the lyrics) may have had this particular production in mind when they wrote it, the song would have fit just as well into a hundred different contexts in as many different shows. And in fact its appearance in *The Man From 'Bam* was not the song's maiden voyage. Five months earlier Ernest Hogan had already introduced "Take Your Time" to Chicago at the Great Northern Theater. Far from concealing this prior association, the sheet music edition issued by the Pekin Publishing Company in 1907 actually used it as a selling point. The cover carries an inset photo not of Stewart but of Hogan, then at the zenith of his fame, with the caption: "Sung by Earnest [*sic*] Hogan in Rufus Rastus Co." The road show *Rufus Rastus* had been traveling around the country since October 1905. It played in Chicago on three separate occasions—at the Great Northern in November 1905, at the Academy in April 1906, and back again for another week at the Great Northern that September, when "Take Your Time" was added to the score. The Pekin edition of the song even includes the additional lyrics that Lester Walton wrote for Hogan's use in *Rufus Rastus*.

"Take Your Time" was popular enough with Pekin audiences that Stewart inserted it into yet a third show, *The Husband,* by Flournoy Miller and Aubrey Lyles, which opened at the Pekin on 22 April 1907. *The Husband* was one of the two shows that the stock company took to New York that August.[52] The song's appearance there at the Harlem Theater led to a second sheet music edition, this one published by Gotham-Attucks. True to its mission, the New York firm presented the song with a number of alterations that reshaped its character and image for domestic consumption. The two covers make the transition from a public to a private sphere immediately apparent.

The Pekin Publishing Company had included on its cover a delightfully unpretentious drawing of a passing scene being enacted on a Chicago street. A playbill in the background advertises *The Man From 'Bam* at the Pekin Theater, while in the foreground one fellow is seen advising another to "Take Your Time," referring no doubt to the latter's interest in the lady passing by (Figure 7.2). The continuity thereby established between stage and street seems to thematize the mediating role of the very sheet music that the drawing graces: the events and images in the song could be as readily imagined in the quotidian life outside on State Street as in Sam Peabody's fictive southern world. The topical references in the lyrics to streetcars, shoveling snow, and even the lightweight boxing champion Joe Gans[53] draw the song even further away from the show's southern setting and closer to the everyday world of Pekin audiences.

The cover of the New York edition, in contrast, transfers the song's sentiments from the theater and street to the sitting room, where they seem to emanate directly from a gentleman enthroned in his easy chair and accoutered with slippers, smoking jacket, cigar, and schnapps (Figure 7.3). No mention is breathed here of any of the three shows or any of the singers with whom the song had been associated in its theatrical career. Far removed from the Chicago edition's pictorial exchange of urban street wisdom, the man of leisure on the New York edition's cover seems to be dispensing advice to no one in particular—advice that will presumably reward whoever heeds it with a life of comfort like the one he him-

Figure 7.2 Cover of "Take Your Time," Pekin Publishing Company. Reproduced from the collection of Thornton Hagert, Cambridge, Md.

self enjoys. Read this way, the New York edition represents a shift from public exchange to private consumption, in which its cover thematizes its role as a commodity destined for the very world it depicts.

The lyrics of the Gotham-Attucks print reinforce what its cover projects. Although they retain Harrison Stewart's two initial verse-chorus pairs, the spelling and scansion are regularized, "whitening" thereby two characteristic features of black dialect songs. Then, in place of Lester Walton's extra verses for Hogan the new edition substitutes a different set of lyrics, which also inch the song closer to the private sphere by invoking such domestic images as a friend who drops by for dinner, furniture for a new flat, the trials of a toothache, and a brother who stutters.[54]

Jordan's music, too, is altered in the Gotham-Attucks edition and in ways that reinforce the new atmosphere created by its visual and textual modifications. The most important changes affect the chorus (see Example 7.2a and 7.2b). Right at the beginning, the Pekin version renders the title lyrics so as to encapsulate the song's central affect with lazy pauses

Figure 7.3 Cover of "Take Your Time," Gotham-Attucks Publishing Company. Reproduced from the collection of Thornton Hagert, Cambridge, Md.

Example 7.2a "Take Your Time," Pekin Publishing Company. Reproduced from the collection of Thornton Hagert, Cambridge, Md.

Example 7.2b "Take Your Time," Gotham-Attcuks Publishing Company.
Reproduced from the collection of Thornton Hagert, Cambridge, Md.

Example 7.2b (*continued*)

between statements of the three-note chromatic motif out of which the first half of the melody is built. This procedure suggests a dialogic—or better, a call-and-response—relationship of singer and orchestra. The program book for the 1907 version of *The Man From 'Bam* specifies the instrumentation of the Pekin Orchestra at the time: two violins, double bass, clarinet, cornet, trombone, piano, and drums. One can almost hear the trombone responding to Stewart's baritone scoops, no doubt in imitation of the famous back-and-forth developed by Bert Williams and the trombone in his signature tune, "Nobody."⁵⁵ In the New York version of Jordan's tune the singer is unable to "take his time," because he is busy singing the orchestra's three-note answers. Gone is the dialogic spirit of both the music and the cover illustration of the Chicago edition, replaced by the repetitive monologuing of the voluble New York protagonist.

Other alterations continue in a similar vein. The most telling of them appear in the last eight-bar strain. Whoever adapted the song for Gotham-Attucks was apparently bothered by the lack of direct resolution of the C-G' tritone in the voice line, and so sacrificed Jordan's unexpected and wonderful low C on "trouble's end" in favor of a more grammatical—and more prosaic—F. This F has been around since the beginning of the chorus, where it provided the point of departure for the chromatic ascent in the first eight bars that the last eight bars will answer. Jordan's low C does not avoid the expected F but rather decides simply to "take its time" getting there—and does so, in fact, to the words "take your time." The New York version palliates these measures with a conventional circle-of-fifths approach and landing on the tonic, complemented by an equally unimaginative melodic itinerary from the dominant F on "trouble's end" to the tonic B♭ in the form of a repetition of the linear chromatic ascent that began the chorus—answered by the piano's descending chromatic thirds, already a cliché, which ooze into the final cadence. For most of the chorus Jordan's vocal line had avoided putting B♭ in a strong position. And when it did appear at "Rush you to" he harmonized it with the diminished triad that supports his striking G♭, yielding to an equally unstable tonic 6-4 chord—yet another adroit dilatory tactic. But the Gotham-Attucks version scotches this judicious 6-4 chord in favor of a humdrum V-I progression that all but insures the inconsequentiality of whatever may follow.

The value judgment embodied in this brief technical analysis of the two printed versions of "Take Your Time," although it appeals to traditional music-aesthetic criteria, rests on a deeper social and historical argument about African-American culture at the beginning of the twentieth century. Beyond the critical pronouncement that the Pekin version is "better" lies a stronger claim, that it is open to a richer set of cultural affiliations and meanings. Its inventiveness and character derive in great degree from its role as a record, or reflection, of what one might actually have seen and heard in a particular theater at a particular time, rather than as an off-the-shelf commodity offered for private consumption. Fittingly, its accompaniment is spare compared with that of the Gotham-Attucks version, for this very lack of finish certifies its credentials as witness to a broader world of social practices.

Yet the Chicago and New York editions of "Take Your Time" have one important feature in common: both reflect a turn-of-the-century entrepreneurial agenda for black print culture that stands clearly apart from the identity politics to which the Harlem Renaissance was to harness print culture two decades later. The issue of racial identity could have scant relevance for these earlier cultural productions, as it presupposes a Du Boisian racial consciousness that rejected as a loathsome stereotype the minstrel mask still worn by songs like "Take Your Time." Instead, the visual, textual, and musical differences between the two sheet music versions of the song suggest that before the Great Migration this mask functioned polysemically, bearing different messages to different strata of a diffracted black urban culture. With the dissolution of that culture's mix of class ideology and enterprise, the distance that separated racial stereotype from racial subjectivity collapsed, and what had regaled a culture of acceptance at the beginning of the century became an object of repugnance at its end.

NOTES

[1]Cited in *The Freeman: A National Illustrated Colored Newspaper* (Indianapolis), 27 September 1897, p. 4.

[2]"Social Bonds in the 'Black Belt' of Chicago," *Charities: A Review of Local and General Philanthropy* 15 (Oct. 1905–Mar. 1906): 40–44 (43).

[3]Ibid., 40.

[4]The attorney Edward E. Wilson painted an unflattering portrait of Chicago's black high society in 1907, emphasizing its tendency to imitate "that mixture of vulgarity, pretentiousness, and vain show that has here among the whites, labeled itself elite." *The Voice of the Negro* 4:7 (July 1907): 306.

[5]For brief biographical information on Williams see Allan H. Spear, *Black Chicago: The Making of a Negro Ghetto, 1890–1920* (Chicago and London: The University of Chicago Press, 1967), 69–70, and *The Story of the Illinois Federation*

of Colored Women's Clubs, 1900–1922, ed. Elizabeth Lindsay Davis (n.p., 1922), 87–88.

[6]*St. Louis Palladium,* 17 Dec. 1904, p. 1.

[7]*Chicago Tribune,* 9 May 1903, p. 4

[8]George M. Fredrickson traces the image of the gentle, loyal, childlike black—one of the cornerstones of what he calls Romantic Racialism—back to the proslavery plantation romances of the 1820s and 1830s in *The Black Image in the White Mind: The Debate on Afro-American Character and Destiny, 1817–1914,* 2nd ed. (Hanover, N.H.: Wesleyan University Press, 1987), 102.

[9]In 1907 the attorney Edward E. Wilson observed: "The colored population of Chicago does not measure its voters at the ratio of one to every four and a half or five persons, because of the large number of young and unmarried men that have come here seeking work and the small number of children. Frequently in a house one finds several men lodgers who run on the railroad, as the phrase goes, while there may be but one woman and no children." "The Chicago Negro in Politics," *The Voice of the Negro* 4: 2 (March, 1907): 99.

[10]See James DeMuth, *Small Town Chicago: The Comic Perspective of Finley Peter Dunne, George Ade, Ring Lardner* (Port Washington, N.Y.: Kennikat Press, 1980).

[11]*The Future in America: A Search after Realities,* "X.—The Tragedy of Color," serialized in *Harper's Weekly* 50 (1906): 1318.

[12]Ibid., 11 Nov. 1907, p. 8. The unsigned article reviews at length and with unstinted praise the production of *Bandanna Land* at the Great Northern Theater.

[13]Augusta De Bubna, "The Negro on the Stage," *Theatre* 3 (1903): 96.

[14]Ann Charters, *Nobody: The Story of Bert Williams* (New York: Da Capo Press, 1983), 115. In return, Ziegfeld promised Williams that he would never have to play in the Deep South, which remained largely hostile to black entertainers of any kind.

[15]Will Foster, "Pioneers of the Stage: Memoirs of William Foster," in *1928 Edition The Official Theatrical World of Colored Artists,* ed. Theophilus Lewis (New York: Theatrical World Publishing Co., 1928), 48. Quoted in Thomas Riis, *Just Before Jazz: Black Musical Theater in New York, 1890–1915* (Washington and London: Smithsonian Institution Press, 1989), 75. The syndicate's concern was well founded. After Cole and Johnson had taken their dauntless company to Canada, a succession of rave reviews finally induced the powerful Klaw and Erlanger booking agency to defy the boycott and bring the show to New York.

[16]*Freeman,* 15 Dec. 1906, p. 6. The occasion was a professional matinee given by Motts to honor two black companies currently playing at downtown theaters, the Smart Set (headed by Dudley) and the *Abyssinia* Company (led by Williams and Walker).

[17]*Freeman,* 13 Feb. 1909, p. 5.

[18]Ibid., 3 Feb. 1906, p. 6. The passage occurs in a letter to the newspaper's editor Elwood Knox, dated 20 January, in which Motts describes a misfortune that had befallen the Pekin earlier that month: "I have recently sustained a thousand dollars damage by fire. A Greek restaurant, close to my place caught fire about three o'clock on the morning of January 10, and the flames, with great maliciousness, leaped out of bounds and attacked the roof of the Pekin auditorium; the fire department did the rest, put me out of business until I can rebuild. It also threw fifty people unexpectedly out of employment."

[19]By far the best description of the Pekin's social role, based largely on oral reports, is given by Dempsey J. Travis, *An Autobiography of Black Jazz* (Chicago: Urban Research Institute, 1983), 12–15.

[20]*Crusade for Justice: The Autobiography of Ida B. Wells,* ed. Alfreda M. Duster (Chicago and London: The University of Chicago Press, 1970), 290.

[21]*Chicago Tribune,* 5 Apr. 1904, p. 3. Ironically, the same day found Booker T. Washington pontificating at Quinn Chapel to a mixed audience, including "many prominent citizens," about the need to "face the fact that ours is a child race."

[22]Plans discussed at the time to create "a colored theatre controlled by colored people and catering only to colored patronage" proved unworkable until Motts resurrected the idea three years later. *Freeman,* 18 May 1901, p. 5.

[23]*Crusade for Justice,* 290.

[24]The first advertisement he ran in a white newspaper appeared in the *Daily News* on 18 October 1904. Among the inducements were "the Pekin Orchestra and male quartet, real plantation songs," a polyscope called *The Great Train Robbery,* and a "symphony concert" (p. 2).

[25]*Inter Ocean,* 5 Nov. 1905, p. 4.

[26]*Freeman,* 15 July 1911, p. 4.

[27]*Chicago Tribune,* 17 Apr. 1901, p. 13.

[28]*Freeman,* 24 Feb. 1906, p. 6.

[29]"The Only Colored Stock Theatre in America," *Theatre* 8 (1908): 28.

[30]In February 1904, the show opened in Louisville. The presence of J. Ed. Green in the cast as Planter Cain signals clearly the conduit through which it found its way to the Pekin when Green arrived there two years later. *Freeman,* 27 Feb. 1904, p. 5.

[31]"Colored People Play," *Daily News,* 24 Feb. 1908, p. 5.

[32]23 Feb. 1907, p. 2. The review is signed "D."

[33]Copies from several shows are now located at both the Newberry Library, Chicago, and Regenstein Library, Special Collections, at the University of Chicago.

[34]As an obituary of Motts in the *Freeman* remarked, "One body of a superior class of men in the show business who were nearest to Mr. Mott's heart were his musicians, and it was better known to others than to the musicians themselves that he idolized them." 15 July 1911, p. 4.

[35]"The members of the organization are clever artists, and the band carries a swell lot of wardrobe." [Warren A. Patrick] "Pat-Chats," *The Billboard* 17: 26 (1 July 1905): 3.

[36]Dan Riley, "A Night at the Pekin," *Chicago Inter Ocean Sunday Magazine*, 5 Nov. 1905, p. 4.

[37]*The Life and Works of Paul Laurence Dunbar*, ed. Leda Keck Wiggins (Naperville, Il.: J. L. Nichols, 1895), 262.

[38]The best scholarly assessment remains Edward A. Berlin's *Ragtime: A Musical and Cultural History* (Berkeley and Los Angeles: University of California Press, 1980).

[39]*Wisconsin Weekly Advocate*, 4 Jan. 1902, p. 4.

[40]*Race Adjustment: Essays on the Negro in America* (New York and Washington: Neale Publishing Company, 1908), 239.

[41]Thomas Riis, *Just Before Jazz*, is one of the few scholars to do more than simply reproduce this music in facsimile. His study of the repertoire of the black musical theater in New York between 1890 and 1915 goes beyond rote musical analysis to include discussions of poetic structures, distinctive traits of individual composers, and the use of quotation (pp. 49–71).

[42]Sensitivity among blacks in the entertainment industry at the time to the public use of "coon" and other offensive epithets in popular songs was clearly on the rise. In 1904, for example, Sylvester Russell had written, "The negro race has no objections to the word 'coon' and no objections to the word 'darkey.' We care nothing for the words black, colored or Negro, but we do object to the word 'nigger.'" *Freeman*, 2 Apr. 1904, p. 5. By late 1905, however, he was reporting with approval on Bob Cole's crusade against the word "coon" and cherishing the hope that the better class of whites would set themselves the task of "teaching the ignorant, degraded classes of white people of this country a few lessons in decency." *Freeman*, 7 Oct. 1905, p. 5.

[43]1: 23 (23 May 1901): 8.

[44]*The Presto*, 21 (31 May 1906): 21.

[45]D. A. Bethea, compiler, *Colored People's Blue-Book and Business Directory of Chicago, Ill. 1905* (Chicago: Celerity Printing Co, [1905]).

[46]12 Jan. 1907, p. 2.

[47]The texts for none of the forty some shows produced at the Pekin between 1906 and 1911 seem to have survived. One must rely on newspaper accounts and program books for information on plots and musical numbers included in the shows.

[48]"Sweetie Dear" provides an especially clear instance of the tenuous connection between the Pekin and the popular songs used in its shows that eventually saw publication. The version issued by the Pekin Publishing Company actually appeared in 1906, well before the song's first recorded use in one of the theater's productions (a revival of the stock company's inaugural show, *The Man from 'Bam,* on 6 February 1907), when it was used as an instrumental entr'acte. Jordan later remarked that he had written the song for Cook's wife, Abbie Mitchell (recorded interview with "Ragtime Bob" Darch, *Golden Reunion in Ragtime,* Stereoddities, Side 2, Band 1).

[49]*Freeman,* 2 Jan. 1904, p. 6.

[50]Ibid., 20 Feb. 1904, p. 5.

[51]Ibid., 29 July 1905, p. 6.

[52]Ironically, on this occasion Lester Walton, who now served as theatrical critic for the *New York Age,* accused Stewart of imitating Hogan in his rendition of "Take Your Time" at the Harlem Theater: "Harrison Stewart . . . should remember that originality wins out nowadays, and he must refrain from either consciously or unconsciously imitating a certain colored comedian, as he was guilty of throughout his entire song, 'Take Your Time,' the other evening." *New York Age,* 22 Aug. 1907, p. 3.

[53]Gans won the championship in a fight with "Battling" Nelson on Labor Day, 1906. The fight was closely followed in Chicago (another black-owned theater that opened shortly after the Pekin, Poney Moore's Palace Theater, carried a direct Western Union wire to the contest, which was held in Nevada), and when Gans was awarded the victory after receiving a blow to the groin in the forty-second round, a riot erupted on Chicago's South Side.

[54]Their aptness is all the more remarkable in that they were supplied by the veteran actor Tom Brown, who at the time was a member of the *Rufus Rastus* Company.

[55]Recorded by Williams on 7 January 1913 in New York on Columbia A. 1289 (mx 38540). A modern transfer is available on Legacy-Art Deco CK 57111. Harrison Stewart was frequently compared to Bert Williams. Mollie Morris does so in a valuable description of Stewart's comedic style in *The Husband:* "He has the art that is Bert Williams' in such a marked degree, he can do almost as much sitting quietly at a table, pretending to read and all the while keeping an eye on his dictatorial wife, as many a comedian would with five times the apparent effort. His telephone conversation, interlarded with laughter, is one of the capital pieces of business which becomes a hit by the simplest means. A catch in the voice, a rolling of the eyes, a broad grin, and the laugh is won." *Daily News,* 2 May 1907, p. 4.

PART III

Music in the Public Sphere

CHAPTER 8

Bénigne de Bacilly and the *Recueil des plus beaux vers, qui ont esté mis en chant* of 1661*

LISA PERELLA

In 1661, the Parisian publisher Charles de Sercy released a book whose format was unique among seventeenth-century French anthologies. The *Recueil des plus beaux vers, qui ont esté mis en chant, Avec le Nom des Autheurs tant des Airs que des Paroles* differed from other poetic collections of the day in anthologizing only song texts, and by including, as the title indicates, the names of the "Authors of the Airs as well as of the Words." Musicologists have long regarded this work as an important bibliographic tool useful in dating and attributing the many anonymous songs contained within printed and manuscript sources of the seventeenth and eighteenth centuries.[1] But if we look at this book in a wider social and political context, we see that its significance is far greater than the status it has been accorded as a reference work. Using the unusual emphasis the *Recueil des plus beaux vers* places on authorship as a starting point, this essay explores the ways in which the book stands apart from previously conceived notions of music publishing in seventeenth-century France. The *Recueil des plus beaux vers* helps us to understand why it is so difficult to date many songs in this period and identify their authors. But more importantly, its publishing context reveals not only the ambivalence many composers felt about print, but also the role it played in altering the commerce of music in the years before Louis XIV founded the academies that marked the beginning of the grand artistic-cultural projects for which he became famous and institutionalized musical practice.

Recent histories of print culture study the physical characteristics of books in order to investigate the manner in which they shape reading and interpretation. Seeking to restore "what writers thought they were doing in writing texts, or printers and booksellers in designing and publishing them, or readers in making sense of them," Donald F. McKenzie envisions a "sociology of texts" that examines not only the material aspects of a book, but also those decisions and practices that determined the book's layout.[2] McKenzie's "sociology" recovers, among other things, the orality of text, editorial intent, and the sociability that the act of reading engenders; thus it dovetails with current scholarship on publishing, reading practices, and literature in early modern France by Henri-Jean Martin, Roger Chartier, and Alain Viala, respectively. Accordingly, this essay extends their approaches to print by discussing the physicality of the *Recueil des plus beaux vers* and by tracing its realization and publication through a number of people (editor, publisher, composers, authors of verse) who brought together in it their complementary, if competing, goals at a moment when the patronage system, advances in engraving techniques, and notions of authorship were all being contested.

The *Recueil des plus beaux vers* was but one of a succession of popular collections of *poésie galante* published after the civil revolts known collectively as the Fronde. Printed in Paris on 18 June 1661, three months after the death of Cardinal Mazarin and the subsequent decision of Louis XIV to govern the realm without the aid of a prime minister, the production of this book coincided with a sweeping redistribution of power initiated by the king himself. The collection was a commercial success: the text could be purchased in many different volumes and editions in the decades following its initial publication, and it spawned many imitations as well.[3] Its title page, frontispiece, *privilège,* dedication, and decoration all offer clues to understanding its contents. The title page (Figure 8.1) employs a standard selling point, announcing a collection of the "most beautiful verse set to music"; for, as Alain Viala explains, "these anthologies offered to the public that which passed for the best of production, either by its novelty or by its well-established reputation."[4] But though printed collections of poetry and, more specifically, words for music were widely available in mid-seventeenth-century France, the publisher's decision to devote a single volume exclusively to lyric poetry was unusual for its time.

Typically, the lyric poetry of a respected writer would appear alongside other genres (plays and *livrets,* as well as sonnets, odes, epigrams, and madrigals) either in a collection of his works alone, or in one containing pieces by many different writers.[5] Lacking the theoretical attention of a group such as Baïf's Academy in the previous century, lyric poetry in itself would not have generated sufficient interest at mid-century to warrant the publication of an entire volume devoted to it.[6] Instead, *recueils* that contained only words for music were most often employed to distribute more "popular" genres of song such as *chansons* and *vaudevilles*.[7] The elegant presentation of this pocket-sized book distinguished it from contemporary collections of such song texts, which tended to be published in larger formats of a cruder design: moreover, these collections usually left the authors of the texts anonymous.[8] Therefore, the inclusion of the "Nom[s] des autheurs" and the reference to them on the title page of the *Recueil des plus beaux vers* were novel and significant.

Despite the volume's apparent emphasis on authorship, however, the "author" of the collection is not indicated. The purchaser probably would have assumed that it was compiled by its publisher, Charles de Sercy. The title page makes no attempt to discourage such an assumption, as it plays on previous expectations—notably, the cachet of the books produced by Sercy and the other printer-publishers of the Palais. At mid-century, the Parisian print industry as a whole was arranged in such a way that printer-publishers who specialized in similar types of material tended to congregate in specific areas of Paris. Clustered around the Palais were those publishers—Charles de Sercy, Toussaint Quinet, his son-in-law Guillaume de Luynes, and Guillaume and Estienne Loyson, among others—who catered primarily to an elite clientele, supplying individuals who were perpetually in search of the "latest," most fashionable items with volumes that would interest them.[9] Charles de Sercy, the publisher of the *Recueil des plus beaux vers,* was a prolific supplier of plays and gardening manuals, and he often remade expensive, large-format books into the pocket-sized editions that his customers preferred. It was, however, as an editor of collections of *poésie galante* that Sercy embarked on what was to become his most profitable venture.[10]

In the seventeenth century, French editors seldom assembled poetic anthologies of this type until Sercy found success with his collections of *Poésies choisies . . .* first published in 1653.[11] He professed that "the beauty of the Verse, and the reputation of the Authors, were doubtless the principal cause of the great vogue that they had."[12] Sercy was explicit about the importance of authorship to his consumers, and he clearly relied upon diversity as well as the renown of his authors as a selling point as he included a lengthy list of their names on the title pages of his books. His reasons for including the works of many different writers in his poetic anthologies are clear from these remarks published in the second of his collections of *Poésies choisies . . .* (1655):

[T]his mixture so pleased that the reputation of a single author could hardly have sold more; and its fortune would be handsome enough if it surpassed that of so good a troupe. Consequently, the most illustrious persons—in rank, and in abundance—could not be angry at me for having forced their modesty, or their reticence, in bringing to light some piece from their youth, or from their secret affairs, [since I] placed them in so pleasant a company. This fortunate success did not surprise me: the currency that these pieces have had in Paris among a few curious persons, from whom I had them, made them arguably the most perfect and the most accomplished that one will see for a long time.[13]

Here, Sercy claims to have assuaged the anxieties of his authors in part by placing their works alongside other writers of repute. This passage is also a reminder that many of these works enjoyed wide distribution in manuscript, and that writers were unwilling to see their works printed in just any venue.

Sercy's mention of the authors' "reticence" was not a conceit, nor was it false modesty on the part of many of the poets to feel uncomfortable about making their writings available to the public. Writers who did not need to rely upon income generated by their works believed that publishing for profit was objectionable. Printing their works and thus claiming authorial status might disrupt their aristocratic status for, as Jonathan Dewald has stated, "writing for the public demeaned anyone of high birth."[14] Rather, these individuals preferred to have their works circulated among their peers, those "curious persons" to whom Sercy refers— literate Parisian elites and professional bourgeois interested in collecting, conversing, and competing through the acquisition of fashionable goods. The distinction between amateur and professional writer was an important one, as the rejection of a career was a mark of prestige among nobles.[15]

Authors relied upon an intermediary to direct the publication—and acceptance—of their works. Indeed, the wariness many nonprofessional writers exhibited about the particular kind of "publicity" that printing accorded them made the role of the editor crucial. Editors were supposed to be what Robert Iliffe has called "trustworthy managers of the transit of private and personal material into the public sphere."[16] Professional writers were concerned with the power these individuals had to establish their reputations and construct public identities for them.[17] But given the very real importance of reputation in seventeenth-century French society, amateurs were equally (if differently) concerned with how their public identities were perceived.

The compiler for the *Recueil des plus beaux vers* was surely confronted with these issues: some hesitancy on the part of many of the writers to see their names in print, and a need to have their public identities as authors treated delicately. Charles de Sercy was clearly quite agile at negotiating this editorial terrain, and the book's arrangement suggests it was an outgrowth of Sercy's fashionable poetry collections—an assumption strengthened by the fact that several pieces from his volumes of *Poésies choisies . . .* appear in the *Recueil des plus beaux vers* as well.[18] However, on closer inspection, we find that it was not Sercy who compiled the *Recueil des plus beaux vers* at all, for the dedicatory letter is signed "B. D. B." As the *privilège* informs us, the same "B. D. B." had been officially granted permission on 10 January 1661 to publish several works:[19]

> Our well-loved Mr. B. D. B. pointed out to us that he composed several Airs that he desires to have engraved, as well as a Treatise on the method of singing, with a Collection of all the most beautiful Verse that has been set to music for the last thirty years, which he wishes to have printed.[20]

The recipient of the *privilège* was a composer authorized to have his musical compositions engraved: more significantly, he was evidently a singer or singing teacher, as there is a reference to a treatise on the art of singing. In this period, there was only one such treatise of note, the *Remarques curieuses sur l'art de bien chanter* (1668).[21] Thus, it can be gleaned from this information that "B. D. B.," the compiler for the *Recueil des plus beaux vers,* was none other than Bénigne de Bacilly (c.1625–1690).[22]

Though biographical information on Bacilly is scarce, scholarly research has shown that he was a composer, pedagogue, and perhaps a priest.[23] But, highly unusual for the important composers and musicians of his time, he does not appear to have held any official position at the court of Louis XIV.[24] Bacilly was a prolific writer of both verse and music for all kinds of songs, and he was also a bookseller ("libraire marchand") who sold his works from his residence, indicated on title pages by the designation "Rue des petits Champs, vis à vis la Croix chez un chandelier."[25] In contrast to the insistence of the *Recueil des plus beaux vers* on establishing and presenting the names of composers and writers, it is difficult to trace Bacilly's activities and identify many of his compositions because of his own ambivalence toward authorship.

Bacilly did not leave a legible signature on many of his works: dedications and title pages have either no indication of his identity or varying, often cryptic, presentation of his initials—sometimes only "D. B." or even a small cursive "B." Most peculiar of all, Bacilly even intentionally misattributed some of his own works to another composer.[26]

Despite the fact that his own authorial signature was often vague or absent, Bacilly's reputation as a composer was already notable at this time and continued to grow in the 1660s. He must have been sufficiently well-known in 1664 when Robert Ballard wrote these remarks at the beginning of a collection entitled *Second livre de chansons pour danser et pour boire. De B. D. B.*:

> I fulfill my promise by continuing to give to the Public the book of *Chansons* by the same Author as last year. If he wished to permit us to place his name on it, the book would doubtless be more highly regarded; but it will be easy to guess what it is, when one reflects upon the paucity of individuals who are capable of publishing so great a number of Airs, and of words, all at the same time and of all kinds, and with such extraordinary ease.[27]

Ballard's words raise questions about anonymity itself as it is understood that the consumer could readily determine who wrote unattributed songs. Indeed, Bacilly claimed sarcastically in the *Remarques curieuses sur l'art de bien chanter* (a work he did sign quite legibly) that the pretensions to anonymity of authors who wrote words for music were just that. Such writers *wanted* their verses to be published, he states, "otherwise they would remain in obscurity which would be contrary to their intention, whatever care they seem to wish to have taken to conceal their Names, . . . they would be most angry if [they were] not known by all the World."[28] If we are to believe Ballard, Bacilly did not want his name on his own *chansons*. Yet Bacilly's statement suggests that it was acceptable to have one's authorship known if it was revealed by an appropriate intermediary in the proper context: in other words, the declaration of authorship had to be couched in the right terms.

In addition to being a *maître du chant* and a composer who had access to and knowledge of the repertory, Bacilly's perspective on the interests and desires of these lyric authors made him the ideal person to compile the *Recueil des plus beaux vers* for Charles de Sercy. Further, his statements are evidence that the open secret of the authorship of songs was not meant to be kept: indeed, the individuals whose names appeared in this anthology wished to make it known that they composed these pieces—not surprising, given the genres of song and names of authors one finds inside its covers.

The 536 pages of the *Recueil des plus beaux vers,* ornamented with decorative borders and woodcuts of flowers, fruits, masks, or stylized designs on every page, contain over 500 pieces. Both the size of the book and the decorations correspond to Sercy's other collections intended for fashion-conscious consumers, as do the works contained in it. Bacilly's editorial procedure, like Sercy's, stresses diversity by including a wide variety of *airs,* villanelles, courantes, sarabandes, gavottes, *récits,* dialogues, and *rondeaux.* Panegyric songs for Louis XIV as well as occasional pieces for the king's father and sister-in-law, Henriette d'Angleterre, appear next to pieces honoring mysterious ladies and gentlemen identified only by their initials. Adding to the breadth of the contents, the collection contains song texts from "the last thirty years," as the *privilège* indicates.

The poets whose texts appear most often in the collection are Jean de Bouillon, followed by Isaac de Benserade, Bacilly himself, and Paul Pellisson; the best-represented composers are Michel Lambert, Sébastien Le Camus, Louis de Mollier, and Antoine Boesset. As in Sercy's collections of *Poésies choisies . . . ,* professional writers and well-known authors—Sarasin, Vion d'Alibray, Quinault, Scarron, Tristan, and Corneille—appear alongside male and female amateurs (often identified only by their initials) both as contributors of verse and of music. Still, it is clear that many of the poets in the *Recueil des plus beaux vers* were less comfortable with their public identities than were the composers as many verses remain unsigned.

The diversity of contents of the *Recueil des plus beaux vers* is apparent from the beginning, and can be seen in an opening of the book (Figure 8.2). For example, these two *airs*—one with music composed by Michel Lambert, the other by Louis de Mollier—reflect the time span of thirty years mentioned in the *privilège:* the earlier piece is Mollier's *air.* The composer Louis de Mollier (c.1615–1688) danced in the *ballets de cour* and was a *musicien de la Chambre* during the regency of Anne of Austria.[29] The celebrated Michel Lambert (c.1610–1696), a singing master and the leading composer of *airs sérieux* in seventeenth-century France, is best remembered today as the father-in-law of Jean-Baptiste Lully. In 1661, Lambert was appointed *maître de la musique de la Chambre du roi.*[30] Though both composers held official positions at court and were professional musicians, a closer examination of the identities of the poets with whom they collaborated illuminates a crucial aspect of French

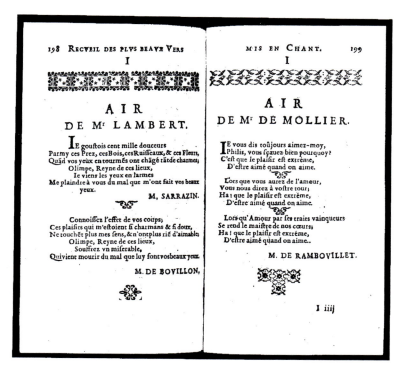

Figure 8.2 "The Name[s] of the Authors of the Airs as well as of the Words," pages 198 and 199 of the *Recueil des plus beaux vers*. By permission of the Houghton Library, Harvard University.

song composition in the period: professional or amateur, they were a part of specific social group, one whose activities centered around the cultural practices of Parisian salons.

From 1630 onward, Catherine de Vivonne, Marquise de Rambouillet, held gatherings at her private residence, the famous Hôtel de Rambouillet.[31] Credited as the leader of a movement to "civilize" manners, comportment, and pronunciation, Madame de Rambouillet gained fame for encouraging all kinds of artistic activity.[32] The weekly gatherings in her salon (usually named after the day of the week on which they regularly met) brought together elites and professional bourgeois who met for conversation, readings of poetry or other selections, and (an activity of which we have less record) musical performance. After the Fronde, the "samedis" held at the residence of Madeleine de Scudéry replaced

Madame de Rambouillet's gatherings as the center of cultural, and especially literary, life in the city. Lambert's *air*—most representative of the type of piece found in the *Recueil des plus beaux vers*—was a creation of Scudéry's *milieu,* as both of its poets frequented her salon. Jean-François Sarasin, a bourgeois poet who advanced into aristocratic circles, wrote *poésie galante* and was notable for his lyric poetry; a second *couplet* for the song was provided by Jean de Bouillon, a poet under the protection of Gaston d'Orléans who was another member of Madame de Rambouillet's circle.

The salons of these two women played a crucial role in the development and dissemination of the repertory contained within the *Recueil des plus beaux vers,* for writing the verses of these songs was an important component of salon sociability. The authors included in Bacilly's anthology reflect the mixing of rank and gender common to the salon where noble and bourgeois, amateur as well as professional, participated in literary activities with the hope of being accepted into polite society. Most of the urban elites and professional bourgeois who promoted this kind of cultural one-upmanship were "mondains." Antoine Furetière defined these "worldly men" in his *Dictionnaire universel* as those "gens de qualité" who maneuvered around the pitfalls of polite society ("le monde poli") with their considerable social skills.[33] Furetière emphasized the importance of reputation to the *mondains* by presenting in his definition of the word "monde" this example: "he is well entered into society, he is placed there . . . in reputation."[34]

For the authors of song texts, the salon was *the* locus for scaling the social ladder and winning patronage. Reputation had its own kind of currency as (in the words of Henri-Jean Martin) "everything depended on the amount of esteem that an author [had] acquired."[35] Salons enabled professional writers ("auteurs de métier") to make contacts and to test the reception of their works by performing public readings.[36] For amateurs, having their names printed in Bacilly's *Recueil des plus beaux vers* identified them as members of this special *milieu,* enhancing their reputations. Thus, by establishing themselves as participants in an activity restricted to their circle, these authors were recognized not as professional writers, but rather as members of a particular group within the ranks of high society.

The arrangement of verse in the *Recueil des plus beaux vers* communicates the social interaction that produced these compositions. Not only does the book reveal that many of these songs were composed collaboratively, but its organization also seems to reflect how they were performed. The book may reproduce the salon activities of reading aloud or singing short pieces—oral practices linked to other activities in the salon, notably conversation and epistolary writing.[37] Creating words for music was a "divertissement" similar to many games ("jeux") in the salon.[38] Writing *couplets* for *airs* (additional verses for pre-existing melodies) was apparently a popular pastime, one often depicted in contemporary fictionalized portrayals.[39] The *salonnières* regarded their writing as an integral part of their social interaction, but one in which authorship was an expression of leisure (versus *métier*).[40] In this way, the *Recueil des plus beaux vers* conforms to one of the models Chartier presents of an anthology which, "when the authors' names are rubricated, construct[s] the book's unity on the basis of the principle of a literary game played within a circle of friends or at a princely court that is a far cry from an individualized work."[41] Though alphabetical, the arrangement of the book still manages, in part, to reflect this configuration, notably in the manner in which some *couplets* are presented as they may have been performed.

Even though it constituted a "divertissement" among friends and "equals," writing verse for music, like all of the games in this society, had very real relevance to personal prospects. Indeed, the composition of these song texts provided a vehicle for social mobility. Individuals frequently used their social triumphs in the salon to ascend in rank.[42] Monsieur Jourdain's failed attempts to pass for noble in Molière's *comédie-ballet* of 1670, *Le bourgeois gentilhomme,* illustrate that using music in this manner was a common strategy. Composing verse for music was part of establishing one's identity—yet another means of constructing an image through apparel, manners, correct pronunciation, conversational ability, and literary facility.[43] In the way in which these activities permitted professional bourgeois to enter into aristocratic circles or win patronage, these songs were used as a means toward advancement, as this conversation from Antoine Furetière's 1666 novel, *Le roman bourgeois,* so explicitly states:

> — Thus you are (said Angélique) of the opinion of those who say that the first step to achieving renown is the madrigal, and the first step to fall therefrom is the *grand poème?*— So it appears to be (added Pancrace).— But how is it that such a little thing could bring renown to people?— You do not mention the best part (added Laurence), which is that they must be set to music to be highly regarded.— Assuredly (interrupted Charroselles); that is why you see all these minor poets

fawn over Lambert, Le Camus, Boisset[44] and the other musicians of repute, who only compose *airs* to the verses of their favorites because
otherwise they would have quite a task.— One cannot deny (said Philalèthe) that this is a good invention to make oneself quite fashionable,
because it is a means to have their verses sung by the most beautiful
mouths at court, and then have them spread around the world.[45]

This fictional exchange in Furetière's novel about his Parisian contemporaries shows how composers wielded power in the salons and how writing verse for music was an activity essential to gaining entry into elite
circles. Bacilly corroborates Furetière's depiction when he states that the
best poets "always give [their texts] to great Composers, and [those] who
are of repute. . . . As a result, there is a very small number of individuals
whose Airs are accepted among high society."[46] Thus, having one's poem
set to music by a renowned composer was one of several ways in which
distinction (in Bourdieu's sense) could be conveyed; for writing lyric
verse separated those who wrote "acceptable" song texts from those who
did not.[47] Much as these activities excluded individuals who were not a
part of the *milieu,* anthologies influenced the dominant tastes of society,
canonized repertories, and permitted elites to create distinction between
themselves and others.[48]

Patrons in the salon reinvigorated the arts, fostering the creation of
new literary genres (such as the novel); they also bestowed a greater cultural weight on printed ephemera. Alain Viala has shown how the *recueils* purchased by the *salonnières* functioned as infrastructures for
publication during the years when a literary field (and a public sphere for
literature) was taking form for the first time in France. Furthermore,
these anthologies extended and at the same time legitimized the literature
contained within their pages while enlarging the public for it.[49] The
printing of Bacilly's *Recueil des plus beaux vers* corresponds to these
tendencies and reveals that there was sufficient interest in sharing these
songs with a public to warrant their publication. But were Bacilly's attempts to capture such ephemeral pieces entirely based on commercial
considerations? What were his motivations for concretizing what were
by their very nature oral practices?

One motive may have been a desire to circumvent the monopoly that
controlled the printing of music in France.[50] During this time, Robert
Ballard (c.1610–1673) was in charge of his family's enterprise, the official "sole printer of the king for music."[51] The principal commodity of
the Ballard family business was printed anthologies of "anonymous"

songs, notably the collections entitled *Livres d'airs de différents au-theurs à deux parties* published from 1658 to 1694, and corresponding collections of *chansons pour danser et pour boire*. Like Sercy, Ballard took care to provide variety in his collections: even collections which advertised a single genre of song would include other kinds of pieces.[52] Although Ballard valued the mixture of authors contained within each collection, he did not find it necessary to identify them. Ballard even chided composers who wanted to publish collections devoted only to their own compositions, claiming that without diversity and novelty, sales would suffer:

> When I printed the Book of Airs by different Authors a few Years ago, I believed I had rendered a considerable service to the Public, which had many times solicited it from me, so that they might save themselves the trouble not only of looking for new Airs and making them accurate, but also of copying them out for themselves and for the others with whom one is obliged to share them. However, I see that many of them are un-grateful, & complain of the fact that I dispense (so they say) pieces too common. Some Authors even complain about seeing their airs among others, maintaining that they ought to print them in a Book on their own, without considering that their Airs are not all of the same strength. The turnover of it would be mediocre, printing in it only those of a single Author, for the reason that, for a whole Book, outdated airs would have to be included. Whereas in a Collection, one places only the Airs of the Year and the most considerable of each Author. Never-theless, I have consented to continue to give to the Public this small work, seeing that if I had stopped producing it (such as I had the inten-tion, to make the clamors of a small number of critics stop) I would have been overwhelmed by the reproaches of a thousand men of honor, who made them daily for my not having started this type of printing earlier, in order to have, in these Collections, the Airs that one goes to a thousand troubles to find, for lack of having the care to send them to press.[53]

Robert Ballard's remarks to his readers inform us that, above all, his edi-torial decisions were dictated by the predilections of his consumers— whether by their desire for new pieces not commonly available, the partiality for gallant themes expressed by his female clientele, or the need of singing teachers to secure songs of a range and difficulty that would suit their students.[54] As a publisher, Ballard concentrated on what would be above all profitable; therefore, the volumes he chose to print had to appeal to a certain purchasing public—the same *mondains* who purchased the books printed by Sercy and the other publishers of the Palais.

Modern scholars frequently lament that the *airs* of seventeenth-century France "may have been the most important vocal music of [their] time only by default, since several generations of Ballards refused to consider any other sort of music and vigorously defended their monopolistic stranglehold on music publishing in France."[55] Yet if we, like Roger Chartier, take into consideration "that publishing strategies depend largely upon the extent and character of the public that constitutes the bookmaker's potential clientele at a given moment in history," we can see that the Ballard catalogue was only supplying the *mondains* with the *airs* (and *recueils*) that interested them.[56] In fact, even when these songs were not printed by Robert Ballard, they enjoyed a wide distribution in Paris, which had the potential to make them quite "common." Robert Ballard's words again remind us that these pieces, like the *poésie galante* found in Sercy's collections, were circulating among friends and acquaintances in manuscript. Therefore, printed works needed to offer to the public what was not available to them otherwise: accuracy, quality, and novelty.

The many "corrected" versions of *airs* that were printed attest to the complications of transmission in this period. Before 1660, copyists ("noteurs") determined how music was distributed in France: the manuscript copies could be purchased at the homes of the copyists themselves. Most often composers would provide or sell music directly to amateur performers, many of whom were their pupils. Scribal publication flourished, but the Ballard family often had a vested interest even in the distribution of these manuscripts. Even though copies were sold both by the composers themselves and the copyists, they could be purchased at the shops in Paris run by the Ballard family as well. Indeed, to assert their position as the leading purveyors of music, the Ballards affixed title pages imprinted with the addresses of their shops to the manuscripts they sold.[57] Thus, the Ballard family's control over the distribution of music was not restricted to printed works, and it extended to manuscripts as well.

But in 1660, the Ballard monopoly faced its first real challenge when copperplate engraving came to music. Engravers were free from *privilège* and composers could have their music engraved (at their own expense) without going through the Ballards; therefore, the engraving of

Michel Lambert's first book of *airs* essentially broke the Ballard monopoly.[58] The new technique was not perfect, however: the engraved plates only produced between 250 to 300 copies before they had to be replaced, and paper was expensive to keep in stock. Because it was necessary to have a publishing run of at least 500 copies to make a book of music financially feasible, it seems that the only practical means of publishing music remained printing rather than engraving.[59] The involvement of a successful printer-publisher with the resources to finance the many stages of the process would have been necessary to any more ambitious undertaking in the realm of music publishing. Thus, it should be noted that the first edition published with the new technique, *Les Airs du Sieur Lambert. Gravez par Richer,* was put into production for none other than Charles de Sercy.

Whether or not Sercy seriously challenged the Ballard monopoly is not clear because Bacilly ended their collaboration. Originally conceived as a three-volume work, the publication of subsequent volumes of the *Recueil des plus beaux vers* was interrupted by a disagreement between the two men, which led to the dissolution of their partnership, recounted by Bacilly in a later volume. The book must have been a profitable venture because, after the parting of ways, Bacilly published a similar anthology under a new title with another publisher.[60] Sercy, meanwhile, began editing his own collections of lyric verse.[61] However, in 1668 Robert Ballard reclaimed whatever ground he may have lost in this area of publishing when he and Bacilly produced the collection's *Seconde & Nouvelle Partie, dans laquelle sont compris les Airs de Versailles.*

Though published later in the decade, Bacilly's comments in his *Remarques curieuses sur l'art de bien chanter* shed light on some of the impulses that may have guided the initial publication of the *Recueil des plus beaux vers.* Even though his treatise primarily involves practical instruction on pronunciation and ornamentation, Bacilly repeatedly invokes marketplace concerns, stressing the consumer culture of music by asserting that "it is still necessary to know how to sing that which is beautiful and good in the commerce of music."[62] His words often reflect the publishing practices of Sercy and Ballard, even though he acknowledges that these printed works rarely received the same attention as those passed from person to person in manuscript:

> And I will say this in passing, that it is better to humble oneself to this point than to pride oneself on singing from [the composer's] Works, which never enter into the commerce of high Society and remain in the

Shop of the Authors where they are unknown except to a few obscure
People who do not have enough credit to give currency to any Works.[63]

His denial of the cult of manuscript *airs* notwithstanding, Bacilly clearly
felt threatened by it, and sought, as his only recourse, to reform the culture of printed vocal music. Acerbically denouncing the manner in which
airs were treated as a commodity by the *mondains,* Bacilly proposed new
channels of publication that would at last provide access to those

> Airs which the Author does not wish to give notated to the Public, ei-
> ther by whim, or [in order] to always have the right to alter them, or to
> have, alone, the advantage over Masters to be able to sing them in all
> their perfection, especially concerning the true meter that he intends to
> be observed there; or not to render them so common, and retain for
> them the title of novelty, which is that which so gratifies our Nation.
>   These sorts of stock Airs are learned only by Tradition, and as as-
> suredly they are much more sought after than others (whether for the
> difficulty of getting them, which is an attraction to the majority of
> Minds who value only things that are difficult to acquire, whether [or
> not] in fact they are more significant in themselves), and because of the
> famous Name of the composer, each takes care to know them and to
> steal them, either from the Author or from those who are allowed to see
> [them] or hear [them]; and it is inappropriate to pride oneself on the
> honor, to not wish to reduce oneself to a beggary of this kind, one
> which can be redressed when one has the right to Trade [*Echange*], and
> when one is able to give in buying [*prenant*], that is to say when one is
> rendered capable of producing Works that can enter in comparison
> with those that one wishes to have from other Composers.[64]

In comparing the dual systems for distributing songs, Bacilly highlights
the rivalry and vying for position that preoccupied composers, as well as
the *mondains,* in the salons and shops of mid-seventeenth-century
Paris.[65] But Bacilly's insistence on providing "the right of exchange"—
to open up competition with other composers in order to reap the financial rewards of consumer interest—is exceptional. His complaints about
how contemporary commercial practice prevented authors from receiving monetary profit from their works are not surprising for a composer
without an official position at court who depended on such income.
Bacilly's perspective on this issue explains his attempts to supplant a
predominantly oral and scribal culture with a more accessible and (he be-

lieved) more equitable one reliant on print. Thus, the desire to open up the commerce of music, make pieces more available, and challenge notions of exclusivity that had traditionally shaped the repertory may have motivated the publication of his verse collections.

Yet the particular format of the 1661 *Recueil des plus beaux vers* was not his idea, and the bitterness Bacilly expressed about the norms of song distribution may have resulted from the circumstances that befell those individuals who stood behind its production. Bacilly dedicated the print to Paul Pellisson-Fontanier, whom he credits with envisioning its structure as a collection:[66]

> Since it is You who inspired the objective of printing this Anthology, permit me to give myself the honor of dedicating it to you. I know that you will find it more voluminous than it ought to be, and that to render it worthy of You, all the bad Verse should have been omitted from it. But since it often happens, and you know it, MONSIEUR, that the most beautiful Poetry is not always the most felicitous, I was compelled to consider instead the currency that the airs that I address to you have had, rather than their proper merit. The number of those who sing being infinite, there is no one who does not have his favorite Chanson; and he would not have approved of this collection if he could not find it there in its rank. There is nothing more true than that beautiful words form the soul of Song and make the most delicate of Poetry; and if those who involve themselves in creating verse knew how to use, as you do, MONSIEUR, elegance, tenderness, and terms sweet to pronounce, the Chansons would have all their charm. But here we must consider the Recueil that I present to you as a parterre composed of all kinds of flowers, in which the small ones set off the great ones. What I included of yours is capable all by itself of diverting that rare Minister by whom you are so especially held in high esteem; and as it is the only purpose for which you proposed to do it, I would consider myself very fortunate, if from the patronage such a Great Man grants to the Muses, it pleased him to give it also to a Musician like myself.[67]

It is clear from this dedication that Pellisson was not Bacilly's patron in the classic sense; rather, he was acting as an intermediary for a more influential patron of the arts, indicated by the reference to a "rare Minister"—Nicolas Fouquet, Louis XIV's finance minister.

As Henri-Jean Martin remarks, "after the Fronde, the great lords of the realm gave up playing the patron and attention focused on the court of the young ruler."[68] But the single most important exception was undoubtedly Fouquet. It was Fouquet who commissioned the often-recognized triumvirate of Charles Le Brun, Louis Le Vau, and André Le Nôtre (in the areas of painting, architecture, and garden design, respectively) to construct his château, Vaux-le-Vicomte—an edifice that would be the model for Louis XIV's Versailles. Fouquet's influence extended beyond this physical space to his identity as a patron of literature and music. Like Mazarin, whom he had hoped to succeed as prime minister, Fouquet was an important arbiter of culture, but he relied upon the management and decisions of Paul Pellisson. By 1661, Pellisson had initiated a variety of literary projects intended to solidify Fouquet's reputation as a patron of the arts, and these efforts form yet another context for the publication of the *Recueil des plus beaux vers*.

Most of the major figures involved in producing *airs* at this time—including Lambert, Pellisson, Pierre Perrin, and Michel de Pure—were habitués of Madeleine de Scudéry's salon and also members of a circle surrounding Fouquet from 1657 to 1661.[69] That the *Recueil des plus beaux vers* was a bid for Fouquet's patronage is confirmed by Pierre Le Doyen's frontispiece (Figure 8.3), which depicts the poet bedecked with a laurel wreath presenting the collection to Apollo and the Muses.

In the distance is the winged horse Pegasus and an allegory of the Hippocrene spring, the source of artistic inspiration, gushing forth. This kind of imagery is most common to musical prints where it notably forms the decorative borders on the title pages of Ballard's collections of *airs de cour* (especially the *airs à quatre parties* in the 1640s and 1650s) and his *Livres d'airs de différents autheurs*.[70] The frontispiece was clearly yet another paean to the finance minister, for those in his circle, notably Jean de La Fontaine, associated Fouquet with this image.[71] But it also suggests that the *Recueil des plus beaux vers* was meant to be a bid for royal patronage as well, as Apollo and the Muses were an integral part of Louis XIV's mythological representation. By this time, as Jean-Pierre Néraudau states, it was "understood that the King *is* the Sun . . . he *is* Apollo, the god of Parnassus, inspirer of the arts."[72] The image of Apollo at the beginning of this book thus established an immediate connection with the monarch.

There are other indications that this collection aspired to Louis XIV's consideration. Pretensions to an "official" document are evident not only in the frontispiece and the long *privilège du roi,* but also the woodcut at the top of the first page (Figure 8.4).

Figure 8.3 Frontispiece by Pierre Le Doyen depicting Apollo and the Muses on Mount Parnassus. By permission of the Houghton Library, Harvard University.

Traditionally, a coat of arms presented in this manner identifies the work that bears it with a particular patron: this mark of royalty resembles—and thus establishes a connection with—the decorative elements of the royal *ordonnances* and the *livrets* of the *ballets de cour*.[73] The inclusion of the *fleurs de lys* of the French monarchy as well as the attributes of kingship (crown, scepter, sword, and *main de justice*) associate it with a project under the aegis of the king's patronage. These features of the book suggest that Pellisson "inspired" this project as part of a larger strategy of cultural production that would eventually enable Fouquet to reach the monarch. But if this, indeed, implied, further down the chain of associates, that Bacilly used the *Recueil des plus beaux vers* to secure royal patronage, he suffered a major turn in his fortunes. For by the time the book was printed, Louis XIV had decided to remove Fouquet from power—a decision reinforced by the king's offense when Fouquet held an all-too-opulent *fête* at Vaux-le-Vicomte in August. Thus, on 5 September 1661, the individuals who stood as intermediaries between Bacilly and his king were imprisoned.

If Bacilly had hoped to receive some sort of royal pension or position by compiling this anthology of lyric verse, it was not to be. As Pellisson and Fouquet were in the Bastille, neither was in any position to aid him: perhaps this explains why Bacilly is one of the rare composers of note in this period who was not in the king's service. For after Fouquet's arrest, Louis XIV immediately became the prime source of patronage.[74] The activities of Pellisson and Fouquet gave way to a patronage system that Jean Chapelain and Jean-Baptiste Colbert created after Fouquet's arrest.[75] Instead of the salon, the artistic activities of the *mondains* and *érudits* now centered upon the Petite académie (also known as the Académie des inscriptions) which, from 1663, sought to institutionalize all the disciplines and bring them into official channels directed toward the glorification of the king. With the new finance minister Colbert as intermediary, a bid for patronage was made by another individual interested in lyric poetry, Pierre Perrin. Perrin's gift—like Bacilly's project, a theoretical treatise and collection of verse—was presented to Colbert just a few years after the publication of Bacilly's *Recueil des plus beaux vers,* and as a result, in 1669 Perrin was awarded the Lettres Patentes to found "Académies d'Opéra" (which would become the Académie royale de Musique).[76]

By the late 1660s, though Bacilly was a successful composer, singing master, and bookseller, he was still not a member of Louis XIV's court. His plans for royal patronage or entry into the Académie did not

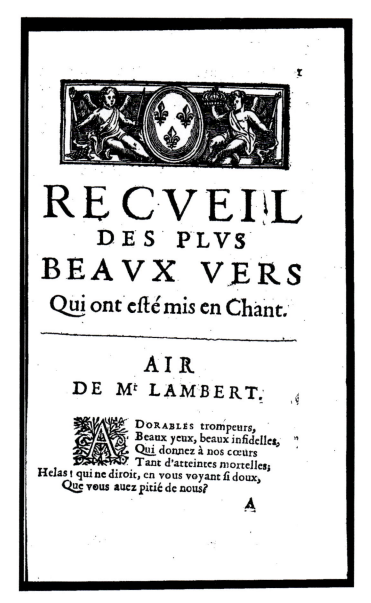

Figure 8.4 Unsigned woodcut on page one with the attributes of kingship and *fleurs de lys*. By permission of the Houghton Library, Harvard University.

come to fruition.[77] But Bacilly continued to publish additional collections of "words for music," stating that

> the principal goal of the Collections of Verse set to Music is to bring back to mind all that which has escaped the memory of those who practice the art of Singing; the Author has but only this consideration: to restore them to completeness, and to see to it that no significant Verse is omitted.[78]

Yet even the language of Bacilly's statement betrays that these anthologies were meant to be more than mnemonic devices. By presenting song texts in a self-proclaimed "definitive" form, selecting pieces he deemed to be "significant," and identifying the authors, Bacilly began to codify ephemeral practices and canonize French vocal music. Consequently, the *Recueil des plus beaux vers* helped transform a repertory that was exclusive and scribally notated into one more accessible and reliant on print: the book's publication brought song into official avenues of royal patronage and was yet another example of the growing number of efforts at arranging and ordering that characterized the first years of Louis XIV's personal reign.

Roger Chartier has written that a "book always aims at installing an order, whether it is the order in which it is deciphered, the order in which it is understood, or the order intended by the authority who commanded or permitted the work."[79] The arrangement of the *Recueil des plus beaux vers*, as we have seen, conforms to all of Chartier's notions of "ordering." Its contents thus invite us to interpret it, as modern scholars have done, as an authoritative guide to the vocal music of seventeenth-century France. More important, however, is how the book records the collaboration of musical production and political power—mediated through print—that defined the French musical canon. In this way, Bénigne de Bacilly's *Recueil des plus beaux vers* of 1661 reveals the union of music, print, and power that would characterize French absolutism more than a decade before the establishment of the Académie royale de Musique and the making of the first French operas.

NOTES

*The idea for this essay was originally formulated in a seminar led by Abby Zanger entitled "The Book and Its Vicissitudes" at Harvard University (Fall 1995). This project is greatly indebted to her work on print culture in seventeenth-century France.

[1]For example, see James R. Anthony, *French Baroque Music from Beau-joyeulx to Rameau,* revised and expanded edition (Portland: Amadeus Press, 1997), 416; Georgie Durosoir, *L'air de cour en France, 1571–1655* (Liège: Mardaga, 1991), 300; Théodore Gérold, *L'art du chant en France au XVIIe siècle* (Strasbourg, 1921; reprint, Geneva: Minkoff, 1971), 110–111.

[2]Donald F. McKenzie, *Bibliography and the Sociology of Texts,* The Panizzi Lectures 1985 (London: The British Library, 1986), 10.

[3]For a complete bibliography and details of the differences between the various editions, see Frédéric Lachèvre, *Bibliographie des recueils collectifs de poésies publiés de 1597 à 1700,* 4 vols. (Paris: Henri Leclerc, 1901–1905), 2: 84–89; 3: 64–73, 75.

[4]Alain Viala, *Naissance de l'écrivain: Sociologie de la littérature à l'âge classique* (Paris: Minuit, 1985), 125: "ces anthologies proposaient au public ce qui passait pour le meilleur de la production, soit par sa nouveauté, soit par sa réputation bien établie." Translations in text are my own.

[5]The mixture of sacred and secular (as well as poetry and prose) was a common practice in this period. The complete title of a posthumous collection of Jean de Bouillon's works illustrates the variety of material it contained: see *Les œuvres de feu Monsieur de Boüillon, contenans l'Histoire de Joconde, le Mary commode, l'Oyseau de passagge* [sic]*, la mort de Daphnis, l'Amour déguisé, portraits, mascarades, airs de cour, et plusieurs autres pièces galantes* (Paris: Claude Barbin, 1663).

[6]See one of the rare discussions of lyric poetry in seventeenth-century France, Alain Génetiot, *Les genres lyriques mondains (1630–1660): Étude des poésies de Voiture, Vion d'Alibray, Sarasin et Scarron* (Geneva: Droz, 1990), 53–56. As Génetiot states, the *chanson* was not, by and large, theorized. On the increasing recognition of lyric poetry in the seventeenth century, see Louis E. Auld, "Text as Pre-Text: French Court Airs and Their Ditties," *Continuum* 5 (1993), 17.

[7]Unlike the *Recueil des plus beaux vers,* such anthologies contained mostly *timbres.* In the 1650s and 1660s, these collections of "popular" songs included the *Nouveau recueil de chansons et airs de cour pour se divertir agreablement* (Paris: Marin Leché, 1656) and the various editions of the *Recueil nouveau des chansons du Savoyard par luy seul chantées dans Paris* (Paris: la vefve Jean Promé, 1665; reprint, Paris: Jules Gay, 1862).

[8]Georgie Durosoir states that the custom of naming the authors of poetry in such collections ceased at the end of the sixteenth century. See Durosoir, *L'air de cour,* 40.

[9]Henri-Jean Martin, *Print, Power, and People in 17th-Century France,* trans. David Gerard (Metuchen, N.J.: The Scarecrow Press, 1993), 231, 442, 487–488.

[10]See Carole Calistri, "La poésie vue par les poètes du premier Recueil Sercy en vers (1653)," in *"Diversité, c'est ma devise" : Studien zur französischen Literatur des 17. Jahrhunderts. Festschrift für Jürgen Grimm zum 60. Geburtstag,* ed. Frank-Rutger Hausmann, Christoph Miething, and Margarete Zimmermann (Paris, Seattle, and Tübingen: Papers on French Seventeenth-Century Literature, 1994), 99–107.

[11]Yoshio Fukui, *Raffinement précieux dans la poésie française du XVIIe siècle* (Paris: Nizet, 1964), 267.

[12]Charles de Sercy, "Le libraire au lecteur," *Poesies choisies de messieurs Corneille. Bensserade. De Scudery. Boisrobert. La Mesnardiere. Sarrasin. Desmarests. Bertaud. DeMontreuil. Cottin. Vignier. Chevreau. Maleville. Vauvert. Petit. Maucroy. Et de plusieurs autres . . .* (Paris: Charles de Sercy, 1655): "La beauté des Vers, & la reputation des Autheurs, ont sans doute esté la principale cause de la grande vogue qu'elles ont eu."

[13]Ibid.: "[C]e meslange a tellement plû, que la reputation d'un seul Autheur ne peut gueres aller plus loin; & que la fortune en seroit assez belle, si elle passoit celle d'une si bonne trouppe. Aussi les plus Illustres personnes, & en condition, & en suffisance, n'ont sçeu sefascher contre moy pour avoir forcé leur modestie, ou leur retenuë, en faisant voir au jour quelque Piece de leur jeunesse, ou de leur intrigue secrete, les ayant mis d'une si bonne compagnie. Cet heureux succez ne m'a point surpris: Le cours que ces Pieces ont eu à Paris parmy quelques personnes curieuses, dont je les ay euës, les font passer avec justice pour des plus parfaites & les plus achevées que l'on ayt veu de long-temps."

[14]Jonathan Dewald, *Aristocratic Experience and the Origins of Modern Culture: France, 1570–1715* (Berkeley and Los Angeles: University of California Press, 1993), 183.

[15]On "amateur" and "professional" writers in seventeenth-century France, see Viala, *Naissance de l'écrivain,* 180–185.

[16]Robert Iliffe, "Author-Mongering: The 'Editor' as Both Producer and Consumer," in *The Consumption of Culture, 1600–1800: Image, Object, Text,* ed. Ann Bermingham and John Brewer (London: Routledge, 1995), 168.

[17]Ibid.

[18]For a complete listing of the contents of this collection, see Lachèvre, *Bibliographie des recueils collectifs,* 2: 86–89.

[19]Whether or not the author had completed these works at this point in time was not an issue. The *privilège,* given upon application after the idea for the book was conceived, functioned as a kind of "informal copyright." See Joan DeJean, *Tender Geographies: Women and the Origins of the Novel in France* (New York: Columbia University Press, 1991), 45.

[20]"Nostre bien amé le Sieur B. D. B. nous a fait remontrer qu'il a composé plusieurs Airs qu'il desire faire graver au Burin; comme aussi un Traitté de la

methode de chanter, avec un Recueil de tous les plus beaux Vers qui ont esté mis en chant depuis trente années, lesquels il desire faire imprimer."

[21]Bénigne de Bacilly, *Remarques curieuses sur l'art de bien chanter, Et particulierement pour ce qui regarde le Chant François. Ouvrage fort utile à ceux qui aspirent à la Méthode de Chanter, sur tout à bien prononcer les Paroles avec toute la finesse & toute la force necessaire; et à bien observer la quantité des Syllabes, & ne point confondre les longues & les brefves, suivant les Regles qui en sont établies dans ce Traité. Par M. B. de Bacilly* (Paris: Rue des petits Champs, Ballard, and C. Blageart, 1668). This treatise has been translated and edited by Austin B. Caswell as *A Commentary on the Art of Proper Singing* (Brooklyn: Institute of Mediaeval Music, 1968). Caswell summarizes the salient features of this treatise and lists its various editions in his *"Remarques curieuses sur l'art de bien chanter," Journal of the American Musicological Society* 20 (1967), 116–120.

[22]The only other French treatise on the subject in this period was Jean Millet's *La belle methode ou l'art de bien chanter* (Lyons: Jean Grégoire, 1666; reprint, New York: Da Capo Press, 1973). However, as Albert Cohen explains in the introduction to the above edition, it is not clear whether or not this treatise ever enjoyed a publishing run and sales. In addition, it was not published in Paris, nor did it ever receive a royal *privilège*. See also Albert Cohen, *"L'art de bien chanter* (1666) of Jean Millet," *Musical Quarterly* 55 (1969), 170–179.

[23]See Henry Prunières, "Un maître de chant au XVIIe siècle: Bénigne de Bacilly," *Revue de Musicologie* 7 [nouvelle série no. 8] (1923), 156–160. An incomplete works list is provided in Austin B. Caswell, "Bacilly [Basilly, Bassilly], Bénigne de," in *The New Grove Dictionary of Music and Musicians,* ed. Stanley Sadie, 20 vols. (London: Macmillan; 1980), 1: 887. It can be supplemented by Elissa Poole, "The Sources for Christophe Ballard's *Brunetes ou petits airs tendres* and the Tradition of Seventeenth-Century French Song," (Ph.D. diss., University of Victoria, 1984), 17 n. 26.

[24]The documents assembled by Marcelle Benoit in *Musiques de cour: Chapelle, Chambre, Écurie, 1661–1733* (Paris: Picard, 1971) do not contain any mention of Bacilly.

[25]See Catherine Massip, "Introduction," *Les Airs de Monsieur Lambert . . .* (Paris: Rue des petits Champs, 1666; reprint, Geneva: Minkoff, 1983), 15. Massip has shown that not only did Bacilly sell his own works from his storefront, but he also sold the compositions of Michel Lambert as well.

[26]Bacilly indicated that his own *airs* were composed by Michel Lambert. See Caswell, *A Commentary,* ix; Prunières, "Un maître de chant," 159.

[27]Robert Ballard, "Au lecteur," *Second Livre de chansons pour danser et pour boire. De B.D.B.* (Paris: Robert Ballard, 1664): "Je m'acquitte de ma promesse, en continüant de donner au Public le livre de Chansons du mesme

Autheur que l'année passée. S'il vouloit permettre que l'on y mist son nom, le livre en seroit sans doute plus consideré; mais il sera aysé de le deviner, quand on voudra faire reflexion sur le peu de gens qui sont capables de mettre au jour un si grand nombre d'Airs, & de Paroles tout à la fois, & de toutes manieres, & avec une facilité si extraordinaire."

[28]Bacilly, *Remarques curieuses sur l'art de bien chanter,* 29: "autrement elles demeureroient dans une obscurité qui seroit contre leur intention, quelque soin qu'ils semblent vouloir prendre pour cacher leurs Noms, . . . ils seroient fort faschez qu'il ne fust pas connu de tout le Monde."

[29]Though few of his other pieces are extant, a collection of his *chansons pour danser* was published by Robert Ballard in 1640. See also Catherine Massip, "Mollier, Louis de," in *Dictionnaire de la musique en France aux XVIIe et au XVIIIe siècles,* ed. Marcelle Benoit (Paris: Fayard, 1992), 471.

[30]See Catherine Massip, "Lambert, Michel," in *Dictionnaire de la musique,* 381–382; James R. Anthony, "Lambert, Michel," in *The New Grove Dictionary,* 10: 397–399.

[31]Bacilly indicates that the text of Mollier's *air* was written by a "M. de Rambouillet." Whether or not he was referring to Charles d'Angennes, the Marquis de Rambouillet, is not entirely clear. Antoine de Rambouillet, sieur de la Sablière, also has been suggested as a possible candidate: see Lachèvre, *Bibliographie des recueils collectifs,* 2: 432. Could this text even have been written by Madame de Rambouillet herself? On the topic of the confusion surrounding the attribution of salon writing and "women's secret publishing," see Erica Harth, "The Salon Woman Goes Public . . . or Does She?" in *Going Public: Women and Publishing in Early Modern France,* ed. Elizabeth C. Goldsmith and Dena Goodman (Ithaca: Cornell University Press, 1995), 181–187.

[32]See DeJean, *Tender Geographies,* 20–22.

[33]Génetiot, *Les genres lyriques mondains,* 17.

[34]Quoted in ibid.: "Il est bien entré dans le monde, il s'y mis . . . en réputation."

[35]Henri-Jean Martin, *The History and Power of Writing,* trans. Lydia G. Cochrane (Chicago: The University of Chicago Press, 1994), 378.

[36]Viala, *Naissance de l'écrivain,* 137.

[37]See Catherine E. Gordon-Seifert, "'La Réplique Galante': Sébastien de Brossard's Airs as Conversation," in *Sébastien de Brossard, musicien,* ed. Jean Duron ([Versailles and Paris]: Éditions du Centre de Musique Baroque de Versailles and Éditions Klincksieck, 1998), 181–201. Gordon-Seifert builds upon Marc Fumaroli's assertion that recited poetry was accompanied by music and proposes that these pieces were sung in dialogue as musical conversations. In a similar vein, another scholar has shown how the art of correspondence extended

to so-called "lettres en chansons" composed on the tune of well-known *airs:* see Renate Kroll, "La Chanson des femmes poètes au XVIIe siècle: Mme de La Suze et Mme Deshoulières—une contribution féminine à la poésie chantée," in *La chanson française et son histoire,* ed. Dietmar Rieger (Tübingen: Gunter Narr Verlag, 1988), 27–45. These two studies show how women contributed importantly to the literary and performance practices of salon society during the second half of the seventeenth century.

[38]See Viala, *Naissance de l'écrivain,* 179.

[39]See, for example, the instances in Michel de Pure's *La prétieuse* and Molière's *Les fâcheux* cited in Gérold, *L'art du chant,* 137. The practice was also a frequent topic of the song texts themselves.

[40]See Roger Chartier, "Leisure and Sociability: Reading Aloud in Early Modern Europe," in *Urban Life in the Renaissance,* ed. Susan Zimmerman and Ronald Weissman (Newark: University of Delaware Press, 1989), 103–120.

[41]Roger Chartier, *The Order of Books: Readers, Authors, and Libraries in Europe between the Fourteenth and Eighteenth Centuries,* trans. Lydia G. Cochrane (Stanford: Stanford University Press, 1994), 56.

[42]See DeJean, *Tender Geographies,* 76. See also Carolyn C. Lougee, *Le paradis des femmes: Women, Salons and Social Stratification in Seventeenth-Century France* (Princeton: Princeton University Press, 1976).

[43]See Domna Stanton, *The Aristocrat as Art: A Study of the* Honnête Homme *and the Dandy in Seventeenth- and Nineteenth-Century French Literature* (New York: Columbia University Press, 1980).

[44]The accomplished theorbist and composer Sébastien Le Camus (c.1610–1677) was named music master to the queen in 1660 and was also viol player of the king's bedchamber. A posthumous collection of his pieces, *Airs à deux et trois parties de feu Monsieur Le Camus, Maistre de la Musique de la Reyne,* was printed by Christophe Ballard in 1678. Anthoine Boesset (1587–1643) was one of the leading composers of *airs de cour* at the time of Louis XIII. Among the many positions he held was that of music master to the queen. Boesset's books of *airs de cour à 4 et 5 parties* and his substantial contribution to French lute song were remembered in France long after Marin Mersenne praised his setting of an *air* in *Harmonie universelle* (1636).

[45]Antoine Furetière, *Le roman bourgeois* (Paris: Gallimard, 1981), 108–109: "— Vous êtes donc (dit Angélique) de l'opinion de ceux qui disent que le premier pas pour aller à la gloire est la madrigal, et le premier pas pour en déchoir est le grand poème?— Il y a grande apparence (ajouta Pancrace).— Mais comment est-ce que si peu de chose pourrait mettre les gens en réputation?— Vous ne dites pas le meilleur (ajouta Laurence), c'est qu'il faut qu'ils soient mis en musique pour être bien estimés.— Assurément (interrompit Charroselles);

c'est pour cela que vous voyez tous ces petits poètes caresser Lambert, Le Camus, Boisset et les autres musiciens de réputation, et qui ne mettent jamais en air que les vers de leurs favoris; car autrement il auraient fort à faire.— On ne peut nier (dit Philalèthe) que cette invention ne soit bonne pour se mettre fort en vogue: car c'est un moyen pour faire chanter leurs vers par les plus belles bouches de la cour, et leur faire ensuite courir le monde."

[46]Bacilly, *Remarques curieuses sur l'art de bien chanter*, 69–70: "les donnent toûjours aux grands Compositeurs, & qui sont en reputation . . . Ainsi il n'y en a que fort peu dont les Airs soient receus parmy le Monde."

[47]Dewald, *Aristocratic Experience*, 175.

[48]Viala, *Naissance de l'ecrivain*, 133.

[49]See ibid., 128–129.

[50]Suggested in Poole, "The Sources for Christophe Ballard's *Brunetes*," 28. Bacilly's *privilège* did not conflict with the Ballard monopoly on printed music. However, Poole's argument—based on the idea that all verse anthologies were free from the necessity of obtaining a *privilège*—is weakened by the fact that the *Recueil des plus beaux vers* was indeed published with a royal *privilège*.

[51]The original *privilège* given to Adrian Le Roy and Robert Ballard (I) in 1551 had been renewed by each successive monarch. The official status of "imprimeur du roi" came into being under the regency and was strengthened during the reign of Louis XIII. For a summary of the family's activities, see Anik Devriès, "Ballard (les)," in *Dictionnaire de la musique*, 41–43.

[52]For instance, other categories of pieces were frequently published alongside the *brunetes*. See Poole, "The Sources for Christophe Ballard's *Brunetes*," 14.

[53]*XII. Livre d'airs de différents autheurs à deux parties* (Paris: Robert Ballard, 1669): "Lorsque j'ay imprimé le Livre des Airs de differents Autheurs depuis quelques Années, j'ay crû rendre un service considerable au Public, qui m'en a plusieurs fois sollicité, pour s'exempter de la peine; non seulement de chercher les Airs nouveaux; & les avoir corrects: mais aussi de les copier pour soy, & pour les autres auxquels on est obligée d'en faire part. Cependant je voy que plusieurs en sont méconnoissans, & murmurent de ce que je rends (disent-ils) les choses trop comunes. Quelques Autheurs mesme se plaignent de voir leurs Airs parmy d'autres, pretendans les faire imprimer dans un Livre à part, sans considerer que leurs Airs n'estant pas tous de mesme force, le debit en seroit mediocre, n'en imprimant que d'un seul Autheur, par la raison, que pour un Livre entier il en faudroit metre de surannez, au lieu que dans un Recuëil on ne met que des Airs de l'Année, & les plus considerables de chaque Autheur. J'ay cependant bien voulu continüer de donner au Public ce petit ouvrage, voyant que si javois cessé de le faire (comme j'en avois le dessein, pour faire cesser les clameurs d'un petit nombre de critiques) j'aurois esté accablé des reproches de

milles gens d'honneur, qui m'en font déja assez tous les jours de navoit pas com-
mencé plustost cette sorte d'impression, afin d'avoir dans des Recuëils les Airs
qu'on a mille peines à trouver, faute d'avoir en le soin de les mettre sous la
presse."

[54]See, for example, Robert Ballard, "Au lecteur," *XXII. Livre de Chansons
pour danser et pour boire. B. D. B.* (Paris: Robert Ballard, 1663).

[55]Auld, "Text as Pre-Text," 18.

[56]Roger Chartier, *The Cultural Uses of Print in Early Modern France,* trans.
Lydia G. Cochrane (Princeton: Princeton University Press, 1987), 145.

[57]Anik Devriès, *Édition et commerce de la musique gravée à Paris dans la
première moitié du XVIIIe siècle: Les Boivin, Les Leclerc* (Geneva: Minkoff,
1976), 3.

[58]Catherine Massip discusses the importance of the new engraving technique and the way in which it effectively broke the Ballard monopoly in her introduction to Michel Lambert, *Les Airs . . . ,* 13–14.

[59]These remarks rely upon Anik Devriès's excellent discussion of music
publishing, "Le commerce de la musique dans le dernier tiers du XVIIème siècle," in her *Édition et commerce,* 1–10.

[60]*Nouveau recueil des plus beaux Airs de Cour contenant plusieurs Gavottes,
Bourrées, Gigues, Vilanelles, Courantes, Sarabandes, Menüets, Entrées de Ballet,
& autres Chansons nouvelles du temps, De differens Autheurs* (Paris: Estienne
Loyson, 1666).

[61]Among them were *Airs et vaudevilles de cour dediez a Son Altesse Royale
Mademoiselle* (1665) and a second volume, *Vaudevilles de cour dediez a
Madame,* published the following year. Although these collections are clearly
modeled on the *Recueil des plus beaux vers,* most of the pieces in them are, as the
titles indicate, anonymous *vaudevilles.*

[62]Bacilly, *Remarques curieuses sur l'art de bien chanter,* 68: "il faut encore
sçavoir ce qui est de beau et de bon dans le commerce de la Musique."

[63]Ibid., 28: "Et je diray cecy en passant, qu'il vaut bien mieux s'humilier
jusques à ce poinct, que de se piquer de ne chanter que de ses Ouvrages, lesquels
n'entrent point dans le commerce du beau Monde & demeurant dans le Magasin
des Autheurs, ou ne sont connus que par des Gens obscurs, qui n'ont pas assez de
credit pour donner du cours à des Ouvrages."

[64]Ibid., 27–28: "les Airs que l'Autheur ne voudra point donner nottez au
Public, soit par caprice, soit pour estre toûjours en droict de les changer, soit pour
avoir seul l'avantage par dessus les Maistres, de pouvoir les chanter dans toute
leur perfection, particulierement pour ce qui regarde la veritable mesure qu'il
pretend y estre observée; soit pour ne les pas rendre si communs & leur conserver
le titre de la nouveauté, qui est ce qui flate extremement nostre Nation.

"Ces sortes d'Airs de reserve, ne s'apprennent que par Tradition; & comme asseurément ils sont plus recherchez que les autres; soit par la difficulté de les avoir, qui est un charme pour la pluspart des Esprits qui n'estiment que les choses qui sont difficiles à acquerir; soit qu'en effet ils soient plus considerables de soy, & par le Nom celebre de celuy qui les a composez, chacun a soin de les sçavoir & de les voler, ou à l'Autheur, ou à ceux qui ont le droict de le voir ou de l'entendre; & c'est mal à propos se piquer d'honneur, de ne vouloir pas se reduire à une mendicité de cette nature, laquelle peut estre reparée, lors que l'on a le droict d'Echange, & que l'on peut donner en prenant, c'est à dire que l'on s'est rendu capable de produire des Ouvrages qui peuvent entrer en comparaison avec ceux que l'on veut avoir des autres Compositeurs."

[65]Martha Feldman has shown how activity in the salons of sixteenth-century Venice was similar to the marketplace. See her *City Culture and the Madrigal at Venice* (Berkeley and Los Angeles: University of California Press, 1995), 21–22. Her comparison is equally applicable to the salons of seventeenth-century Paris.

[66]Pellisson's own collections of *poésie galante* included the *Recueil de pièces galantes, en prose et en vers, de Mme la Ctsse de La Suze et de M. de Pélisson* (Paris: G. Quinet, 1664); *Nouveau recueil de pièces choisies de Mme la Ctsse de La Suze et de M. Pélisson, seconde partie d'une autre dame et de M. Pélisson . . . Tome ppremier* [*sic*] (Paris: G. Quinet, 1668). On Pellisson's contribution to *poésie galante,* see Viala, *Naissance de l'écrivain,* 170. See also Orest Ranum, *Artisans of Glory: Writers and Historical Thought in Seventeenth-Century France* (Chapel Hill: The University of North Carolina Press, 1980), 236–268.

[67]Bacilly, *Recueil des plus beaux vers,* "Epistre": "Puis que c'est Vous qui m'avez inspiré le dessein de faire imprimer ce Recueil, permettez que je me donne l'honneur de vous le dédier. Je sçay que vous le trouverez plus ample qu'il ne devroit estre; & que pour le rendre digne de Vous, il en falloit retrancher tous les mauvais Vers: Mais comme il arrive souvent, & vous le sçavez, MONSIEUR, que la plus belle Poësie n'est pas toûjours la plus heureuse, j'ay estê contraint de considerer plûtost le cours qu'ont eu les Airs que je vous adresse, que leur propre valeur. Le nombre de ceux qui chantent estant infiny, il n'y a personne qui n'ait sa Chanson favorite; & tel n'auroit pas approuvé ce Recueil, s'il ne l'y avoit trouvée en son rang. Il n'y a rien de plus vray, que les belles paroles font l'ame du Chant, & le plus delicat de la Poësie; & que si tous ceux qui se meslent d'en faire y sçavoient employer comme Vous, MONSIEUR, l'elegance, la tendresse, & les termes doux à prononcer, les Chansons auroient toute leur grace: mais icy il faut considerer le Recueil que je vous presente, comme un Parterre composé de toute sorte de fleurs, & où les petites font valoir les grandes. Ce que j'y ay mis du vostre peut tout seul divertir ce rare Ministre de qui vous estes si particulierement estimé; & comme c'est le seul but que vous vous estes proposé en le faisant, je

m'estimerois bien heureux, si dans la protection qu'un si Grand Homme donne aux Muses, il luy plaisoit de la donner encore a un Musicien comme moy."
[68]Martin, *The History and Power of Writing,* 379.
[69]See Alain Niderst, *Madeleine de Scudéry, Paul Pellisson et leur monde* (Paris: Presses Universitaires de France, 1976), 353–448.
[70]One exception is the engraving "Le Matin" from the "Four Times of Day" (1643) by François de Poilly and Balthazar Moncornet, which depicts the royal family outside a château that appears to be located next to the Hippocrene spring (and Pegasus), and thus represents Louis XIII as the source of artistic inspiration. The image is reproduced in Sue Welsh Reed et al., *French Prints from the Age of the Musketeers* (Boston: Museum of Fine Arts, Boston, 1998), 49. Returning to musical prints, it should be noted that the printing device of the Ballard firm, Pegasus on Mount Parnassus, was an integral element of the books produced by Le Roy & Ballard (and later Ballard) beginning in the 1560s. Thus, it may be significant that when Pierre Le Doyen remade the frontispiece of the *Recueil des plus beaux vers* for other books printed by Charles de Sercy in the years that followed, Pegasus is notably absent. Le Doyen's later depiction of Apollo and the Muses (minus Pegasus) is reproduced in Maxime Préaud, *Inventaire du fonds français: Graveurs du XVIIe siècle, vol. 10, Leclercq-Lenfant* (Paris: Bibliothèque Nationale, 1989), 68. I would like to thank Kate van Orden for acquainting me with the history of the Ballard printing device, and Sue Welsh Reed for helping me locate information about Pierre Le Doyen and his frontispiece.
[71]Jean de La Fontaine was the poet laureate of Fouquet and hoped to be that of the king. He wrote *Clymène,* a work associating Fouquet with Apollo, during the same period as the compilation of the *Recueil des plus beaux vers.* See Marc Fumaroli, *Le poète et le Roi: Jean de La Fontaine en son siècle* (Paris: Éditions de Fallois, 1997), 61–63. Le Brun's decoration of Vaux-le-Vicomte's Salon des Muses makes a similar association. See also Jean-Pierre Néraudau, *L'Olympe du Roi-Soleil: Mythologie et idéologie royale au Grand Siècle* (Paris: Les Belles Lettres, 1986), 172–178.
[72]Néraudau, *L'Olympe du Roi-Soleil,* 63: ". . . entendu que le Roi *est* le Soleil . . . il *est* Apollon, le dieu du Parnasse, inspirateur des arts."
[73]On the decoration of the *livrets* and *ordonnances,* see Françoise Karro, "Marques de royauté dans les livrets de L'Académie royale de Musique entre 1672 et 1687," *Revue de la Bibliothèque Nationale* 49 (1993), 12–25. I would like to thank Gregory Brown for bringing this article to my attention.
[74]Ranum, *Artisans of Glory,* 252.
[75]Ibid., 245.
[76]Perrin presented his *Recueil des paroles de musique* (Bibliothèque Nationale, MS F. Fr. 2208) to Colbert circa 1666. A transcription of this text can be

found in Louis E. Auld, *The* Lyric Art *of Pierre Perrin, Founder of French Opera. Part 3:* Recueil de Paroles *de Musique de Mr Perrin* (Henryville, Ottawa, and Binningen: Institute of Mediaeval Music, 1986).

[77]Philippe-Joseph Salazar argues that Bacilly's *Remarques curieuses sur l'art de bien chanter* may have been the composer's bid to gain entrance into the Académie as a theoretician of pronunciation and to write a *Rhétorique* (a project which never came to pass). See Salazar's important discussion of Bacilly, including the *Recueil des plus beaux vers,* in his *Le culte de la voix au XVIIe siècle: Formes esthétiques de la parole à l'âge de l'imprimé* (Paris: Champion, 1995), 172–177.

[78]Bacilly, "Avertissement," *Recueil des plus beaux vers qui ont esté mis en chant. Avec le nom des autheurs. Seconde & Nouvelle Partie, dans laquelle sont compris les Airs de Versailles* (Paris: Ballard, Rue des Petits-Champs, and Pierre Bienfait, 1668): "le principal but des Recueils de Vers mis en Chant, est pour se ressouvenir de tout ce qui pourroit avoir échapé à la memoire de ceux qui pratiquent le Chant, l'Autheur n'a eu seulement égard qu'à les rendre complets, & faire en sorte qu'il n'y eust aucun Couplet considerable d'obmis."

[79]Chartier, *The Order of Books,* viii.

CHAPTER 9

Cheap Print and Street Song following the Saint Bartholomew's Massacres of 1572*

KATE VAN ORDEN

"Do books make revolutions?"

Historians of the French Revolution have traditionally answered yes to this question. If the intellectual origins of the Revolution rested in Enlightenment philosophy, as Daniel Mornet argued in *Les origines intellectuelles de la Révolution française, 1715–1787,* then print was responsible for disseminating the new philosophy.[1] Through political pamphlets, newspapers, gazettes, and books, Enlightenment ideals were spread to a broad public which read and internalized the new ways of thinking promoted by philosophers such as Voltaire and Rousseau. The idea that books make revolutions and that the *République des lettres* made the *République française* certainly requires qualification, but even the most sophisticated recent analyst of the origins of the Revolution, Roger Chartier, begins with the hypothesis that "if the French of the late eighteenth century fashioned the Revolution, it is because they had in turn been fashioned by books."[2]

Historians of sixteenth-century France hesitate to make such claims about printing and the people during the Wars of Religion (1562–1629). The civil wars in France were certainly just as riotous as the Revolution and just as deadly for the king, yet they have never been viewed as popular revolts. Only recently have historians begun to examine the role of France's third estate in the course of the wars and to discover how ordinary people—peasants, laborers, merchants, and petits bourgeois—*did* take part in what has hitherto been characterized as a power struggle among nobles. Thanks to the work of Natalie Zemon Davis, Barbara

Diefendorf, and Denis Crouzet among others, the eruptions of mob violence in French cities during this period are now being reckoned as decisive factors in the wars.[3] For example, Diefendorf re-examines the causes of the Saint Bartholomew's Day massacre of Protestants (August, 1572), concluding that it was not initiated by a Machiavellian command from Catherine de' Medici or Charles IX, but more likely resulted from a wave of popular violence that swept through Paris. Histories of the religious wars are thus shifting from noble whodunnit to more inclusive cultural histories.

From Paris the August riots spread to the provinces where towns with significant Protestant populations exploded from pent-up animosity. Lyon was one such place: a city with a vocal Protestant constituency supported economically by healthy trade and intellectually by nearby Geneva. At the height of Protestant zeal in the 1560s, one third of the city professed the reformed faith, a large number compared to the average of ten percent in the rest of France. Emotions ran high in Lyon, which made the *vespres lyonnaises* (a local term in Lyon for the Saint Bartholomew's massacres) particularly savage. This essay studies, in part, the reactions of a Lyonnais merchant, Benoist Rigaud, to this climax of religious violence in his city. Rigaud's story is one of ambivalence and political expediency, for he sympathized with the Protestants early on in the wars but quickly renounced the faith when the tide turned against the new religion.

Lyon is of particular interest because the city sustained a large number of printers. She was France's second city of print after Paris and strategically situated at a European crossroads far from "the King's France" of the north and just down the Rhône from the printing capital of Geneva. The city enjoyed a healthy and independent culture of print and, as Davis has shown in her "Strikes and Salvation at Lyon," a large number of those in the printing business were Protestants. This made print a nexus of tensions between the Catholic majority and the Huguenot minority in Lyon. Rigaud, who ran presses and sold books from his shop in the rue Mercière, saw many close friends and associates murdered during the wars. What can his output tell us, then, about religious strife in Lyon?

Rigaud generally printed material that either avoided political topics or served the state directly—he printed royal edicts and ordinances, for example—but throughout his career, he also printed war songs that unavoidably took a political stance (see Appendix 9.1). The books and pamphlets containing these songs were cheap and circulated widely. Although never brazenly seditious, these printed songs matched the favorite vehicle of pamphleteers who used print to attack everything from Protestantism or Catholicism to the monarchy. During the civil wars, all manner of political pamphlets and posters flew from French presses to be received by a populace suddenly—and unusually—engaged in the political trajectory of their country. For religious sentiment colored politics in such a way that those who cared little about power struggles among nobles did care desperately that France was being polluted with heresies. Protestants hated the Mass and holy sacraments. In turn, their iconoclasm and reformation of devotional practices seemed to threaten the eternal salvation of Catholic folk.

Commoners voiced their religious concerns in age-old expressions of popular sentiment such as satire and song, and these, in turn, inflected cheap forms of print aimed at a broad public. As Natalie Zemon Davis says in "Printing and the People,"

> though most early polemical literature disseminated outward and downward the political and religious views of persons at the center, . . . it occurred to some city people on the margins of power to use the press to respond. . . . The addition of printed pamphlets to traditional methods for spreading news (rumor, street song, private letters, town criers, fireworks displays, bell-ringing, and penitential processions) increased the *menu peuple*'s stock of detailed information about national events.[4]

By using the traditional modes of communication in sixteenth-century French cities as a context in which to study printed matter, Davis shows us how print adopted expressive devices that would have been familiar to city folk. Such is the case with Rigaud's political songs, where we find the oral tradition of singing and crying the news elaborated in print. The printing of these street songs does not mark out a trajectory away from the oral toward the written, however. Oral practices structure the printed forms that emerge from them, coding reading as performance. Back in the street, these printed songs stood a fair chance of intersecting the lives of ordinary people in Lyon. In this essay, I would like to suggest some particular ways in which the songs printed by Rigaud arose from and invigorated the religious and political debates of their urban audiences. As fragments of a culture on the margins of the official, in which printed ephemera and street song encouraged the voice of public opinion if not outright revolt, Rigaud's political songs afford us the opportunity to ask for this early period of print, "Do books make revolutions?"

SONGS PUNISHABLE BY DEATH

The monarchy was well aware of the seditious potential of certain songs and tried to contain the problem by punishing those who sang them. Early in December of 1564, the town crier of Lyon traveled through the city and its surrounding areas to announce a royal ordinance against the singing of "dissolute songs." It was but one of a number of edicts made by the king's provincial governor, de Losses, that aimed to quell the religious violence lingering in the wake of the first civil war. The edict of pacification of 1563 had promised liberty of conscience to Protestants, but had been accepted only unwillingly by the town council of Lyon, and skirmishes between Huguenots and Catholics continued to disrupt the calm of daily life in the city. Most of the ordinances supported the conciliatory policy of the Valois, which aimed for religious toleration, but in Lyon, with its large Protestant population, tensions ran high. In the 1564 ordinance, singing seditious songs comes under attack along with vagrancy, gambling, and blaspheming the Virgin Mary, suggesting that this sort of dangerous singing took place in the city's streets and public houses. A translation of the printed record follows (see Appendix 9.2 for the original French):

> Decree of the King and of Monseigneur de Losses . . . not to blaspheme, gamble, nor sing dissolute songs, all upon pain of death by hanging. Lyon: Benoist Rigaud, 1564.
>
> Very express command is made to all vagrants and people without employment or trade, being in the said city, that, after the publication of the present [commands], they should forthwith vacate and go out of the said city and its faubourgs, upon pain of hanging.
>
> It is charged upon the above pains to all hoteliers, innkeepers, and other persons of whatever quality and condition that they might be, not to seclude, give lodging to, nor administer any board to the said persons beyond one night, without our express leave.
>
> And to remove the means of supporting and secluding the above-said vagrants and idle people, all people living in this city as well as in its faubourgs are forbidden to hold casinos in their homes and gardens, and to permit the playing of dice, cards, ninepins, and other prohibited and forbidden games there, upon the said pain of hanging, as much against those who operate these said casinos as against those who would be found playing.
>
> Also in following the old Decrees and saintly constitutions of the King our Master, it is very expressly forbidden and prohibited to all

persons of whatever estate, quality, and condition that they might be to swear, blaspheme, spite, and renounce the name of God, to make other vile and detestable sermons against the honor of God, the Virgin Mary, and the Saints, to sing or say dissolute songs and songs leaning toward sedition, or to agitate by insults or otherwise and under the pretext of Religion, upon the pains contained in these said Decrees.

Copy checked against the original, by myself, Secretary to Monseigneur de Losse, Lieutenant general of the King . . .

DAVOST

The present decree here above was cried, read, and publicized by loud voice, public cry, and the sound of the trumpet at each and every one of the crossroads and public squares usual for making announcements, proclamations, and publications in the said city of Lyon by myself, Claude Thevenon, clerk and assistant of Mister Jean Bruyeres, public crier of the said city, today, the fifth day of December, fifteen hundred sixty-four.

THEVENON.

Through the expulsion or execution of vagrants, gamblers, and blasphemers, Charles IX hoped to cleanse the body politic in a process that emphasizes song as a transmitter of social disease and religious unrest. We must wonder, first and foremost, which songs are being outlawed here, and secondly, why singing them warrants capital punishment. Clearly several motives stand behind such a radical attempt to silence the religious agitators who employed songs in their sectarian goals. The social clime that produced this edict was one of religious vigilantism in which songs were hypercharged with meanings that could rally a crowd to violence. And popular violence threatened the authority of the state. Songs criticizing the monarchy before a crowd gave focus to collective dissent, and so the ordinance aims to silence crowds, not just singers.

In the first instance, de Losse's ordinance was directed at Huguenot psalms. As early as the 1550s, psalms had been sung during public protests. In 1551, printers' journeymen in Lyon staged an armed procession in which they led their wives and other artisans through the streets singing psalms and shouting insults at Catholic onlookers.[5] Owing to events such as this, Henry II banned the public singing of psalms in 1558, though to little avail. The ban had to be reiterated innumerable times, and it is likely that de Losse's allusion to "old decrees" refers to prior proscriptions against these "battle cries" of the reformed religion. In the summer of 1564—just before the issuance of this ban—the

Protestants of Lyon had obstreperously constructed a new temple in a vacant ditch known as Les Terreaux, which had been allotted to them by the city. Claude de Rubys reports that "all of them—large and small, men and women—threw themselves into carrying the earth required to fill in the ditches, and it was good to watch the young ladies, two by two, with their skirts hitched half-way up their legs, carrying the bucket by the handles, singing their songs of Marot and de Bèse."[6] The songs of Marot and Bèze were, of course, the French translations of the psalms made by the poet Clément Marot and the Calvinist pastor Théodore de Bèze. Antoine Vincent, a rich merchant-publisher from Lyon, produced the Huguenot Psalter in exile, commissioning an astounding 27,400 copies from the Genevan presses alone in 1562, while others were printed in Lyon.[7] The Lyonnais were hardly alone in coupling psalm-singing and religious activism: among the most noteworthy occurrences we find a minister enjoining his "flock" of 500 to kneel and sing Psalm 31 when they found themselves ambushed by Catholic forces; Psalm 144 was the victory cry of Huguenots in Sancerre to mark their initial resistance during the siege there in 1572; and when Huguenots seized Bourges in 1562, they sang Psalm 124. Little wonder, then, that psalms were considered seditious given their status as insurrectionary hymns, particularly when their texts condoned militancy and holy war: "Blessed be the Lord my strength which teacheth my hands to war and my fingers to fight (Ps. 144)."[8] The proscription against singing psalms in assemblies and communal gatherings led to the frequent arrest of Protestants, even for singing psalms at home. Although Henry II and his son, Charles IX, continued to support the right of Protestants to sing privately without threat of imprisonment, the ongoing petitions made by Protestants attest to the inability of the king to protect their rights in the face of local opposition. Psalm-singing, whether public or private, generated antagonism in onlookers.[9] Congregational singing arose in France in conjunction with the religious fervor of Calvinism, and the forms of communal prayer so touted by Luther—who penned chorales himself—worked both inside and outside the Temple to foster unity and demonstrate faith by singing together in groups.

Despite the well-documented cases of psalm-singing during religious protest and the central role of psalms in the Reformation, we should not necessarily read de Losse's 1564 ban as one exclusively targeting Huguenot psalms. Catholic factions, too, used liturgical music to rally believers in open demonstrations. One analogous example is the use of the *Te Deum laudamus*. At the height of the religious wars, Charles IX, Henry III, and Henry IV ordered the singing of the *Te Deum* hymn more

and more often at Notre Dame de Paris and throughout the realm to cele-
brate victories and to reconsecrate the country after Protestant distur-
bances. Accompanied by a public procession and Mass, the singing of
the *Te Deum* glorified kingship both earthly and divine with lines such as
"Te per orbem terrarum sancta confitetur Ecclesia, Patrem immensae
majestatis" ("the holy Church proclaims your greatnesses throughout the
universe, O Father of immense majesty"). *Te Deum* processions winding
through the Ile de la Cité and around the Louvre, the Châtelet, and the
Université, emphasized the king's dominion over the capital.[10] As a signature of Catholic authority, the hymn became a perfect weapon for the
humiliation of Protestants. Catholics dressed Protestants in holy vest-
ments and paraded them through the streets on asses, forcing them to say
the Mass while the accompanying crowd sang a mocking *Te Deum* or requiem.[11] In addition to the use of the *Te Deum* in such carnivalesque rituals, loose French translations of the *Te Deum* circulated as spiritual
chansons not unlike Protestant psalms, and other liturgical chants also
worked their ways into the memories of congregants, who sang them out
of church: the Gallic litany for Rogation days, "Te rogamus audi nos,"
was popular both in its own right and as a tune to which one sang pro-
Catholic spiritual songs.[12]

Later in the wars, when the Catholic League pursued a policy of
zero toleration, Catholic hymns came to be used in the same public and
insurrectionary ways as Protestant psalms: pilgrims in white sheets criss-
crossed the countryside in "white processions," singing, according to one
observer, "diverse sorts of songs, prayers, litanies, psalms, and verses of
proses such as *Ave Maria* from the proses of the Nativity and the Assumption of Our Lady, *Deus benigne, stabat mater, christi fideles, Averte
faciem,* and many others things of great devotion."[13] In the late 1570s, the
Duke of Savoy ordered *processions blanches* in the diocese of Lyon, and
in 1583 alone, some 72,000 pilgrims descended upon the arch-Catholic
cathedral of Rheims from all parts of Lorraine, Champagne, Picardy, and
Upper Normandy, hoping that by marching and singing they could eradi-
cate the heresy gripping the kingdom.[14] Singing bound the pilgrims together and helped them march together in time, and this physical
bonding in turn produced precisely the sense of regimentation and col-
lectivity that served soldiers, violent mobs, and city militia during the
civil wars.[15]

Church music galvanized congregations in both church and temple
and rallied crowds without, yet liturgical songs count for only the smallest portion of sectarian songs that might have fallen under bans. A much

larger repertory of semi-spiritual songs addressing religious and political issues circulated during civil wars. These *chansons nouvelles* or "new songs" fitted new texts on current affairs to familiar tunes, continually replenishing a popular repertory with songs that were easy to sing and relevant to the lives of city people. Their form made them highly accessible, for they required no musical literacy to perform and, because the tunes were simple—with limited range, conjunct motion, and inner repetitions—almost anyone could sing them. Based on standard dance tunes and the melodies of well-known songs, the music was so widely disseminated that there was no need to write it down. The texts, on the other hand, were new, lengthy, and hard to remember; thus they came to be printed as *aides mémoires* on single sheets of paper, in pamphlets, and in small books.

Both Catholics and Protestants wrote political songs in this way, which is not surprising given that the singing of new words to old tunes had been a common practice for centuries. Indeed, in his fanciful *Propos rustiques* or "rustic tales," Noël du Fail depicts a rural gathering at which the peasant Robin Chevet could be found "singing most melodiously—for he sang well—some *chanson nouvelle,* while Jouanne, his wife, on the other side answered him in like manner as she spun."[16] Robin's "chanson nouvelle," which is "answered" by his wife, suggests the practice of singing new texts to familiar tunes, and, in fact, the crafting of just such a "chanson nouvelle" is described later in the novel.[17] Du Fail calls the process "contrepoincter," "mettre en cantique," and "encantiquer," which, as with our political songs, involved rigging out a known melody with new words.

At their most fleeting, these songs were printed up as single or "flying" sheets known as "feuilles volantes" or "placards" (posters). An example of one is shown in Figure 9.1.

At approximately eleven inches in height, it is little larger than a piece of notebook paper, yet it would have been posted on walls, as the designation *placard* suggests, or sold in city streets. *Placards* had a very short life-span, and rare are the examples that survive. This one was conserved by Pierre de l'Estoile, court diarist during the reigns of Henry III and Henry IV, who amassed a large scrapbook of *placards* and engravings from the period of the League, the radical Catholic faction active circa 1576 to 1594 whose militancy was at least partially responsible for the regicide of Henry III.[18] Whether posted in city squares or held in the hand, *placards* sporting song texts were certainly meant to be sung. Convocations of the League surely included the singing of songs, for the

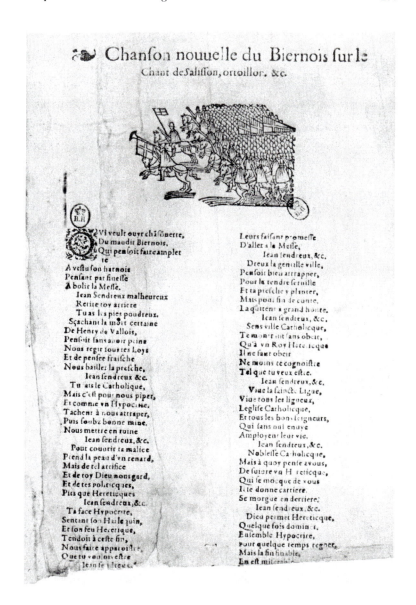

Figure 9.1 *Placard* from the scrapbook of Pierre de l'Estoile, F-PBn Rés. fol. La 25.6, fol. 25ʳ. Photo courtesy of the Bibliotheque nationale, Paris.

Leaguers even had their own hymn identified as "le chant de la Ligue." Its text was printed on *placards* and its melody served as a "timbre" or stock tune for other chansons, achieving enough renown to become detached from the original text and to serve new texts written to the rhyme scheme of the original poem.[19] The title of this *placard* announces the tune for the contrafactum text ("Sallison, ortoillon") with the standard formula "chanson nouvelle . . . sur le chant de . . ." ("new song . . . to the tune of . . ."). Henry III was dubbed "Biernois" (fool) by the Leaguers, and this song denounces him as a heretic who will not act decisively and crush the Hugenots.[20]

   Placards blur the distinction between song and proclamation, reminding us that the walls lining the streets and squares used for the crying of public news were often plastered with posters both official and inflammatory. In the streets, cries mixed with song, and vendors trafficking news and propaganda plied their cheap print with regularity. In the face of libelous songs such as the "Chanson nouvelle du Biernois," it is easy to understand the royal suppression of this kind of speech and the printed forms upon which it relied. To the extent that these songs voiced opinions contrary to the king in public forums, they defied the authority of the monarch and subjected it to open scrutiny. In this way, city squares, church steps, market places, and fairgrounds became contested sites where the monarchy asserted its program of religious toleration and where zealots preached, marched, fought, sang, and prayed.

THE PRESSES OF BENOIST RIGAUD IN LYON

Owing to their fragility and timely nature, only a handful of sixteenth-century *placards* have survived to this day—even fewer with song texts. Moreover, all the printed engravings, *placards,* and pamphlets produced by the League were destroyed at the command of Henry IV after he abjured Calvinism in 1593: he ordered booksellers to destroy their stocks of libelous literature and prohibited its sale with stricter enforcement.[21] But whereas *placards* rarely surmounted the trials of time, songs printed in books and pamphlets fared much better. Dozens of small seidecimo prints collected song texts under the title of *recueil de chansons,* and, among the *recueils,* a unique series published by Benoist Rigaud in Lyon includes political songs (see Appendix 9.1).[22] Great portions of the chansons in these *recueils* abandon the usual theme of love and favor that of war instead. In a world of lyric utterance completely geared toward the expression of love—a world in which ninety-five percent of polyphonic chansons took love as their subject—these war songs stand out in bold contrast to the rest of the repertory. Their themes range from the hardships of living under siege to stories of artillery battles and prayers for peace. They are often signalled in the titles of prints such as *Petit recueil de chansons nouvelles tant de l'amour que de la guerre, Nouveau recueil des chansons qu'on chante a present, tant de la guerre & voyage de la Fère, de la Mure, & des chansons amoureuses,* and *La fleur des chansons nouvelles, traittans partie de l'amour, partie de la guerre* (see Figure 9.2). But in other *recueils,* songs of war lie hidden like thorns within prints advertising charming bouquets of songs: *Le plaisant jardin des belles chansons* or *Le rosier des chansons nouvelles.* The size of a typical *recueil* is twenty-four to eighty-six folios, with thirty-two and sixty-four folios being the most common given the seidecimo format. Occasionally Rigaud printed single songs in larger formats with far fewer pages: the *Chanson nouvelle de la paix, par le peuple de France* (in-8, 4 ff.) is a good example.

Unlike so many of his contemporaries in the printing industry, Rigaud sent material to press that had broad appeal.[23] He printed books of vernacular poetry, French histories, books on law, arithmetic, and trade routes that were useful to merchants, and books of entertainment such as the *Amadis de Gaule* cycle and our *recueils de chansons.*[24] At least once Rigaud issued printed music, *Le premier livre de chansons spirituelles* (RISM 1568[9]), an attempt to produce a cheap book of four-voice chansons by printing all of the parts in the same seidecimo book.[25] In the early part of his career he served as the printer of government documents in Lyon, printing, among other things, the 1564 ordinance against seditious songs.[26] Despite the time involved in typesetting and printing, Rigaud issued other pamphlets that functioned like proto-newspapers, recounting the details of various battles and giving lists of casualties, or describing the negotiations leading up to a treaty, and so forth. Polemic pamphlets recorded responses to royal declarations, denouncements of various political acts, and all sorts of editorializing. Finally, Rigaud printed up pamphlets that functioned as public statements of celebration or mourning by commemorating special occasions such as royal entries, weddings, or funerals. Alongside this official and newsy line of pamphlets, which generally took the form of octavo prints containing four to eight folios, Rigaud dealt a much more sensationalist genre of news to the public in the form of *canards* or chapbooks, which generally contained six to sixteen pages.[27] They propagated stories of the bizarre

Figure 9.2 *La fleur des chansons nouvelles, traittans partie de l' amour, partie de la guerre,* titlepage and fol. 2ʳ. Reproduced with permission of the Bibliothèque nationale, Paris.

and marvelous, including tales of monstrous births, unusual crimes, supernatural prognostications (usually involving comets or other heavenly appearances), miracles, sacrileges, gruesome murders, and stories of floods or plague. For almost forty years—from 1553 until his death in 1597—Rigaud produced inexpensive vernacular prints with the broadest possible appeal.

The material aspects of Rigaud's *recueils* certainly imply a printing method geared toward the rapid production of cheap print rather than the laborious production of expensive volumes for bibliophiles and connoisseurs. Rigaud used an inexpensive grade of paper called "commung," which was sometimes of very uneven thickness (see the ink bleed in Fig. 9.2), and he continually recycled the small and tired woodcuts decorating his title pages (such as that in Fig. 9.2). Gatherings of many *recueils* are poorly folded and the type worn, yet these prints do not imply a sloppy shop, for they contain few typographical or printing errors (most typos appear in the foliation numbers, which are occasionally inverted or out of order). Compared to other sorts of books, Rigaud's *recueils* were thus cheap but good, and they could be had for about one sou (the cost of a pound of beef or a week's worth of wine in Lyon in 1580),[28] just a bit more expensive than *canards* and single sheets, which cost but a denier or two like the penny ballad sheets sold in London.[29]

Rigaud marketed his books in at least four very different ways. His print shop in the rue Mercière was located in the heart of Lyon's commercial district, where one might call in at the store front to buy books *sur place*. With the burgeoning industries of silk manufacturing, printing, and metalworking all concentrated in the streets around his shop, trade must have been fairly brisk right off the street. Lyon bustled with merchants, journeymen, craftsmen, artisans, day laborers, bourgeois, and peasants. At the crossroads of trade routes joining Paris, Brussels, and London to the north, and Milan, Venice, Florence, and Rome to the east, Lyon handled goods from the whole of Europe and the Orient, its commerce fueled by cash from Florentine bankers who had settled in the city and established it as one center of the international money market. Nestled at the confluence of the Rhône and Saône rivers, Lyon also drew trade from north and south along these great waterways. Since 1463, Lyon's fairs at Easter, in August, at All Saint's, and at the Feast of the Kings had made it an unusually privileged site for commerce, and Rigaud regularly sold quantities of books at the fairs to merchants from Le Puy, Montpellier, the Dauphiné, Lorraine, and Navarre.[30] It is likely that Rigaud sold some material by subscription, particularly prints of royal edicts, ordinances, and letter patents.[31] Finally, we know that

Rigaud sold small books to traveling vendors, who in turn resold them in city streets throughout the country.[32]

Street vendors or "colporteurs" likely sold the *recueils* containing war songs, or at least the shorter and less expensive ones, alongside their stock of *canards*. But it is not just their low cost and small size that seems to place the *recueils* in the *colporteur*'s basket: as we will see, many of their songs explore the same themes as *canard* literature, and, moreover, *colporteurs* commonly hawked their wares in song.

SONG AND *COLPORTAGE*

Colporteurs were urban vendors who trod the major streets, squares, and crossroads of cities, singing the songs they sold and crying out the sensationalist titles of their *canards* in counterpoint to the official public announcements of town criers.[33] Pierre de l'Estoile called these peddlers "contre-porteaux" (a bastardization of "colporteurs") or "port-paniers" (basket-carriers); more commonly they were known as "colporteurs" because the tray of goods they carried was suspended from a neck strap.[34] (See Figure 9.3.)

This sixteenth-century engraving of a *colporteur* shows him displaying his wares and speaking or singing as he walks along. His cry of "beaulx abc, belles heures" serves as a title and gives us some idea of the sorts of print hawked through *colportage*—books for the marginally literate, like abc's, and books of hours. Written accounts of *colporteurs* describe them with baskets full of almanacs, romances, indexed literature, stories of marvelous events, and *recueils de chansons* containing, according to a seventeenth-century report, "dirty and nasty secular songs, written down by an unclean spirit, vaudevilles, vilanelles, airs de cours, [and] chansons à boire."[35] Print crowded their trays alongside mirrors, gloves, tape, ribbons, and other odds and ends.[36] *Colporteurs* were often little better off than beggars—L'Estoile describes them as "poor" and "dejected"—and they plied city streets selling whatever cheap print and trinkets came to hand.[37]

Colporteurs often sang the songs they sold as a form of advertisement that drew attention to their stock in trade. Indeed, singing and peddling cheap print went hand in hand, as songs pitched the sale of the print to those who paused to listen—hence the bounty of rhetorical hooks used in the songs, opening formulae such as "Who would like to hear a little song . . ." (see Figure 9.1) or "Listen, ladies, listen to the story. . . ." One of the problems for *colporteurs*, however, was that there was little to

Figure 9.3 Engraving of a *colporteur* from a collection of sixteenth-century engravings entitled *Les cris de Paris,* Arsenal Estampes Rés. 264, fol. 1ʳ. Photo courtesy of the Bibliothèque nationale, Paris.

separate them from beggars who used song and minstrelsy to glean hand-outs from passersby. Vagrants haunted cemeteries offering to sing "bizarre little hymns for the dead" for a few coins;[38] instrumentalists reg-ularly faked blindness and perched themselves on chairs before the church to play the lute for alms;[39] and errant minstrels and jongleurs who might dance, do acrobatics, play on the flute, and sing for money had a bad reputation as "loathsome and vile" sorts.[40] The associations conjured up at the thought of street musicians were so unsavory, in fact, that in the sixteenth century the verb "ménestrauder" commonly meant both to practice minstrelsy and to live in beggary.[41] Looking back to the Lyon-naise ordinance of 1564 in this light, it is perhaps not so surprising that the laws expelling vagabonds from the city and restricting singing should come in the same breath. Furthermore, because *colporteurs* so often sold libelous *placards, canards,* and indexed literature, they naturally came under surveillance from the authorities. Strict interdictions were levelled against the *colportage* of print during the years of the League. In re-sponse, *colporteurs* disguised seditious material by crying other titles; they claimed illiteracy and thus ignorance of what they sold; they worked at night; and some books were "colportés" (vended) by confectioners be-neath their cakes and rolls.[42] As a subversive activity, most of what we know about *colportage* is recorded in rulings attempting to curtail its practice. In time *colportage* was brought under government control, and eventually street song, too, was forced into the service of social nor-malcy. By the end of the nineteenth century, both practices had been regulated and stripped of the insurrectionary potential they once pos-sessed.[43]

THE *POLITIQUE* OF RIGAUD'S SONGS

Rigaud had a particularly difficult time negotiating the shifting sands of religious politics in Lyon. Not that it was easy, for the political situation was decidedly unstable. Rigaud began his career in 1555 in partnership with a zealous Protestant, Jean Saugrin. Although Saugrin's marriage to Rigaud's niece in 1558 strengthened their relations, the business alliance broke up in the same year owing to religious differences.[44] Saugrin went off to print Protestant material on his own and Rigaud, from all appear-ances, remained a Catholic.[45] But appearances change. The spring of 1562 brought a revolution to Lyon resulting in Huguenot rule of the city council for over a year. Although the Catholics regained control of the city in 1563, the next four years saw a period of relative tolerance fostered by the large number of powerful Huguenots in the city and their (minority) representation on the city council. Rigaud printed works sympathetic to their cause during this time, such as the little four-folio *Chanson chrestienne et nouvelle de la Royne de Navarre* [Jeanne d'Albret], *avec une autre chanson chrestienne d'un gentil'homme provençal respondant a icelle* from 1564.[46] In the fall of 1567, however, the tide shifted once again, the second religious war got underway, and Protestants in Lyon suffered a sudden onslaught of persecution. The temple at Les Terreaux was destroyed. The government imprisoned Protestants, seized their property, confiscated the stocks of Protestant booksellers, and drove a number of Rigaud's fellow printers from the city.[47] Although fortunate enough not to have been included on the list of 240 Lyonnais Protestants who lost their possessions in January of 1568, Rigaud did not escape altogether, for he was "taxed" 100 livres for his apparent empathy with those of the reformed faith. He quickly abjured Protestantism and, as Natalie Zemon Davis observes in her study of his output, he never again published a "heretical" (i.e., Protestant) work.[48] His religious temperament, inasmuch as it can be discerned from the prints that came off his presses, was moderate. This moderation is most evident in Rigaud's prints following the Saint Bartholomew's Day massacre in 1572. The bloodshed, which had begun in Paris with the murder of Admiral Gaspard de Coligny and turned into a riot of violence against all the Protestants in the city, was not contained within the walls of Paris but spread throughout the country. Of the other affected cities—all of them at one time or another Protestant strongholds—Lyon suffered the greatest butchery. The gates of the city were closed, Protestants were rounded up and imprisoned in jails, and eventually angry hoards broke open the royal prisons and massacred those being held there.[49] Claude Goudimel, one of the foremost composers of his time and the first to set the psalm translations of Marot and Bèze to music, also perished in the *vespres lyonnaises.*

Rigaud must have been horrified by the *vespres lyonnaises,* during which even others like himself, who had abjured Protestantism, were killed. The carnage was appalling: somewhere from 600 to 800 men, women, and children were slaughtered. Their bodies were dumped in the river and created a terrifying spectacle down the length of the Rhône to Avignon. Rigaud printed five Catholic pieces on the Saint Bartholomew's massacres in 1572 and 1573 and, perhaps unsurprisingly, it is at this time that his *recueils de chansons*—which previously had been devoted to love songs—begin to contain numerous war songs. The songs generally approach their subjects using styles that I describe in the three sections that follow as newsy, lamenting, or preaching, but in most cases the tone is the same: one of Catholic moderation and conciliation. I argue that this "politic" position—politic in that it favors the political entity that is France even if it means tolerating religious difference—found sympathetic ears (and voices) among the city folk of Lyon.

NEWSY SONGS

One reason Rigaud printed so many pamphlets about the Saint Bartholomew's massacres must have been because they sold. Ghastly reports filled the pages of his *canards* and fed demand in the market for sensational news. Songs, too, pitched their tales in dramatic tones, and many of the war songs report news from the front. Notorious sieges generated whole families of songs as all eyes turned toward a series of walled Protestant strongholds continually beset by Catholic forces. Most of these cities lay well away from Paris, on or near the great rivers that flowed westward through central France to the sea. La Rochelle, the de facto capital of Protestant France, looked out across the sea for support from Protestant England. Inland, the ramparts of Sancerre, La Charité, Issoire, Sommière, and La Fère bristled with halberds and arrows. Some of the most common timbres for war songs name the fortified cities: "Le chant de Sommières," "Le chant de La Rochelle," and "Soldatz de Charité." Sieges often lasted several months and reduced life in these cities to virtual nightmares. Jean de Léry, a Huguenot minister living in Sancerre, reported that the famine there became so extreme that—having already eaten hides, leather, and even deer's feet from keychains—people ate parchment books by soaking, boiling, and then fricasseeing the pages. With terror Léry also tells of a couple he saw sit down to dine upon the cooked remains of their little daughter who had died of hunger. Rigaud printed an account of the siege at Sancerre as a *canard* that included a song: the *Nouveau discours sur la siege de Sanserre . . . plus une complainte de la France en forme de chanson* from 1573, a little 16–folio pamphlet by Jean de la Gessée that exemplifies a system of information fluid enough to bind a prose account and a song together.

Topical songs struck an immediate tone with first person diction and the rhetoric of street cry, full of eyewitness narrative that contrasts with the timeless love stories most often told in chansons. The following song captures the spirit of storytelling as it describes the fall of La Charité from the vantage of someone inside the city walls:

Chanson nouvelle de la prinse de la Charité, rendue en l'obeissance du Roy nostre Sire, Et se chante sur le chant, Quand j'estoy libre (Fleur, fol. 57ʳ)

O Terre ô Ciel, voyez la grand detresse
Voyant l'aussaut la grand fleur de noblesse,
Tant de Soldats François,
Doubles Canons de furieuse audace
Sa grand furie des rempars nous dechasse
Tremblant d'un grand effroy.
    Ja la bresche aussi le bastillon
Tout renversé de grands coups de canons
Les soldats preparez
A nous monstrer nostre dol & fallace
Je les vois tous de furieuse audace
S'emparer des fossez.
    Et nous voyans les canons de furie
Brisant, tuant, nous ravissant la vie,
Avons parlementé:
Prians le Roy d'appaiser la furie
Voyans les murs brisez d'artillerie
Nous ont espouventez.
    . . .
    Monsieur d'Anjou Prince tresdebonnaire,
Nous a servy de tresfidelle pere
Nous prenant à mercy,
En sauveté sous sa protection
Faisant cesser la furie du canon
Qui nous eust tous occis.
    . . .
    Monsieur de Guise s'exposa au hazart
Et à toute heure approchoit du rampart
N'avoir peur de la mort,
Dans les trenchees il estoit en personne
Ne craignant point l'artillerie qui donne
Ruynant tout nostre effort.
    . . .
    Car le haut Dieu qui tient tous sous dextre,
En un moment fera par l'univers
Vivre dessouz sa loy,

Tranquilité, une paix & concorde,
Fera cesser les querelles & divorce,
Recognoissant son Roy.
   Prions le Roy Henry de grand valeur,
Puis que sur nous a monstré sa faveur
En toute loyauté:
Prions sans fin ce grand Dieu souverain:
Nous prosternant priant à joinctes mains
Nous tenir effacé.

[Oh earth oh heaven, see the great distress watching the great flower of nobility assault. So many French soldiers, double canons of furious boldness, its great fury chases us from the ramparts trembling with a great terror. Already the breach also the stronghold, all destroyed by great canon shots. The soldiers prepare to show us grief and our fallacies. I see them all seize the ditches with furious boldness. And we, seeing the canons of fury breaking, killing, carrying off our life, negotiated: Begging the King to abate the fury, seeing the walls broken from artillery, we were terrified . . . . Very debonnaire Prince d'Anjou served us for his faithful father, taking mercy on us and rescuing us with his protection, making the fury of the canon stop, which would have slain all of us. . . . M. de Guise was exposed to hazards and went each hour to the rampart, having no fear of death. In the trenches he came in person, not fearing the artillery shots at all, ruining all our effort. . . . For God, who holds all in his right hand, in a moment he will make the universe live under his law, tranquility, one peace, and concord. (He) will make the quarrels and divorce end, recognizing his King. We pray to King Henry of great merit, since he has shown us his favor in all loyalty: We pray without end to this great sovereign God: We prostrate ourselves praying with clasped hands, forgive us.]

La Charité was one of the fortified towns on the Loire river that had been ceded to the Protestants in the treaty of May 1576 and one of the first to be besieged when the wars against the Protestants were renewed in 1577. It fell on 2 May 1577 to royal forces headed—according to the song—by François, the Duke of Anjou (the king's brother) and the leader of the League, Henry, Duke of Guise. Rigaud issued a little eight-folio pamphlet right away in 1577 entitled *Le discours du siege tenu devant la*

Charité, ensemble de la prise par Monsieur frere du Roy avec le nombre des morts, tant d'une part que d'autre that described the siege and fall of the city and gave information such as the number of dead on each side. This song, which came out three years later in a *recueil de chansons,* clearly does more. It is not just a sung version of the same news related in the earlier pamphlet, but a vivid and cautionary recollection of the siege that celebrates the heroism of the Duke of Guise and the clemency of Henry III and the Duke of Anjou. In the song, La Charité is made to emblemize royal victory, peace, forgiveness, and the benefits of surrender to any who would oppose the crown, telling of the artillery barrages, the terrifying breach in the town walls, and the even-handed peace restored by the Duke of Anjou in the name of the king. La Charité becomes a poster child for surrender three years after the event and presumably long after listeners had forgotten that the Duke of Anjou never actually commanded the royal troops (he had too little experience in the field) and that the badly equipped army ran out of steam shortly after La Charité and was itself forced to surrender. The song's real message is that old French standby: *un roi, une foi, une loi* or "one king, one faith, one law," whose party line makes it not unlike the official sorts of proclamations announced by town criers or the songs sung in *Te Deum* processions and royal entries.[50]

The song's melody is just as royal as its message, for the timbre "Quand j'estois libre" began as a courtly chanson. Pierre de Ronsard, court poet, first published the text in 1556, and Nicolas de la Grotte published a tuneful setting of it for four voices in 1569.[51] By 1574, La Grotte was installed at court along with his master, Henry III, and his setting of "Quand j'estois libre" was reprinted five times in the 1570s by Le Roy & Ballard, the royal printers of music. The melody is based on the complex rhythm of a galliard, an exhibitionary dance popular at bourgeois festivities and at court. The timbre's origins thus remind us that urban minstrelsy and courtly music-making often shared musical material. And as we wonder about the connections between courtly lyric production and street songs, this song cautions us not to assume a blunt correlation between cheap print and lower class consumption.

The songs printed by Rigaud do reflect city or "bourgeois" culture, but there is no doubt that courtiers purchased and enjoyed them as well. As late as the eighteenth century, the king's librarians were copying songs from cheap prints into large manuscript collections such as the Chansonnier Maurepas and the Chansonnier Clairambault.[52] The compilers of these collections occasionally drew material from sixteenth-century prints: their sources include an octavo print from 1553 that provided the text of "un discours de la guerre de metz en Lorraine" (Rigaud included the same song in his 1557 *Recueil de plusieurs chansons*), a *recueil* of timbres printed in 1575, and even a tattered sixteenth-century *placard,* which was pasted directly into one volume. The Bibliothèque Royale may have acquired these sources already in the sixteenth century, either for the amusement of the court or, like L'Estoile's scrapbook of *placards,* for the annals of state. L'Estoile, we should recall, bought pamphlets from the *colporteurs* outside the Louvre, and other courtiers no doubt did the same. Whatever the acquisition history, eighteenth-century conservators copied songs from cheap little sixteenth-century prints into beautiful folio manuscripts bound in red leather, showing that prints with broad circulation traverse all rungs of the social ladder. The cultural cleavages defining the audience for cheap print do not run along the social divisions separating merchants from nobles any more than the urban spaces in which these songs circulated effectively divided commoners from the upper classes.[53]

COMPLAINTES

If one genre of song, by definition, registered the sentiments of *le menu peuple,* it was the *complainte.* A relative of the *planctus,* the political *complainte* marked the anonymous reaction of the people to the great events of history, expressing the suffrage of those who had neither the consolation of glory nor material compensation to soften the hard reality of war.[54] Such songs of lamentation abound in the *recueils* printed after 1572, and with good reason, for there was much to lament. In addition to the many deaths, the ravages of war shattered the economic and agricultural pulse of life in Lyon. Taxes increased as the wars at home and in Flanders dragged on, prices skyrocketed, and the periodic lean years that always accompanied commerce followed one another in the relentless succession of a true crisis. The lower and middle classes suffered particularly at the hands of soldiers, who sacked shops and homes. Because both Catholics and Huguenots hired foreign mercenaries to bolster their troops, many soldiers cared little about the French people. They stole food, grain, livestock, and money while billeted among the citizenry and acted little better than marauders. Those unfortunates who lived in the open countryside without the protection of city walls made especially susceptible victims, as this song makes clear:

Chanson nouvelle de la complainte des pauvres Laboureurs & gens de village sur le chant Dames d'honneur, je vous prie à mains jointes (Lyon 1572, 232)

Dieu tout puissant, que nul ne peut desdire,
Voy le tourment, & le cruel martyre,
Que tous les jours j'endure sans cesser,
Entens ma voix, vueilles moy exaucer.
  Guerre civile m'a mis nud en chemise,
Helas, helas c'est bien pauvre devise
Rien que le corps il ne m'est demeuré,
J'ay tout perdu ce qu'avois labouré.
        . . .
  Femmes et enfants sans cesse apres moy crie,
Du pain, du pain, pour soustenir leur vie,
Morceau n'en ay, gensdarmes ont tout mangé,
Mon bien batu, nauré & outragé.
        . . .
  Helas bon Roy faites une ordonnance
Que vos soldats n'usent pas de violence
Au laboureur, quoy qu'ils mangent son bien
S'ils continuent ils ne trouveront rien.
        . . .
  Gentils soldats qui marchez en campagne,
Qui que sayez de France, ou d'Alemagne,
Changez voz moeurs & vos complexions
Ottant de vous ces imperfections:
  Ayez pitié de nous pauvres Rustiques
Vives en paix sans faire de repliques
Considerant que nous sommes Chrestiens
Comme vous autres & non pas des Payens.
  Ne nous traiste ainsi que bestes brutes
Et ne nous faites coucher emmy les rues,
Ce que trouvez, mangez paisiblement
Vous contentant tousjours honnestement.
  Dieu tout puissant qui tiens tout sous ta dexte
Aye pitie de ton peuple champestre
Qui crie à toy, se voyant affligé
Par les gensdarmes & tous les jours pillé.

[All powerful God, whom nothing can make retract a promise, see the
torment & cruel martyrdom that I incessantly endure. Hear my voice,
please grant my prayer. Civil war left me naked in a shirt. Alas, alas, it
is surely a poor device. Nothing but my body remains to me, I lost
everything for which I labored. . . . Women and children cry after me
incessantly, bread, bread, to sustain their life; I do not have a crumb,
soldiers ate all my food, beat, harrassed, and insulted me. . . . Alas,
good King, make a ruling that your soldiers not use violence upon the
laborer. Though they eat his food, if they continue, they will find nothing. . . . Kind soldiers who march in the country, whether from France
or Germany: Change your morals and your dispositions, get rid of
these vices. Have pity on us poor Rustics. Live in peace without making retaliations. Considering that we are Christians just like you & not
heathens, do not treat us like brute beasts, and do not make us sleep in
the streets. That which you find, eat peaceably; always satisfy your-
selves honestly. All powerful God who holds all under your right hand,
have pity on your rural people, who cry out to you, seeing themselves
afflicted by soldiers and pillaged each day.]

The melody, "Dames d'honneur," bears the characteristic traits of
timbres—conjunct motion, repetitive rhythms, and melodic repetitions—
although its range of an octave is somewhat larger than normal (see Figure 9.4). Despite its musical commonplaces, however, "Dames d'honneur"
is not just a blank slate that might accommodate all contrafacta equally.
It was always associated with the *complainte* and, in Rigaud's prints, was
used for songs about the difficulties of living in besieged Protestant
strongholds (La Charité, Issoire, La Rochelle, and La Fère), songs on
royal deaths, general lamentation over the war, and a song about an unusual crime.[55] Many of the songs based on the "Dames d'honneur" timbre are cast in feminine voices, which relate to the *complainte* genre
itself and to its two traditional themes: love and the hardships of ordinary
people. The political *complainte,* as we know, registered the suffering of
commoners in anonymous or collective language. The amorous *complainte,* on the other hand, was essentially a feminine genre, a melan-
choly song of sadness at ill-fated love or the death of a loved one. The
"Dames d'honneur" songs call upon a society of women to raise their
voices in lamentation, and the songs address women as well. Those
about La Charité, Issoire, La Rochelle, and La Fère, for example, speak
in the voices of women living in those cities, who warn other women not

Figure 9.4 The timbre "Dames d'honneur, je vous prie à mains jointes," reproduced from Jean Chardavoine's monophonic chansonnier *Le recueil des plus belles et excellentes chansons en forme de voix de ville,* fol. 123ᵛ, where it is underlaid with a different text. Reproduced with permission of the Bibliothèque nationale, Paris.

to make the mistake of converting to Protestantism and tell of the rape and victimization that befalls women in Protestant communities. These songs send strong messages in the form of sisterly confidences: the ladies of La Fère describe the atrocities committed by the Huguenots who seized their town, the ladies of Issoire counsel other women that it would be wiser to move than to stay in a Protestant enclave, and the ladies of La Rochelle—probably Protestants—pray that the walls will hold and beg the king's troops to spare them and their children. They end their chanson with the words "adieu, oh foreign women, you should not be like us. . . ." Both political and feminine, these *complaintes* grieve over the war's destruction and call upon women to express the nation's regrets. They are *complaintes* of the third estate, relating the commonplace tragedies of faceless victims.

What we know of earlier *complaintes* relies on courtly examples from the fourteenth and fifteenth centuries. But by the sixteenth century, the genre had ceased to interest court poets.[56] In contrast to its place in literate traditions, the *complainte* always enjoyed a healthy life in the repertories of jongleurs. Thus, what appears to be a sudden flowering of the genre in *recueils de chansons* is probably an instance of an oral repertory with a venerable history making its way into print. Owing to its traditional function as an expression of *le menu peuple* when confronted with political violence, we have every reason to suppose that the *complainte* was a genuinely popular mode of lamentation. In the seventeenth century, *marchands des complaintes* hawked *complaintes* and stories of crimes in city squares and markets, and it is not difficult to imagine how prints such as Rigaud's *recueils* and the flyaway four-folio *Complaincte et Querimonie des pauvres laboureurs fuyant la calamité du temps present sur Da pacem* (1568) gave rise to the complaint-seller's stock-in-trade.[57]

Nonetheless, historians of the book often warn us not to presume that popular subject matter was aimed at a popular audience. Of the poor laborers singing in our *complaintes,* only the most exceptional would have been able to read. Nobles recalled bucolic pleasures over their Almanacs and Shepherd's Calendars far more often than these books made it into the hands of rustics, and even Rigaud's *Placart pour connoître le point et aube du jour . . .* (n.d.) must have graced far more townhouses than farm kitchens.[58] On the whole it is clear that printing transformed only the lives of city folk, and that *colporteurs* worked city streets, not country roads. Some buyers must have bound Rigaud's little *recueils* and placed them alongside Ronsard's poems on their shelves, others wore them out more quickly, but certainly most buyers came across them in the city.

What distinguishes these *recueils* as popular is not their content, but their use of a printing formula designed to satisfy a style of reading common to a less adept public of readers.[59] Levels of literacy varied greatly in the sixteenth century: some people could read print but, never having learned to write, could not read script; others could sound out biblical texts they already knew by heart; some could read in numerous languages. For those who found lengthy, unfamiliar texts difficult, the form of the *recueils* was, by contrast, quite inviting. The brief songs, jumbled together, satisfied readers who were pleased to sacrifice the coherence of a lyric cycle for ready comprehension. The randomly assembled chansons, enlarged initial letters, and italicized headings that comprised the *recueil* formula visibly broke the text into manageable bits and identified the poems, aiding the less skilled reader's errant passage through the book.[60] Compared to the blocks of text crushed onto the pages of elitist books—pages without paragraphs or other breaks in the text—the *recueils* presented a much less challenging form to the marginally literate (see Figure 9.2).

Moreover, books designed for easy consumption enlisted their readers' previous knowledge. As Roger Chartier has written in his study of the *Bibliothèque bleue,* the seventeenth-century manifestation of this printing formula:

> By the recurrence of extremely coded forms, by the repetition of motifs that return from one work to another, and by reuse of the same illustrations, an acquaintance with texts that the reader had already encountered was mobilized into serving for the comprehension of unfamiliar reading matter.[61]

In this way, the Rigaud *recueils*—to gloss Chartier—"organized a manner of reading that was more recognition than true discovery."[62] Because the realization of the song texts rested on a stock of common musical material held in the memories of the readers, the texts always activated a background store of knowledge, rendering them more readable. Moreover, contrafacta texts recycled stock phrases from one song to another, loading *chansons nouvelles* with lines from timbres readers already knew. The interlocking relationships between text, memorized timbres, and contrafacta texts shaped a matrix of familiar idioms, thus revealing to the historian's eye what is truly "popular" about the newsy songs and *complaintes.*

Let us return to our *Complainte des pauvres laboureurs.* "Dieu tout puissant" is set in the voice of a rural laborer, though we can hardly suppose that it was written by one, as most peasants were illiterate. But if the fictional attribution is unbelievable, we still should not dismiss it out of hand, for it locates the production of the *complainte* in a cultural sphere concerned with the third estate.

Complaintes play off the juridical sense of "se plaindre"—to register a legal complaint—and in the fifteenth century, writers often composed *complaintes* as formal objections to a ruler's actions in war or governance. "Dieu tout puissant" is more politic than those earlier *complaintes,* and addresses the "good king" of France who keeps the peace and protects the poor. A petition of this sort—one that anticipates a helpful response—is most like those made by provincial lawyers on the behalf of commoners, and I would suggest that a lawyer may have penned this song. The French legal bureaucracy supported a whole society of jurists, parliamentarians, lawyers, clerks, notaries, judges, and legal administrators, a society whose nobility took the title *noblesse de la robe* (nobility of the robe) for the long robes of their judicial offices and whose more common members counted among the notables and bourgeois of French cities. In general, strong connections tied these legal professionals to the people, for they were often the sons of local merchants and petits bourgeois who worked their way up the economic ladder with college educations in law, for which reason law supported Frenchmen from diverse socioeconomic backgrounds. Not lacking in musical talents, Lyon's law clerks organized their own play-acting society of *Basochiens* who entertained guests with theatrical chansons and were old hands at writing new texts to popular tunes for their plays.[63]

Jurists and lawyers concentrated in cities and usually dealt with taxes, property, and commerce, but sometimes the rights of peasants made it onto their docket. In 1574, the Parisian jurist René Choppin wrote a handbook for country lawyers entitled *De Privilegiis Rusticorum: Lib. III* ("On the Privileges of Rustic Persons"), which must have met some need, judging from its three editions during his lifetime (1575, 1582, 1590), and we also know that lawyers drew up petitions to the king based on the complaints of peasants.[64] When, in 1579 and 1580, noble brigands preyed brutally upon the peasantry, Jean La Rouvière, a small-town lawyer in the Vivarais just south of Lyon, petitioned the king for aid with a list of atrocities like those reported in *complaintes:* raping women, kidnapping children or roasting them alive, burying peasants alive, throwing them in wells, nailing them in boxes without air, burning their feet, torching their houses, ransoms, sackings, and exorbitant levies and taxes.[65] Henry III sent commissioners to keep the peace and made edicts that were cried and posted and that in this way arrived at the same places where *complaintes* registered dissatisfaction in song.[66]

Singing "Dieu tout puissant" would have been an ineffectual way to petition the king, of course. If anything, singing it would only have reinforced the fear and anger shared by listeners. Conversely, it would also have reinforced the law with its expectation that justice would be served. I suspect that lawyers professed this faith in the systems of justice much sooner than the man in the street, which would mean that "Dieu tout puissant" expresses both a peasant's grievances and a lawyer's "solution" to the problem, but even so, the song would—like a petition—have been heard as coming from the third estate. Its tacit support of the king should not brand it a piece of courtly propaganda, for many commoners supported their Catholic king, and legal professionals generally supported the state, which meant supporting the monarch as well. Indeed, when the wars against Protestantism threatened the institutions of monarchy, it was jurists and administrators who argued that the state should be preserved even at the expense of spiritual purity. The views of moderate Catholics eventually coalesced as a political philosophy known as *politique,* a middle road that proposed the temporary toleration of Protestantism in order to restore peace to the kingdom.[67] The *politiques* included many of the king's commissioners who had been dispatched to the provinces to uphold the edicts of toleration ordered by the king, and their first-hand experience with the petitions or *remonstrances* of the people made them keen legislators of peace. The moderate attitudes toward religious difference in most of Rigaud's *recueils* align well with this *politique* philosophy of toleration, a philosophy eventually accepted by a country exhausted from religious violence and the financial burden of war.

SONGS AND PREACHING

Let us be clear, though, that the *politiques* only exerted significant influence after Henry IV was crowned in 1594. The 1570s saw an apex of conflict between Catholics and Huguenots that was fought out in the Saint Bartholomew's massacres and in the fourth, fifth, sixth, and seventh civil wars. Churchmen in particular called for battle, not truce. Preachers such as René Benoist inflamed Catholic hatred from the pulpit and in printed sermons, and Huguenot pastors such as Jean Ruffy helped sack the Cathedral of Saint Jean in Lyon. With the blessing of ministers, Protestant iconoclasts broke open reliquaries filled with "animal bones" and destroyed holy wafers before Catholic congregants worshipping their "God of paste," while Catholics speared Huguenot bibles with halberds and stuffed their pages into the mouths of corpses in the name of Christ.[68] Preaching all too often suggested and condoned these violent rites of purification, suspending the commandment "Thou shalt not kill" in the crusade against idolatry and heresy.[69]

Protestant ministers had to preach to clandestine conventicles, but Catholic preachers could make their pulpits where needed, be it in or out

of church. Luther's threat to the Catholic church had provoked a wave of
missionary preaching designed to convert and fight heresy. As Larissa
Taylor relates in her *Soldiers of Christ: Preaching in Late Medieval and
Reformation France,* Louise of Savoy sent twelve doctors of theology
into the provinces to preach the Catholic faith in the 1520s, and in 1544,
Brother Germain Lamy was dispatched to Normandy "to preach the
faith, stop the progress of heresy, and pacify tempers."[70] Much preaching
took place in the open air, for which a pulpit or raised platform was
erected against the wall of the church, in the square before the church, in
the church cemetery, the market place, or even in a field, and to which a
bell summoned the congregation. Mendicants, whose traditional charge
was the preaching of missionary sermons, delivered their sermons before
or after Mass on Sundays and daily during Lent. Special events also merited public sermons, particularly the death of a heretic, when a sermon
was always delivered for the soul of the condemned and for the edifica-
tion of onlookers.[71] Public exorcisms, too, provided spectacular occasions for sermons, as priests cast out blasphemous devils and restored
good Catholics to rights.

City councillors in Lyon felt a strong need for missionary preaching,
given the city's reputation as a second Geneva. As Philip T. Hoffman tells
us in *Church and Community in the Diocese of Lyon,* the Catholic majority of the city council awarded subsidies to the Catholic preaching orders
during the 1570s in order to "further the Catholic religion" as Dominican, Franciscan, Carmelite, Minime, Jesuit, and Capuchin monks took
the pulpits of parish churches during Lent and Advent, on holy days, and
for special occasions.[72] Some of these preachers delivered such engaging
sermons that parish laity began to request certain preachers for the
Lenten and Advent series. Whereas Lyon's parish clergy tended to be
most concerned with shepherding the elite among their parishioners, the
sermonizing priests of religious orders looked to the spiritual needs of
the masses. In the business of charismatic preaching, it was these priests
of the religious orders who wrote most of the religious pamphlets, sermons, and surely also some of the evangelizing songs flying from the
city's presses.[73] Certainly the forms and subjects of sermons provide a
structure for this song, printed by Rigaud in 1580:

Memoire de deux signes fort espouventables advenus au pays d'An-
gleterre de deux hommes lesquels se sont apparus au ciel l'un en feu &
l'autre en sang, sur le chant de La Parque (Jardin, 115)

    Chrestiens ne vous desplaise
J'ay osé sans faillir
Ce beau discours a l'aise
A tous vous faire ouyr
D'un signe merveilleux
Qui est fanticieux.
    O grand Dieu salutaire
Tu permets ce jourd'huy,
Qu'au Sainct ciel de bonnaire
L'on descouvre luy
De tes faicts precieux
Qui sont miraculeux.
    Au pays d'Angleterre
Lequel nous est fiel,
C'est apparu sur terre,
Dans un arc en Ciel
Un homme en feu bruslant
Qui estoit tout ardant.
    Seigneur ce ne sont fables
Croyez le fermement
Pour dire veritable
Qu'au ciel presentement
C'est apparu d'orreur
Un signe de fureur.
    C'est une forme d'homme
Qui estoit tout en sang
En forme de fantosme,
Couroit comme le vent
Dans le ciel divin
Helas ce n'est en vain,
    O Anglois plein de rage
Contre Dieu & raison
Voyez l'Emant courroucé
De vostre trahison
Le grand Roy de là sus
Vous monstre vos abus.
    Vous voyez chose insignes

Afin vous advertir
Au ciel voyez les signes
Afin vous convertir,
Nostre Dieu gracieux
Lever vous fait les yeux.
Helas ce n'est sa faute
Si vous estes damnez
Il vous crie à voix haute
Que vous vous amendez,
La fin approche fort,
Pensez à vostre mort.

[Christians, do not be upset, I dared without fail to let you all hear this beautiful discourse about a marvelous sign, which is uncanny. Oh great beneficent Lord, you allow us to see today with our own eyes in the heavenly sky your precious deeds, which are miraculous. In the country of England, which is gall to us, there appeared on the earth in a rainbow, a man burning in flames who was all scorched. Sir, these are not stories. Believe in it wholeheartedly as a truthful claim that in the sky today there appeared, in horror, a sign of rage. It was the shape of man who was all bloodied, a phantom in shape, running like the wind in the divine sky. Alas, it is not in vain. O English, full of ire against God and reason, see the wrathful issue of your treachery. The great King above shows you your wrong. You are seeing remarkable things in order to warn you. You are seeing the signs in the sky in order to convert you. Our gracious God makes you raise your eyes. Alas, it is not his fault if you are damned. He cries out to you in a loud voice that you should change. The end approaches quickly: Think of your death.]

The little drama scripted by this song is not hard to imagine: the preacher-singer steps up before the crowd convened to hear about the "two very dreadful signs that came to the country of England, of two men who appeared in the sky, the one on fire and the other [bathed in] blood" announced by the title of the song. In the first stanza, the preacher quells the crowd—"Christians," he begins—and promises them uncanny news. Then he looks to heaven in the second stanza and speaks directly to God, thanking him for the miraculous messages inscribed in the sky. Furious with the English church, God's signs warn heretics to convert and predict their impending doom: "The end approaches quickly, think of your death." The sensational language and direct address of the song imply a public transaction between a preaching singer and his audience,

while the pictorial quality of the warning signs—two men in the sky—
plays upon the ways moralizing emblem books, posters, and church win-
dows conveyed their messages to viewers.[74] These iconographies come
alive as the song denounces the Protestant heresy with the tactics of hell-
fire and brimstone sermons by reporting the fate of wrongdoers and calling upon miraculous proofs to seal its claims. The form and language of
canard literature inflects "Chrestiens ne vous desplaise" just as surely as
preaching does, and its message fits well with the prognostications cried
by vendors of cheap print. Whether sung by preacher, lay evangelist, *colporteur,* or in private, the very idioms of song anticipate its public declamation in a sermonlike gathering.

The timbre of our "preachy" song, "La Parque si terrible," was popular in Rigaud's political *recueils,* and Rigaud included it in three different collections between 1572 and 1580. New songs written to its tune
number a dozen in the same eight years, as can be seen here:

"La Parque si terrible" and Songs Written to Its Tune[75]

*"La parque si terrible" (Sommaire, 51^r; Lyon 1572, 199; Jardin, 72r) [J.
Du Bellay]

*"Amy entens mes plaintes" (Sommaire, 51^v)

"D'ou vient l'amour soudaine" (Sommaire, 48^r) [J. de la Péruse]

"Las je mourray d'angoisse" (Sommaire, 53^r)

"Ton doux parler m'attire" (Ample, 31^v)

"Si j'avois la feconde" *chanson nouvelle d'Anvers* (Beauté, 10)

"La fortune amiable" (Lyon 1572, 188)

"Jamais tel cas terrible" *chanson nouvelle de la plus terrible chose advenue en la ville de Bar en Lorraine, d'un marchant de draps &
laines nommé Jean Godard & Claude Caboret son gendre qui se
sont desfaicts pour avoir veu les biens beaux, estans possedez des
Diables, comme appert sur la copie imprimee à Paris avec permission: et se chant sur la Parque* (Rosier, 25^r; Fleur, 31^r)

"La peine fatiguante" *Complaincte de treshaute & excellente Dame Elizabeth d'Austriche sur la mort de ma Dame fille unique d'elle & de
feu Roy Charles* (Printemps, 5^r)

"Qui d'une maladie" (Printemps, 10^r)

"Chrestiens ne vous desplaise" *Memoire de deux signes fort espouventables . . .* (Jardin, 115^r)

"O mort tant inhumaine" *chanson nouvelle des complainctes et regrets
d'une dame, laquelle lamentoit la mort de son mary qui fut tué devant Sainct Valery* (Jardin, 54^r)

"O Dieu, quelle nouvelle" *chanson nouvelle des complaintes & regretz de Madame d'Aumale, sur la mort de son mary, lequel fut tué en parlementant avec les traistres de la Rochelle. Et se chante sur la chant, La Parque si terrible* (Jardin, 52ʳ)

Written by the Parisian poet Joachim Du Bellay, "La parque si terrible" also went by the title "Le chant du Desesperé," which tells us much about the family of contrafacts that grew up around it. At first glance, Du Bellay's poem masquerades as a love song that treats the subject of ill-fortune in the language of unrequited love. But the poet's cold mistress is absent from this song, and the reader soon discovers that the poem is simply about fate and pain. The first stanza gives a good idea of how it proceeds:

La parque si terrible
A tous les animaux,
Plus ne me semble horrible,
Car le moindre des maux,
Qui m'ont fait si dolent
Est bien plus violent

[The Fates (which are) so terrible to all the animals no longer seem horrible to me, since the smallest pain, which makes me so mournful, is much more violent.]

Du Bellay's reference to the Parcae (Fates) recurs in all the texts written to this melody, probably because the first line—and "La Parque"—became the song's identifying incipit. In Roman mythology, the Parcae were three hags who controlled human destiny and life: the first (Clotho) spun the thread of life; the second (Lachesis) determined its length; and the third (Atropos) cut it off. Their use in a chanson signifies a new and bleak understanding of the human condition. Traditionally, the French typified destiny with Fortune and her wheel: a beautiful blonde woman, blindfolded, turned the wheel upon which we are fixed in our passage through life. Fortune's random gyrations assured that some person rose to success even as someone else took a fall from power. In contrast, Du Bellay's witchlike Fates symbolize a far grimmer world view, for good luck plays no role in their machinations (though Fortune does appear briefly further on in the poem).

The sense of impending disaster that gripped French consciousness during these years emerges fully formed in the family of songs on "La Parque si terrible" as the contrafacts transform the Fates of the musical model into heavenly signs and prognostications. "Jamais tel cas terrible" tells of demonic possessions, "O mort tant inhumaine" and "O Dieu quelle nouvelle" are *complaintes* of women whose husbands were killed in the religious wars (and Madame d'Aumale might well complain, as her husband was killed quite unfairly during negotiations), and "La peine fatiguante" is the queen's lament on the death of her daughter. In six-teenth-century Lyon, "La Parque si terrible" expressed a crisis of faith in the holy ordering of the world that made it particularly susceptible to laments and evangelical doom-saying.

Preachers were not the only zealots who might have penned an in-flammatory song. The thirty or more stipendiary priests of Lyon's Cathe-dral of Saint-Jean themselves came from modest backgrounds, sons of local artisans who cared for the spiritual welfare of their families and so-cial peers. They usually began as choristers and thus had a special affin-ity for music that other priests might lack.[76] Certain staunch Catholics among the lay elite of Lyon may also have turned their efforts toward contrafacting evangelical songs.[77]

Finally, we must not forget the potential authors among the business-men and literate artisans who worked in the print industry. Lyon supported a large population of printers, from enterprising merchant-publishers such as Antoine Vincent and publisher-printers such as Rigaud and Saugrin to the master craftsmen and printers' journeymen who ran the presses. Many of these men could have penned pro-Catholic songs, and one group in particular—the journeymen pressmen, typesetters, and proofreaders—had already demonstrated their propensity for public song. As Natalie Zemon Davis relates in her essay on the printers' jour-neymen in Lyon, the self-directed spiritual paths of Protestantism at-tracted this proud group in the 1550s, and in 1551, journeymen took to the streets in an armed procession, singing psalms and professing their faith in public.[78] By 1566, however, the journeymen realized that no place would be made for them in the administration of the Reformed Church of Lyon, which had come to be run by citizens of higher rank, and, disappointed, they drifted back to the Catholic Church. By 1572, the movement back to Catholicism was all but complete: as Davis says, "the psalm-singing printers' journeymen became in the late sixteenth century Catholic *politiques* who regretted that France should tear herself to pieces for the sake of religion."[79] The general trend among printers' jour-neymen in Lyon matches Rigaud's own circular relationship with the

Reformed Church in the same years, and the moderate pro-Catholic, proto-*politique* messages in Rigaud's *recueils* may express a shared attitude in his shop and among the smaller people in the print industry. Printers' journeymen no doubt kept right on singing after they abjured the Protestant faith, and songs like "Chrestiens ne vous desplaise" would have been apt replacements for psalms.

PUBLISHING AND THE PUBLIC SPHERE

Sixteenth-century technologies of information were vastly different from our own. First of all, the exchange of news and information most often took place in public. It was in public locales that urban folk beheld spectacles such as royal entries, heard official edicts proclaimed in a loud voice, read *placards* pasted to the doors of the church, and received news by rumor, town crier, street song, or tocsin (alarm bell). All of these technologies rely on speech and sound. So fundamental is this connection between things public and the spoken word that to "publish" was, by definition, an oral act.

In sixteenth-century France, the term public—or *public*—bore two separable categories of meaning. The first arose from the understanding of the king as the head of state. For this reason Brantôme declared that "he who kills his king offends and kills not only his father, but an entire public." Heritor and guardian, first owner of public property, the king was, in effect, France. His participation in processions and entries represented his embodiment of divine authority and likewise, his lieutenant governors to the provinces served the public by representing the king. It is in this royal sense, then, that we may also understand the work of town criers when they declaimed edicts and decrees. These royal proclamations were "leu, crié & publié à son de trompe & cry public"—that is, "read, cried & published by trumpet and public cry"—and those who read them aloud, announced them with trumpet calls, or subsequently printed them were "public" representatives of the king before the people in the royal sense of the word.

The second meaning of "public" in the late sixteenth century presages our modern usage, a sense increasingly distanced from the essentially feudal one just adduced. *Publier* and *publicquer* meant to confiscate and sell by auction, to put private goods up for sale by force. It is difficult to prise apart that which belonged to the people from that which belonged to the king—here we would have to know who benefited from the profits of such a sale—but the notion of communal property is nascent in these uses. Even more proximate to our modern definitions of public are the currency of *publicateur* and *publieur:* one who spreads or makes something known. Yet sixteenth-century mechanisms of publication differed from subsequent technologies in that they were based on oral communication. We will search in vain for the use of *publié* in reference to printing. Books were not yet to be *publié* (published), but only literally *imprimé* (printed), and there existed only the most fragile semblance of a press to disseminate information on paper.

What we know of town criers is recorded in pamphlets documenting the material they proclaimed. Like de Losse's ordinance banning dissolute songs, pamphlets reprinting letter patents, edicts, ordinances, and other royal declarations usually ended with specific information about the vocal publication of the text and were signed by the crier, who was an official employee of the city or, in Paris, of the king. The attestations, like that of the 1564 ordinance, follow a formula: "the present decree here above was cried, read, and publicized by loud voice, public declamation, and the sound of the trumpet at each and every one of the crossroads and public squares usual for making announcements, proclamations, and publications in the said city of . . . ." They are signed by the crier or his deputy, and include the name of the official trumpeter, the name of his deputy when appropriate, the number of trumpeters accompanying him if there was more than one, and the date—to the day—of the cry. For particularly important cries, up to five trumpeters would be used. In Paris we know that the palace, the Châtelet, and the Hôtel de Ville were among the first spots to receive news from criers; in Lyon criers began their route with stops at each end of the bridge over the Saône, just a few blocks from Rigaud's shop.[80] In every instance, the authorization of official pamphlets by civic criers signals that the paper pamphlet only registered the actual publication preceding it, which was made in a loud voice in the city's public spaces.

Oftentimes the publication of an ordinance on paper was meant to work in tandem with public crying. In the seventeenth century, official broadsheets or *affiches* were posted in the regular sites for cries, and "affichée par les carrefours" became part of the regular formula reporting cries at the end of prints. Another typical case in which print supported oral declamation was the process for announcing public sales, in which information was cried, announced at public markets, and "posted by *affiche* on the post at the market and at the entrance to the auditorium where the sale would take place."[81] Print thus entered into urban life in conjunction with the spoken word. *Affiches* and printed copies of edicts recollect the oral as soon as they verify it, shadowing the actual publication with far less certain trajectories than the "ceremonies d'information" that institutionalized the work of town criers. So, too, with printed song texts, which both produced and recalled public singing, whether official or seditious.

Readers will recognize that the foregoing discussion of publicness and publicity relies to a large extent on the theories Jürgen Habermas expounded in his *The Structural Transformation of the Public Sphere*.[82] The bourgeois public sphere as he defines it was created by coalitions of private people—that is, those who did not participate in the rule of the state—who eventually asserted themselves in the public sphere that had initially been created by princely authority.[83] By the eighteenth century, merchants had turned the systems of publicity established for ceremonies of monarchic representation to their own uses. The fully developed bourgeois public sphere was marked by the moment when public authorities—representatives of the king—were engaged by the people in open debate over political issues.

Of course, merchants and bourgeois in late sixteenth-century Lyon did not claim enough power against public authority to garner control in the public sphere. The commercial identity of the city enabled men from these middle classes to fill the majority of seats in the city council—a highly unusual state of affairs in other French cities at the time—yet even so, royal authority checked the council's government of the city through the king's officers, commissioners, and the *sénéchausée* (the city's royal court).[84] The governmental structures of Lyon favored merchants and bourgeois, but the city never loosed itself from monarchic rule. Nonetheless, citizens enjoyed relatively good local representation and the freedoms of speech it supported, which made Lyon a prime site for the kinds of political debate that would eventually produce the eighteenth-century bourgeois public sphere and, at the end of that century, the French Revolution.

Another crucial mechanism of bourgeois power in the public sphere—the press—was only just forming in the sixteenth century. Still, Habermas identified the sixteenth-century oral mechanisms of publicity as important precursors to the seventeenth-century press. Just as the press would serve both the monarchy and the bourgeoisie, so the traffic of news in the sixteenth century was controlled partly by the monarchy and partly by merchants. As they engaged in long-distance trade, merchants relied on news of distant events in order to calculate the fluctuations of their markets, and they traded in news along with other commodities. Merchants, for example, organized the first mail routes between major trade cities. As Habermas remarks, "almost simultaneously with the origin of stock markets, postal services and the press institutionalized regular contacts and regular communication."[85]

Habermas was well aware that cheap print and street songs were early analogues to the bourgeois newspapers of the seventeenth century. But he felt that their ability to create a bourgeois public sphere was overwhelmed by their traditional functions in the public sphere created by ritual appearances and announcements of the monarch:

> . . . Sixteenth-century single-sheet prints still bore witness to the strength with which an unbroken traditional knowledge was able to assimilate communications whose rising stream, to be sure, already pointed to a new form of public sphere. Such sheets indiscriminately spread the news of religious wars, campaigns against the Turks, and Papal decrees as well as news of rains of blood and fire, freaks, locust plagues, earthquakes, thunderstorms, and heavenly phenomena; of Papal Bulls, electoral agreements, and discoveries of new continents as well as of baptisms of Jews, punishments by the devil, divine judgments, and resurrections of the dead. Often . . . [they] were written in the form of songs or dialogues, i.e. were meant to be declaimed or sung, alone or with others. In this process, the novelty moved out of the historical sphere of "news" and, as sign and miracle, was reintegrated into that sphere of representation in which a ritualized and ceremonialized participation of the people in the public sphere permitted a merely passive acceptance incapable of independent interpretation . . .[86]

Habermas argues that singing changed the message of the song, transforming it from news into just another performance of monarchic public authority. If I read him correctly, the public singing of the song strips it of its bourgeois newsiness and casts it back into the old public sphere created by and for the first estate. Habermas rightly observes that many of the historical songs serve the state in the same way as other monarchic publication, and I agree that songs such as "O Terre, ô Ciel" glorify the Valois and equate royalty with godliness in a traditional way. I must argue, however, that not all songs relegated performers—or listeners, for that matter—to "merely passive acceptance incapable of independent interpretation." The bans against seditious songs aimed to curb the mob violence that often accompanied singing, and, as we have seen, French kings responded to the insurrectionary potential of song with force. The songs calling for and celebrating the regicide of Henry III, it seems to me, contested the absolute authority of the king in the public sphere. Pace Habermas, songs like the *placard* "Chanson pleine de resjouissance, avec action de graces sur la mort advenue à Henry de Valloys . . . pour mettre les Catholiques en liberté" adopted the systems of monarchic publicity to express views that precisely opposed the conciliatory policies of the Valois. (This is one of the *placards* in L'Estoile's scrapbook; also see Figure 9.1.)

The *ancien régime* emerged in tandem with an unruly third estate, which it tried to suppress and which eventually destroyed it. The civil wars may have resulted in a stranglehold of royal control rather than revolution, but we should recall that absolutism began in a climate of popular revolt: as the billeting of soldiers took its toll on the countryside, the issues at stake in the wars turned from religion to economic oppression, and just to the south of Lyon, in the Vivarais, Dauphiné, and further south in Provence, peasants took up arms against the soldiers who had been torturing them and the noblemen who had been sheltering and defending the murderers (1575–1580).[87] The peasants took little note of the religious or political affiliations of their targets, for what rallied them against the soldiers was material hardship. For these reasons, social tensions flared during the religious wars, and armed bands sometimes coalesced within classes rather than along the lines drawn by Catholic and Huguenot factions. The peasant revolts show the third estate up in arms against local nobles. And while it is not a revolutionary document, the petition to the king that Jean La Rouvière drew up for the peasants of Vivarais in 1579 did make revolutionary demands, such as representation for the third estate in provincial government and the establishment of a special court to deal with military violence. Citizen militias sprang up in the cities of Dauphiné to expel the king's garrisons and defend against their return. Although city consuls argued that they acted to enforce the edicts of peace made by the king, commanders of royal troops beheld citizens arming themselves against the monarchy. In the countryside of Dauphiné, peasants attacked nobles who provoked them, killing them and burning their estates to the ground.

In March 1579, popular insurrection targeted Laprade, a noble brigand growing fat off his plunder of Dauphiné.[88] The battle began when four thousand peasants laid siege to Laprade's stronghold at Chateaudouble, and it ended several weeks later when the king's lieutenant governor, Maugiron, intervened. Maugiron wanted to control the uprising and did so by aiding the peasants in order to end the conflict and disband them, for the mob proved to be far more threatening to the king than

Laprade and his soldiers. The victory was enormously important to the demoralized citizens of Dauphiné, and Rigaud wasted no time in printing two songs on the peasants' revenge, which came out in 1580.[89] The first song, "Rossignoletz des boys sauvages," makes no mention of Maugiron, celebrating instead the peasant soldiers who "lived by the sword" and "risked their lives in a thousand hazards for the cause" (ll. 47–48, 38–40). In the language of a people's tribunal, Laprade and his band are made to answer for the corn, wine, flour, meat, and thousands of francs they stole from rustics and townspeople:

> *Chanson de la prise de chasteaudouble en Dauphiné au mois de Mars 1579. Sur le chant* de Petit Rossignolet sauvage (Fleur, fol. 79[r])

> *Je leur demande en concience,*
> *D'où est sorty si grand tresor*
> *Et s'ils n'ont du peuple de France*
> *Dedans leurs coeur quelque remord*
>   *D'avoir mis bas & tout à plat,*
>   *Tous ceux qui sont du tiers estat.* (ll. 49–54)

> [I ask them in good conscience whence these great treasures came, and if they have no remorse in their hearts for the French people for having put down and laid out flat all those who are of the third estate.]

The second song, "Pensons amis," lauds the brave folk of Romans who successfully attacked two companies of light cavalry—one led by Henry d'Angoulême, the Grand Prior of France—and overthrew the town's oligarches before setting off to the north some fourteen thousand strong to stir rebellion in Valence.

> *Autre chanson sur la prinse de Chasteaudouble en Dauphiné, sur le chant de* Sommière (Fleur, fol. 81[r])

> *Le tambour bat deça dela par tout:*
> *Chacun armé veut chasser telle peste,*
> *Qui plus luy nuit qu'une forte tempeste.*
>   *Hardy on voit marcher par la campagne*
> *Le Roumanois, qui à ce rien n'espargne*
> *Deliberé devant le lieu mourir,*
> *Ou ces voleurs bien tost faire perir.* (ll. 52–58)

[The drum beats here there everywhere; every armed man wants to
hunt the menace who harms him more than a strong storm. One sees
boldly marching in the countryside the Romans, who spare nothing and
die resolutely before the place where these thieves will soon perish.]

Romans, Valence, and Chateaudouble all lay within fifty miles of Lyon,
which sat at the northern tip of Dauphiné. In this song we can hear the tocsin calling men to arms and the sound of peasants and villagers marching
against the soldiers, tax men, and marauding noblemen who had op-
pressed them during fifteen years of civil war. Sung before a crowd, sung
to a drum, to clapping hands, or sung while marching, "Pensons amis" co-
ordinates all of the sentiments necessary for popular uprising.

Singing and marching together invested individuals with the
strength of numbers and directed free-floating anger into the regular
physical motions of a collective. It empowered lone souls with group
strength. Lutherans sang during services, Huguenots sang during their
martyrdoms, soldiers and pilgrims sang while marching, and protesters
sang during demonstrations. Indeed, I would suggest that during the civil
wars, street songs made revolution sooner than books did.

The songs printed on *placards* and in *recueils* arose first and foremost from oral practices of publication. Making up new songs to the
tunes of old ones produced repertories at all levels of society, to be
sure—from the court to the farmhouse, if we believe Noël du Fail—and
long before the invention of the printing press, news was transmitted by
oral means in cities and towns. Street songs, bell ringing, the tocsin,
rumor, town crier, fireworks, and processions remained the first avenues
by which local and national news reached city notables and the *menu
peuple* in the early age of print. Printing song texts about current affairs
expanded an oral repertory of songs, making more and longer song texts
available to literate singers and more songs available to city folk both
orally and in print. Yet song spread the word faster than print, even while
print spread songs along the pathways of literacy faster than word of
mouth. Within the third estate, political and religious songs were only
truly effective when singing sent them from print back into the oral
sphere where they could produce or reinforce public opinion.[90] No
République des lettres produced these songs, nor a bourgeois public
sphere defined by writing and reading—though these communities of
print were fast on their way. Rather, this repertory emerged from oral traditions of voicing public opinion that would later come to revise the public sphere through print.

Appendices

APPENDIX 9.1

Short-Title List of *Recueils de chansons* and Pamphlets Containing Political Songs Published by Benoist Rigaud (with abbreviations for frequently cited prints)

Recueil de plusieurs chansons divisé en trois parties: en la premiere sont les chansons musicales: en la seconde les chansons amoureuses & rustiques: & en la tierce chansons de la guerre . . . . With Jean Saugrin, 1557. In-16, 208 pp.

Chanson Crestienne et nouvelle de la Royne de Navarre. Avec une autre chanson Chrestienne, d'un Gentil'homme Provençal respondant à icelle. 1564. In-8, 4 ff.

Avant-chant nuptial, faict sur le mariage du Roy & Elizabet d'Autriche par Am. Jamyn. 1570. In-8, 8 ff.

Lyon 1572: *Le recueil de plusieurs chansons nouvelles* . . . . No publisher, 1572. In-16, 281 pp.

Jean de la Gessée, *Nouveau discours sur la siege de Sanserre* . . . *plus une complainte de la France en forme de chanson.* 1573. In-8, 16 ff.

Hymne triomphal, sur l'entree et louange du tres illustre & serenessime Prince Henry, esleu Roy Auguste de Pologne, grand Duc de Lituanie: faicte à Paris le 14. jour de Septembre 1573. 1573. In-8, 8 ff.

Petit recueil de chansons nouvelles tant de l'amour que de la guerre, contenant la pluspart des heureuses victoires obtenues en Auvergne et ailleurs. 1577. In-12, 48 ff.

Sommaire: *Sommaire de tous les recueils des chansons, tant amoureuses, rustiques que musicales* . . . 1579. In-16, 112 ff.

Ample recueil: *Ample recueil des chansons tant amoureuses, rustiques, musicalles qu'autres* . . . 1579. In-16, 112 ff.

Fleur: *La fleur des chansons nouvelles, Traittans partie de l'amour, partie de la guerre, selon les occurrences du temps present* . . . 1580. In-16, 87ff. Another edition in 1586.

Printemps: *Le printemps des chansons nouvelles* . . . 1579 and another undated edition. In-16, 64 ff.

Rosier: *Le rosier des chansons nouvelles* . . . 1580. In-16, 64 ff.

Jardin: *Le plaisant jardin des belles chansons* . . . 1580. In-16, 128 pp.

La Fère: *Nouveau recueil des chansons qu'on chante a present, tant de la guerre & voyage de la Fère, de la Mure: & des Chansons amoureuses.* 1581. In-16, 47 pp.

Nouveau recueil: *Nouveau recueil de toutes les chansons nouvelles, tant de l'amour que de la guerre* [1580]. In-16, 64 ff.

Bouquet: *Le joyeux bouquet des belles chansons nouvelles* . . . No publisher, 1583. In-16, 32 ff.

L'excellence des chansons les plus joyeuses et recreatives . . . . 1584. In-16, 80 ff.

Nouveau vergier florissant des belles chansons nouvelles . . . no date.

Chanson nouvelle de la paix, par le peuple de France. 1588. In-8, 8 pp.

Beauté: *La beaulte des belles chansons nouvelles* . . . No date. In-16, 32 ff.

Chansons joyeuses et recreatifves avec ceux de la guerre . . . No publisher or date. In-16, 32 ff.

Le cabinet des plus belles chansons nouvelles, tant de l'amour que de la guerre . . . No publisher, 1592. In-16, 80 ff.

APPENDIX 9.2

British Library 5423.AA.23 (1), in-8, 3 ff, unnumbered.

Ordonnance du roy, et de Monseigneur de Losses, Gouveneur general pour sa Majesté, en la ville de Lyon, pays de Lyonnois Beaujollois &c. En l'absence de monseigneur le Duc de Nemours: Touchant de ne blasphemer, joüer, ne chanter chansons dissoulues, le tout sur peine de la hart. [printer's mark or royal seal—Charles IX looking to the right, surmounted by the three fleurs de lys and a crown above that. A banner across the top says "pietate et justicia"]

A Lyon, Par Benoist Rigaud. 1564 avec permission.

De par le Roy.

Et monseigneur de Losses, Chevalier de l'Ordre, premier Capitaine de ses Gardes, Gouverneur & Lieutenant general pour sa Majesté, en l'absence de monseigneur le Duc de Nemours, en la ville de Lyon, pays de Lyonnois, Beaujollois &c.

Est faict tresexpres commandement à tous vaccabons, & gens sans adveu ou trafficq, estans dans ladicte ville, qu'ilz ayent incontinent apres la publication des presentes, à vuider & sortir hors la-dicte ville, & fauxbourgs d'icelle, sur peine de la hart.

Est enjoinct sur les peines que dessus, à tous hosteliers, cabaretiers, & autres personnes de quelque qualité & condition qu'ilz soient, ne retirer, loger, ne administrer aucuns vivres ausdictes personnes, plus que d'une nuict, sans expres congé de nous.

Et pour oster le moyen d'entretenir & retirer les dessusdictz vaccabons, & gens oisifz: Sont faictes deffences à toutes personnes demeu-
rans tant en ceste ville que fauxbourgs, de tenir berlans en leurs maisons
& jardins, & d'y souffrir joüer à jeuz de detz, carres, quilles, & autres
jeuz prohibez & deffenduz, sur ladicte peine de la hart, tant contre ceux
qui tiendront lesdictz berlans, que contre ceux qui seront trouvez joüans

Aussi en ensuyvant les anciennes Ordonnances, & sainctes constitutions du Roy nostredict Seigneur, sont faictes tresexpresses deffences &
inhibitions, à toutes personnes de quelque estat, qualité & condition
qu'ilz soyent, de jurer, blasphemer, maulgreer & renier le nom de Dieu,
faire autres vilains & detestables sermens, contre l'honneur de Dieu, de
la vierge Marie & des Sainctz, & de ne chanter ny dire chansons dissoulues & tendans à sedition, ne se provocquer par injures ou autrement,
& soubz pretexte de la Religion: soubz les peines contenues esdictes Ordonnances.
DE LOSSE
Copie collationé à l'original, par moy Secretaire de monseigneur de
Losse: Lieutenant general du Roy au gouvernement de Lyonnois, Beaujollois &c. en l'absence de monseigneur le Duc de Nemours.
DAVOST.
La presente Ordonnance cy dessus, a esté crieé leuë & publiée à haute
voix, cry public, & son de trompe par tous & chascuns les carreffours &
places publicques accoustumees à faire crys, proclamations & publications en ladicte ville de Lyon: Par moy Claude Thevenon clerc & commis
de maistre Jean Bruyeres, crieur public de ladicte ville, aujourdhuy
cinquiesme jour de Decembre, Mil cinq cens soixante quatre.
THEVENON.

NOTES

*Many of my ideas about print culture were formulated during the spring of
1995 in seminars taught by Roger Chartier at the University of Chicago and
Martha Feldman at the Newberry Library, Chicago. Earlier versions of this paper
were read at the Society of Fellows, Columbia University—an institution that
supported my work on this project during 1996–1997—and in the Morrison
Library Inaugural Lecture Series, University of California, Berkeley. I would like
to thank my colleagues in New York and Berkeley for their innumerable helpful
comments. Special thanks goes to Frank Dobbins, Martha Feldman, and Donna
Cardamone Jackson, who read the article as I was preparing it for publication.

[1]Mornet, *Les origines intellectuelles de la Révolution française, 1715–1787* (Paris: Armand Colin, 1933, reprint, 1967). Also see Robert Darnton, *The Literary Underground of the Old Regime* (Cambridge, Mass.: Harvard University Press, 1982), the essays in *Revolution in Print: The Press in France, 1775–1800,* ed. Robert Darnton and Daniel Roche (Berkeley and Los Angeles: University of California Press and the New York Public Library, 1989), and especially Roger Chartier, *The Cultural Origins of the French Revolution,* trans. Lydia G. Cochrane (Durham and London: Duke University Press, 1991).

[2]Chartier, *Cultural Origins,* 68. Chartier concludes that the transformation of reading practices in eighteenth-century France allowed for freer interaction with texts—whether favorably disposed or antagonistic toward the monarchy— and that it was this new way of reading that supported new relationships with authority.

[3]Natalie Zemon Davis, *Society and Culture in Early Modern France* (Stanford: Stanford University Press, 1975); Barbara Diefendorf, *Beneath the Cross: Catholics and Huguenots in Sixteenth-Century Paris* (New York and Oxford: Oxford University Press, 1991); Denis Crouzet, *Les guerriers de Dieu: La violence au temps des troubles de religion, vers 1525–vers 1610,* 2 vols. (Seyssel: Champ Vallon, 1990).

[4]Davis, *Society and Culture,* 218–219.

[5]Ibid., 4–5.

[6]Rubys cited in Pierre Clerjon, *Histoire de Lyon depuis sa fondation jusqu' à nos jours,* 6 vols. (Lyon: Théodore Laurent, 1829–1837), 5: 197.

[7]Mark Greengrass, *The French Reformation* (Oxford: Basil Blackwell, 1987), 64.

[8]Diefendorf, *Beneath the Cross,* 136–144.

[9]See, for example, *Articles respondus par le Roy en son conseil privé sur la requeste presentée par plusieurs habitans de la ville de Bourdeaux, & Seneschaulcée de Guyenne sur le faict de la Religion qu' on dict reformée* (Paris: Charles Perier, 1565), sig. A, iii^r, and *Edict du Roy sur la pacification des troubles de ce royaume* (Paris: F. Morel, 1576), fol. 3^v.

[10]See Michèle Fogel, *Les cérémonies de l'information dans la France du XVIe au milieu du XVIIIe siècle* (Paris: Fayard, 1989), 133–188, 293–326, and, for an example in Lyon, see Clerjon, *Histoire de Lyon,* 1: 220.

[11]Davis, "The Rites of Violence," in *Society and Culture,* 180.

[12]Frère Leger Bontemps, "'Nous te louons majesté souveraine' Chanson au Cantique contenant la louange de nostre Dieu, suyvant le Te Deum, sur le chant 'Estant assis aux rives aquatiques'," and Christophe de Bordeaux, "'Voulez ouyr chanson chanter' autre chanson nouvelle qui se chante a plaisir de ces apostats regniez sur le chant 'Te rogamus audi nos,'" both in Bordeaux, *Beau recueil de plusieurs belles chansons spirituelles avec ceux des huguenots heretiques & en-*

nemis de Dieu & de nostre mere saincte Eglise (Paris: for Magdeleine Berthelin, [after 1563]), 69ᵛ and 3ᵛ respectively. Pierre de Ronsard also wrote lyrics to be sung to the tune of "Te rogamus audi nos." See Ronsard, *Oeuvres complètes,* ed. Jean Céard, Daniel Ménager, and Michel Simonin, 2 vols. (Paris: Gallimard, 1993), 2: 617.

[13]On the "white processions" see Crouzet, *Les guerriers de Dieu,* 2: 297–310.

[14]See ibid. and Philip T. Hoffman, *Church and Community in the Diocese of Lyon, 1500–1789* (New Haven and London: Yale University Press, 1984), 47.

[15]See William McNeill, *Keeping Together in Time: Dance and Drill in Human History* (Cambridge, Mass.: Harvard University Press, 1995).

[16]Cited in Roger Chartier, "Leisure and Sociability: Reading Aloud in Early Modern Europe," in *Urban Life in the Renaissance,* ed. Susan Zimmerman and Ronald Weissman (Newark: University of Delaware Press, 1989), 112.

[17]The chapter cited here was one of two large interpolations made after the first edition of the *Propos* in 1547. See *Les propos rustiques de Noël Du Fail, Texte original de 1547, interpolations et variantes de 1548, 1549, 1573,* ed. Arthur de la Borderie (Paris: Lemerre, 1878), 167.

[18]L'Estoile dates his collection 1586, but clearly many items were included later, such as the song on the death of Henry III, who was murdered in August of 1589.

[19]Le chant de la Ligue is named as a timbre for "Bien que le malheur," Printemps, fol. 61ʳ, and "Rendés-vous, rendés bourgeois de la Mure," Nouveau recueil, 20. L'Estoile includes a placard entitled "Chanson de la Ligue" in his collection (fol. 27ᵛ). These three texts do not have identical rhyme schemes, however, so we must presume that more than one melody came to be known by this title.

[20]Fol. 25ʳ is entitled by L'Estoile "Chansons des Gueux de la Ligue trouvées dans la grande cage des oisons, a Paris, ou les Ligueurs, continuans en leurs folies et fureurs, trainent par les fanges de leurs sottes boufonneries, sales et ordes medisances, le nom du Roy d'aujourd'huy qu'ils appellent Le Bearnois: qui, enfin berne si bien et eux et leur ligue, qu'ils cognoissent le peu d'acquest qu'il y a de se jouer a son maistre."

[21]L'Abbé Reure, *La presse politique à Lyon pendant la Ligue (24 février, 1589–7 février, 1594)* (Paris: Alphonse Picard & Fils, 1898), 24–25.

[22]For a general account of contemporary *recueils de chansons,* see my "Vernacular Culture and the Chanson in Paris, 1570–1580," (Ph.D. diss., The University of Chicago, 1996), 239–303.

[23]For background information on the publishing industry in Lyon see Richard Gascon, *Grand commerce et vie urbaine au XVIe siècle: Lyon et ses marchands, environs de 1520–environs de 1580,* 2 vols. (Paris and The Hague: École Pratique des Hautes Études and Mouton, 1971), 1: 104–106; 2: 628–637.

[24]For Rigaud's output see Henri-Louis Baudrier, *Bibliographie lyonnaise: Recherches sur les imprimeurs, libraires, relieurs et fondeurs de letters de Lyon au XVIe siècle,* 12 vols. (Lyon: Louis Brun and Paris: A. Picard et Fils, 1895–1921), 3: 175–448.

[25]On music printed in the city see Frank Dobbins, *Music in Renaissance Lyons* (Oxford: Clarendon Press, 1992), and Laurent Guillo, *Les éditions musicales de la Renaissance lyonnaise* (Paris: Klincksieck, 1991). Dobbins (164) and Guillo (335) give the format of *Le premier livre de chansons spirituelles* as seidecimo, whereas RISM lists the print as an octavo format.

[26]See Baudrier, *Bibliographie lyonnaise,* 3:177–178, for the renewal of Rigaud's privilege to print royal ordinances and edicts dated 1566. He printed less and less official material in the course of the 1570s, and by 1587 we find him being petitioned by Jean Pillehotte, the new holder of the royal privilege, to stop infringing on his rights (ibid. 3: 182–183).

[27]For examples see Jean-Pierre Seguin, *L'information en France avant le périodique: 517 canards imprimés entre 1529 et 1631* (Paris: Éditions G.-P. Maisonneuve et Larose, 1964).

[28]Gascon, *Grand commerce et vie urbaine,* 2: 922–923.

[29]On English religious ballads see Tessa Watt, *Cheap Print and Popular Piety, 1550–1640* (Cambridge: Cambridge University Press, 1991).

[30]Baudrier, *Bibliographie lyonnaise,* 3:176–183, and Gascon, *Grand commerce et vie urbaine,* 1: 237–263.

[31]Reure, *La presse politique à Lyon,* 28.

[32]Baudrier reprints notarial records relating to a contract between Rigaud and "Jehan Guynot, marchant contreporteur," who owed him 611 livres tournois on a purchase, which no doubt included some larger books, but which would have been thousands of *recueils* and pamphlets if they sold for a sou a piece, *Bibliographie lyonnaise,* 3: 479, 481.

[33]Seguin, *L'information en France,* 15.

[34]See Edmond Huguet, *Dictionnaire de la langue française du seizième siècle,* 7 vols. (Paris: Champion, 1925–1973), 2: 507.

[35]Cited by Robert Mandrou, *De la culture populaire aux 17e et 18e siècles: La Bibliothèque bleue de Troyes* (Paris: Éditions Imago, 1985), 23.

[36]See Shakespeare's ballad-seller Autolycus in *The Winter's Tale,* esp. IV, iv, ll. 590–593.

[37]Roger Chartier, *The Cultural Uses of Print in Early Modern France,* trans. Lydia G. Cochrane (Princeton: Princeton University Press, 1987), 168, 175–178.

[38]Diefendorf, *Beneath the Cross,* 13.

[39]Luc Charles-Dominique, *Les ménétriers français sous l'ancien régime* (Paris: Klincksieck, 1994), 220–221.

[40]See François de Thierriat, *Trois traictez sçavoir 1. De la noblesse de race, 2. De la noblesse civile, 3. Des immunitez des ignobles* (Paris: Lucas Bruneau, 1606), 122, and Pontus de Tyard, *Solitaire second,* ed. Cathy M. Yandell (Geneva: Droz, 1980), 74–75.

[41]Charles-Dominique, *Les ménétriers français,* 222.

[42]Reure, *La presse politique à Lyon,* 20, 28–29.

[43]Jacques Attali, *Noise: The Political Economy of Music,* trans. Brian Massumi (Minneapolis: University of Minnesota Press, 1992), 72–74.

[44]Baudrier, *Bibliographie lyonnaise,* 3:175.

[45]On Saugrin's music prints see Dobbins, *Music in Renaissance Lyons,* 164, 268, 309.

[46]Natalie Zemon Davis, "On the Protestantism of Benoît Rigaud," *Bibliothèque d'Humanisme et Renaissance* 17 (1955): 246–251.

[47]Arthur Jean Kleinclauz, *Histoire de Lyon des origines à 1595* (Lyon: Librairie Pierre Masson, 1939), 424–425.

[48]Davis, "On the Protestantism of Benoît Rigaud," 251.

[49]Jacques-Auguste de Thou, reprinted in Jean-Baptiste Monfalcon, *Histoire de la ville de Lyon,* 2 vols. (Lyon: Guilbert et Dorier and Paris: Dumoulin, 1847), 2: 687–692.

[50]Another song about La Charité in the same print takes the city to task for its resistance to the crown and tells the story of its fall in harsher language: "'O Charité ne dois estre nommée,' chanson nouvelle de la prinse de la Charité sur le chant, 'Dames d'honneur je vous prie.'"

[51]Nicolas de la Grotte, *Chansons de P. de Ronsard, Ph. Desportes, et autres mises en musique par N. de la Grotte* (Paris: Le Roy & Ballard, 1569). For a modern edition see Jane A. Bernstein, ed., *The Sixteenth-Century Chanson,* 30 vols. (New York: Garland Publishing, 1992), 15: 53–55. Le Roy even arranged the song for lute and voice in his *Livre d'airs de cour miz sur le luth par Adrian Le Roy* (Paris: Le Roy & Ballard, 1571).

[52]Chansonnier Maurepas, F-Pn, F. Fr. 12616–12659; Chansonnier Clairambault, F-Pn, F.Fr. 12676–12743.

[53]See Roger Chartier, "Communities of Readers," in *The Order of Books: Readers, Authors, and Libraries in Europe between the Fourteenth and Eighteenth Centuries,* trans. Lydia G. Cochrane (Stanford: Stanford University Press, 1994), 1–23.

[54]I gloss Daniel Poiron, *Le poète et le prince: L'évolution du lyrisme courtois de Guillaume de Machaut à Charles d'Orléans* (Paris: Presses Universitaires de France, 1965; reprint, Geneva: Slatkine, 1978), 415.

[55]Chansons on this timbre printed by Rigaud include "La complainte des pauvres laboureurs & gens de village" (Lyons 1572, 232); "Des regretz d'une dame de

Rouen estant à l'article de la mort, se repentant de s'estre mal gouvernee durant sa jeuness" (Lyon 1572, 246; Printemps, fol. 28^v), "Complaincte & regret d'une Dame ayant perdu son honneur" (Printemps, fol. 42^v), "Les regrets des Princesses & Dames de la Court sur le decez de tresillustre Princesse, Madame fille unique de feu Roy Charles" (Printemps, fol. 8^r), "La prinse de la Charité" (Fleur, fol. 7^v; Rosier, fol. 2^r), "Des regrets & lamentations des Dames de la ville d'Yssoire" (Rosier, fol. 7^r; Fleur, fol. 11^v; Nouveau recueil, 21), "Des regrets douloureux et pleurs lamentables de tres-haute et tres-verteuse dame, Elizabeth d'Autriche, royne de France, sur la mort du roy Charles IX, son espoux, avec les doulences des dames de la court" (Jardin, 3), "La douloureuse complainte des dames de La Rochelle aux soudards du camp du Roy" (Jardin, 69), "Deploration des Dames de la ville de la Fère, tenues forcemens par les ennemies de la Religion Catholique" (Fère, 9), "Lamentation du roy à tout son peuple de France" (Jardin, 16), "Derniers propos de haulte & vertueuse Princesse madame Claude de Valois, duchesse de Lorraine" (Nouveau recueil, 35). On the *complainte* genre and this family of songs see my "Female Complaintes: Laments of Venus, Queens, and City Women in Late Sixteenth-Century France," forthcoming in *Renaissance Quarterly.*

[56]Songs of parting, an important exception, are studied by Donna G. Cardamone, "The Prince of Salerno and the Dynamics of Oral Transmission in Songs of Political Exile," *Acta Musicologica* 67 (1995): 77–108.

[57]The timbre of this song, the antiphon "Da pacem," gives us another example of liturgical chant being used for contrafacts.

[58]On peasants and print see Davis, *Society and Culture,* 194–209.

[59]In the seventeenth century, this formula produced the so-called *Bibliothèque bleue.* On this phenomenon see Chartier, "The *Bibliothèque bleue* and Popular Reading," in *The Cultural Uses of Print,* 240–264, and the bibliography included there.

[60]On the related topic of how visual images are used as mnemonic hooks see Mary Carruthers, "Memory and the Book," in *The Book of Memory: A Study of Memory in Medieval Culture* (Cambridge: Cambridge University Press, 1990), 221–257.

[61]Chartier, "Communities of Readers," 14.

[62]Ibid.

[63]Dobbins, *Music in Renaissance Lyons,* 72–73, 108, 117, 267.

[64]Davis, *Society and Culture,* 207–208. For more on Choppin see idem, "René Choppin on More's Utopia," *Moreana* 19–20 (1968): 91–96.

[65]Mack P. Holt, *The French Wars of Religion, 1562–1629* (Cambridge: Cambridge University Press, 1995), 112–114; Henry Heller, *Iron and Blood: Civil Wars in Sixteenth-Century France* (Montreal and Kingston: McGill-Queen's University Press, 1991), 90–93.

⁶⁶For an example of the king's response to petitions reporting the theft of goods, casting people from their homes, raping women, and killing children, see *Commission expediee par le Roy* (Paris: R. Estienne, 1563), which is listed in Doris Varner Welsh, *A Checklist of French Political Pamphlets, 1560–1644, in the Newberry Library* (Chicago: The Newberry Library, 1950), 4.

⁶⁷Holt, *The French Wars of Religion,* 109, 126–127, 168–169, and idem, *The Duke of Anjou and the Politique Struggle during the Wars of Religion* (Cambridge: Cambridge University Press, 1986).

⁶⁸Davis, *Society and Culture,* 156–157.

⁶⁹On the role of Catholic preachers in encouraging violence in Paris see Diefendorf, *Beneath the Cross,* 145–158.

⁷⁰Taylor, *Soldiers of Christ: Preaching in Late Medieval and Reformation France* (New York and Oxford: Oxford University Press, 1992), 19. The following is summarized from the chapter, "The Sermon as Event," 15–36.

⁷¹Ibid., 212.

⁷²Hoffman, *Church and Community,* 30–42.

⁷³All of the songs in Rigaud's *recueils* are anonymous, but a Parisian print of similar Catholic contrafacts offers a useful comparison, as its authors are named. The second half of Bordeaux's *Beau recueil de plusieurs belles chansons spirituelles* is entitled *Nouvelles chansons spirituelles pour recreer les esprits des catholiques, afliges des ennemis, & adversaires de la Foy. Par F. Legier Bontemps.* Bontemps was a Catholic priest—his title is "Frère" or "le Père" in other prints—and is a prime example of a holy man who wrote inflammatory songs.

⁷⁴Most emblem books were more expensive than *recueils de chansons,* owing to their length and the costs of engraving their images, but they still functioned as visual counterparts to the *recueils.* Some of the smaller emblemata printed in Lyon in these years include Andrea Alciati's *Emblematum libellus* (Macé Bonhomme, 1548, in-8, 168 pp.), Barthéleym Aneau's *Picta poesis* (Macé Bonhomme, 1552, in-8, 120 pp.), and Georgette de Montenay's *Emblemes, ou Devises Chrestiennes* (Jean Marcorelle, 1571, in-4, 116 fols). On emblem books see most importantly Mario Praz, *Studies in Seventeenth-Century Imagery,* 2nd ed. (Rome: Edizioni di Storia e Letteratura, 1964). Not always emblematic, stories about heavenly apparitions were fairly common at this time and seemed to make good reading. In his *Thresor d' histoires admirables et memorables de nostre temps,* 2 vols. (Paris: Samuel Crespin, 1620), I: 46–64. Simon Goulart includes an entire chapter on "Apparitions diverses en l'air" that occurred between 1500 and 1556 (drawn from Conrad Licasthenes, *De prodigiis & ostentis*). Goulart relates three different occasions upon which Europeans saw armies battling in the air (once with audible shouts), two stories of individual combatants facing off against one another, and numerous other tales of astrological abnormalities,

such as two suns, a black ball emerging from the moon, the sun appearing at night, and a cross in the sky.

[75]The timbre can be found in Jean Chardavoine, *Le recueil des plus belles et excellentes chansons en forme de voix de ville* (Paris: Claude Micard, 1576; reprint Geneva: Minkoff, 1980), 39[r].

[76]Hoffman, *Church and Community,* 13.

[77]For an example from Paris see Bordeaux, *Beau recueil de plusieurs belles chansons spirituelles.* Judging from his other writings, "maistre" Bordeaux (a layman) specialized in religious pamphlet literature. The form of his *Beau recueil* matches that of Rigaud's *recueils* and included pro-Catholic songs such as "Huguenots retirez vous" and "O malheuruex heretiques, scismatiques." Huguenot laymen, too, collected and penned "preachy" songs, though few survive in print. The surgeon Rasse des Noeux amassed a manuscript collection of Protestant contrafacta entitled *Recueil de pièces de vers, chansons, sonnets, triolets, sur les guerres de religion formé par le chirurgien protestant Rasse Des Noeux* (F-Pn F. Fr. 22560). Few of the songs copied there are concordant with printed sources (though Des Noeux did paste a tiny *placard* into his collection). Rather, they must come from a destroyed repertory of Huguenot prints, from a manuscript tradition, or Des Noeux's own pen. For another example of a manuscript collection of the time containing songs on the religious wars see F-Pn Rothschild 411.

[78]Davis, "Strikes and Salvation at Lyon," in *Society and Culture,* 1–16.

[79]Ibid, 16.

[80]See Fogel, *Les cérémonies de l'information,* 23–59, and Reure, *La presse politique à Lyon,* 34–35. For an example of a particularly well documented cry in Paris, consider the *Edict du Roy sur la pacification des troubles de ce royaume* (Paris: Morel, 1576), which was cried "À la Table de Marbre du Palais de Paris, heure de dix heures du matin, levee de la Court: & depuis & au mesme instant en la Court dudict Palais, Chastellet, Maison de ville, & autres lieux accoustumez, estans assistez de Pierre Sudour, Gerault Chancel, Gerard de Madieu, dict Montaigne, François de Chef-defaux, & Michel de Noiret Trompettes ordinaires de sa Majesté" (fol. 22[r]).

[81]Henri III, King of France, *Edict du Roy sur la pacification des troubles de ce royaume* (Paris: Morel, 1576), ordonnance 29, fol. 10[r].

[82]Jürgen Habermas, *The Structural Transformation of the Public Sphere: An Inquiry into a Category of Bourgeois Society,* trans. Thomas Burger with Frederick Lawrence (Cambridge, Mass.: MIT Press, 1989).

[83]Ibid., 27–31.

[84]Gascon, *Grand commerce et vie urbaine,* 1: 412.

[85]Habermas, *The Structural Transformation of the Public Sphere,* 16.

[86]Ibid., 254 n. 35.

[87]Here and following see Holt, *The French Wars of Religion,* 111–116; Heller, *Iron and Blood,* 86–104; and J. H. M. Salmon, "Peasant Revolt in Vivarais, 1575–1580," in his *Renaissance and Revolt: Essays in the Intellectual and Social History of Early Modern France* (Cambridge: Cambridge University Press, 1987), 211–234.

[88]Heller, *Iron and Blood,* 96–97.

[89]"Chanson de la prise de Chasteaudouble en Dauphiné au mois de Mars 1579. Sur le chant de 'Petit Rossignolet sauvage'" and "Autre chanson sur la prise de Chasteaudouble en Dauphine. Sur le chant de Sommière," both in Fleur, fols. 79^r and 81^r, respectively.

[90]For a special example of the effectiveness of political songs see Herbert Schneider, "The Sung Constitutions of 1792: An Essay on Propaganda in the Revolutionary Song," in *Music and the French Revolution,* ed. Malcolm Boyd (Cambridge: Cambridge University Press, 1992), 236–75.

Afterword: Music in Print

ROGER CHARTIER

The publication of music—and, more generally, the published forms of musical scores and the texts associated with them—has long been neglected by historians of the book. Proof in the guise of a *mea culpa* exists in the four volumes of the *Histoire de l'édition française* that I edited with Henri-Jean Martin and which was published between 1982 and 1986: not one of its essays is devoted to the publication and sale of music.[1] Other national traditions have been a little more generous in this regard, but, nearly everywhere, historians of the book must accept the severe diagnosis given by A. Dunning for the Netherlands: "The world of scholarship in the history of book printing, publishing, and trading in the Dutch Republic has never really shown that it was much aware of the significance of related endeavors in the field of music."[2] Fortunately, a few musicologists have undertaken the task neglected by their colleagues in the history of the book for too long. This volume is one of the finest results of this new and original scholarship. Too generously cited by many of its authors, I would like to convey in this afterword all that I have learned from the case studies presented here, and to signal the relevance of their contributions to the emerging field of research that links the study of texts (both canonical and ordinary), the description of the forms (manuscript, print, orality) that transmit these texts to their readers (or listeners), and the analysis of their uses and interpretations by different communities of readers (or listeners). I must, however, reveal my bias toward the time period with which I am most familiar, that of a "typographical *ancien régime*" which was born with the invention of movable type and the printing press in the middle of the fifteenth century and which faded as printing became more industrialized in the early nineteenth century.

THE FORMS OF MUSIC PUBLICATIONS

The leading contribution of the essays collected here is their demonstration of the complexity involved in any classification of music printing. For material printed before 1800, the factors controlling such a classification include the techniques used for publication, the formats and contents of musical publications, and the modes of their attribution or, to put it another way, of their authorship. Music publishing also introduces a primary and fundamental difference between objects that offer music itself, sometimes with vocal texts, and those that consist only of texts, with or without an indication of the tune to which they should be sung. This distinction must lead us to differentiate clearly between scores without text and texts without music, even while recognizing that both belong to the domain of music publishing.

As for the publication of music, the essays that constitute this volume—setting aside the classic question of the evolution of musical notation—make two important claims. The first claim acknowledges the enduring, and no doubt increasing, recourse to manuscript publication for the circulation of music in the seventeenth century. Contempt for print, which supposedly devalued aesthetic creations, the desire for tighter control over the precision of musical notation, and the urge to protect the secrets of performance were sufficient reasons to justify faithful adherence to manuscript publication for all genres of music, including opera. This conclusion is fully consistent with many recent studies of the history of the book, which have concentrated on the role of "scribal publication" in the age of print.

In seventeenth-century England, the genres whose circulation remained widely, perhaps even predominantly, in manuscript form consisted of three distinct groups: political texts (parliamentary debates and declarations, published in the form of "separates," newssheets, or satires), volumes of poetry collecting works by a single poet or by many authors, and scores destined for musicians who played in consorts.[3] There were also three categories, without strict boundaries between them, of manuscript publication: "authorial publication," "entrepreneurial publication," and "user publication." Authorial publication put into circulation texts in manuscript form that had been either copied or corrected by the author. This practice, which had its origins in the efforts of a few medieval authors (Petrarch, for instance) to maintain control over the precise form given to their works, was reinforced in the sixteenth and seventeenth centuries by a heightened (and lamented) awareness of the errors introduced by print. Often print was perceived as corrupting a text in three ways: it distorted the text itself, altered by the errors of incompetent typesetters; it destroyed the selfless ethos behind intellectual or aesthetic creation by handing the work of humanists, poets, or scholars over to greedy and dishonest booksellers; and it perverted the true significance of works by making them available to ignorant readers incapable of understanding them properly. From these attitudes grew suspicions about the printed book and a preference for manuscript publication that permitted tighter control over the text, its circulation, and its interpretation. This choice was also made by a number of female writers, who in this way could more easily protect their works from public exposure. And, even when printing a text was necessary or desirable, authors chose manuscript for the presentation copies that were offered to a prince or to other important figures in exchange for, or in hopes of receiving, their patronage.[4]

But publishing was also a business. Satires and newsletters were copied in series in *"scriptoria"* resembling the *ateliers* in eighteenth-century France that produced manuscript newssheets and clandestine texts.[5] Even more common was the activity of individual scribes who worked at the request of a private client or for a bookseller of the Stationers' Company. Finally, next to autograph manuscripts and the products of workshops or professional scribes, an important portion of manuscript publication originated with readers themselves, or, rather, by members of those "scribal communities" whose connections formed around the copying or loan of manuscripts, the transcribing of documents, and correspondence. Various such communities appeared at different times, consisting of readers who wrote in order to read and who read in order to write. In seventeenth-century England, they consisted of literate and aristocratic circles at court, in the Inns of Court, among educated friends, and within the family. Between 1680 and 1730, the Republic of Letters itself constituted a scribal community whose ethos of generosity and of reciprocity was nourished by the manuscript in all its forms: letters, copied texts, memoranda.[6] The common thread among these different types of scribal communities in the age of print lay in the desire to withhold from public access—and therefore from the risk of corruption or debasement—precious knowledge, select literary texts, or, in the case of readers of unorthodox manuscripts, dangerous texts. This profound reevaluation of the forms and genres of manuscript publication in the age of print could be a valuable tool for delving even further into the coexistence or competition between these two forms of publication for music between the fifteenth and the nineteenth centuries.

The second broad claim advanced by the present studies concerns a technical opposition. It distinguishes between two techniques of printing music: one that used movable type and another that resorted to the engraving of scores. The use of these two procedures varied with time and place. Yet, as the situation in France reveals, the issue at stake was not merely technical, but also legal and commercial, since it was the introduction of pewter plate engraving after 1660 that made it possible to circumvent the exclusive privilege over music printing granted in 1551 to a single publisher, the house of Le Roy and Ballard.[7] Likewise, it was the engraving of music, and not the use of movable type, that guaranteed the pan-European success of the Amsterdam-based enterprise of Étienne Roger and Michel-Charles Le Cène during the first forty years of the eighteenth century.[8] The history of printed editions of texts presents no equivalent opposition between different techniques of printing once the dominance of the printing press and the peripheral importance of engraved texts solidified. Nevertheless, a similar duality occurred in the printing of texts in the East, with the extremely limited use of movable type and the predominant use of wood engraving, and for illustrations in the West, with the successive or contemporaneous uses of xylography and copperplate engraving.[9]

The essays that make up this volume demonstrate the diverse forms musical prints might take: from posters plastered on walls to thick anthologies, from folio choirbooks to oblong octavos for instrumental music, from full scores to separate parts, from deluxe editions destined for members of the court to books sold by peddlers. In this complex typology—which juxtaposes the materiality of printed objects, the readers for whom they were destined, and the compositions contained within them—a fundamental tension exists in the contrast between the forms of publication that put into circulation a single work or the works of one composer, and those that brought together in the same volume pieces belonging to different genres and/or written by different composers.

This very opposition is now accepted as fundamental to understanding the modes by which texts were perceived and attributed, in the age of manuscripts just as surely as in the age of print. In seventeenth-century England, an essential feature of scribal publication was the perpetuation of anthologies or collections of miscellany—the predominant type of book since the seventh or eighth century, except in the case of ancient or Christian *auctoritates*.[10] The modern manuscript book inherited this textual structure that assembled works by different authors and in different genres in a single volume. This made it impossible to attribute a book to any one name that could be indicated as the sole author, for a number of reasons: books took a form that could contain both manuscript and printed pages, copyists and owners were uncertain in their attributions, and, in a transfer of the authorship of a work, the scribe himself might be named as the author.[11] In this way manuscript publications perpetuated the ambiguity of the very term *writer,* which was understood as the person who had copied the book as well as the one who had composed the text. Even though printed books strongly enforced the logic of a "unitary" book that linked an object, a work, or a series of works to a single name, collections and anthologies bringing together works, excerpts, or citations of multiple authors remained a fundamental book type from the sixteenth to the eighteenth century. There are many examples of this practice, ranging from volumes of commonplace books to miscellany, and from selected works to compilations.[12] In this light, publications taking the form of anthologies of poems set to music or of musical compositions are merely specific examples of a more generalized practice wherein books resisted material expression in the unitary book of a single work and an identifiable author.

Yet music publications, even more than literary ones, multiply the forms of their attribution. At opposite ends of the spectrum lie the celebration of an individual composer, who is identified by name and praised in various preliminary texts (Josquin des Prez, for instance, or Orlando di Lasso), and anonymity, common to certain genres that are taken to be inferior or to the lesser composers assigned to produce the works necessary to round out a collection of madrigals or chansons. Between these two systems of attribution for musical compositions exist numerous other situations in which different names are used either to attribute entire books, or to attribute each of the works contained within a book. The position of the "author" of an anthology can be occupied by the editor who assembled the different compositions, by the bookseller or printer who published it, or even, in an anonymous or implicit way, by the social sphere in which the different compositions were performed or sung—as in the world of the salons in seventeenth-century France. As for the pieces themselves, they can be attributed either to the poet who wrote the text while the composer who set the text to music remains unnamed, or, inversely, to the composer of the song without, in this case, naming the writer of the text.

This plurality of possible "authors" is not without parallels in literary publications, and particularly in publications of theatrical works. In quarto editions of Elizabethan plays, for example, the published text was only rarely attributed on the title page to the playwright who wrote it. Either it was presented as anonymous, or the author had to share his "authorship" with the name of the troupe that performed the play, the places where the play was performed—hence, implicitly, the audiences who saw it—and, if there were any, the playwrights who revised or adapted it. The title page of the first quarto of *Hamlet* thus announced: *The Tragicall Historie of Hamlet Prince of Denmarke By William Shake-speare As it hath beene diverse times acted by his Hignesse servants in the Cittie of London: as also in the two Universities of Cambridge and Oxford, and else-where.* The instability of the "author function" in music publications as well as in poems set to music is a reminder that, as in the publication of plays, the process of publication always implicates a plurality of actors. These actors can, for different reasons, disappear behind the anonymous work; they can also share, either peaceably or contentiously, in its authorship.

MUSIC PUBLISHING

The essays brought together in this volume enable us to outline a geography and typology of music publishing between 1501, the date of Ottaviano de' Petrucci's publication of the first volume of printed music in Venice, and the end of the eighteenth century. During these three centuries the center of music publishing, long dominated by Venetian printers,[13] shifted to Paris—especially after pewter plate engraving ended Ballard's monopoly—and to the Netherlands. This displacement reflects a more widespread shift of publishing activity, in which the primacy of Venice gave way to the preeminence of northern European cities. From the beginning of the seventeenth century, in fact, Italian printed production decreased in northern markets, followed by the diminishing role of Antwerp and German cities as active centers for the production and sale of books. Dutch publishing dominated the European market in the second half of the century. The house of Elzevier paved the way beginning in 1640 by pirating growing numbers of Parisian publications and printing Jansenist works for the readers of the realm. The influx of Huguenot refugees, before and after the revocation of the Edict of Nantes, further strengthened the position of booksellers in Amsterdam, The Hague, Leiden, Rotterdam, and Utrecht, and thus assured the triumph of Dutch publishing.[14]

Within each country, this geographical shift was accompanied by a change in the kinds of people who published musical compositions. Composers persevered for a long time as publishers of their own music. Orlando di Lasso, for instance, received two privileges—granted by the king of France in 1571 and by the emperor ten years later—that allowed him to retain ownership of his works and to entrust his music to the printers of his choice. In this way Lasso applied to the domain of music publishing a practice that some authors had tried to impose on booksellers and printers since the early sixteenth century. Authors in Paris attempted to control the circulation of their works by requesting privileges for themselves while bringing lawsuits against printers who had published their texts without their permission; the first example of this type of lawsuit dates to 1504.[15]

In the seventeenth century, a few unspecialized booksellers and printers added music publishing to their other activities. This was the case in England with John Playford, who began his publishing career in 1647 by printing political texts, primarily monarchistic ones. In 1651, he began to specialize in publications of airs, poems set to music, and works about music, without, however, abandoning his political preferences, which surfaced in his decision to publish the works of musicians and poets who formed a "royalist coterie culture."[16] Likewise, in Amsterdam Étienne Roger published around five hundred music publications next to three hundred works on other topics between 1696 and 1722.

A third kind of publisher emerged in Paris during the second half of the eighteenth century in the domain of engraved music. "Merchants of music" combined music publishing with other activities, such as teaching, performing, building instruments, and engraving scores. The proliferation of this new kind of publisher brought a number of changes that transformed publishing practices: subscription sales, periodical publications that took the form of "journals," memberships that allowed one to borrow scores for a given length of time, and advertisements of new titles in general-interest as well as specialist journals.[17]

Music publishing was therefore not immune to the changes that profoundly transformed the production of printed matter in the second half of the eighteenth century, even as techniques of typesetting and printing remained the same.[18] Without a doubt the most spectacular change was seen in the multiplication and transformation of journals. The number of new journals (some enduring, others ephemeral) grew impressively, accompanied by the appearance of new genres of periodicals. In Germany, for instance, erudite and literary journals were eclipsed by the appearance of moral weeklies (*Moralische Wochenschriften*) preoccupied by the values of usefulness and the common good, and by political and historical journals that, after 1770, offered discussions of affairs of state to enlightened readers. Meanwhile books themselves became more accessible. The success of small formats (in-12, in-16, in-18) turned books into versatile companions. Reading became freer. Books no longer needed to be placed somewhere to be read, and readers no longer had to be seated to read: a new relationship with the written text, more familiar and immediate, could now be established. More manageable, books also were easier to acquire or consult. Granted, prices rose: in Germany the price of a novel in its original edition increased by eight or nine times in the last three decades of the eighteenth century. But a double corrective limited or canceled out the effects of growing costs.

On the one hand, the widespread practice of pirating editions (that is, publishing a given work in violation of the rights of the printer who owned the privilege or copyright) inevitably lowered book prices because the pirate publisher paid neither the author of the manuscript nor the chancellery fees required to obtain a privilege. On the other hand, all across Europe institutions proliferated where it was not always necessary to purchase a book in order to read it. One institution was the lending library. Diverse names (circulating library, rental library, *Leihbibliothek, cabinet littéraire, bureau littéraire*) describe the same phenomenon: in exchange for a monthly or annual membership fee, readers could either consult on the premises or take home all the books that a bookseller's catalog offered on loan. This system was a great success in England. Inspired perhaps by the coffeehouses that made newspapers and pamphlets available to their customers, circulating libraries appeared early in the century and took off dramatically after 1740 with the establishment of 380 more or less permanent libraries in 119 different locations. The situation was similar in France, although it emerged later and on a smaller scale. Another kind of institution was the voluntary association, endowed with collectively approved statutes. Members who paid an annual fee could borrow books that were acquired collectively. At the end of the year the books were then either sold at auction (this was the case for book clubs) or kept in the library of the society (for subscription libraries and *Lesegesellschaften*). The reading societies participated fully in three essential processes of the Enlightenment: they encouraged democratic sociability insofar as all decisions were subject to the principle of majority vote, which disregarded differences of social status; they constituted a tool for regulating civilization because their statutes censored uncivil behavior; and, finally, they contributed (alongside literary societies and

Masonic lodges) to the construction of an intellectual and social network that made possible a new public sphere in which, at a distance from the authority of the monarch, private individuals debated affairs of state and the actions of their prince.

Even if music publishing in the second half of the eighteenth century did not mirror all of the changes that so profoundly transformed publishing activity as a whole, its own innovations took place in the midst of these new publishing practices—sometimes for the better, but also for the worse. Pirated editions formed a significant, even predominant, share of music books printed in Paris as well as Amsterdam. A. Dunning estimates that "reprints and/or pirated editions" made up 85 percent of Dutch production in the eighteenth century, and composers and publishers in Paris complained often about this practice, which harmed the economic interests of those who held privileges at the same time as it corrupted the works themselves.[19]

The distribution of music in print relied on various forms of commerce: the shops of booksellers (both specialized and not), the stores where one sold musical instruments and staff paper alongside musical scores, and the peddlers who sold their wares in the countryside as well as in town and who sang and sold ballads. The peddlers were not professional singers but merchants who sang in order to attract customers, either by singing the ballads they hoped to sell, or by itemizing in song the other merchandise they had to offer.

In *The Winter's Tale,* Shakespeare put on the stage a peddler who sells his wares and sings ballads: Autolycus, who appears many times in the fourth and fifth acts of the play.[20] Many traits define his character, not least the deceit signaled in his name, which is that of the son of Hermes (Mercury to the Romans), a deity known for his slyness. Autolycus, in fact, is not merely a merchant and a singer of ballads. He also steals linens ("My traffic is sheets") and picks pockets ("My revenue is the silly cheat"). A cunning thief, expert in clever tricks, Autolycus is also a successful peddler, whose character Shakespeare created from the features that typified the profession in Elizabethan England.

First, he is a character who "performs," singing not only the ballads that he sells—for, as he puts it, "I can bear my part, you must know, 'tis my occupation"—but also the inventory of his merchandise, as in the two songs "Lawn as white" and "Will you buy." The fiction here is construed in reference to actual peddlers' songs, which appear in other plays of the time, and which were later collected by folklorists. Introduced by the Servant as a singer of ballads ("He sings several tunes faster than you'll tell money. He utters them as he had eaten ballads") and of goods ("he sings 'em over as they were gods or goddesses"), Autolycus is closely related to all wandering merchants who, like the blind sellers of prints in Spain[21] or the peddlers of *canards* in Paris (whom Pierre de L'Estoile calls *porte-paniers* or *contre-porteux*), cried out, announced, or sang titles and the texts they hawked to customers.

A second feature that characterizes Autolycus's trade is the link between the songs and the goods. Although ballads are the only printed matter he sells, he offers to the imaginary Bohemian peasants of the last two acts of *The Winter's Tale* all the objects found in the packs of seventeenth-century English peddlers: pieces of cloth, necessary supplies for sewing and embroidery, clothing accessories, jewelry, perfume, and also writing tablets ("table books"). In this way a close connection is forged, in the schemes that are hatched around Autolycus, between the ballads that are, for the most part, love songs, and the many items offered by young men to young women in their attempts to seduce them. This connection between the ballads that speak of love and the objects that are proof of that love is central to the quarrel between the Clown and the peasant girl Mopsa, to whom he has promised "a tawdry-lace and a pair of sweet gloves."

Autolycus "hath songs for man or woman, of all sizes," and, among these, "the prettiest love songs for maids," whose proclaimed innocence the Servant ironically refutes with extremely coarse double-entendres. Of the "ballads in print" sold by Autolycus, Shakespeare lets us hear three ballads that comically play on the repertoire of the genre. The first, "to a very doleful tune," tells "how a usurer's wife was brought to bed of twenty money-bags at a burden, and how she longed to eat adders' heads and toads carbonadoed." The second tells the fantastical story of a girl who is changed into a fish because she rejected the advances of her lover. The third is a "merry ballad," a love song that "goes to the tune of 'Two Maids Wooing a Man'"—a situation identical to the one in the play in which the Clown is chased by Mopsa and Dorcas, the very characters who join Autolycus in singing this ballad. The ballads that appear on stage (or at least the first two) are parodic inventions, yet they rely nevertheless on the tone of monstrous births, fantastical beings, and terrifying exemplary punishments so common to the repertory of ballads published by London booksellers and their French colleagues who published chansons and *canards*.

The ballads sold by Autolycus, like the chansons distributed by Parisian peddlers, make it possible for us to grasp the forms of publication and circulation used for the most broadly disseminated kinds of music.[22] As we know, the ballad was a fundamental poetic, musical, and editorial genre in England between the mid-sixteenth and mid-seventeenth centuries. The number of different ballads printed during this hundred-year period has been estimated at around three thousand, and their very low price made them available to even the humblest customers. Ballads were generally printed on a single side of a printer's sheet, and included the following material arranged from top to bottom according to a regular pattern: the title, the indication of the tune to which the ballad was to be sung, a woodcut, and the text disposed in two columns. These "broadside ballads" were affixed to walls (either inside private homes or in public places) and were also circulated by hand.[23]

Ballads constituted a large market, one gradually mastered by specialized booksellers who established a quasi-monopoly over the genre. Beginning in 1624, in fact, the "ballad partners"—five printer-booksellers of the Stationers' Company—took over the widespread distribution of printed sheets of songs. It was as the history of the genre unfolded that its characteristic features became fixed: woodcut illustrations appeared more frequently after 1600 (they are found in five out of six ballads); the page layout of the text reached its canonical form, a two-part folio sheet; and the tune to which ballads were to be sung was indicated more often. In addition, between the mid-sixteenth and mid-seventeenth centuries, religious ballads lost ground to secular ones, as if legitimate religious culture gradually excluded song as it inclined toward other forms such as psalms that might be sung at home or in church. The ballad, linked with a more popular and communal culture, thus became a fundamentally secular genre—witness the ballads sold by Autolycus and those composed in rural communities.[24]

This close examination of English ballads in the sixteenth and seventeenth centuries enables us to remember that music publishing (even if in this case only the texts to be sung are published) also concerns the most popular forms of print (chapbooks, the books of the *Bibliothèque bleue, pliegos sueltos*); and, at the same time, that a musical culture that is shared, nourished by easily remembered tunes, and mobilized by diverse texts constitutes the widest possible context of reception for all genres that associate words and notes.

THE USES OF PRINTED MUSIC

It is difficult to characterize precisely, with its disparities and changes over time, the public of purchasers and consumers of musical compositions and of texts accompanied by music. One must first make a distinction between the limited clientele of professional musicians and amateurs who made music in society, and the wider public who purchased, either to sing or to have sung, chansons, *complaintes,* and ballads. The market of the former ought not to be underestimated, even if the print runs of music publications remained limited—especially in the case of engraved music, which rarely surpassed two or three hundred copies. But from the sixteenth century onward, in Italy at least, this market was large enough to accommodate a great number of editions and reeditions of chansons, airs, and madrigals.[25] In seventeenth-century France, composing, reading aloud, and reciting or singing lines of poetry destined to be set to music counted among the literary games dear to the sociability of the salons.

In contrast to the domestic and aristocratic uses of music in print (or manuscript), the music for which peddlers sold the words circulated publicly. This being the case, the tunes—known to all and frequently reused—mattered less than the effect or the veracity of the words set to music. Chansons and *complaintes* from the Wars of Religion to the Fronde (or even later, to the Revolution) endeavored to express strong feelings of belonging or to mobilize the crowd.[26] Ballads worked the same way. Shakespeare presents with irony the strategies employed to substantiate the authenticity of the extraordinary tales heard in song. Autolycus, in fact, multiplies the number of signs meant to make credible the improbable events narrated by the ballads. A midwife ("Here's the midwife's name to't") and "five or six honest wives that were present" attest in writing to the truth of the monstrous birth. And the story of the girl changed into a fish has "five justices' hands at it, and witnesses more than my pack will hold." The appeal of the genre therefore seems to depend on making it possible for the reader to believe in the stories he or she sings or hears sung. Mopsa and Dorcas question Autolycus on several occasions to be reassured of the veracity of the stories that he sells: "I love a ballad in print, alife, for then we are sure they are true," Mopsa says while Dorcas asks "Is it true, think you?" The pleasure of reading or listening presupposes that the ballads can be taken as true. Yet at the same time, this desire for authenticity and the signs of authentication are always mockingly refuted. The midwife who supposedly attended to the usurer's wife is named "Mistress Tail-Porter," and the date of the insensitive girl's metamorphosis into a cold fish is "Wednesday the fourscore of April."

This tension between the expectation of truth by the ballads' purchasers and the parody (which occurs not only in Shakespeare but also in ballads published by London booksellers) places the texts squarely in the realm of the incredible. It delineates a relationship to literary fiction in which the singer and his audience are both persuaded and dissuaded, believe and do not believe, and vacillate between—or combine—adherence and rejection. Perhaps this is also a way of describing the relationship between spectators and the play itself, which is just as unbelievable as old tales or ballads, and which must simultaneously captivate the spectators, persuade them of its plausibility, and make them believe in the unbelievable. The relationship of Mopsa and Dorcas to the songs of Autolycus ("Is it true, think you?") is thus transformed into a figure of dramatic art, with or without music, which is always defined for the listener or spectator by the pleasure of believing in the artifice without being deceived by that belief.

One theme runs through all of the essays collected here: the idea that it is impossible to reduce music to its many possible forms of transcription and publication. This is a condition that music shares with works written for the pulpit and the theater. Numerous playwrights in the sixteenth and seventeenth centuries emphasized the loss that occurs when a text moves from the stage to the printed page. In 1606, Marston addressed the reader of the second edition of his play *Parsitaster, or the Fawn* with the following: "Reader, know I have perused this copy, to make some satisfaction for the first faulty impression; yet so urgent hath been my business that some errors have still passed, which thy discretion may amend. Comedies are writ to be spoken, not read; remember the life of these things consists in action." Over a half-century later, in 1666, Molière used the same words to alert the reader of his comedy *L'amour médecin:* "It is unnecessary to warn you that many things are dependent on the action: one knows full well that plays are written only to be performed; and I would advise the reading of this one only to those persons who have eyes capable of discovering in the act of reading all the action of the theater."

Yet just as plays must be published, so must works of music. The same question then applies to both arts: what are the effects on the hearing, understanding, and criticism of works when this necessary (and sometimes, despite the denials of the authors, strongly desired) sacrifice of performance to the printed page is made?[27] While there is no easy answer, an important transformation seems to characterize the second half of the eighteenth century, especially after 1770, when piano-vocal reductions allowed more faithful access to major genres of music—operas, oratorios, cantatas, passions—than the separate publishing of parts and excerpts. From this point on, critics could devote themselves to the music score rather than prioritizing the libretto, and it was possible for amateurs of music to train their ears and tastes in the privacy of their own salons. Like the history of the gaze in painting, the history of listening in music must overlap with, on the one hand, the study of the conventions that govern the relationship of listeners to performance, and, on the other, the analysis of the very forms in which works are made available for hearing, seeing, and "reading."[28]

The reflections in this afterword have no intention other than to demonstrate how the history of the publication and appropriation of musical compositions (or of their texts) cannot be separated from the intellectual project that endeavors to link the history of works, the history of the forms of their transmission, and that of their reception. It is fortunate that music historians have taken charge of an area of study ignored by scholars of written and print culture for too long. My own experience as a historian of the typographical *ancien régime* has led me in this short essay to privilege the early centuries of music publishing and printing, to the detriment of changes that have modified techniques and forms from the nineteenth century to the present. But it seems to me that a single fundamental issue is at work for all periods: namely, to discover how different modes of publication and performance affect the way music is composed and heard. In this volume, written by many different hands, one can find stimulating variations on this common theme studied in a perspective shared today by historians of texts (literary or not), and of works of art.

—Translated by Leslie Sprout

NOTES

[1]Roger Chartier and Henri-Jean Martin, eds., *Histoire de l'édition française,* 4 vols. (Paris: Promodis, 1982–1986; 2nd ed., Paris: Fayard/Editions du Cercle de la Librairie, 1989–1991).

[2]A. Dunning, "Music Publishing in the Dutch Republic: The Present State of Research," in *"Le Magasin de l'Univers": The Dutch Republic as the Centre of the European Book Trade,* ed. C. Berkvens-Stevelinck, H. Bots, P. G. Hoftijzer, and O. S. Lankhorst (Leiden and New York: E. J. Brill, 1992), 121–128.

[3]Harold Love, *Scribal Publication in Seventeenth-Century England* (Oxford: Clarendon Press, 1993; reprinted as *The Culture and Commerce of Texts: Scribal Publication in Seventeenth-Century England,* Amherst: University of Massachusetts Press, 1998).

[4]Armando Petrucci, "Copisti e libri manoscritti dopo l'avvento della stampa," in *Scribi e colofoni: Le sottoscrizioni di copisti dalle origini all'avvento della stampa,* ed. Emma Condello and Giuseppe De Gregorio (Spoleto: Centro Italiano di Studi Sull'alto Medicevo, 1995), 507–525.

[5]*De bonne main: La communication manuscrite au XVIIIe siècle,* ed. François Moureau (Paris: Universitas, and Oxford: Voltaire Foundation, 1993).

[6]Ann Goldgar, *Impolite Learning: Conduct and Community in the Republic of Letters, 1680–1750* (New Haven and London: Yale University Press, 1995).

[7]Anik Devriès, *Édition et commerce de la musique gravée à Paris dans la première moitié du XVIIIe siècle: Les Boivin, Les Leclerc* (Geneva: Minkoff, 1976).

[8]François Lesure, *Bibliograhie des éditions musicales publiées par Estienne Roger et Michel-Charles Le Cène (Amsterdam, 1696–1743)* (Paris: Heugel, 1969).

[9]Roger Chartier, "Gutenberg Revisited from the East," *Late Imperial China* (Special Issue: Publishing and the Print Culture in Late Imperial China) 17, no. 1 (June 1996): 1–9.

[10]Armando Petrucci, "Dal libro unitario al libro miscellaneo," in *Tradizione dei classici, trasformazioni della cultura,* vol. 4 of *Società romana e impero tardoantico,* ed. Andrea Giardina (Rome and Bari: Laterza, 1986), 173–187. Published in English translation as "From the Unitary Book to the Miscellany," in Armando Petrucci, *Writers and Readers in Medieval Italy: Studies in the History of Written Culture,* ed. and trans. Charles M. Radding (New Haven and London: Yale University Press, 1995), 1–18.

[11]H. R. Woudhuysen, *Sir Philip Sidney and the Circulation of Manuscripts, 1558–1640* (Oxford: Clarendon Press, 1996).

[12]Ann Moss, *Printed Commonplace-Books and the Structuring of Renaissance Thought* (Oxford, Clarendon Press, 1996); Barbara M. Benedict, *Making the Modern Reader: Cultural Mediation in Early Modern Literary Anthologies* (Princeton: Princeton University Press, 1996); Hans-Jürgen Lüsebrink, " 'L'Histoire des Deux Indes' et ses 'extraits': Un mode de dispersion textuelle au XVIIIe siècle," *Littérature* 69 (1988): 28–41.

[13]Jane A. Bernstein, *Music Printing in Renaissance Venice: The Scotto Press, 1539–1572* (New York and Oxford: Oxford University Press, 1998); Mary S. Lewis, *Antonio Gardano, Venetian Music Printer, 1538–1569: A Descriptive Bibliography and Historical Study,* 2 vols. (New York and London: Garland Publishing, 1988 and 1997).

[14]Henri-Jean Martin, *Livre, pouvoirs et société à Paris au XVIIe siècle (1598–1701)* (Geneva: Droz, 1969) 2: 690–695.

[15]Elizabeth Armstrong, *Before Copyright: The French Book-Privilege System, 1498–1526* (Cambridge and New York: Cambridge University Press, 1990);

Cynthia J. Brown, *Poets, Patrons, and Printers: Crisis of Authority in Late Medieval France* (Ithaca and London: Cornell University Press, 1995).

[16]Peter Lindenbaum, "Music and/as Politics in the Interregnum" (paper presented at the Lily Library, Bloomington, Ind., April 1999).

[17]François Lesure, "L'édition musicale en France au XVIIIe siècle. État des questions," in *Le livre et l'historien: Études offertes en l'honneur du Professeur Henri-Jean Martin,* ed. F. Barbier, A. Parent-Charon, F. Dupuigrenet Desroussilles, C. Jolly, and Dominique Varry (Geneva: Droz, 1997), 229–234.

[18]Roger Chartier, "Libri e lettori," in *L'Illuminismo: Dizionario storico,* ed. Vincenzo Ferrone and Daniel Roche (Rome: Editori Laterza, 1997), 291–300.

[19]A. Dunning, "Music Publishing in the Dutch Republic," 126.

[20]Citations of *The Winter's Tale* are from *The Norton Shakespeare,* ed. Stephen Greenblatt (New York: W. W. Norton, 1997), 2873–2953.

[21]Julio Caro Baroja, *Ensayo sobre la literatura de cordel* (Madrid: Ediciones de la Revista de Occidente, 1969); María Cruz García de Enterría, *Sociedad y poesía de cordel en el barroco* (Madrid: Taurus, 1973); Joaquín Marco, *Literatura popular en España en los siglos XVIII y XIX (Una aproximación a los pliegos de cordel)* (Madrid: Taurus, 1977); Jean-François Botrel, "Les aveugles colporteurs d'imprimés en Espagne," *Mélanges de la Casa de Velazquez,* vol. 9 (1973), 417–482, and vol. 10 (1974), 233–271.

[22]Kate van Orden, "Vernacular Culture and the Chanson in Paris, 1570–1580" (Ph.D. diss., The University of Chicago, 1996).

[23]Tessa Watt, *Cheap Print and Popular Piety, 1550–1640* (Cambridge: Cambridge University Press, 1991).

[24]Adam Fox, "Ballads, Libels, and Popular Ridicule in Jacobean England," *Past and Present* 145 (November 1994): 47–83.

[25]Tim Carter, "Music Publishing in Italy, c. 1580–c. 1625: Some Preliminary Observations," *Royal Music Association Research Chronicle* 20 (1986–1987), 19–37; Martha Feldman, *City Culture and the Madrigal at Venice* (Berkeley and Los Angeles: University of California Press, 1995).

[26]Laura Mason, *Singing the French Revolution: Popular Culture and Politics 1787–1799* (Ithaca: Cornell University Press, 1996).

[27]Abby E. Zanger, "Paralyzing Performance: Sacrificing Theater on the Altar of Publication," *Stanford French Review* (Fall–Winter 1988) 169–185.

[28]Many essential studies outline a history of listening and the history of music's social, political, and aesthetic determinants: William Weber, *Music and the Middle Class: The Social Structure of Concert Life in London, Paris, and Vienna* (London: Croom Helm, 1975) and idem, *The Rise of Musical Classics in Eighteenth-Century England: A Study in Canon, Ritual, and Ideology* (Oxford: Clarendon Press, 1992); Jane Fulcher, *The Nation's Image: French Grand Opera*

as *Politics and Politicized Art* (Cambridge and New York: Cambridge University Press, 1987) and idem, *French Cultural Politics and Music: From the Dreyfus Affair to the First World War* (New York: Oxford University Press, 1999); James H. Johnson, *Listening in Paris: A Cultural History* (Berkeley and Los Angeles: University of California Press, 1995); and Esteban Baruch, *La Neuvième de Beethoven: Une histoire politique* (Paris: Gallimard, 1999).

Contributors

Thomas Bauman is Professor of Music at Northwestern University. He received his Ph.D. from the University of California, Berkeley in 1977. Since then he has taught at the University of Pennsylvania, Stanford University, and the University of Washington, Seattle. He has published books and articles on Mozart's *Abduction* and Requiem, Verdi's *Falstaff,* eighteenth-century German and Italian opera, and cultural classification in the Progressive Era. Currently he is writing a book on Chicago's Pekin Theater.

Katherine Bergeron is Associate Professor of Music at the University of California, Berkeley. She is the author of *Decadent Enchantments: The Revival of Gregorian Chant at Solesmes* (1998) and co-editor of *Disciplining Music* (1992). She is currently working on *Voice Lessons,* a study of the mélodie and the Parisian bourgeoisie circa 1900.

Tim Carter was born in Sydney, Australia, and he studied in the UK at the Universities of Durham and Birmingham; his books include *Jacopo Peri (1561–1633): His Life and Works, Music in Late Renaissance and Early Baroque Italy,* and the Cambridge Opera Handbook on Mozart's *Le nozze di Figaro,* and he is currently working on theoretical and analytical issues in the music of Claudio Monteverdi. He has taught at the Universities of Leicester and Lancaster, and is currently Professor of Music at Royal Holloway and Bedford New College, University of London.

Roger Chartier is Director of Studies at the École des Hautes Études en Sciences Sociales, Paris. Among his many books are *Forms and Meanings: Texts, Performances, and Audiences from Codex to Computer, Cultural*

History: Between Practices and Representations, The Cultural Uses of Print in Early Modern France, The Cultural Origins of the French Revolution, and *The Order of Books.*

Thomas Christensen is Associate Professor of Music at The University of Chicago. He received his Ph.D. from Yale University in 1985 and has taught at the University of Pennsylvania and the University of Iowa. His research interest lies predominately in eighteenth-century historical music theory and aesthetics. His book, *Rameau and Musical Thought in the Enlightenment* (Cambridge University Press, 1993), won the 1994 Wallace Berry Prize from the Society for Music Theory. Thomas Christensen is also a pianist and has performed in numerous chamber concerts and recitals over the years.

Martha Feldman is Associate Professor of Music at The University of Chicago. She is the author of *City Culture and the Madrigal at Venice* (1995) and volume editor of three volumes of madrigals in the Garland series *The Sixteenth-Century Madrigal.* Much of her recent work involves rethinkings of opera in eighteenth-century Italy and France from the anthropological perspectives of ritual, exchange, myth, kingship, and sacrifice.

James Haar is W. R. Kenan Jr. Professor Emeritus of Music at the University of North Carolina at Chapel Hill; he also taught at Harvard, the University of Pennsylvania, and New York University. He has published books and articles in his chief fields of interest, the Italian madrigal, Renaissance humanism, and problems of music theory in the early modern period.

Robert Holzer is Assistant Professor of Music at Yale University and has published articles on Italian music of the seventeenth century and on the Second Viennese School.

Lisa Perella is a doctoral candidate at the University of Pennsylvania, working on a dissertation entitled "Mythologies of Musical Persuasion: The Power and Politics of Song in France, 1653–1673."

Kate van Orden is Assistant Professor of Music at the University of California, Berkeley. She has published on the Renaissance chanson and on French symbolism and music. She also specializes in historical performance on the bassoon and has performed and recorded with ensembles such as William Christie's Les Arts Florissants, Jeanne Lamon's Tafelmusik, and Nicholas McGegan's Philharmonia Baroque Orchestra.

Index